GAME OF SPIES

ALSO BY PADDY ASHDOWN

The Cruel Victory: The French Resistance, D-Day and the Battle for the Vercors 1944

A Brilliant Little Operation: The Cockleshell Heroes and the Most Courageous Raid of WW2

A Fortunate Life: The Autobiography of Paddy Ashdown

Swords and Ploughshares: Bringing Peace to the 21st Century

The Ashdown Diaries (two volumes)

Beyond Westminster

Citizens' Britain

PADDY ASHDOWN

In Collaboration with
SYLVIE YOUNG

GAME OF SPIES

THE SECRET AGENT, THE TRAITOR AND THE NAZI

WILLIAM
COLLINS

William Collins
An imprint of HarperCollins*Publishers*
1 London Bridge Street
London SE1 9GF
WilliamCollinsBooks.com

First published in Great Britain by William Collins in 2016

3 5 7 9 8 6 4 2

A catalogue record for this book is
available from the British Library

HB ISBN 978-0-00-814082-3
TPB ISBN 978-0-00-814938-3

Maps by John Gilkes

Printed and bound in Great Britain by
Clays Ltd, St Ives plc

MIX
Paper from
responsible sources
FSC
www.fsc.org   FSC™ C007454

FSC™ is a non-profit international organisation established to promote
the responsible management of the world's forests. Products carrying the
FSC label are independently certified to assure consumers that they come
from forests that are managed to meet the social, economic and
ecological needs of present and future generations,
and other controlled sources.

Find out more about HarperCollins and the environment at
www.harpercollins.co.uk/green

To the young men and women whose lives were changed in Room 055 of the Old War Office Building in London – and ended in the death camps of Nazi Europe.

CONTENTS

Introduction		xi
Author's Note		xv
Maps		xix
Prologue: The Execution		1
1	Bordeaux – Beginnings	3
2	Roger Landes	17
3	Friedrich Dohse	27
4	André Grandclément	33
5	A Happy Man and a Dead Body	41
6	Scientist Gets Established	53
7	A Visitor for David	59
8	Crackers and Bangs	69
9	Businesses, Brothels and Plans	81
10	'Je suis fort – Je suis même très fort'	89
11	A Birthday Present for Friedrich	101
12	The Wolf in the Fold	113
13	The Trap Closes	125
14	The Deal	133
15	Arms and Alarms	141
16	Progress and Precautions	149
17	The Battle of Lestiac	159
18	Maquis Officiels	171
19	Lencouacq	179

20 Of Missions and Machinations   185
21 Crossing the Frontier   199
22 Cyanide and Execution   209
23 Aristide Returns   221
24 'I come on behalf of Stanislas'   233
25 'Forewarned is Forearmed'   243
26 'This Poisoned Arrow Causes Death'   253
27 A Deadly Charade   263
28 The Viper's Nest   275
29 Two Hours to Leave France   287
30 Nunc Dimittis   295

    Epilogue: Post Hoc Propter Hoc   313

    Acknowledgements   317
    Dramatis Personae   321
    Notes   329
    Select Bibliography   359
    Credits   363
    Index   365

'O look, look in the mirror,
  O look in your distress:
  Life remains a blessing
  Although you cannot bless.

'O stand, stand at the window
  As the tears scald and start;
You shall love your crooked neighbour
  With your crooked heart.'

It was late, late in the evening,
  The lovers they were gone;
The clocks had ceased their chiming,
  And the deep river ran on.

From 'As I Walked Out One Evening'

W. H. Auden

INTRODUCTION

The three main characters of this book – Roger Landes, André Grandclément and Friedrich Dohse – appeared as fleeting shadows in my book *A Brilliant Little Operation*, the story of the 'Cockleshell Heroes' raid on Bordeaux in 1942. And that's the way they would have remained had it not been for a chance email from a friend. Richard Wooldridge, who I had got to know while researching my Cockleshell heroes book, runs the remarkable little Combined Services Military Museum at East Maldon in Essex, of which I am a sometime patron. He had been gifted some documents which had come to light after the death of the owner of a house called 'Aristide' in Liphook, Hampshire. The papers had first been passed to a retired gentleman in the Isle of Wight, who asked Richard if his museum could provide a home for them.

Recognising the name 'Aristide' from the work we had done together, Richard contacted me and asked if I would be interested. I was, but, due to pressure of work could not visit the museum myself to look at the archive. So my colleague and collaborator in this book, Sylvie Young, made the journey to East Maldon and brought back around 400 photographs of letters and papers from the museum. It soon became clear that what we had was the personal archive of one of the Second World War's most remarkable secret agents – Roger Landes.

And that is how this book began.

Since tracing Tito's progress across the mountains of Bosnia (mostly on foot) and reading the remarkable accounts of F. W. D. Deakin and Fitzroy Maclean, who marched with Tito's partisans, I have always been fascinated by that part of the Second World War in which Britain supported, fostered, and sometimes even created, bands of 'freedom fighters' (the Germans called them 'terrorists') dedicated to the liberation of occupied Europe.

Looking back today, it seems to me extraordinary that our besieged little country commited so many of its young men and women and so much of its resources to secret and extremely hazardous operations to free the countries of Europe, which we have now chosen to be no part of. It seems extraordinary that a nation which today does less than any other member of the European Union to help those fleeing the misery of war, was, so short a time ago, their only refuge. After the shock of the Referendum result, I still cannot bring myself to believe that our country, which has now turned its back on solidarity with our European neighbours, was then so much their last hope that, from the alpine pastures of Norway to the mountaintops of Greece, those desperate for freedom from every nation in Europe gathered on moonlit nights to listen for the tiny reverberation in the air which would tell them that the dark shadow of an RAF Halifax from London would shortly pass over them, with its largesse of weapons and its message that they were not alone.

Of course, I know that that is the romance of the story. I know that there is more to it than that. There are legends, and myths, and very black deeds – as well as brilliantly shining ones; and cowardice along with courage, and stupidity too, and vanity – a lot of vanity – and, it must be said, a good deal of betrayal as well. How could it be otherwise, since the basic ingredient of these stories is how ordinary, untrained, unsifted, unselected and unprepared individuals faced the great questions of life and death, which most of us have never had to face in our carefully pasteurised, cotton-wool worlds?

Fortunately, there is now a new mood amongst historians of the Resistance – and especially the French Resistance. A much more granular picture is emerging. The role of women is, at last, coming to light. The failures and betrayals are being analysed, as well as the triumphs, and a much more objective view about the overall achievements – and lack of them – is beginning to appear. This is especially so in France, where the fashion for debunking the Resistance may now even be distorting the picture in the opposite direction.

The role of organisations such as the Gestapo in the story of the European resistance movements remains, on the other hand, a monochrome black. Little has been written in popular form about how the Gestapo worked, how it fitted into the German hierarchy and especially about the individuals involved. In the popular imagination, Klaus Barbie – the 'Butcher of Lyon' – is the model for a Gestapo officer, and it is assumed they were all more or less like that. But of course they weren't. It is time for a much more rounded description of what life was like then, not just for the secret agent operating in enemy territory, but also for the German security apparatus dealing with this so-called 'terrorist' threat, bearing in mind that in our age too we are faced with challenges which are, in practical terms even if not in moral ones, not totally dissimilar.

Following up on the leads in the Aristide archives, we stumbled across the fact that Friedrich Dohse, a Gestapo counter-espionage officer in Bordeaux, had written his memoirs (the only such ones in existence, I believe). These covered the period when his overriding priority was to catch British SOE agent Roger Landes. The opportunity now presented itself to write something which gave both sides of the story.

The third person in the triumvirate at the heart of this book is André Grandclément. He was responsible for one of the most controversial betrayals in wartime France. Much has been written on him, but little about his psychology and the deeper reasons for his 'betrayal' (if that, indeed, is what it was).

In this book I hope to give a picture of those times seen through the eyes of these three men – three enemies – who all lived and operated in wartime southwest France. In these pages, I trace their lives, almost on a day-to-day basis, over the two and a half years from the early months of 1942 to the final liberation of Bordeaux in August 1944.

This is not a book of moral judgements. The three men's stories are presented, as far as possible, plain and unvarnished. Ultimately it is up to the reader to judge what to make of them. But if in the process of making those judgements, a more complete and detailed picture of this fascinating period and of some of the people who lived in it emerges, then this book will have achieved its purpose.

AUTHOR'S NOTE

This is a work of non-fiction, based chiefly on primary historical sources. The key details of the story remain disputed even today. With very few exceptions the accounts which form the basis of this work were written shortly after the war, and often by participants whose reputations were at risk – either because they faced accusations of collaboration, or because they were subject to legal action. For instance, a principal source in this book is the unpublished memoirs of Friedrich Dohse, written while he was awaiting trial by a French military tribunal in Bordeaux after the war. These were plainly designed to put the Gestapo officer's wartime activities in the most favourable light and form part of his defence against the charges he was facing. The same caveat must also apply to the descriptions of events given by others who, while not necessarily preparing for formal court cases, were nevertheless explaining their actions before the court of post-war French public opinion, or simply leaving a record for posterity. There are, in consequence, often radically different versions of the same event. In these cases, difficult judgements of historical evaluation have had to be made. Where an account exists which is substantially different to the one used in this narrative, this fact has been identified in the endnotes.

Sometimes it has been necessary to include some minor speculation in the narrative, where the basic facts surrounding an event have been already established. For example, on 24 September 1943, André Grandclément rode a bicycle through Bordeaux to pay a clandestine visit to the house of Charles Corbin. A visit to the Corbin house for research revealed that the building is very small with a tiny back garden and no back access. Based on these facts and bearing in mind that Grandclément was paying a secret visit to the Corbin family, it seems reasonable to speculate that his bicycle would have been wheeled through the Corbin house into the back garden, rather than leaving it outside.

The dialogue in the Prologue has been reconstructed in a manner consistent with the known facts of the event described. On all other occasions dialogue has only been included where it was either recorded at the time, recorded later by one of the protagonists, or subsequently verified as an accurate representation of what was said.

There are also some important issues regarding terminology. The term 'Gestapo' originates from the first letters of the three words used for the Nazi state secret police (GEheimeSTAatsPOlizei). But the 'true' Gestapo was only a small element within the overall, highly complex German state security apparatus. However, the Gestapo gained such a reputation during the war that very soon (and with the active encouragement of SOE) the word 'Gestapo' became a generic word used to cover all parts of the German security system. In an attempt not to test the sanity of the reader too far with unnecessary complexity, the term 'Gestapo' in this narrative is, in almost all cases, used in its wider more 'popular' sense, rather than its narrower more technical one.

In the 1930s and 1940s the term 'spy' carried pejorative overtones of cheating and underhand activity which it does not have today. For this reason – and perhaps also in the vain hope that their operatives behind enemy lines might gain some flimsy protection from the Geneva Convention provision that spies could be shot – the Special Operations Executive was very particular not to call its operatives 'spies', but 'secret agents'. However, any such distinction was rejected by the German authorities at the time: they ignored SOE's terminological niceties and treated all their captured agents as spies, liable to immediate execution.

In addition to one or more false identities with which every SOE agent was equipped, each also had a number of aliases or codenames: one which was used under training, another for SOE files and correspondence, and a third for when they were in the field. For example,

Roger Landes's false identities in France were 'René Pol' on his first mission and 'Roger Lalande' on his second. Under training he was known to his colleagues as 'Robert Lang'; the internal alias by which he was referred to in SOE papers was 'Actor' (all F-Section agents had internal aliases based on occupations) and the nom de guerre by which he was known to his French colleagues was 'Stanislas' on his first mission and 'Aristide' on his second. In addition, SOE agents often accumulated nicknames while in France: Victor Charles Hayes, codename 'Printer', alias 'Yves', was more frequently known to his French colleagues as 'Charlot' – or, because of his prowess with explosives, 'Charles le Démolisseur'. Although almost all the participants in this story would have used their aliases when communicating with each other I have used personal names throughout, except where the needs of the story dictate otherwise (for example, when it is appropriate to refer to Roger Landes by the *noms de guerre* by which he was known to the Gestapo officer Friedrich Dohse – that is, 'Stanislas', and later 'Aristide').

During the war, the French resistance, diverse and diffuse as it was, was neither referred to nor seen as a single body. It was only after the war that the disparate resistance organisations were regarded as part of a single overarching structure known as the French Resistance (with capitals applied to both words). For ease of reading, I have, in this book, adopted the post-war habit of referring to the French Resistance (with capitals) when referring to the overall organisation, and French resistance when the noun is employed more generally. Latitude and longitude for places of key importance (such as parachute sites and places of execution) are included in the endnotes. For certain military operations, timings are given according to the twenty-four-hour clock and have been converted into Central European Time (Greenwich Mean Time plus one hour from 16 August to 3 April, and GMT plus two hours from 4 April to 15 August) – which was the standard time used throughout all Nazi-occupied Western Europe for the duration of the war.

As is often the case, there are a bewildering profusion of characters who people this historical narrative. In an attempt to make things easier for the reader, I mention characters by their names only if they appear more than once. For those interested in the names of the others mentioned, these, where known, can be found in the endnotes. Even so, the reader may find the number of names challenging. I have therefore provided a dramatis personae of all the main characters on page 321.

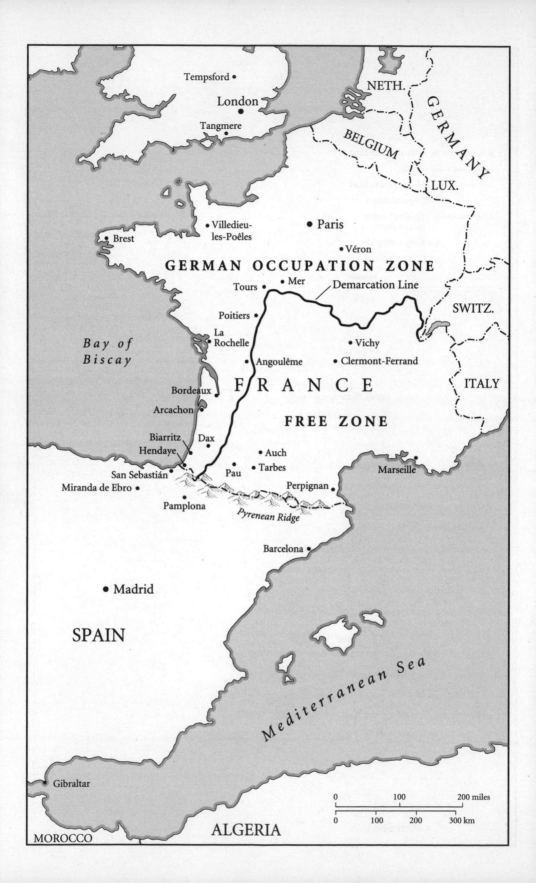

Tempsford •

London

Tangmere •

NETH.

GERMANY

BELGIUM

LUX.

• Villedieu-
les-Poêles

• Paris

• Véron

Brest •

GERMAN OCCUPATION ZONE

Tours •   • Mer

Demarcation Line

SWITZ.

Poitiers •

La
Rochelle •

*Bay of
Biscay*

• Vichy

Angoulême •   • Clermont-Ferrand

ITALY

F R A N C E

Bordeaux •

FREE ZONE

Arcachon •

Biarritz •   • Dax

Hendaye •

San Sebastián •   • Pau

Miranda de Ebro •

• Auch

• Tarbes

Marseille •

Perpignan •

Pamplona •

Pyrenean Ridge

Barcelona •

• Madrid

SPAIN

Mediterranean Sea

• Gibraltar

0   100   200 miles

0   100   200   300 km

MOROCCO

ALGERIA

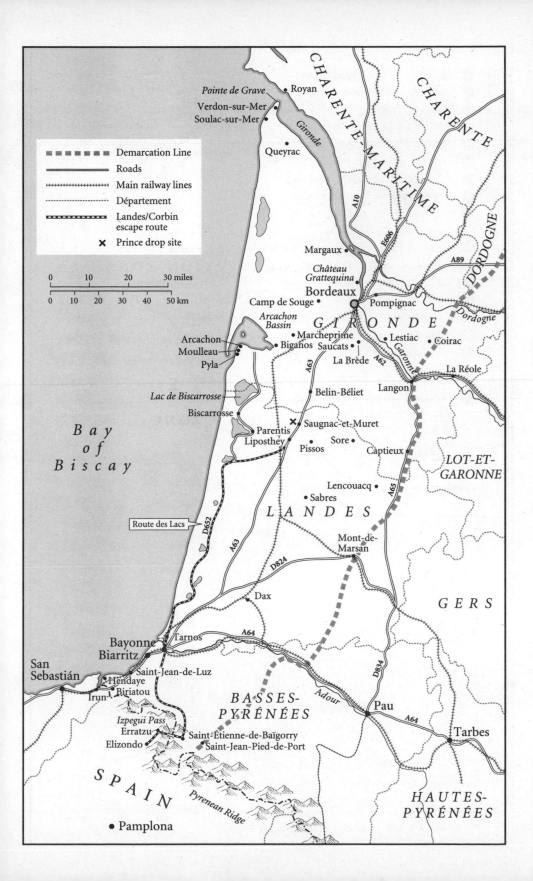

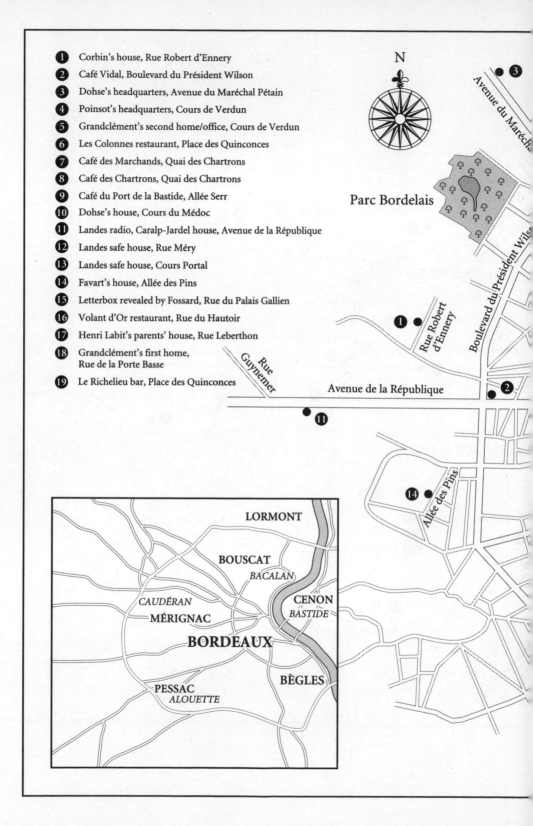

1. Corbin's house, Rue Robert d'Ennery
2. Café Vidal, Boulevard du Président Wilson
3. Dohse's headquarters, Avenue du Maréchal Pétain
4. Poinsot's headquarters, Cours de Verdun
5. Grandclément's second home/office, Cours de Verdun
6. Les Colonnes restaurant, Place des Quinconces
7. Café des Marchands, Quai des Chartrons
8. Café des Chartrons, Quai des Chartrons
9. Café du Port de la Bastide, Allée Serr
10. Dohse's house, Cours du Médoc
11. Landes radio, Caralp-Jardel house, Avenue de la République
12. Landes safe house, Rue Méry
13. Landes safe house, Cours Portal
14. Favart's house, Allée des Pins
15. Letterbox revealed by Fossard, Rue du Palais Gallien
16. Volant d'Or restaurant, Rue du Hautoir
17. Henri Labit's parents' house, Rue Leberthon
18. Grandclément's first home, Rue de la Porte Basse
19. Le Richelieu bar, Place des Quinconces

N

Parc Bordelais

Avenue du Maréchal

Boulevard du Président Wilson

Rue Robert d'Ennery

Rue Guynemer

Avenue de la République

Allée des Pins

LORMONT

BOUSCAT

BACALAN

CAUDÉRAN

CENON

BASTIDE

MÉRIGNAC

BORDEAUX

BÈGLES

PESSAC

ALOUETTE

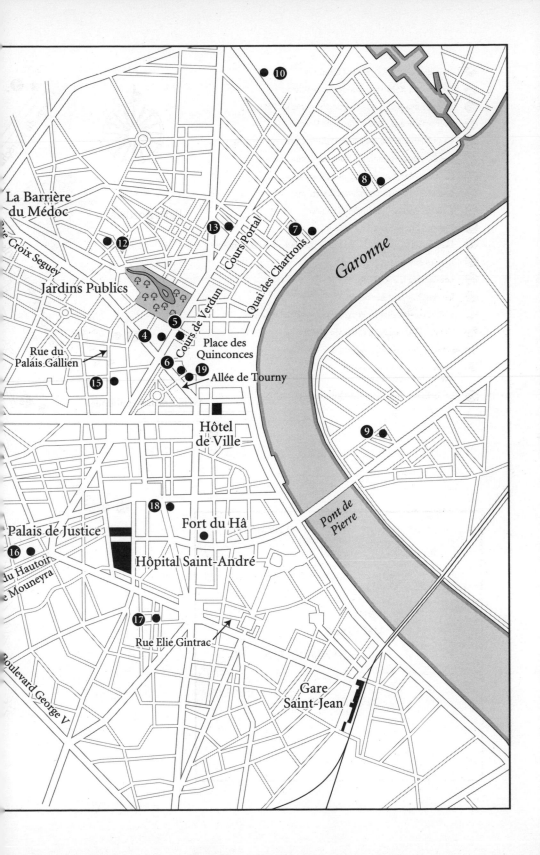

THE EXECUTION

The man's index finger slid forward along the cool metal surface of the Colt in his overcoat pocket and curled gingerly around the trigger. The signal would come soon now.

The young woman walked half a pace ahead of him and a little to his right: she was lithe and pretty with auburn hair. Her wooden-soled sandals clacked on the dry path, and her wedding ring glinted in the last rays of the evening sun. She had dressed for London carefully, before leaving the house: slingback sandals with raised heels, a deep V-neckline green dress, which swung on her hips as she strode lightly along the forest track. She was happy: by the morning she and the husband she adored would be far away from this snake pit of betrayal and treachery.

In a few moments he would have to kill her. He had agreed to this when they had decided on the executions an hour previously. He had not killed before – though he had ordered others to be killed. But he was calm. It had to be done and he was ready for it.

On the woman's right walked a second man, his hands too plunged deep into the pockets of a heavy coat, though it was a warm summer's evening.

They strolled along the track, between the fir trees, chatting amiably.

'When will the aircraft arrive?'

'After dark I suppose. We'll hear when we get to the landing site.'

'How long will it take?'

'To London? About three or four hours I should think.'

'Oh! As long as …'

The sentence died in a cacophony of shots and screams coming from the other side of a small copse to their left.

With a flick of the wrist, the Colt was out of his pocket, its muzzle pressed against the back of the woman's skull. He pulled the trigger. But it wouldn't yield. In the millisecond it took him to push the safety catch down, the woman, feeling the cold of the muzzle, turned her head. He could already see the flared white of her left eye and the terrified gape of her mouth when the gun fired. She dropped silently to the ground, a crumple of green and red lying incongruously on the forest path, as his shot echoed through the woods, startling a small cloud of evening birds.

They half-carried, half-rolled the woman's body into a stream, which ran quietly in a nearby ditch. Her fresh blood billowed in the clear water.

They were joined by two men half dragging another corpse, which trailed a wide smear of blood on the woodland path.

'Both dead?' the man with the Colt asked.

'Yeah, but Christian botched the young man. I had to finish him off. He shouted for mercy.'

'Put him in the ditch and we'll collect the other. The guys will clear up in the morning.'

Ten minutes later the two men's bodies lay heaped in an awkward jumble on top of the woman's. Their blood mingled with hers, turning the little rivulet into a meandering of crimson among the grasses and ferns.

They covered them with branches, walked back to their vehicles in the gathering dusk and drove to Bordeaux, arriving just before the start of curfew.

1

BORDEAUX – BEGINNINGS

After Paris, probably no French city was more affected by the drama of the fall of France and the early months of the German occupation than Bordeaux.

On 10 June 1940, with the sound of German artillery ringing in their ears, the French government fled Paris. Four days later they set up their new emergency wartime capital in Bordeaux. As newcomers, they were not alone. The city was already bursting with a vast tide of humanity, which the French christened the *Exode* – the great exodus of refugees desperately fleeing south to avoid the advancing German armoured columns.

Historically this was not a new experience for Bordeaux. Twice before the city had acted as the emergency capital and chief refuge of France: during the Franco-Prussian War of 1870 and again in 1914. But everyone sensed that this time was going to be different. This time it was going to be not just a military defeat, but a national catastrophe in which all would be engulfed.

The last scenes of France's tragedy were swiftly acted out.

On the evening of 16 June 1940, General de Gaulle, who had been sent to London to secure the support of the British, flew back to Mérignac airport outside Bordeaux in a plane which Churchill had placed at his disposal. He booked into the Hôtel Majestic and arranged an urgent interview with Marshal Pétain, who was headquartered next door at the Hôtel Splendid. The interview was short and fruitless. De Gaulle promised Churchill's help and pleaded with the old marshal to begin the fight back. But it was too late; the die was already cast. Later that day the

French prime minister resigned and Marshal Philippe Pétain, the hero of Verdun in the First War, began negotiating an armistice with the Germans. Disgusted, de Gaulle returned to Mérignac and, on the morning of 17 June, took off for London accompanied by four clean shirts, a spare pair of trousers, 100,000 gold francs and the honour of France. The day after, he made the first of his great speeches from the British capital, appealing to all French men and women to rally to his cause and rescue their country from the shame of defeat.

Initially, however, the general's impassioned pleas fell mostly on deaf ears. The mood in France following its rout was predominantly one of stunned apathy. 'The population was, if not pro-German, at least disposed to do nothing if they were left alone,' one senior German intelligence officer put it.

Under the terms of the armistice signed by Pétain, France was divided by a demarcation line – in practical terms, an internal frontier – running from the Lake of Geneva to the Pyrenees. This separated the northern, occupied zone – a virtual annex of Germany – from the *zone non-occupée*, governed by Pétain's Vichy government in the south. In the Bordeaux region the demarcation line ran along a north–south axis forty kilometres east of the city, and encompassed in the German zone not just the great port itself, but also the entire Atlantic coast south of the Médoc peninsula. Security along the Atlantic coastline was further supplemented by a ten-kilometre-deep *zone interdite* from which all French citizens were banned, unless in possession of a special pass.

The Germans acted swiftly to take control of the occupied zone, not least by requisitioning a number of key addresses in the French capital, most infamously 82–84 Avenue Foch (soon rechristened by Parisians 'Avenue Boche'). Here they established the headquarters of the main state security organisations – the Abwehr (officially the spy service for the German army); the Gestapo (which from mid-1942 would be responsible for all intelligence-gathering on Resistance movements in occupied territories); the Geheime Feldpolizei (GFP), the police arm of the Abwehr; and the Sicherheitsdienst (SD), reporting directly to Heinrich Himmler at his headquarters in Berlin. The SD was originally tasked to root out domestic dissent in Germany, but it soon also expanded its activities into the occupied territories, establishing a strong intelligence presence in Paris and Bordeaux, where it would increasingly use the Gestapo as its action arm for arrests and interrogation.

At 11 a.m. on 28 June, less than a fortnight after de Gaulle left the city, the newly appointed German commandant of Bordeaux and its region, General von Faber du Faur, entered his new residence in the city, an imposing townhouse on the Rue Vital Carles. Here the *préfet* of the Gironde presented him with a magnificent welcoming bouquet of flowers in a fine cut crystal vase.

The city which formed the heart of the general's new command was – and still is – one of the most beautiful and venerable in all France. Lying along a crescent-moon-shaped curve of the Garonne river (from which the city gets its nickname, the '*Port de la Lune*'), Bordeaux had been a port since Roman times, shipping iron and tin from its quays; in later centuries, slaves, coffee, cotton, indigo and agricultural products were added to the trade. But the most valuable of all Bordeaux's commodities – and central to the region's wealth and dignity – was wine. From the great clarets of the Médoc, to the Graves and Sauternes of the Garonne valley, to the cognac grapes of Charentes – Bordeaux's rich hinterlands of vineyards made the city affluent, proud, and uncompromisingly mercantile in its outlook.

In the pre-war years the entire port area had been rebuilt and renovated, from the working district of Bacalan at the northern end, south along the sweep of the Quai des Chartrons, to the elegant parks and apartments near the city centre. The most modern cranes were installed, a small-gauge railway was constructed, new warehouses were established, tarmac was laid in place of cobbles and a brand-new tram system was inaugurated to link the port to the rest of the city. Bordeaux was, at the fall of France, not only one of the most beautiful, but also one of the most modern ports in the whole of Europe. On still days a thin diaphanous haze, caused by the incessant bustle of the great port, hung over the city. In stormy weather, the wind funnelled down narrow streets, whipping the harbour into white-topped rufflets and sweeping fallen leaves from the city's plane trees into drifts along the gutters and neat piles in the sheltered corners of alleyways and squares.

Back from the waterfront, the city of 1940 was little changed from the previous two centuries. Its imposing centre, dominated by the town hall, the eighteenth-century Hôtel de Ville, boasted impeccably manicured tree-lined squares, fine restaurants and elegant frontages. These led to broad boulevards radiating out towards the port's trading and residential quarters. Beyond the main roads, this was a city of little restaurants, cafés, scurrying markets and narrow cobbled streets, lined with shops and first-floor apartments. Here a cacophony of humanity jostled with a jumble of cars, vélo-taxis, bicycles, lorries, barrows and horse-drawn carts.

The city's political landscape was also one of contrast. During the 1930s, communism found a strong foothold amongst France's intellectuals and working classes. Most of the dockworkers, who lived in the city's crowded Bacalan quarter – where the restaurants were as rough as the wine they served – were, if not communist, then communist sympathisers; as were the *cheminots* (the railway workers) and the post office workers. In the countryside, too, especially in the Landes region lying between Bordeaux and the Pyrenees, communism and socialism had strong roots. Many of the Bordelais, however, regarded communism with a fear amounting almost to paranoia – seeing it as some kind of modern reincarnation of the *sans-culottes* of the French Revolution. A secret British wartime report observed that '[amongst] the upper bourgeoisie [there is] an apprehension of Russia and a real fear of the former French Communists and of the mob ... [they believe that] only evil can come to France from the disorder which would follow the coming to power of the extreme left'.

Those in charge of mercantilist Bordeaux were above all pragmatists. What was good for trade was good for the city. Foreigners came and foreigners went. But if trade (and especially the wine trade) went on, the city prospered, whoever was in charge. The city's bourgeoisie and petit-bourgeoisie embraced the politics of conservatism and of 'order'. Among these classes, right or centre-right views were dominant, extreme right nationalism not unusual, and anti-Semitism commonplace.

'England', regarded by some in France as the centre of modern Jewry, was often thrown into this mix of political foes. 'The English, the yids, the capitalists, these are the true enemies of France which is threatened, like every other country, by the Bolshevik sword of Damocles,' declared one local right-wing activist of the time. When it came to anti-Semitism, Bordeaux was by no means unusual in the France of the 1930s and '40s. 'The Jewish question was a subject of lively discussion in France at the time,' one respected French commentator wrote. 'There was a strong resurgence of anti-Jewish sentiment in the period before the war and during the years of the Vichy government.'

Von Faber du Faur did not waste time imposing his rule on the city. He laid on a grand military parade through the streets of Bordeaux, designed not just as a spectacle, but also as a show of force. The salute was taken by, amongst others, Erwin Rommel (who requisitioned a nearby château for holiday use). On 1 July 1940 a curfew, enforced by armed soldiers with dogs, was imposed between 2300 and 0500 hours, with curfew-breakers risking long terms of imprisonment or forced labour. All clocks were advanced one hour to match German time. All firearms, including hunting weapons, had to be handed in to the local *mairies*; all official notices (including street signs and administrative requests) had to be in German as well as French, and the swastika emblazoned on a red banner was hung outside all principal official buildings. Controls were introduced on traffic in the Gironde estuary and on all major road inter-sections and railway stations. In time, German oversight would be extended to cover the postal service, telecommunications, newspapers, cinemas, cultural events, agriculture (including, inevitably, wine), commercial transactions, the refining and distribution of petroleum products and the passage of goods and people over the demarcation line into Vichy France. Laws were passed to require farmers to give up a percentage of their produce to the German occupiers – though in most cases, thanks to peasant cunning, these were honoured more in the breach than the observance. German soldiers were under strict instruc-tions to behave politely towards the French, and mostly did. But the terms of occupation were clear. On 10 October 1940 the city's military administration published a decree stating: 'Anyone who gives shelter to a member of the British Forces will be condemned to death.'

Almost overnight, it seemed, the German authorities also established an iron grip on the region, turning the whole of the Gironde estuary and the Médoc peninsula into one gigantic military base. Concrete pens were constructed in Bordeaux harbour to house the German submarines engaged in the deadly business of cutting the Atlantic lifeline on which Britain depended to save it from starvation. Italian submarines also had a base in the city. The Bordeaux quays were fortified with concrete pillboxes, a system of interlocking trenches and underground bunkers. This would soon also become the base for a small fleet of converted merchantmen which – fast, lightly armed and German-crewed – acted as blockade-runners, bringing in vital raw materials from Japanese-occupied territories in the Far East.

The Atlantic beaches running south from the mouth of the Gironde, considered a likely place for an Allied invasion, were fortified with a network of defences, including heavy coastal guns in thick concrete casemates; searchlights; numerous machine-gun nests, and a small fleet of riverine patrol vessels. Some 60,000 German troops were stationed in and around Bordeaux. By the end of the war, this would include two infantry divisions, a Panzer division and an army headquarters. A Luftwaffe force of 150 aircraft was assembled at Mérignac airport and on small local airfields. Kriegsmarine units were brought in to protect the Gironde and the coastal waters of the Gulf of Aquitaine.

The city itself was soon crammed full of German troops and dotted with a profusion of headquarters for the major military units, which jostled with buildings housing the German harbour authorities, civil government and the various security organisations charged with keeping order. A requisitioned passenger liner, the *Baudouinville* – last used by the Belgian cabinet when they took the fateful decision to surrender – was brought to Bordeaux and tied up along the quay at the Place des Quinconces as overflow billeting for German and Italian troops. There was also an array of soldiers' brothels and watering holes: the Lion

Rouge nightclub was specially reserved for Wehrmacht officers, the Côtelette for Abwehr intelligence officers, and the Blaue Affe (the Blue Monkey) for ordinary soldiers.

For most citizens of Bordeaux, shortages now became a way of life. The price of baby milk rose by fifty per cent; fish was limited to one tin of sardines per month and sugar was almost unobtainable. Even saccharine tablets were rationed to a hundred pills per person for every six months. Shopkeepers had to accept the Reichsmark at an exorbitant fixed rate of exchange and butchers were prohibited from selling meat on Wednesday and Thursday, with Friday reserved for horsemeat and tripe only. Most metal came from recycled stock. Leather was only available on the black market, or with an official authorisation; gloves and belts were difficult to find and most shoes had only wooden soles. There was a severe shortage of elastic (though this did not affect the availability of ladies' suspenders, one British secret agent noted, cheerfully). German soldiers had priority on public transport, and horses were used extensively. Real coffee was such a valuable commodity that it became an article of barter, with most cafés and restaurants serving a roasted acorn substitute christened 'café Pétain'. Unsurprisingly – and very quickly – a flourishing and all-pervasive black market was established, as the French population in both town and country tried to find ways round these new discomfitures in their daily lives.

Despite this – and contrary to the early hopes of the intelligence community in London, who claimed that 'occupied Europe was smouldering with Resistance to the Nazis and ready to erupt at the slightest support or encouragement' – secret feelers put out by the British and the Free French reported that the 'spirit of Resistance' in the city was depressingly frail. 'Bordeaux was not a town for Resistance. It was more a town for collaborators. Most of our activity was outside Bordeaux,' one early British agent concluded.

It was not long before a climate of suspicion began to infect Bordeaux city life. People tended not to speak to each other in the streets and tried to avoid speaking at all to those they did not know for fear of agents provocateurs and collaborators. One commentator said, 'Neighbours reported confidentially on one another. People were denounced for anti-German sentiments and for listening to foreign news broadcasts.' Another, describing the attitude of the average Bordelais, reported, tartly: '[They believed] their duty as patriotic Frenchmen was more than adequately fulfilled by listening to BBC London in their slippers in front of the fire,' adding, 'influenced by German propaganda [the Bordelais] were terrified of Communism and of losing their money'.

Though they found German rule irksome, the people of Bordeaux were, for the most part, content to continue with their lives quietly and as best they could in the circumstances. The great biannual spring and autumn fair took place as usual in the Place des Quinconces. Photographs from 1940 show unarmed German soldiers mingling with local crowds on the fairground rides. That year, as every year in the past, the Amar Circus – complete with lions, elephants, tigers and clowns – made the journey from Paris to play to full houses on the Bordeaux quays. *La Petite Gironde*, a broadly collaborationist Bordeaux daily newspaper, advised that the proper attitude to the occupation should be to 'understand and be resigned' – a proposition which many in the city followed.

Even when the Germans began a drive against the city's Jews, sentiment in the city remained largely unmoved. On 27 August 1940, a Jewish man, Laiser Israel Karp, was summarily condemned to death for raising his fist at a German parade. On 17 October a notice was issued requiring all Jews and Jewish enterprises in the city to register. Five days later, 5,172 Jews and 403 Jewish businesses had complied. Early in 1941, Jews were banned from seventeen public places in the city, including all parks, theatres and cinemas and many schools. A year later the Vichy authorities in Bordeaux hosted a travelling exhibition with a strong anti-Semitic theme. Entitled 'The Jews and France', it proved a huge success in the city, attracting 60,000 local citizens through its doors.

During the course of 1941, however, as the German occupiers reacted to provocations and attacks with increasing ferocity, the mood in Bordeaux – as across the rest of France – began to shift. On 20 October the German military commander in Nantes was assassinated and the following day the weighted-down body of Hans Reimers, an officer in the Wehrmacht, was discovered in Bordeaux harbour. Hitler insisted on responding to these 'outrages' with maximum severity, overruling appeals from German military commanders in France for a more restrained response. In Bordeaux, fifty civilian hostages, most of them suspected communist sympathisers, were taken to the old French military camp at Souge, fifteen kilometres west of the city, and executed. They were the first of 257 'Resistance martyrs' who would die before German firing squads at Souge before the war was over. More attacks were followed by more reprisals and, as French outrage grew, the ranks of resistants began to swell.

In November 1941, a special French police brigade under the command of a ruthless pro-German Frenchman called Pierre Napoléon Poinsot, was established in close cooperation with the German authorities to tackle the new threat. His first act was to launch a major drive against the communists. In sweeps, notably in the Bacalan quarter of the city, and in a number of rural communities in the Gironde region, hundreds of suspects, men and women, were arrested and incarcerated in an internment camp at Mérignac.

By now executions and deportations had become an established part of the German system of control and repression. According to secret British estimates, across France a total of 5,599 people were executed and 21,863 deported in the last quarter of 1942 alone. Resistance organisations started to spring up in Bordeaux and its hinterland. Some of these were small, personal and informal. Others were part of larger information-gathering networks. Many were under the control of foreign intelligence services, notably the British Secret Intelligence Service (SIS – also known as MI6), the Free French in London and the Polish secret service. By the end of 1941 there were no less than nine of these foreign-controlled spy networks tripping over each other in Bordeaux and the Gironde. In addition there were also numerous smaller 'private' Resistance fiefdoms, such as the one run by Raymond Brard, the head of the Bordeaux port fire brigade, whose network was based on the membership of a weight-lifting and 'Gironde wrestling' club in a city backstreet.

One of the first of these 'private' initiatives was established at the end of August 1940, just ten weeks after de Gaulle left France. Its founders were two neighbours who lived on the Bordeaux waterfront.

Jean Duboué, a strikingly handsome man of imposing build with a strong face and a direct, challenging gaze, was already an established figure in Bordeaux. Forty-three years old when the Second World War began, this was not Duboué's first conflict. He had been wounded in one of France's bloodiest calvaries of 1914–18: the battle of the Chemin des Dames. A self-made man, Duboué had left school in Bordeaux aged twelve to work down the coal mines of the Basque Country. Returning to Bordeaux, he began a new career as a restaurateur, managing the Grand Café du Commerce et de Tourny, one of Bordeaux's most prestigious restaurants. From here he branched out with his own businesses. One was the Café des Marchands, a modest restaurant and boarding house frequented by dockers and travelling salesmen on the Quai des Chartrons. By the end of the 1930s, Duboué's businesses were doing well enough for him to purchase a country retreat southeast of Bordeaux, where he, his wife Marie-Louise and daughter Suzanne spent every weekend and most holidays.

His co-conspirator, Léo Paillère, recently demobilised and an ex-captain of infantry in the First World War, was, at fifty, older than Duboué. A man of distinctly right-wing tendencies, Paillère lived with his wife Jeanne and their five sons next door to the Café des Marchands.

During late 1940 and early 1941, Duboué and Paillère set about recruiting a number of friends as agents. They gathered intelligence on German positions, troop movements, weapons and ships in the port – especially the blockade-runners and submarines. The intelligence was smuggled out of Bordeaux by Suzanne Duboué (sixteen years old at the time and known in the family as 'Mouton', or 'lambkin' in English). She took the secret reports to a restaurant owner called Gaston Hèches in Tarbes, 140 kilometres south of Bordeaux. Hèches then passed them along a clandestine escape route he controlled, over the Pyrenees to the SIS representative in the British consulate in Barcelona. When this route was closed, or too dangerous, Suzanne carried the intelligence hidden in a basket across the border to the Spanish Basque coastal town of San Sebastián, where the British consulate doubled as the gateway to another escape line and courier service to Madrid, Gibraltar and London.

The Duboué–Paillère reports on German activity first began to reach London early in 1941, the year which was, for Churchill and the British, the *annus horribilis* of the war. The heady days of solitary defiance and the Battle of Britain were over. Now British forces were engaged in a long struggle of retrenchment and attrition, and losing on all fronts: in the Atlantic, in the deserts of North Africa, on the plains of Russia and against the Japanese in the Far East. Churchill knew that after Dunkirk it would take time – probably years – to turn the tide. He knew too that if Britain was not to retreat into passive defence, then apart from RAF attacks on German cities, his only means of carrying the war to the enemy was through clandestine and unconventional warfare.

In 1940 he created three new organisations to wage this secret war: Combined Operations, charged with conducting commando raids on the European coastline; MI9, tasked with helping escaped Allied prisoners and downed pilots to get back to Britain; and the Special Operations Executive (SOE), established in July of that year and ordered, in Churchill's inimitable words, to 'set Europe ablaze'.

Staffed mainly by amateurs in the spying game, the 'Baker Street Irregulars' (as SOE swiftly became known, after their headquarters near Marylebone station) were regarded by Britain's professional spies in SIS with a sniffy disdain, bordering, when occasion arose, on murderous enmity. Malcolm Muggeridge, himself an SIS officer, commented: 'Though SOE and SIS were nominally on the same side in the war, they were, generally speaking, more abhorrent to one another than the Abwehr was to either of them.'

Operationally, SOE was run by a regular army brigadier, Colin Gubbins, and was an autonomous organisation which, for cover purposes, pretended to be part of the War Office. It was divided into country sections for each of the occupied countries of Europe – except for France which had two country sections: F (for France) Section,

13

staffed mainly by British officers, and RF (République Française) Section, staffed mainly by the French. Both sections sent their own agents into France, but their approaches were entirely different. The British-run F Section favoured small discrete spy networks built on independent 'cells', which had no contact with each other. This, they hoped, would limit the damage of penetration and betrayal. The French-run RF Section acted mainly as a logistics organisation for de Gaulle's Free French spy service in London, the BCRA (Bureau Central de Renseignement et d'Action). Unlike F Section, it preferred large, centrally controlled networks, more akin to an underground army.

SOE was nearly a year old and under considerable Whitehall criticism for delivering little of value to the wider war effort at the time that Jean Duboué's intelligence started to arrive in Baker Street. Up to this moment almost all the secret agents SOE had dispatched to France had been sent to the Vichy *zone non-occupée*. Suddenly, here was an opportunity to get involved in the spying business, not just in the occupied zone, but also, given Bordeaux's role as a submarine base, in an area of real strategic importance to the battle of the Atlantic.

SOE decided to send a secret agent of their own to Bordeaux to see what was going on.

Robert Leroy was in many ways an unsuitable person for such a pioneering and precarious mission. A former marine engineer from the Brest area, Leroy's SOE training reports describe him as 'shrewd ... [but] suffering from the weaknesses of his class – a proneness to alcoholic indulgence and women' – and add, in a comment which tells us more about SOE's snobbery than it does about Leroy's table manners, that he was 'out of place in an Officers' Mess'.

Under the codename 'Alain', Robert Leroy was landed from an SOE 'ghost ship' on a beach at Barcarès near Perpignan on the night of 19 September 1941. His orders were to make his way to Duboué's contact, Gaston Hèches in Tarbes, and thence to Bordeaux, where he was to liaise with Jean Duboué, get a job in the port and assess the possibilities of attacking the German submarine pens. Unfortunately, the explosives Leroy was supposed to take with him somehow got lost during the landing, leaving him with no option but to set off on his mission without them. His journey to Bordeaux appears to have been both leisurely and bibulous, for he did not reach the city until mid-November, leaving behind a trail of debt and unpaid bar bills.

Arriving in Bordeaux, Leroy contacted Duboué, who used his influence to get the newcomer a job as a tractor driver in the docks. The new arrival quickly established a relationship with the director of warehouses in the *Port de la Lune*, to whom Leroy hinted that he was involved in black-market operations which could be of mutual profit to both of them. In return he had his card stamped '*Indispensable pour le Port de Bordeaux*'. This meant that Leroy, provided he wore his docker's blue blouse, could roam anywhere he liked, safe from German checks and roll calls.

Other early information came from a fellow Breton marine engineer, who furnished Leroy with intelligence on the blockade-runners. These merchantmen were using Bordeaux in increasing numbers, unloading the precious raw materials (tungsten, molybdenum, rubber) needed by the German war machine and reloading their holds with blueprints and examples of new German technology – such as radar and proximity fuses – for the Japanese. In early 1942, Leroy sent back 'detailed reports on the shipping and also a map of the docks' to London. They arrived at a most propitious moment. On 9 May that year, the head of SOE and Minister of Economic Warfare, Lord Selborne, wrote to Prime Minister Churchill drawing his attention to the Bordeaux blockade-runners and their 'most vital cargoes' and proposing that it was now crucial to the national interest to '[stop] the trade altogether'.

Suddenly SOE found themselves, through the unlikely person of the ever-convivial Robert Leroy, with a ringside seat on what had just become a national strategic war target. London immediately recalled their secret agent to make a full report. It seems probable that Leroy returned to Britain via San Sebastián with Suzanne Duboué acting as his guide, for one of his first acts on reaching London on 29 May 1942 was to send a message back to Bordeaux through the BBC French Service, announcing his arrival with the words: '*Bonjour à Mouton*'.

After a full debriefing and a few days' leave, Leroy was sent back to Bordeaux with instructions to continue his work and prepare for reinforcements. Bordeaux was about to become, along with Paris, SOE's most important centre for spying and sabotage in occupied France.

2

ROGER LANDES

The piece of paper that changed Roger Landes's life appeared on the noticeboard of No. 2 Company, 2nd Operations Training Battalion of the Signals Training College in Prestatyn, North Wales, sometime during the last week of February 1942.

It was brief and to the point: Army Number 2366511 Signalman Roger Landes to report to Room 055 of the War Office in Whitehall on Wednesday 4 March 1942. A military rail warrant for a return journey to central London could be collected from the company office.

Given the vagaries of wartime travel it is likely that young Landes (he had celebrated his twenty-fifth birthday just before Christmas) went down to London the day before his interview, and spent the night at his parents' apartment at 48 Carlton Mansions, Holmleigh Road, London N16. Although the crescendo of the London blitz had passed by midsummer 1941, the city's overground rail system remained in many places unrepaired and everywhere prone to breakdown and delay. Most Londoners used the Underground to get around.

No one would have paid much attention to the small man in the ill-fitting serge uniform of a private of the Royal Signals, making his way this cold grey March day on the Piccadilly line towards central London. If he had spoken, they would have noted his heavy accent, and concluded that he was just another foreigner in a city full of foreigners – from the 'exotic' to the ordinary, from kings and queens to commoners – all taking refuge from the German onslaught across the Channel.

Born in December 1916 and brought up in Paris the son of a family of Jewish immigrants of Polish–Russian extraction, Roger Arthur Landes had inherited his British citizenship from his father, Barnet, a jeweller in the French capital, who, through an accident of fate, had been born in London. Sometime in the early 1930s, Barnet Landes was bankrupted by the Great Depression. Roger was forced to leave school at the age of thirteen and start work in a firm of quantity surveyors, while attending technical classes at night school. His parents emigrated to London in 1934, where they rented a small flat off Stamford Hill, an area much favoured by the Jewish community. Roger stayed on in France where, despite not having taken his baccalauréat, he managed to obtain a place at the prestigious École des Beaux-Arts in Paris. On graduating (with the École's *Prix d'Honneur*, among other prizes), he took furnished rooms in the French capital and set about learning the practical aspects of his trade as an architect and quantity surveyor.

By 1938, however, it was clear to all that war was coming. Landes knew that if he stayed in France he would soon receive his call-up papers for the French army, which, even half a century after the Dreyfus affair, still had a reputation for anti-Semitism. He left for England, moved in with his parents in Stamford Hill and secured a position as a clerk in the architectural department of London County Council. Later he was to say that his time in the LCC was one of the most enjoyable of his life.

On the outbreak of the war, Landes signed up immediately and was posted to the Rescue Service in Islington, where he used his architectural skills to assess bomb damage during the blitz. Two years later he was redeployed to the miserable, windswept, wintry conditions of Prestatyn holiday camp in North Wales for training as a radio operator. It was here in 1942 that the mysterious note on the No. 2 Company noticeboard found him and ordered him to attend the War Office on this March Wednesday morning.

Short (five foot four), slender and unprepossessing, Roger Landes was olive-skinned, with a narrow heart-shaped face, a rather sensitive (even feminine) mouth, oiled black hair carefully coiffed in the fashion of the day, and heavy eyebrows jutting out above eyes which combined humour and cunning in equal measure. He spoke English imperfectly and with a strong French accent, overlaid with the distinctive guttural 'r' and nasal cadences of the Jewish community of Stamford Hill. Though proud of being a Jew, he wore his religion lightly and was a rare practicant. Perhaps the most remarkable thing about this slight figure amidst the press of wartime Londoners going about their daily business was that he was unusually unremarkable. A fellow British agent later observed: 'his smallness and … particular facial features' gave him an uncanny ability to vanish into the crowd, making him, even when undisguised, 'a difficult man to track'.

The early months of 1942 were the coldest in northern Europe since 1895. The ground remained frozen solid under a carpet of thick hoar frost, which persisted into the early weeks of March. The scene that would have greeted Landes as he emerged from the London underground and walked along the Embankment would have been a sombre one. The parks by the river's edge had long ago been dug up for vegetable allotments and air-raid shelters. A leaden Thames, indistinguishable from its mud banks, flowed sullenly under a blanket of freezing fog. The trees lining the north side of the river appeared as a row of ghostly mourners emerging from the mist, their lopped branches raised like stumps in supplication to a vengeful sky. Thin drifts of unswept snow still lay in gutters and along the sheltered edges of buildings.

Set back from the Thames, Whitehall, grimy from two centuries of coal fires, now also bore the pockmarks of the recent blitz. Every window was white-taped against bomb blast and curtained with condensation from the human fug inside; every door was protected by a tunnel of sandbags manned by soldiers with fixed bayonets. The War Office building itself had been hit and some of the great buildings of state had been turned into bombsites, which now sprouted young buddleia bushes, stalwart against the cold, and withered mats of brambles whose tentacles reached out across the rubble, hoping for the spring.

Landes made his way to Whitehall Court and the back entrance to the War Office building, where a sentry barred his way. He showed his orders and was passed on to a reception desk. From there an escort took him down long ill-lit corridors with black-and-white mosaic floors and brown panelling to a large room used only for interviews, whose grimy windows looked out onto the inner courtyard. The space, carpeted in linoleum which peeled back in one corner, was empty of ornament or furniture, save for a bare desk behind which sat a forlorn, out-of-place-looking secretary. Landes produced his letter and was ushered into a second, smaller room. Here seated at a desk facing him was a cadaverous-looking man in the perfectly cut uniform of a British major. A small coal fire glowed bravely in the middle of one wall but made little headway against the entrenched cold of a room which had been inadequately heated all winter.

The major rose, extended his right hand and – waving the other at the upright chair positioned opposite him – said: 'I am Major Gielgud. Do sit down.'

The interview did not last long, for the major's speech was terse and his manner brusque in the fashion of these urgent times. 'We are sending British personnel into France who can speak fluent French and use wireless sets – radio operators who will be able to pass for French people. From the report I have on your skill in wireless communications, and as you have lived in France for so long, you are the perfect man to send, should you be willing to go. There are three ways to send you to France; by parachute, by motor-boat, or by fishing boat from Gibraltar. The danger is you may be caught, in which case you will probably be tortured and sent to a certain death. The fact that you are a Jew is not going to make life easier for you, as I am sure you understand. Will you accept? Yes or no? You have five minutes to think about it.'

Landes thought about it very little, before saying yes.

'Good,' said Gielgud, who was the brother of the great actor, John. 'Then return to your unit. Say nothing to anyone, even your parents, and we will be in touch.'

Some days later Landes received another order: he was to report on 17 March to a flat in Orchard Court, Portman Square, and introduce himself as 'Robert Lang'.

* * *

The door at Orchard Court, a 1930s mansion block, was opened by a man in butler's uniform, who welcomed him with a butler's smile. His name was Arthur Parks, and he spoke perfect French, having worked for Barclays Bank in Paris before the war. Parks led the new recruit to a grand room where he was introduced to Captain André Simon, who in peacetime had been a wine merchant. Simon was also brief, informing Landes that he was now formally a member of the Special Operations Executive, with the rank of temporary second lieutenant. He was, henceforth and for the rest of his life, subject to the Official Secrets Act and would receive an initial salary of five guineas a week. Captain Simon then gave Landes £10 with which to buy two khaki shirts and ordered him to report back to Orchard Court with a small overnight bag the following day.

Arriving the next morning at Orchard Court, Landes found he was not alone. He and another nine students, all young men and all of them looking equally uncomfortable in ill-fitting army uniforms, were swiftly introduced to each other using the aliases by which they would be known throughout their period of training. They were a hybrid collection, whose only common feature, as far as Landes could see, was their ability to speak French as a native. Most had dual identities, having been brought up in France as the children of mixed French–British marriages. Some had British parents who had chosen to educate their children in local French schools. One was the son of a well-known Francophone family from Mauritius; he was the first, but by no means last, SOE recruit to come from the tiny British colony.

Introductions over, they were bundled into a small bus and driven out of London, along the A30 through Guildford to the little village of Wanborough, close under the northern flank of the Hog's Back. Here they turned up a small farm track to a brick-built three-gabled Elizabethan house set about with outhouses, sheds and workers' cottages.

Wanborough Manor (known by SOE as Special Training School No. 5) was in many ways an odd choice for a spy school. Plainly visible from the road only 200 metres away, and famed for having one of the largest medieval wooden barns in southeast England, it sat right in the middle of the small hamlet of Wanborough. The house had a cellar, used for indoor instruction, a kitchen, a substantial sitting room and a dining room on the ground floor, bedrooms on the top two floors dedicated to staff accommodation and a small church in the grounds, where interdenominational services were held to cater for the needs of SOE's wide variety of students. Physical training was held on the two lawns, back and front, which during fine weather in the summer months were also employed as occasional outdoor classrooms.

SOE's trainee agents were not the first unusual visitors to Wanborough. Gladstone's parliamentary secretary had lived there and the Grand Old Man wrote his resignation speech in the Manor's study. During Gladstone's time as prime minister, Queen Victoria had also paid a visit to Wanborough, accompanied by Bismarck. The two marked the occasion by planting two giant sequoias on the front lawn, each adorned with a cast-iron memorial plaque recording the moment. What SOE's new recruits thought about sitting in the shade of the Iron Chancellor's memorial tree, while being trained to set Nazi-occupied Europe 'ablaze', is not recorded.

There was almost nothing in the hitherto quiet and fastidious life of young Roger Landes that could have prepared him for the next four weeks. Wanborough Manor was a French-speaking microcosm. Its students were cut off from the world, save for carefully vetted letters and occasional accompanied trips over the Hog's Back to the local pub The Good Intent (Landes drank alcohol only very abstemiously), or to the nearby gravel pit for hand-grenade practice. Landes was woken at dawn every morning from a hard army bed and went straight into PT, followed by a run around the manor house grounds. Then lessons all day, most of them requiring hard physical exertion, which cannot have been made any easier for Landes by his habit (which continued unabated all his life) of smoking sixty cigarettes a day. Soon every muscle of his slight, city-softened body ached. He ate voraciously and without discrimination. And at the end of the day sleep came to him as swift as the click of a camera shutter.

Landes had never held, let alone fired, a gun in his life. But by the end of his four weeks' intensive training he knew how to strip down and reassemble, even in the dark, every German, Italian, French, American and British small arm in common use. He knew how to fire them too – and found he was a surprisingly good shot. He also learnt how to move unseen across open country; how to prime and throw a hand grenade; how to find his way, even at night with a map and compass; how to kill a man without a weapon; how to disarm an enemy and how to dissemble convincingly in the face of inquisitive questions.

At the end of the Wanborough Manor stage of the course, two of the original ten 'disappeared'. By this time Landes's colleagues had begun to resolve themselves into personalities. Of the eight remaining, three would feature prominently both in SOE's history and in Roger Landes's life as a secret agent. 'Clement Bastable' (real name, Claude de Baissac) was ten years older than Landes. An imposing man with the air of some-one who expected to be obeyed, he too was of dark complexion and had a neatly trimmed moustache in the style of many Hollywood actors of the time – Clark Gable, say, or Errol Flynn. He had indeed been a film publicist in France before the war. 'Hilaire Poole' (Harry Peulevé) was the same age as Landes, but he was taller and more powerfully built, with a finely chiselled, handsome face and deep, rather disconcerting eyes. 'Fernand Sutton' (Francis Suttill) was thirty-two, but looked much younger. Fair-haired, blue-eyed, clean cut, with the fresh-faced look of an English public school boy, he was, in the words of a fellow secret agent, 'magnificent, strong, young, courageous and decisive, a kind of Ivanhoe; but he should have been a cavalry officer, not a spy …'.

Among these fellow students, Landes was the exception – perhaps sufficiently even to feel, and appear, a little out of place. Most of his colleagues were, like SOE itself, ex-public school and from the upper echelons of British society. Claude de Baissac was of course French – or to be precise Mauritian French. But he too had been to one of the best schools, the Lycée Henri IV in Paris. His family were not by birth from the upper reaches of French society, but they aspired to be so, adding the aristocratic 'de' in front of their name when de Baissac's mother accom-panied her son to Paris to begin his education, in the late 1920s. Landes's Wanborough Manor colleagues were also, in one way or another, strong characters, bursting with charisma and natural leadership. Landes, the little clerk from the Architectural Department of London County Council, son of an immigrant Jewish jeweller from Paris, who had managed to educate himself at night school, was none of these things. His SOE reports refer to him, somewhat dismissively, as a 'cheery little Frenchman'; he was less impressive, less significant and much, much less noticeable than his fellow recruits. Qualities which, whether SOE valued them or not, were precisely those he would require to be a successful secret agent.

In early 1942, the eight students caught the train north for Scotland and four weeks' intensive training at Meoble Lodge, beside Loch Morar in Inverness-shire. Here, where moor and mountain sweep down to the back door, they marched long distances carrying heavy loads, spent nights in the open under rough shelters made of bracken and fir branches, learnt how to set a snare for rabbits and how to skin, gut and cook them afterwards. Two ex-Shanghai policemen taught them how to kill a man noiselessly with the SOE's specially designed fighting knife, and an ex-chartered accountant showed them how to pick a lock and blow a safe. They also learnt the strange artefacts and sacred rituals of explosives: how to place the primer, just so; how to crimp (but gently) one end of the fuse in the detonator so it wouldn't pull out, and how to scarf the other end at an angle, waiting for the match. How to light it, even in a gale, by holding the match end against the scarfed face of the fuse and striking it with the box, rather than the other way round. Why, with the fuse lit, you should always walk away, never run.

Parachute training at Ringway near Manchester followed, after which, in early May, Landes and his colleagues attended SOE's 'finishing school' at Beaulieu, Hampshire. Here they learnt, among other things, codes and cyphers; disguise; how to follow someone and know if you were being followed; how to hide in a city; and how to place an explosive charge in just the right manner to cut a rail, slice through a bridge girder or blow the giant flywheel off a power station turbine, causing a hurricane of damage to everything it careered into.

After Beaulieu, most of Landes's colleagues were given leave, while waiting for an aircraft and a full moon to parachute into France. In Claude de Baissac's final report he was assessed as 'an excellent operator' destined for leadership. Not seeing the same qualities of 'leadership' in Landes, SOE marked him out for a radio operator and sent him to their wireless school at Thame, near Aylesbury. Here he met another fellow student, destined to join him in France. Gilbert Norman, also an ex-public school boy, was an imposing figure whose regular features, permanent suntan and moustache gave him the air of an actor who specialised in playing cads – or perhaps army captains – in a seaside repertory company. In fact, he was a chartered accountant from Llandudno. In July 1942 the two men passed out as fully qualified SOE wireless operators.

Roger Landes had done well. 'He has the eye of a marksman ... works well with others ... liked for his keenness ... very fit and tries hard ... did exceptionally well on his own,' his trainers wrote on his various reports: 'a pleasant little man who takes great interest and trouble in what he does ...'. Of all Landes's attributes it would be his ability to work alone and his unobtrusiveness which would make him a truly great secret agent.

But Roger Landes was now much more than the sum of his good reports.

He had been transformed – and he had transformed himself – from a young Jewish refugee from Paris, working as an architect's clerk in the LCC, into a fully capable secret agent and radio operator, ready to take the fight to the enemy in occupied France. To be sure, he still looked as he had always done: small, pleasant, unremarkable. But inside, he was now something completely different. Something hard, uncompromising, focused – even a little cold; always alert, always suspicious, always watchful. Above all, he was confident of his own strength and his ability to survive and to endure.

3

FRIEDRICH DOHSE

On 26 January 1942, a fortnight or so before Roger Landes saw the message on the company noticeboard at Prestatyn, a young German officer stepped down from a first-class carriage at Saint-Jean station in Bordeaux. His Gestapo uniform, if anyone had glimpsed it, might have attracted attention, for few if any of these had been seen in Bordeaux at this time of the war. But muffled and greatcoated against the exceptional cold that had gripped France that January, he would have seemed to most to be just another German officer making his way in the throng that pressed towards the checkpoint at the station exit. Yet, over the next few years, Dohse would come to dominate the city and shape its events more than any other German who had come to Bordeaux since the occupation.

Six foot three and of athletic build, with sharp grey eyes deep set under a heavy brow in a pale oval face; chestnut, but fast vanishing hair; an easy smile and regular features (apart from rather small a mouth) – twenty-eight-year-old Friedrich Wilhelm Heinrich Dohse (pronounced 'dosuh') was a man who commanded attention quite as much as Roger Landes deflected it.

His journey to this moment had been a long one. Although his grandfather had been a peasant farmer in Silesia, his father, Hinrich, had risen to become a French teacher in the little Schleswig-Holstein town of Elmshorn, north of Hamburg. Here, Friedrich was born in July 1913. His family was respectable, bourgeois, Lutheran and of moderate political views (which he shared). Like his sisters and brother, he attended the local secondary school, before moving on to commercial college in

Hamburg, where he excelled in French. Leaving school at seventeen, he travelled the short distance to the city's port where he joined the merchant marine, serving on passenger liners to South America and East Africa. In 1933, at the height of the German Depression and finding himself unemployed, the twenty-year-old Friedrich joined the Hamburg police and local Nazi party. Later he would insist that he became a Nazi because it was the only way to get a job, though it was often remarked that, on the rare occasions he wore his Gestapo uniform, he never failed to emblazon it with the 'Golden Party Badge', awarded only to those in the Nazi party of 'special merit', or who had been amongst the first 100,000 to join.

Whatever Dohse's motives, becoming a Nazi seems to have worked, for after five months as an ordinary policeman he was offered a job with the criminal police in a Hamburg suburb. Dohse soon transferred to the Gestapo in Kiel, where he was employed in counter-espionage against marine saboteurs. He continued his progress into the hierarchy of Hitler's Germany by joining the Sturmabteilung (SA), the Nazi paramilitary wing, on 1 June 1934. Just weeks later Hitler destroyed the organisation in the great 'blood purge' of 30 June. Nothing daunted, two years after this reverse, Dohse became a member of the Schutzstaffel, or SS, Hitler's 'protection squadron', and wore its badge, with the letters SS in the form of two jagged lightning bolts, for the rest of his wartime career. In 1937, Dohse completed his eight weeks' infantry training and on the outbreak of war was called up, quickly rising to the rank of sergeant. It is difficult not to see the young Dohse during these years as a man of ambition and strong patriotic convictions, dedicated to serving his country, while scrambling up the Nazi ladder as fast as he could.

After brief spells first in the army, and then the Luftwaffe, Dohse was posted back to the Gestapo as a sergeant in the spring of 1941. Now married and with two young children, he was sent on 15 June to Paris. Here he was seconded to the counter-espionage section of the newly established German directorate of security (the BdS), headquartered at 82–84 Avenue Foch – an address which was already becoming one of the most feared in France. At the time the Gestapo was not formally permitted to operate in France, making Dohse one of the first Gestapo officers to work on French soil.

It was this posting, more than any other event of his young life, which transformed Dohse from a junior up-and-coming member of the Gestapo into a subtle, cunning and accomplished counter-intelligence operator. For it was here that he met the man who would become both the mentor from whom he learnt his skills and the protector who would cover his back in the dangerous times ahead.

Karl Bömelburg, aged fifty-six in 1941, was the son of a pastry cook and a man of many skills, disguises and aliases (including 'Charles Bois', 'Herr Bennelburger' and 'Colonel Mollemburg'). According to both Paris rumour and British intelligence records, he was also – very unusually for a high-ranking Nazi – known to have homosexual proclivities. Elegant and cultivated, Bömelburg was a notable bon viveur, fluent in French, an enthusiastic Francophile and a master of the art of spying. 'Though not a *political* Nazi', according to his superior in Berlin, 'he was completely loyal and a committed anti-communist.' According to one account, he had spent eight years before the war operating undercover as a silk merchant in Lyon. Other records suggest that he was part of the German embassy in Paris in 1938, where, with the knowledge of the French government, he was tasked with rooting out communist subversives from the German immigrant population in France. During these interwar years, under the cover of his anti-communist work, Bömelburg built a German spy network which extended deep into French society and commercial life.

Regarded by his close colleagues as a 'little God', Bömelburg seems to have immediately spotted something unusual and appealing – a kindred spirit perhaps – in the new arrival from Schleswig-Holstein. He dispatched Dohse first to the Berlitz school in Paris to perfect his French, and then on a month's detachment to each of the departments in the Avenue Foch to get him acquainted with every part of the German security apparatus in Paris. His initiation complete, Bömelburg appointed his young protégé as his personal secretary and, though Bömelburg would not have needed it, his official interpreter.

It was in this capacity that, in July and August 1941, Dohse accompanied his chief and another senior SS intelligence officer on a two-month tour across occupied and Vichy France and into Italy. The three men travelled in some state in Bömelburg's pride and joy, a requisitioned armour-plated Cadillac chauffeured by his personal driver. The main purpose of the tour was for Bömelburg to reactivate and debrief his old spy network, but the trio did not ignore the opportunity to have fun as well. Their itinerary included Vichy, Dijon, Lyon, Saint-Étienne, Montélimar, Aix-en-Provence, Marseille, Toulon, Saint-Raphaël, Cannes, Ventimiglia, San Remo and Monte-Carlo, where Dohse won 25,000 francs at the gaming tables (enough to have a fur coat made up in Paris and sent to his wife in Elmshorn).

What Bömelburg taught Dohse during their escapade of the summer of 1941, and in the months which followed at BdS Paris, is that counter-espionage is an art in which the techniques of subtlety and persuasion are more important, and usually more successful, than those of brutality and threat. Dohse was neither squeamish about torture, nor morally opposed to it. He argued that 'enhanced interrogation' – a euphemism used by the Nazis which is still in active use today – could be 'necessary … in situations where the lives of German soldiers were at imminent threat'. Dohse had, moreover, no qualms at all about leaving brutality to others if it meant that he could use the techniques of persuasion, personal charm and the disarming power of an act of kindness to better effect. In his own words: 'I didn't need to dirty my hands – others did that.' Later, after the war, Dohse was to invest this way of working with moral principle, claiming that it was all intended to 'humanise' (his word again) the struggle against Resistance 'terrorists'.

What, above all, Dohse the interrogator learnt from Bömelburg was the importance of knowing his subjects and their psychologies, weaknesses and desires, the better to turn them to his purpose. As one commentator later put it, Dohse 'did not terrify, he demobilised'.

Neither these more subtle skills – nor Dohse's habit of easy superiority, nor his elegant style of dress, nor his cultivated tastes, nor his pragmatic, non-ideological approach to his task; nor his Francophilia, nor his preference for French company over that of many of his German colleagues (he was referred to disparagingly as 'half French'); nor the high level of protection he enjoyed in Paris made the young, pushy, newly arrived Gestapo officer at all popular amongst his more hardline colleagues in Bordeaux. He was, in many ways, a man apart amongst the more traditional Nazis who dominated the German security structures of the time. His loyalty to the German cause was unchallenged – and unchallengeable – at this stage of the war. His pride in his professionalism as a police officer, his sense of personal honour and his duty of loyalty to his superiors made it easy for him to be ambivalent to the excesses of National Socialism. Nazi politics and prejudices held no interest for him, beyond the point that they were necessary for the pursuit of his ambition and his ability to serve his country. Dohse was not intelligent in the intellectual sense of the word. But he was wily and clever and quick to win people to his point of view. Nor was his spirit a heroic one. He liked Bordeaux because it was congenial, and because he liked France. But he liked it most of all because it was not the Russian front.

Dohse's arrival in Bordeaux in January 1942 coincided with the centralising of the city's security structure – chiefly the SS and the police – into the one new grouping known for short as 'KdS Bordeaux'. The organisation would eventually grow to around a hundred German officers, assisted by a large number of French men and women in various supporting roles. They were housed in four large requisitioned residential properties in what was virtually a KdS colony, stretching along a 200-metre section of the Avenue du Maréchal Pétain in the northern Bordeaux suburb of Bouscat. The new office was split into seven departments: I: Administration; II: Liaison with the French authorities and Jewish matters; III: Political affairs (also including Jewish matters); IV: Intelligence-gathering and the suppression of the Resistance; V: Economic crime and the black market; VI: Internal security; and, last but not least, Department VII: Archives and Records. The site also boasted a canteen converted from an old casino, indoor and outdoor recreation areas and staff accommodation.

When Dohse arrived, the commander at KdS Bordeaux was twenty-nine-year-old SS-Sturmbannführer Herbert Hagen, a close friend of Adolf Eichmann's. Dohse was given command of Department IV: 'Intelligence and the suppression of the Resistance'. His remit was the elimination of all threats to German troops, organisations and installations, and his department was the largest and – by common acceptance – the most important of the newly fledged organisation.

This irked his new colleagues even more. Before the formation of KdS Bordeaux, security in the region had been more or less the exclusive preserve of the Sicherheitsdienst (SD). Now the long-established SD officers would have to share the role with the uppity Gestapo man with well-connected friends in Paris. To make matters worse, Dohse's initial role in Bordeaux was hazy. He was not at first sent to the city as a member of the KdS, but as a kind of liaison officer, representing the security police structures in the French capital. The fact that Dohse, a mere detective superintendent, was of more junior rank than most of the KdS section heads added insult to injury. Hagen – who despite being eight weeks younger than Dohse was the overall head of KdS – initially assigned only translation work to the unwelcome new arrival, and had him billeted in a pokey little bedroom which he had to share with a Spanish agent. 'I took the first train to Paris [to tell Bömelburg] that this would not do,' Dohse later explained. Things changed immediately. The Gestapo officer was, albeit with bad grace, given accommodation suitable to his status, his own office to work in and the space and support he needed to begin assembling his new department.

It was a demonstration to all that the young interloper's power did not lie in his modest rank, but in the fact that Bömelburg was his high-level protector in Paris. It was because of this, as one colleague later said of Dohse, that 'everyone in KdS feared him'.

4

ANDRÉ GRANDCLÉMENT

André Grandclément was born with everything – except steadfastness of purpose, good judgement, and a father who loved him.

Captain Raoul Gaston Marie Grandclément, Chevalier de la Légion d'Honneur, was serving as a staff officer to the French Second Naval Squadron in Rochefort-sur-Mer, 150 kilometres northwest of Bordeaux, when his son, André Marie Hubert François, was born in the local hospital on 28 July 1909.

In his father's absence (the future admiral was posted to Morocco two years after André's birth), the boy was brought up by his mother, Amélia, the daughter of a colonel of infantry. When André was seven, Amélia died and his father married again. Care of the young boy passed to his stepmother, Jeanne, who he loved greatly. The couple lived in a grand house in the sixteenth arrondissement of Paris, an area famously known as 'the invisible ghetto' because of the many members of the French establishment who lived there. Often criticised as being immune and insensible to the social upheavals that rocked France in the 1930s, the prevailing culture of the invisible ghetto during André's early years was one of conservatism, a firm belief that national order depended on the preservation of the national hierarchy, and a fierce and unshakeable belief, come what may, in *La gloire française*.

André, like many of the sons of France's military, was sent to the Franklin Jesuit College just a few hundred metres from his home. Here the values of the invisible ghetto were as much part of the curriculum as the rote learning of mathematics, foreign languages, French history and literature. It was at Franklin that the young Grandclément met and befriended a fellow student, Marc O'Neill. Descended from one of the 'Wild Swans' who had fled an oppressed Ireland in 1688 and subsequently fought for revolutionary France in the eighteenth century, O'Neill would, in the years to come, show that the family instinct for fighting oppression had not diminished in the intervening centuries.

In what was to become something of a pattern in André Grandclément's young life, he failed to finish his studies at Franklin College, leaving at the age of twelve to join his father, now an admiral and Grand Croix de la Légion d'Honneur, who had been posted to command a French naval division in Syria in 1921. Admiral Grandclément had won acclaim in the First World War, including two terms as naval attaché to President Raymond Poincaré, and in action at the battle of Verdun, where he was wounded while 'showing the greatest dynamism and a superb disregard for danger'. Grandclément senior spent his time in Syria, adorned with medals and a feathered hat, saluting everything military that moved as they passed him in review. Grandclément junior, meanwhile, looked on in distant admiration from first Beirut and then Tunis, where he continued his studies under the Jesuits. Finally, in his late teens André changed schools for the fourth time and returned to Paris to take his Baccalauréat.

Grandclément senior, whose brother and cousin were also admirals, had long made it clear that he expected his son to follow the family tradition and join the navy. It was now time for André to do his duty and prepare for the entrance exams for France's naval college, the École Navale, at Brest. But something seems to have snapped in young André during his period of preparation for the great naval school. One day, he peremptorily resigned his place and joined up as an ordinary soldier in a Senegalese rifle regiment in Sfax, North Africa. Writing to a friend he said: 'So now I am going to be with the negroes, with whom, if truth be told, I find a greater affinity than with the whites.' André Grandclément had become – and would remain for the rest of his life – the outsider who longed to be inside.

Explaining his sudden and perplexing flight from a naval career, Grandclément junior later wrote: 'At eighteen, I rejected my father as a result of a foolish row. If that had not happened I would have maintained the family tradition … [but then] I would have ended up less human – like my father.'

A little later, on a weekend visit to the Bizerta home of one of his father's friends, the twenty-year-old André, ever romantic, ever impetuous, fell in love with the colonel's daughter, Geneviève Toussaint, known as 'Myssett'. Almost immediately he announced his intention to marry his new sweetheart. The admiral was predictably furious, but his son was adamant.

The couple married in Bizerta on 6 November 1929. Though he did it with bad grace and complained of the expense, the old admiral made the journey from Paris to join a small flotilla of senior naval Grandcléments who sailed into the cathedral of Notre-Dame-de-France in Bizerta for the ceremony, complete with clanking swords, heavy encrustations of medals, elegantly trimmed naval beards and, of course, the inevitable feather-festooned cocked hats.

André and Myssett had five children in quick succession. Three died young, leaving two daughters: Ghislaine, paralysed as a result of brain damage at birth, and Francine, four years her junior.

A year after the wedding, André suddenly announced yet another change of course: he was thinking of leaving the army. The young Grandclément family, now feeling the pinch financially (another regular feature of André Grandclément's life), transhipped to Toulon. Here, in 1932, André declared that he was not after all leaving the army, but would instead attend the officer school at Saint-Maixent in the Somme valley. As ever, full of hope and resolution, he wrote to his wife: 'I am very happy … and well aware of the value of two years of engagement once again in the business of learning and study.'

All seemed set fair once more. But then, fate again intervened – this time in the form of a serious riding accident which left him unfit for military service as a result of a damaged lung and, according to his doctor, tuberculosis as well. A short period of work in the wine business on the Côte d'Or followed. Then thanks to the patronage of a cousin, he was offered a job as a salesman with the insurance company Mutuelle Vie in Bordeaux. He and his family moved into a cramped first-floor apartment above a garage on the Rue Basse, a narrow street set back from the Pont de Pierre. It was all a long, long way from the pomp, gilt and glitter of the Bizerta cathedral wedding, just six years previously.

The twenty-six-year-old Grandclément who arrived in Bordeaux in 1935 was tall, slim, elegant, suntanned and clean cut. Though he had a curiously expressionless face, he was considered handsome, with blue eyes, a slightly hooked nose, a prominent chin and meticulously coiffured hair. Many who knew him commented on his verbal dexterity and his ability to carry an audience, albeit with a tendency, on occasion, to sound pompous. This together with a certain grace made him impressive – even beguiling – on first acquaintance: 'intelligent, amiable, sensitive, good looking and with considerable presence,' said one contemporary. Others were less enamoured. 'He greatly overestimated his own importance. He was a kind of [ideological] gigolo,' remembered one close colleague, while another described him as carrying 'himself badly with a stooping head and shoulders as a result of some chest affliction. He has a pale face and a prominent nose.'

André Grandclément's early opinions were those of his class and upbringing: Catholic and conservative, but not active in either cause. Later, preparing for the navy, he apparently shared the royalist sympathies of his classmates. After his marriage to Myssett the couple affected a bohemian lifestyle; there are even some suggestions of left-wing views during André's time with the Senegalese rifle regiment. By the mid-1930s, however, he was close to the Croix-de-Feu, a right-wing political organisation, subsequently banned for its fascist leanings. Later police reports reflect these internal ambivalences, one noting him as a 'dangerously militant communist', suspected of hiding arms, while another described him as 'a faithful partisan' of the Vichy government. In reality, in these immediate pre-war years, André Grandclément, the perennially restless optimist who was always certain that the next chance was the best one, was still seeking a safe harbour for his views, just as he was looking for a secure financial future for his young family and a fitting purpose for his life.

The truth was that behind what was, at first sight, an imposing front, there lay a weak man in everything except his attachment to his daughters – especially little Ghislaine. The chief drivers of his personality were vanity, a hunger for recognition and the certainty that, despite the low opinion of his father and the moderate opinions of his contemporaries, there was nevertheless some important purpose to his life to match his hitherto unrecognised talents.

On 24 September 1939, just days after war broke out, Grandclément met a pretty young divorcée who worked in the same office building in Bordeaux. Not long after, the two became lovers and in due course he declared Lucette Tartas – vivacious, intelligent, firm in her views, and in many ways much stronger than her lover – his 'official mistress'. In this capacity, according to the curious French custom of the time, Lucette was recognised by the family and his wife. Myssett, her heart broken, took to the country with the two girls and began an official separation from her husband.

The love affair between Grandclément and Lucette Tartas was deep, genuine and endearing. 'Their love for each other dazzled ... like a couple straight out of one of those pre-war musical comedies,' one contemporary observed.

Weeks after meeting Lucette, and despite his physical incapacity, Grandclément managed to pull enough strings to be declared 'fit for service'. He joined the battle for France, fighting with an infantry regiment engaged in the frantic attempts to stop German armour breaking through the Ardennes forest. Here he showed considerable military ability and was mentioned in dispatches for bravery. But this too did not last. When France surrendered, he was demobilised and returned to the role of a humble insurance agent in Bordeaux.

By 1940, with burgeoning medical expenses for the treatment of Ghislaine, the Grandcléments were once again in difficult financial straits. It was all too much for Myssett, who now sued for divorce. But by early 1941 the insurance business started looking up again – so much so that in September of that year André and Lucette were able to move house. They rented an elegant and spacious apartment at 34 Cours de Verdun, in a fashionable neighbourhood of central Bordeaux and just opposite the main headquarters of the special French police brigade under Pierre Poinsot.

By now, the public face of André Grandclément was hiding a deeper and much more dangerous life. The war had finally provided him with a secure political anchorage. He was, he decided, conservative, republican and, like many of his class (especially the fascist-leaning revolutionary group known as the '*Cagoule militaire*' in the army, with whom he had both connections and sympathy), intensely patriotic, right-wing and nationalist. To start with he was a fervent supporter of Pétain's Vichy administration. But, though he remained loyal to Pétain himself, he became disenchanted with the armistice and the Vichy government and began looking elsewhere for an organisation which would give him the opportunity to resist the German occupation, whilst remaining true to the right-wing authoritarian France in which he believed.

Sometime in 1941 Grandclément began to get involved in Resistance activities, working at a senior level in two relatively minor covert organ-isations. It was the beginning of a new enthusiasm in his life. But it was not enough. He needed something larger to match his talents.

In September 1941, a school teacher from Bordeaux set up a local branch of an underground organisation called the Organisation Civile et Militaire (OCM). The OCM's roots lay in a group of eight French ex-army officers who had set up a minor escape line to London in August 1940. By 1942 the organisation had expanded from these small beginnings into a vast, hierarchical, rambling movement made up chiefly of ex-army officers, intellectuals and government servants, covering the western half of the German occupied zone. Its activities included gathering intelli-gence, organising arms depots, managing escape routes, minor sabotage, setting up Maquisard units and hunting down collaborators.

This was the kind of secret network that immediately appealed to André Grandclément's sense of scale, romance and adventure – and these were his kind of people, too: ex-military, Catholic, conservative, strongly anti-communist and in many cases anti-Semitic as well.

Jean Duboué and Léo Paillère, the neighbours from the Quai des Chartrons who were by this time sending regular secret intelligence reports to London, were also early members of the OCM. Indeed from late 1941 Paillère was its chief of staff in southwest France. But in 1942 he was arrested and imprisoned for six months for black-market offences involving no less than 1.5 million francs' worth of Armagnac and illegally distilled *eau de vie*. The regional OCM was left without a leader. OCM's national head in Paris, Colonel Alfred Touny, sought a replacement and solicited the advice of two key southwest OCM members, both of whom just happened to be close to André Grandclément. One was his old Jesuit College friend, Marc O'Neill; the other, his uncle, General Paul Jouffrault (who was already head of the OCM in the Vendée). Both agreed that André would be perfect as the new head of the southwest chapter, which covered a vast swathe of France, from the Loire valley to the Pyrenees.

This was a fateful and extraordinary decision. For, apart from high-level family connections and an ex-school friend in the right place at the right time, André Grandclément, though a good organiser and a patriot, was temperamentally completely unsuitable for the task with which he was now entrusted. For Grandclément, however, his moment had arrived at last. Here was a role worthy of his talents as a mover of men and a shaper of events: a position of truly national importance. And if the Allies landed in 1943, as everyone believed they would – possibly even nearby, in the Gulf of Aquitaine – then here was a role which would assure him a place in history, too. What would his father, the admiral, think of that!

In the spring of 1942, as Roger Landes was busy training as a spy, and Friedrich Dohse was setting up his counter-espionage department in Bouscat, André Grandclément, the thirty-three-year-old insurance salesman, was given the leadership of the largest and most powerful Resistance organisation in southwest France. The change in him was immediate and dramatic. 'With Lucette on his arm, André Grandclément was now a man who was utterly content and sure of himself,' wrote one close observer. 'He was no longer the insurance agent always complaining about life's unfairness and injustices … Now he was living another life, with entirely new aims. Now he was fighting for his country and need no longer concern himself with such petty matters as finances and money. The transformation in him was complete – both morally and physically.'

5

A HAPPY MAN AND A DEAD BODY

The cold of January 1942 held on tenaciously into February and March. The vines of the Médoc and the plane trees of Bordeaux remained stubbornly and unseasonably bare.

These had been frustrating months for Friedrich Dohse. Constrained by the passive obstructionism of his boss, Herbert Hagen, and open hostility in KdS Bordeaux, he was also held back by the fact that, until a special decree was issued by Hitler on 1 June 1942, the Gestapo (soon to be rechristened, in French argot, '*La Georgette*') were not formally permitted to operate in France.

But Dohse was not a man to waste time. Using the skills he had learnt in the criminal police in Hamburg, he spent the first few months of 1942 gathering information, creating a filing system and recruiting staff to his new department. Here too he had to cope with interference from his German intelligence colleagues – in this case the Abwehr, who made determined attempts to poach his new recruits; things got so bad that he finally had to ban their officers from all contact with his team.

Despite these impediments, over the next months Dohse managed to recruit forty-eight German officers, who, supported by about twenty French assistants (including interpreters, typists, cooks and clerks), would form the base of his organisation. Amongst these, three were of particular note.

Rudolf Kunesch was an Austrian Wehrmacht soldier drafted into KdS and, though senior to Dohse in rank, was assigned to be his deputy. This clumsy arrangement meant that Dohse could not give Kunesch direct instructions, except through Hagen. While Dohse himself normally initiated operations, it was Kunesch who frequently commanded them, leaving his 'chief' to attend only in the technical role of 'observer'. Tensions were not improved by the fact that when prisoners were brought in, it was Kunesch, not Dohse, who interrogated them first. Overweight, balding, thick-lipped, an energetic drinker, with a face straight out of a 1930s gangster film, Kunesch was regarded as 'brutal and stupid'. His heavy-handed approach stood in sharp contrast to Dohse's preference for more subtle techniques. These differences, exacerbated by the lack of clarity about their relative seniority, meant that relations between the two men were very often strained to the point of open warfare – though there is no record of Dohse ever complaining about his deputy's brutal methods.

Kunesch was in due course supported by his 'chief torturer', Anton Enzelsberger. Known as 'Tony the Boxer', Enzelsberger had been heavyweight boxing champion of Austria. With only one working eye (ice blue) and a shaven head, Enzelsberger was as close as one could get to the caricature of a dyed-in-the-wool, hatchet-faced Nazi thug. He was also a regular soldier, untrained in police skills, and had been released from a sentence for murder when Hitler annexed Austria. Kunesch, Enzelsberger and their subordinates preferred torture to all other means of extracting confessions from their subjects. Among their favourite instruments of persuasion were a rubber cosh (Kunesch was known as 'the cosher-in-chief'); a whip similar to a cat o' nine tails; and an arrangement consisting of two braziers backed by a reflector, in front of which prisoners were placed to slowly roast like pieces of meat on a barbecue.

Another new recruit was forty-two-year-old Marcelle Louise Sommer. Born in the Swiss Romande, Marcelle Sommer had been interned with her mother by the French during the First World War and spoke flawless French. She spent some years between the wars working first at a department store in Paris and then in – and very probably spying on – the Michelin factory in Clermont-Ferrand. Hated and feared in equal measure, she became known locally as the 'lioness of the Gestapo'. Though she had started as Dohse's personal assistant (and had been one of those the Abwehr had tried to poach), she quickly rose to become head of Department IV's intelligence section. Tall, imposing and statuesque, even without the high heels she habitually wore, she was the mistress of one of Dohse's section chiefs (and one of his few close personal German friends), SS-Obersturmführer Schöder. Dohse trusted Sommer completely and gave her full autonomy to run her own network of French agents, which included many women and prostitutes employed as agents provocateurs.

Dohse's personal assistant was twenty-five-year-old Claire Keimer, whose blonde tresses and Wagnerian proportions soon became well known in Bordeaux. Intelligent, quick-witted, ambitious, fluent in French and a natural in the spying business, it was not long before the two became lovers. Her role, however, extended well beyond being Dohse's mistress, for over time she also became his chief confidante and adviser – often attending his interrogations and participating in conferences to decide strategy and policy.

The main elements of Dohse's staff assembled, he and Sommer set about creating a network of agents. Among the most important of these were 108 individuals each paid 5,000 francs a month (the equivalent of around £1,000 today), plus expenses. These included 'agents of influence' – senior officials in the French administration and police, key leaders in pro-Gestapo French paramilitary units – and undercover agents who were used to infiltrate Resistance groups and organisations. The financial resources available to Dohse's section were, like those of all the German secret services, almost unlimited. French counter-intelligence at the time commented that '[German] officers, civil servants and agents … spend without limit and enrich themselves without scruple'. There was even a fixed tariff for information and betrayal:

denunciation of a Jew or a Communist = 1,000 francs
denunciation of a Gaullist = 3,000 francs
information leading to the discovery of a weapons cache = 5,000–
    30,000 francs (depending on the size of the horde)

One French collaborator, the appropriately named Johann Dollar, is calculated to have earned, in a single year, the equivalent (at today's prices) of £18,600, for information passed to the Germans.

Dohse's most important collaborator on the French side was the local police chief, Pierre Poinsot, the scourge of the communists in 1941. Now, as the head of the new Vichy French police brigade known as the Section des Affaires Politiques (or SAP), he also ran his own network of agents. Dohse made Poinsot a paid informer, supplementing his meagre French policeman's salary with occasional bonuses (amounting on one occasion to 10,000 francs, accompanied by a further 20,000 to be distributed to his men). Poinsot and his unit, who soon became known as the 'murder brigade' for their habit of killing and extreme torture, now became, to all intents and purposes, an extension of Dohse's Gestapo organisation. Poinsot reported to Dohse daily, arrested whoever Dohse wanted, tortured (or refrained from torturing) whoever Dohse wanted, and did nothing unless Dohse approved of it. On one occasion Dohse 'interrupted' one of Poinsot's torture sessions on a young resistant: 'I said to Poinsot "Enough! Get him dressed"', Dohse later claimed. 'Then I put the young man in my car and sat him next to me. He was not chained or handcuffed. I said "Listen. Tell me the truth … or I will hand you back to the French police" … it was not a nice thing to do – but it was my job … I took the young man to my home and had him fed – and he gave me everything.'

It is fair at this stage to point out that, although torture, extreme brutality and executions were largely institutionalised among the Nazi security forces and Poinsot's SAP, the Resistance were also not squeamish about using 'enhanced techniques of persuasion' and punishment. A female SOE agent connected with Bordeaux describes in a post-mission report how two newspaper journalists in Poitiers suspected of collaboration were executed by the local Resistance, one by being shot and the second by being first tortured and then killed using a metal file, with which he was stabbed more than twenty times.

In all, Dohse and Sommer recruited more than a hundred low-level French, Russian and Spanish agents scattered across the region. A headquarters for this spy network was established in the Place de la Cathédrale in Bordeaux. This was supplemented by the establishment of a number of safe houses around the city and by the formation of right-wing French paramilitary organisations, which provided Dohse with information and operational support as required. In due course, the French forces which Dohse could rely on also included the much-hated, black-shirted Milice française ('French militia'). Raised with the help of the Germans in 1943, but not active in Bordeaux until the spring of 1944, this paramilitary force, created to fight communism and 'terrorism', was drawn largely from the ranks of the French fascists and the criminal fraternity.

In early May 1942, Dohse finally found a proper home for his now fast-growing unit. He requisitioned a large property at 197 Avenue du Maréchal Pétain, opposite the main KdS headquarters in Bouscat. The building, a substantial nineteenth-century château on three floors, stood in its own grounds and was protected by a low wall which supported a fence of robust cast-iron railings. Substantial wine cellars beneath the house were converted into prison cells and, when occasion arose, torture chambers. Dohse chose an airy room on the ground floor at the rear of the building, adjacent to a handsome glass veranda which gave access to the garden and stables, as his office. The stables, too, were converted for use as interrogation cells. The most notorious of these was christened the *Chambre d'action*. Above the door was a notice instructing 'No water, no food'.

At the start, Dohse was assiduous when it came to protecting his back, making a point of taking the train to Paris to brief Bömelburg almost every weekend. He also acted as secretary and translator to a Franco-German body based in the French capital called the Cercle Européen. This discussed a future united Europe formed around an axis between Germany and France. As time passed, however, Dohse felt secure enough to visit Paris less and enjoy southwest France more.

In the second week of April 1942, a mini-heatwave hit Bordeaux, bringing spring to the city in a rush. The vines in the Charente and the Médoc flowered early and the restaurants threw open the doors they had kept firmly closed all the long bitter winter and spilled out onto terraces and pavements in gay profusion.

On 1 May, Dohse's obstructive boss, Hagen, was posted to Paris. His replacement was a thirty-three-year-old ex-judge from Frankfurt called Hans Luther. Though Luther was punctilious and sociable, Dohse did not have a high opinion of his new commander, whom he regarded as lazy and 'just an administrator ... not qualified for this kind of post ... he just gave the orders, that was all'. However, with Hagen gone and a chief who seemed more interested in having a good time than interfering, Dohse's life became much easier. He was by now beginning to be recognised by fellow Germans in KdS Bordeaux as an effective, even if not likeable, colleague, while at the same time enjoying a certain notoriety – popularity, even – among the local population.

Dohse at this stage could do more or less as he pleased. He moved his personal accommodation out of the Bouscat Gestapo colony and took up residence in a small town villa at 145 Route du Médoc, in the northwest of the city, which he shared with three colleagues. Here he held frequent dinners, inviting many of his French friends as well as those closest to him among the German contingent in the KdS. Soon the villa, permanently guarded by two French policemen, became something of a hub of social activity in the city. Each morning if the weather was fine, Dohse's personal chauffeur would collect him in an open-topped car – invariably dressed in an elegant suit, set off with a fashionable tie – and carry him in state on the short journey to his office in Bouscat. At lunchtime his habit was to be driven to his favourite restaurant, where he would enjoy a glass or two of champagne and a convivial lunch with his French friends.

Around this time Dohse seems to have copied his patron in Paris, Bömelburg, acquiring, probably through requisition, a large black Cadillac which he used for longer journeys. At weekends, he and Claire Keimer would frequently be driven to the little seaside resort of Pyla on the gulf of Arcachon, where Dohse took a villa; or, if he had business to conduct with German intelligence colleagues in Spain, he would drive with Claire to the picturesque Spanish coastal town of San Sebastián, which had by now become a hotbed of spying, centred on the British and

German consulates and a restaurant called Casa d'Italia. Here all the resident spies gathered to drink and regard each other with suspicion and as much enmity as they could muster in such convivial surroundings. Dohse even boasted he had literally rubbed shoulders with 'Mr Gutsman, my British opposite number'.

'I liked the good life and had lots of parties. And I had a host of French friends – not collaborators … (just friends) with whom I had many good dinners at which not a word of politics was spoken,' Dohse claimed after the war. 'I did not want to die on the Russian front. Life in France was much more pleasant – much more fun. One was able to enjoy all the things one could wish for.'

'Dohse loved Bordeaux,' one observer wryly commented. 'His table was refined, and his mistress, beautiful. Dohse was a happy man. And those are the most dangerous.'

At this point in the war, danger seemed rather far away to Friedrich Dohse and his German compatriots in Bordeaux. True, in mid-1941, agents parachuted in by London had attacked and destroyed a power station in the Bordeaux suburb of Pessac. But the damage had been slight, the interruption of power short and, apart from a dozen German soldiers shot for their failure to protect the installation, little of consequence had resulted from the British raid. On 23 April 1941, for the first time, a British parachute drop of weapons was discovered near the little village of Cestas, fifteen kilometres southwest of Bordeaux. This caused much astonishment among the locals and dramatic reports from the local French police. There had also been RAF bombing raids on the port of Bordeaux – but these had been infrequent, haphazard and poorly targeted, often killing many more French civilians than German personnel and causing damage to many more residential properties than military installations. If anything, the raids served to fuel anti-British sentiment in the city.

Leaving aside the regular drives against the communists (there was one in June 1942, following Poinsot's success in turning a senior communist), things on the security front were quiet and life for Bordeaux's occupiers rather congenial.

But beneath this seemingly placid surface, things were changing. By the middle of 1942, OCM, now numbering some 800 Resistance fighters and 100 officers, had expanded to cover almost the whole of southwest France, from the Charente region west to the Pyrenees and from the Aquitaine coast south to Toulouse. Among the local Resistance organisations which had by now been fully subsumed into the OCM was the Duboué–Paillère network centred on Duboué's Café du Commerce at 83 Quai des Chartrons. This group had grown too, and by this time consisted of fourteen active units with, between them, eight parachute sites in the area. Its new recruits included nine living along the Bordeaux waterfront. Two of these were Marcel Bertrand and his wife, who ran the Café des Chartrons at the Bacalan end of the quay. Duboué used the Bertrand café as his chief clandestine 'letterbox' through which he passed his reports and messages to London and to other members of his group.

Meanwhile, the new head of OCM Southwest, André Grandclément, had also been busy – recceing potential parachute drop sites, overseeing the hiding of arms, establishing escape routes, issuing orders, setting up a hierarchy of command and devising a system of secret communication. The pity was that, in almost every other way, the OCM was not secret at all. Its existence was by now widely known of and boasted about in the Bordeaux area. Grandclément's meetings – which tended to be a cross between a meeting of the golf club committee and a cocktail party – were held regularly and in the same place – at 34 Cours de Verdun, the home he shared with Lucette. Worst of all, members of the OCM could and did belong to other Resistance organisations as well. This meant that if one secret organisation was penetrated the rot could quickly spread to endanger all of them.

In the spring of 1942 an event occurred which made it explicitly clear to the German authorities that this burgeoning underground activity was not just a local matter: London, too, was getting involved in Bordeaux.

On the morning of Sunday 3 May 1942, the weather in Langon, a market town bisected by the demarcation line in the Gironde, was as bright and glorious as a spring morning could be. At 8.38, the regular Sunday morning country train from the small market town of Luxey, seventy kilometres south of Bordeaux, puffed slowly into Langon station, which stands astride the main junction between the rural lines which serve south Gironde and the express line from Toulouse to Bordeaux. Among the passengers who climbed down onto the platform and lined up to have their papers checked was a smartly dressed man who had joined the train at 0549 that morning at the tiny railway halt in the village of Sore, twenty kilometres away. He was young and handsome, with a round face enlivened by alert brown eyes and a small, rather unkempt moustache. He carried a rucksack and a small brown suitcase and, despite the warm day, wore a navy gabardine mac, a suit (light grey with white and blue stripes), a short-sleeved pullover, a shirt, tie (blue, with red and white spots), blue socks and dark brown shoes. When his turn came, he stepped forward and handed his papers to the German customs official for inspection. The official studied them carefully and, finding something out of place, ordered the young traveller to step into the customs office for further enquiries and a search of his luggage.

It may have been Henri Labit's suitcase which attracted the unwelcome attention – for at this stage of the war SOE was in the habit of issuing the exactly same make and colour of cheap cardboard suitcase (and, for that matter, the same make of pyjamas) to all their agents – something which the Gestapo had already spotted. Karl Schröder, the head of the small German section at Langon, opened Labit's case to discover a radio transmitter. Labit's response was instantaneous. He pulled a Colt automatic out of his pocket, shot Schröder dead, wounded three other guards in the room and made a run for it. Some of the wounded men gave chase, firing after the fugitive. The local gendarmes were called in. Someone reported that they had seen a man running near the town cemetery. The area was quickly surrounded and the young man was spotted leaning, seemingly wounded, against a wall with his Colt in his hand. Before the pursuers could get to him, he collapsed. By the time they reached him, his lips were blue and white foam was frothing from his mouth.

Henri Labit (alias 'Leroy'), twenty-one years old and originally from Bordeaux, had been trained by SOE and parachuted into France the previous day with false identity papers in the name of 'Gérard Henri Laure'. Rather than be captured, he had swallowed the 'L' (for 'lethal') cyanide tablet, which he had been given before leaving London. The Germans stood to attention alongside the young man's body as he passed through his last agonising convulsions.

Among the incriminating papers found on the dead man's corpse was a letter from a certain 'Ginette'. No address was given, but there was reference to a pharmacy in Bordeaux. The Gestapo eventually narrowed their search down to a young girl called Ginette Corbin, the daughter of Charles Corbin, an ex-pharmacist turned wartime policeman, who, unknown to the Germans, was also active in the local Resistance. Ginette Corbin was Henri Labit's cousin, and it seems clear that the letter was intended as a device by which Henri Labit could make contact with Charles Corbin and then, through him, with the Resistance in Bordeaux.

Ginette and her mother were taken to Dohse's headquarters and interrogated. They initially denied all knowledge of Labit, until, confronted with the letter found on Labit's body, Ginette blurted out that she was trying, for personal reasons, to hide that she was, in fact, engaged to Labit. It was a complete invention intended to avoid having to reveal that the Corbin family were, in reality, related to Labit. But it worked. Ginette and her mother were released. Next, the Germans arrested and interrogated Henri Labit's mother, Henriette, insisting that the dead man was her son. She too denied any relationship. So she was taken down to the cellars of the château and shown the body of her son hanging on a meat hook. Mme Labit coldly examined the cadaver and declared she did not recognise the young man.

The orders given to Henri Labit before he left London were to establish a Resistance network in and around Bordeaux, identify parachute sites where weapons could be dropped, and reconnoitre amphibious landing grounds on the beaches south of the Gironde estuary. His mission was the first in a planned programme of British/French expansion into the whole of the German occupied zone, with special emphasis on Paris and Bordeaux.

On 20 April, an SOE radio operator with orders to open up wireless communications from Tours, 250 kilometres northeast of Bordeaux and also in the occupied zone, was landed on the south coast of France. He arrived in Tours on 23 June and was joined three weeks later by an ex-RAF officer called Raymond Henry Flower.

Quite why the tremulous and easily frightened Flower was sent to France as leader of a delicate and dangerous mission is difficult to understand given his SOE training reports: 'no powers of leadership, very little initiative', 'lacking in strength of mind and body', 'very slow mentally and an uneducated type of brain', '… probably only useful in a minor capacity, under sound leadership'.

Ten days later, on the night of 29/30 July, a forty-five-year-old grandmother called Yvonne Rudellat was secretly landed on a beach near Cannes, with orders to make her way to Tours. Attractive, physically tough, with greying tousled hair, Rudellat had moved to London before the war and worked as, among other things, a shop assistant and the club secretary at the Ebury Court Hotel and Club, near Victoria, where SOE had found and recruited her. At Tours, Rudellat was to act as courier to Raymond Flower's circuit, codenamed 'Monkeypuzzle'. Another person who joined Monkeypuzzle at about this time was a locally recruited Frenchman called Pierre Culioli. Of Corsican-Breton extraction, twenty-eight-year-old Culioli – described as having 'cold grey eyes behind his spectacles … resolute mouth … deeply cleft chin' – was small of stature and slight of frame. This, together with the Hitler moustache he grew, half as a joke and half as hirsute protection against German inquisitiveness, resulted in him being nicknamed 'Adolphe' by his Resistance colleagues.

Culioli and Rudellat, both strong characters, were ordered to work under the nervous Flower. Their task was to prepare parachute sites and receive the agents London now planned to drop in to create two new secret organisations in the German-occupied zone: the 'Scientist' network in Bordeaux and a new network in Paris, which was to be codenamed 'Prosper'. Given the mix of personalities, relations within Monkeypuzzle were never going to be easy. In due course, they would become literally murderous.

The day after Yvonne Rudellat landed from a *felucca* (fishing vessel) off the Côte d'Azur, two of Roger Landes's fellow spy students from Wanborough Manor, Claude de Baissac and Harry Peulevé, were back in Orchard Court, Portman Square, receiving their final briefing before being parachuted into France.

De Baissac, the 'natural leader', was given the key role of heading up the Scientist network in Bordeaux; Peulevé was to be his radio operator. After parachuting in, their orders were to make their way first to Gaston Hèche's restaurant in Tarbes and thence to Bordeaux, where they were to 'investigate the possibilities of the Duboué organisation'. Their primary task was to plan, organise and carry out sabotage attacks on the blockade-runners and the submarine pens in Bordeaux harbour.

SCIENTIST GETS ESTABLISHED

At 1.15 a.m. on 30 July 1942, above the town of Nîmes in southern France, the sky was starlit, with a full moon and scudding clouds driven on a boisterous mistral. In truth, the wind was too strong for safe para-chuting, but the risk of a jump tonight had to be balanced against the risk of flying a second sortie down the length of enemy-occupied France a few days later. As he flew south over Nîmes, Pilot Officer Leo Anderle lowered his Halifax to 2,000 feet and, spotting the little village of Caissargues, its canal sparkling like a ribbon of tinsel in the moonlight, warned his two passengers, Claude de Baissac and Harry Peulevé, that he was running into their target and they should get ready to jump. He made a first pass over the drop site, a deserted aerodrome, while his co-pilot flashed the agreed recognition signal. There was no response from the reception committee on the ground. Anderle made a second pass and then a third – still no signal. He was nervous now that he was spending too long in the area – and drawing too much attention.

He passed a message to his passengers. They had two options: aban-don and turn for home, or drop blind on a field nearby and take pot luck. The two secret agents decided that they had come this far and did not want to go back. Anderle brought the big aircraft down to 500 feet and began his final run, choosing an open field west of the deserted aerodrome.

De Baissac got into trouble almost as soon as he jumped. His para-chute opened with a sharp jerk, pulling his left shoulder out of the harness. To make matters worse the brown cardboard suitcase strapped to his left leg had somehow broken free in the turbulence of the aircraft slipstream and become entangled in the parachute rigging above him. He tried to disengage it but couldn't, thanks to the buffeting of the wind, which now carried him along at an increasing pace. Then it was too late. The ground was coming up fast to meet him. He crashed into the soil of France awkwardly and on one leg, spraining it badly. With some difficulty, he gathered his parachute in the strong wind, peeled off his jumpsuit, dug a shallow grave and buried both. Picking up his case and, dressed now as any wartime French traveller, he set off to find Peulevé.

It was eventually Harry Peulevé's cries which drew de Baissac to him. He had suffered an even worse landing and was lying in a ditch with a broken leg. The two men agreed that there was no option. De Baissac would have to continue alone, without his radio operator. Peulevé would wait until dawn, then drag himself to a nearby farmhouse and throw himself on the mercy of the local population. De Baissac buried his colleague's parachute, jumpsuit and wireless, and limped off to Nîmes railway station, arriving not long after the curfew was lifted at five in the morning.

Two weeks later, in the second week of August 1942, Claude de Baissac – codenamed 'Scientist' after his network, known in France as 'David' and travelling under the false identity of a publicity agent named 'Claude Boucher' – arrived at Tarbes station, close to the Pyrenees. He had not had a trouble-free journey. At one stage his papers had been checked by a suspicious Vichy policeman.

'And how long have you been here?'

De Baissac – who had fled the country for London just months previously with his sister, Lise – insisted that he had always lived in France and was on business.

'Your papers are obvious forgeries. Tell London to be more careful in future!'

It was the second time in a matter of weeks that SOE had put the life of one of their agents at risk through a careless mistake in documentation. The difference between Henri Labit's death and Claude de Baissac's survival rested only on the good fortune for de Baissac that his flawed papers were first exposed to a sympathetic French official, rather than a hostile German one.

De Baissac made his way from the station to Rue Avezac-Macaya near Tarbes cathedral, where he found Gaston Hèches's restaurant and guesthouse, a substantial four-storey building with rooms on the top floors where 'guests' awaiting passage over the Pyrenees were accommodated. Entering the restaurant, de Baissac found a large, beamed, ground-floor room, full of rough tables and the chatter of Hèches's lunchtime clientele. A huge cast-iron stove belching smoke occupied almost the full length of one wall, presided over by a small man so stricken with rheumatism that he could barely move his head or walk without the aid of two sticks. This was Gaston Hèches, the *patron* of the establishment, which he ran with his wife Mimi and their two daughters. To the casual eye this was no more than a thriving country restaurant in a market town. But behind the façade, the building performed a second, more secret, function. It was the local headquarters for the Édouard line, one of SOE's most successful escape lines over the Pyrenees. By the end of the war it would also become the base for a highly successful sabotage network, also run by Hèches.

De Baissac installed himself at an empty table and waited for the opportunity of a quiet word with the *patron*.

'I am a traveller and I am looking for Édouard,' de Baissac said, using the password sequence he had been given by London.

'Where are you coming from?' Hèches asked, following the script.

'From Switzerland.'

'And you are going to?'

'To the United States.'

Shortly afterwards de Baissac met up with Robert Leroy, who had been sent to escort him across the demarcation line into the occupied zone. The two men had to wait for a few days while Hèches contacted a local priest who arranged for new documents to be forged for 'David'. Finally, after paying off Leroy's latest bar bill from the 100,000 francs de Baissac carried in a money belt, the two agents took the little one-track railway line north from Tarbes, which wound its way under a sweltering August sun, through 150 kilometres of pine forest and heathland, to Langon. At Langon their papers would have been checked on crossing the demarcation line, just as Henri Labit's had been. Then they continued on the final leg of their journey to Bordeaux.

Arriving in the city at the end of August, de Baissac would have witnessed the aftermath of the first transportation of Bordeaux's Jews. The French authorities in the occupied zone had wrestled with a demand to deport 40,000; eventually the German authorities accepted that the transportation should be limited to stateless Jews. Bordeaux was set a target of 2,000. That month the initial wave – 614 people, including, on Berlin's insistence, their children – were taken from their homes and crammed into railway carriages at the Gare Saint-Jean. From here they were taken to a French internment camp, in a derelict housing estate at Drancy, on the outskirts of Paris, and then – though no one knew it at the time – onwards to the death camps of Nazi Europe.

In Bordeaux, de Baissac wasted no time getting started. A few days after his arrival Leroy introduced him to Duboué and the Bertrands at the Café des Chartrons. The café, a favourite haunt of dockers and labourers, was situated on the ground floor of a four-storey building with bedrooms on the upper floors and a rear entrance leading to the tangle of little streets and narrow ill-lit alleys of the working-class district of Bacalan. The café's first-floor front windows directly overlooked Scientist's primary target: the blockade-runners moored alongside the quay just a hundred metres away. It was, de Baissac decided, the perfect place for his headquarters. In return for a regular subvention of 8,000–10,000 francs a month, the Bertrands undertook to provide free daily meals to members of the Scientist network, and to give de Baissac access to the rooms on the first floor which could be used, without the need to fill in the usual police forms, by any who needed urgent refuge and by those visiting Bordeaux on Scientist business. What neither de Baissac nor the Bertrands knew was that two of Dohse's agents lived less than 200 metres away.

The most pressing problem, having lost his radio operator, was how de Baissac was going to communicate with Baker Street. As a stopgap, Yvonne Rudellat was tasked by London to courier between Scientist and SOE's nearest radio operator in Tours, 300 kilometres northeast of

Bordeaux. It was by this means that, on 14 September 1942, de Baissac sent his first brief report to London informing them that he had established the Café des Chartrons as his headquarters and primary 'secret letterbox' in the city, and giving the details of his first parachute drop site at the Moulin de Saquet, close to the little hamlet of Coirac in the commune of Targon, sixteen kilometres east of Bordeaux.

On 19 September 1942, a further, more detailed report from de Baissac was carried from Bordeaux to Tarbes by young Suzanne Duboué. From Tarbes it was taken over the Pyrenees to the British consulate in Barcelona for coded transmission to London. It reported that Scientist was preparing sabotage attacks on the blockade-runners at the Quai des Chartrons: 'Louis [Robert Leroy] is only waiting for the necessary material [explosives] in order to get on with the job. He can then work on the painting of the boats down in the hold. He has already informed you how he needed the goods [in small packages] which could easily go into a workman's haversack.'

De Baissac had been too fast off the mark. On 7 October, Baker Street responded with alarm instructing him not to carry out any attacks until ordered. For the moment, Whitehall, not wishing to give the Germans any excuse for an invasion of the Vichy zone, had prohibited all sabotage in the occupied zone, unless it was completely untraceable to British hands. The time would come to take the gloves off. But it wasn't yet.

Meanwhile, SOE urgently needed to find a radio operator to replace the injured Peulevé. Roger Landes, at the time enjoying some leave at Carlton Mansions after completing his wireless course, was the obvious choice. On 16 September Landes was recalled, promoted to lieutenant and told to prepare to be dropped onto the Moulin de Saquet site as Scientist's new radio operator.

On the same day an instruction from German headquarters in Paris arrived at KdS Bordeaux. Forty-one Germans had been killed in Resistance attacks; under the German reprisal policy, two hostages would be executed for every German death caused by the Resistance. Eighty-two hostages chosen from those already in German captivity would now have to be shot. But the Germans in Paris could only find thirty-two 'suitable' hostages for execution. So Bordeaux would have to produce the extra fifty demanded by Berlin. Some suggest that this extra number was imposed on the city in retaliation for Bordeaux's failure to find more Jews for transportation.

On the evening of the following day, 17 September, French communists threw a bomb into the Rex Cinema in Paris, killing one German soldier and injuring thirty. In response, Paris raised the number of hostages to be executed in Bordeaux to seventy. Friedrich Dohse contacted his chief, Bömelburg, complaining that the decision would serve only to increase hostility in the area. He suggested that, if the number could not be reduced, then at least the condemned should be taken to Paris for execution, rather than being shot at nearby Souge. But even the appeals of Bömelburg's personal representative in Bordeaux were rejected. Dohse spent the next few days making summaries of the files of the most likely candidates for execution in local prisons and submitting them to Hans Luther for his decision.

At midday on 21 September, seventy coffins were delivered to Souge. They were followed that afternoon by seventy male hostages; most were communists and many were very young. They were executed by firing squad in batches of ten, in the gathering dusk, among the camp's pine trees, that still autumn evening.

Luther attended the executions. But it was not the only thing he did that day. At 09.10 he sent a message to Paris: 'In the morning, a transport consisting of seventy Jews left Bordeaux. The Jews have been placed in three railway wagons, connected to a fast freight train. As instructed, the destination was Drancy. The Jews are expected to arrive on 22 September,' Luther ended.

A VISITOR FOR DAVID

As his fellow Jews were travelling to Paris crowded into railway wagons, Roger Landes was being driven up the Great North Road to RAF Tempsford, eight miles from Bedford.

A few days earlier he had been instructed to leave all unnecessary belongings at his parents' home and make his way to Orchard Court. Here, after being dressed in his French clothes, he was minutely searched for anything incriminating and closely cross-examined on his cover story. Then, equipped with his brown cardboard mock-leather suitcase containing everything he would need as a traveller in France, he was taken to an SOE holding unit – a substantial Georgian mansion in Huntingdonshire – where he stayed for a few days in the company of other SOE agents waiting to be parachuted into occupied Europe.

At Tempsford, Landes was given as good a meal – with wine – as the RAF could muster in wartime, before being escorted to a large farm-house at the edge of the base. Another search for incriminating traces of British life – matches, receipts, theatre tickets etc. – ensued, together with a repeat examination of his cover story and a briefing on how to use his suicide 'L' tablets, which were handed to him in a small rubber box. Finally, he was equipped with French ration cards and documents made out in his new false name: René Pol, a quantity surveyor working for the German military construction operation, Organisation Todt.

An hour before departure, the RAF dispatcher, who would now escort Landes all the way to the moment he jumped, helped him into voluminous parachute overalls covered with pockets. These contained a folding shovel, a parachutist's knife, a small flask of rum, a compass, a torch, a .38 Luger automatic, some Benzedrine tablets and a tin of emergency rations. On top of his overalls Landes wore a single-piece camouflaged parachute smock, buttoned up between the legs and closed by a zip at the front. On top of that came his parachute and harness, secured by two straps passed over his shoulders and two more under his buttocks. All four straps were clipped into a quick-release buckle on his chest.

Thus, trussed up like a chicken, and carrying his parachute helmet, Roger Landes was led to a converted Halifax and installed in the back, along with a sleeping bag, a flask of coffee laced with rum, a brown paper bag containing sandwiches and four metal cylinders packed with his radios, weapons and ammunition. The dispatcher checked that his charge was comfortably installed and advised him to get as much sleep as he could. There was a long cold night ahead.

Sadly, it was all in vain.

There was no sign of the promised reception committee at de Baissac's new Moulin de Saquet site. Landes, remembering what had happened to de Baissac and Peulevé, declined the offer to drop blind and the aircraft turned for home. Three further attempts were made to parachute Landes into France, but all were frustrated. (One because the wrong Morse recognition letter was sent by the reception committee; one because an incautious owl flew into the engine of Landes's Halifax; and one because of a signal miscommunication.)

Finally, at 1.40 a.m. on 1 November 1942, after yet another cancelled drop and an attempt to fly him to Gibraltar and send him by fishing vessel to the southern French coast, Roger Landes, codenamed 'Actor', alias 'Stanislas' and carrying the false identity of 'René Pol', landed at Bois Renard, near the village of Mer in the Loire valley. Parachuted in with him that night was Gilbert Norman, his colleague from the SOE wireless school at Thame.

Buffeted by strong winds, Landes and Norman had had an uncomfortable journey as their Halifax made its way south across France. To offset the wind, the Halifax pilot took his aircraft down to a spine-chilling 150 metres for the jump. Norman went first; then Landes.

As the dark bulk of the aircraft passed away over Landes's head, he felt the sharp jerk of his parachute opening. A moment or so later, he was down – in the middle of a muddy field. Looking around, he found himself alone with the sound of the Halifax fading away into the darkness. No reception committee, no lights, no Gilbert Norman: no one and nothing in sight. He stripped off his jumpsuit and buried it – along with his parachute – and started to consider his options. Perhaps he would have to make his own way to Bordeaux?

He decided to hide in some bushes and wait to see what would happen next. Ten minutes later he heard the sound of Norman's voice softly calling his alias: 'Stanislas, Stanislas.' He emerged to find Norman accompanied by a slender man with a slightly ridiculous Hitler moustache: it was Pierre Culioli. Raymond Flower, the head of the Monkeypuzzle reception team, should have been there, but he had become so frightened of almost anything that he could not be relied on and so Culioli had taken his place.

The real cause of Flower's petrified condition, however, was far worse than Culioli knew. Flower had convinced himself that both Culioli and Rudellat were Gestapo agents, and had sent to London for cyanide tablets to kill them both. The lethal tablets to do the job were contained in a special unmarked package which Norman had been given that night, with firm instructions that they were to be delivered personally into Flower's hands only. In the end, the killing never happened because the petrified Flower could neither bring himself to do the deed nor persuade anyone else to do it for him. In reality, Culioli and Rudellat's supposed 'treachery' was no more than the product of Flower's fevered imagination. Nevertheless, Culioli's survival, whether justified or not, would cost Gilbert Norman, his colleagues in Paris and the whole of SOE, very dear in the months to come.

That night Culioli took Landes and Norman to the house of a local mayor, who also happened to be Culioli's father-in-law.

The following morning there was a knock on Landes's bedroom door. Suddenly wakened from a deep sleep, the new arrival from London sat bolt upright and shouted: 'Come in!' – in English. Fortunately, Landes's early morning caller was not the Gestapo, but his host, come to collect him for the next stage of his journey to Bordeaux.

After breakfast, Norman left to take up the role of radio operator for the new Prosper network in Paris, headed by one of Landes's ex-Wanborough colleagues – the young 'Ivanhoe', Francis Suttill. Norman took the morning train to Paris with his 'guide', Francis Suttill's courier, Andrée Borrel. Small-boned, dark-complexioned and twenty-three years old, Borrel was an ex-Paris 'street urchin', who had fought in the Spanish Civil War and worked in an escape line before fleeing to London in 1941, making her the most battle-experienced of any of the Prosper or Scientist agents. One of the first women to be dropped into France, she had arrived in late September, with orders to join Suttill in Paris.

As Borrel and Norman made their way to the station, Landes was loaded onto a cart which, with him at the reins, carried him in lonely state to a nearby farm. Neither SOE's training, nor Landes's city life in Paris and London had equipped him with the skills to drive a horse and cart. But luckily, as he explained afterwards, 'the horse found its own way home. Though it was a very strange feeling being on a public road, full of uniformed Germans, when only the night before I had been in England ...'

At the farm, Landes was surprised to find the jumpy Raymond Flower, together with Flower's radio operator Marcel Clech and two of SOE's most important women agents, waiting for them and a merry party in progress. Landes, who never relaxed his obsession with security, later complained that it was 'more a social event than a business meeting'. He was of course right. If the farm had been raided that night the Gestapo would have netted Landes, Rudellat, Flower, Clech and Lise de Baissac, Claude de Baissac's sister, who had been parachuted in a month previously and was on her way to establish a new SOE circuit in Poitiers.

At six o'clock the following morning, 2 November, Landes set off on foot for the local station, while Rudellat and Lise de Baissac followed separately on bicycles, each with a suitcase strapped to a carrier rack. Rudellat's suitcase contained Landes's radio and revolver, which she was to carry for him to Bordeaux. (It was not her first experience of carrying compromising articles. She had already become famous in Baker Street for cycling round Tours distributing sticks of dynamite to the Resistance from a stock hidden in her underclothes.)

The three secret agents took the train to Tours, the two women sitting together in one carriage and Landes separately in another. At Tours, Lise de Baissac caught a train south to the Charente, where she had contacts to meet. Rudellat had her own flat in the town, but decided that, as a single woman with an inquisitive landlord, it would attract too much attention if Landes stayed the night with her, so she directed him to a small hotel near the station. The two agreed to meet the following morning in the station buffet and catch the early train to Bordeaux, travelling as a married couple. In case the rendezvous failed, Rudellat gave her 'husband' the address of the Café des Chartrons, before they parted.

Checking in to the hotel that evening, Landes made a mess of writing his new name on one of the five forms he was required to complete in order to register. He amended it as best he could, hoping the manager wouldn't notice.

The following day, 3 November, there was no sign of Yvonne Rudellat at Tours station. Landes had no option but to continue the journey to Bordeaux by himself. Now he was totally on his own. They had told him in training to invent a cover story for every journey, so as always to have a convincing explanation for what he was doing. Over time, this would become one of his cardinal rules for survival and one he would always impress on others who he trained. Now, however, with no previous experience in wartime France, he had to do the best he could with what little London had given him. He was returning to his job in Organisation Todt after a visit to Tours, where he had been seeing friends. But who were the friends? What were their names? What was their address? What was his address in Bordeaux? He had neither a past nor a future to draw on. If he survived, he would accumulate enough back history to create both. Looking out of the window as the train ground labori-ously south through Poitiers, Angoulême and the Charente vineyards, where the leaves flamed with the gold and red of autumn, Landes felt alone, out of place and very vulnerable.

Finally, late in the morning, the train rattled over the iron girder bridge spanning the muddy waters of the Garonne and pulled into the glass and cast-iron cavern of Bordeaux's Gare Saint-Jean, full of steam and noise and bustle. Safely through the German checkpoint at the end of the platform, he went to register at a local hotel which Yvonne Rudellat had recommended, and then set off for the Café des Chartrons.

In general, cities are the most congenial places to conduct the business of secrets. The advantages of anonymity, a facility for easy contact and the ability to vanish into the crowd make spying, like any impropriety, easier in an urban setting than anywhere else. In due course, Roger Landes would become a master of his trade in this environment. For the moment, though, it was enough to feel safer amongst the crowds in Bordeaux than he did being drawn around the Loire valley behind a horse with homing instincts.

That first day among the faceless throng filling the streets and squares of a foreign city must nevertheless have been a nerve-jangling one, even for someone trained to the task and used to living in France.

After the huddled coats of London in November, it would have been strange to see people sitting outside street cafés, soaking up the last warmth of summer. Stranger still to have to root his feet to the ground to stop them taking flight when the turn of a corner brought him face to face with a crowd of German soldiers coming in the opposite direction. He cut down onto the waterfront and, turning left, followed the crescent-shaped sweep of the quay north, towards the Pont de Pierre with its seventeen graceful arches, one for each letter in Napoléon Bonaparte's name. He was passing through elegant Bordeaux now, with its magnificent eighteenth-century frontages, balconied apartments and spacious tree-lined parks. Turning briefly left into one of these, he found himself in the Place des Quinconces. Here, strolling idly through yellow drifts of fallen leaves from the park's plane trees, he saw a little bistro, the Café des Colonnes, and noted it as a possible future meeting place. Back on the waterfront once more, he walked north, up the Quai des

Chartrons, crowded with small merchant vessels and German warships and busy with the clatter of cranes, small goods trains and lorries. Here were quayside bars and chandleries and the imposing shop windows of great wine merchants. On the opposite side of the road a line of new warehouses marched along the quay, stretching north into the haze. It was there, in the Bacalan quarter – as he remembered from the map he had studied back in London – that he would find number 101: the Café des Chartrons, the rendezvous he had fixed with Yvonne Rudellat the previous day.

It was *midi*, the sacred French lunch hour, when he arrived at the café. The restaurant was crowded, smoky and full of the noise of shouted meal orders and the clatter of plates. Landes ordered himself a drink and settled into a corner to wait for the place to empty enough for him to call the *patron* over. Using Claude de Baissac's alias in France, he began: 'I have a letter for David.'

'David? I don't know any David.'

'You are Monsieur Bertrand?'

'Of course I am. But there is no David here. I don't know what you are talking about.'

Landes asked him if he could leave a letter for his friend. Bertrand, not wishing to give any indication to this stranger that he knew de Baissac, shrugged and answered that of course he could. But since he didn't know anyone called David, there was no guarantee it would be delivered. On a slip of paper Landes wrote:

My dear David,

I am briefly passing through Bordeaux and would love to see you. If you can make it I will be in the Café des Colonnes in Place des Quinconces from 11 in the morning and dining at around 7 in the evening in the Café Gambetta. I do hope we can meet,

Stanislas

Handing the note to Bertrand, Landes returned to his hotel near the station.

That evening, Landes entered the Café Gambetta at seven o'clock sharp and was reassured to see Yvonne Rudellat already installed at a corner table with a thick-set, dark-haired stranger, who she introduced as 'Monsieur Jean Duboué'. She had had an accident while cycling to Tours railway station the previous day, she explained. She was only bruised, but her clothes had been badly torn. She didn't want to attract attention on the train, so she had gone back to her flat, changed and caught a later connection. She had looked for Landes at the Café des Chartrons. Marcel Bertrand told her that a stranger had left a message. And so, here she was.

'David is out of town waiting for your parachute drop,' Rudellat continued. 'If you missed each other, I was to tell you to go every morning to the Bar de Petit Louis, order a glass of wine and wait for him to arrive.'

The three of them went back to the Café des Chartrons, where Landes unpacked his radio and, relieved to find that it had not been damaged in Rudellat's bicycle accident, tried to get through to Baker Street. He could hear London well enough. But they couldn't hear him. He would have to find somewhere else to make his transmissions.

On that same day, 3 November 1942, while Landes was trying to radio London, Admiral Raoul Gaston Marie Grandclément, Grand Croix de la Légion d'Honneur, pillar of the French navy, head of the Grandclément family and pitiless mirror to his son's failures, died at his home in Paris, with André Grandclément at his bedside.

In Bordeaux, two days later, Claude de Baissac finally met Roger Landes. They discussed where the newly arrived radio operator should live and decided that he should move in with de Baissac that evening until somewhere more permanent could be found. That afternoon, trying to kill time, Landes went to the cinema and nearly gave himself away again by lighting a cigarette. The cinema manager rushed over and warned him in an urgent whisper that, under the Germans, smoking in cinemas was strictly forbidden.

Although Friedrich Dohse in Bouscat knew nothing of the new arrivals in his city, he knew something was going on. Luftwaffe reports sent to his office highlighted a substantial increase in clandestine night flights into the Bordeaux region. They were probably, he was told, parachuting in arms and agents. Dohse ordered daily updates and persuaded local Wehrmacht commanders to provide roving raiding parties to intercept the new threat.

Up to now, Bordeaux had been, for Friedrich Dohse, quiet, pleasant and comfortable. All this was about to change.

8

CRACKERS AND BANGS

Eight days after Roger Landes's arrival in Bordeaux, German tanks smashed through the flimsy barriers which marked the demarcation line and occupied Vichy France.

Operation Attila was triggered by the Allied landings in North Africa and the German realisation that they were now vulnerable to invasion, not just on France's northern Channel coastline, but on its southern Mediterranean one as well. From this moment, Pétain and his government, who had enjoyed a measure of genuine autonomy up to now, became little more than German puppets.

The German invasion of Vichy France also marked the beginning of a new phase in the French Resistance and in the activities of SOE. Now there was no need for squeamishness in unleashing what Baker Street euphemistically referred to as 'crackers and bangs' (i.e. sabotage) wherever and whenever London wished. On 13 November 1942 Baker Street sent out a message to circuits across France calling for 'sabotage immediately and on as large a scale as possible'. These were accompanied by specific instructions to de Baissac to take 'action against all shipping that used the port of Bordeaux'.

Events immediately started to move at an increasing pace.

On 18 November, a week after the German invasion of the *zone non-occupée*, Victor Charles Hayes, a pharmacist and dental mechanic whom SOE had turned into an explosives expert, was parachuted into a site just south of Tours with instructions to make his way to Bordeaux. Thirty-four years old, balding, short in stature (five foot four), with a tendency to plumpness, Hayes (known to all as Vic) looked like a comfortable country lawyer or bank manager of the day. After the armistice he had fled France for Spain, where he had taken a boat to Liverpool, leaving his wife, Raymonde, and their baby daughter to follow him on a later ship. On his SOE training course, he heard that both had been drowned when their ship was torpedoed in the Bay of Biscay.

Vic Hayes arrived in Bordeaux on 28 November to find his explosives already waiting for him. They had been parachuted in a week before when, at the third attempt, a Whitley bomber dropped four containers to the Coirac reception committee. They were packed with sixty pounds of explosives, twelve Sten guns, twelve revolvers, sixty-six hand grenades and fifteen small clam mines, suitable for attacking coastal craft and cutting railway lines.

Around the same date, a Slade School of Art graduate, fluent in French, Italian, Spanish and German, cycled into Tarbes and made her way to Gaston Hèches's restaurant. Mary Herbert, alias 'Claudine', known to her friends as 'Maureen' and travelling under the identity of 'Marie Louise Vernier', was, at thirty-nine, the oldest of the Scientist team. A woman of pronounced Catholic views and a trusting character, she was pretty rather than striking, with a tall, willowy figure, blue eyes, a face enlivened by a winning smile and hair so fine that it had a natural aptitude for disorder. Mary Herbert had been stranded in Plymouth earlier in the month with Landes, waiting for a flying boat to take them to Gibraltar. In the end, she and four other agents had been infiltrated into France by submarine and fishing boat, landing fifteen kilometres southeast of Marseille on the same night that Landes was parachuted into Bois Renard. Her orders were to join the Scientist network as Claude de Baissac's courier.

Gaston Hèches installed Mary Herbert in one of the third-floor bedrooms above his restaurant, where she passed the time waiting to hear from Bordeaux by embroidering handkerchiefs and table linen for the Hèches family. On 22 November, Robert Leroy, now demoted to courier and rechristened 'Robert the Tipsy' by his Resistance colleagues, arrived in Tarbes with orders to smuggle Herbert over the demarcation line. She left her expensive leather handbag with one of Hèches's daughters ('too sophisticated for my new life') and accompanied Leroy to a village near Bordeaux, where de Baissac was waiting for her.

Yvonne Rudellat, sent down from Tours to warn de Baissac of his courier's impending arrival, now busied herself with finding accommodation for her newly arrived colleague, eventually settling on an apartment in the same road as de Baissac's flat.

As Scientist's courier, Mary Herbert was responsible for arranging de Baissac's meetings, carrying his messages (often in a matchbox, hidden beneath the matches, or between the pages of a novel) and transporting Landes's radios around the city. On one occasion in Bordeaux, struggling off a Paris train with a hefty case containing a wireless set, a German naval officer stopped her and demanded to know what was inside. She was moving flats, she replied. It looked heavy, the German suggested – and offered to carry it for her to the tram. He was rewarded with a charming smile and a mildly flirtatious 'thank you' for his trouble.

It was in the nature of Mary Herbert's job that she and Claude de Baissac spent a lot of time together, often late at night when she picked up or delivered the day's messages. Sometime around December 1942, the two became lovers.

Roger Landes spent the first weeks of November 1942 making further attempts to get through to London. He tried several locations in the city, but always with the same result; he could hear London, but they could not hear him. Eventually Marcel Bertrand suggested an empty villa which he owned, in the Bordeaux suburb of Cenon, a middle-class district situated on an escarpment above the city, on the east bank of the Garonne. The house, which was located in a sunny spot and had four bedrooms, was what the French call a *pavillon* and the English refer to as a bungalow. It was perfect for Landes's needs. The front-door lock could only be opened in a certain way, so that it was detectable if a stranger who did not know the lock's eccentricities attempted entry in the owner's absence. There was a sizeable urban garden surrounded by high walls in which were set two doors, each giving access onto a different street. Best of all (and in what would become Landes's trademark habit of hiding 'in plain sight'), the house lay almost in the shadow of a powerful medium-wave radio mast serving the nearby headquarters of the German anti-aircraft batteries in Bordeaux. Landes knew that the tiny sliver of a signal from his little short-wave radio would be completely hidden from Gestapo detector vans among the forest of powerful German transmissions from the much larger station next door.

Landes moved into the villa in the second week of November 1942, spreading the word amongst his neighbours, most of whom were billeted Germans, that he needed an airy house because he was recuperating from tuberculosis (an impression reinforced by his hacking smoker's cough). This cover story had a double advantage. It explained why he lived by himself, while at the same time discouraging neighbourly inquisitiveness. He transmitted to London from the kitchen table and kept his radio set, when not in use, under his bed. His transmission schedules and ciphers were hidden in the garden shed, while six spare crystals, each on a different frequency, were buried in a tin box in the kitchen garden.

On 15 November, after some aerial adjustments, Landes finally succeeded in getting through to SOE headquarters, 'strength 3 to 4'. Scientist was, at long last, in direct touch with Baker Street. There would be no need for Rudellat to make any more hazardous journeys from Tours, or for Suzanne Duboué to travel to Tarbes with de Baissac's reports hidden under the shopping in her basket.

Aware that the Germans knew that an irregular lifestyle was a tell-tale sign of a secret agent, Landes always followed the same daily routine. He left his house at 9 a.m. and went for a long walk. When he was sure he was not being followed, he collected his messages and cleared his letter-boxes. The afternoons were spent in a local cinema, sleeping. Returning home around 5 p.m., he would have an early meal and then, after dark and with all the blinds pulled down, he began his transmissions to London, often continuing until late into the night.

With his radio operating, Landes now needed to find himself a courier to carry messages to and from Claude de Baissac. He chose Ginette Corbin, the pretty cousin of young Henri Labit, who had died in agony in Langon rather than be taken prisoner. What Ginette did not know at the time was that Roger Landes had fallen for her at their first meeting, but kept his feelings secret. After the death of Labit, he would explain to her later, he did not wish to involve her and her family in more pain. But there was another reason for his reticence. He regarded serious long-term emotional involvements as dangerous to security. They were for after the war, not during it.

The Scientist network was now complete. With five British SOE officers in Bordeaux and Claude de Baissac's sister, Lise, running a support network in the Charente, east of the city, Scientist was now the largest and best-resourced SOE network in all of occupied France.

Unusual cold gripped the whole of Europe in the last week of November 1942. Temperatures of minus eight degrees were recorded in Bordeaux and Toulouse. It was the advance guard of winter – the winter of Stalingrad. The parasols and tables outside Bordeaux cafés retreated out of the cold, and summer strollers in the Parc Bordelais gave way to muffled stragglers taking shortcuts past frost-scorched flower beds and the leafless skeletons of trees. In the first week of December, a light dusting of snow fell across the whole of France.

Sometime during these weeks, a tall and handsome man with an air of authority, startlingly blue eyes and a markedly retroussé nose, knocked at the door of 34 Cours de Verdun. It was Charles Corbin, the father of Ginette, Roger Landes's new courier. He was calling on Grandclément, ostensibly in his capacity as a policeman investigating some minor infraction of economic law (Grandclément's cavalier attitude to finance and the law was a persistent feature of his life, both public and secret). What exactly happened during this encounter is not known, but by the end of it – in a move which would be full of consequence for both men – Corbin accepted Grandclément's invitation to join him in the OCM. Perhaps one of the things which brought the two men together was the fact that both had expressed strong anti-communist views and had close contact with the proto-fascist Croix-de-Feu.

By now de Baissac, comfortably installed in the Café des Chartrons, had both the expertise and the materials to mount his attack on the blockade-runners he could see from the café's front windows. A small team of saboteurs, under Jean Duboué and Vic Hayes, began to prepare the explosive charges. The attack was set for 12 December when the explosive, timed to go off that night, would be taken on board in dockers' haversacks while the ships were being loaded.

Of this impending sabotage attack right in the heart of his area of responsibility, Dohse, in his office at KdS headquarters in Bouscat, just three kilometres from the Café des Chartrons, knew nothing. Indeed, the Germans had only recently woken up to the fact that they had a substantial armed Resistance, supported by London, planted in their midst.

But Friedrich Dohse was not the only person who would be surprised by what happened next.

When Vic Hayes's demolition team arrived at the Quai des Chartrons a little before dawn on the morning of 12 December, they found the dock area swarming with German troops against a background of general pandemonium and chaos. Someone said that bombs had gone off on one of the blockade-runners. Suddenly, as if to confirm the fact, there was a dull thud and a tall column of water shot up the flank of a ship moored almost precisely opposite the Café des Chartrons. Already one of the other ships was leaning over, threatening, in the words of a German officer on the quayside that morning, 'to capsize, but for her hawsers, stretched like violin strings, which are still able to hold her'.

Throughout the morning and into the early evening the explosions continued, not only on ships alongside the Quai des Chartrons, but also on those tied up along the quays on the opposite bank of the Garonne. Fire broke out on a small oil tanker, the *Cap Hadid*, sending a pall of smoke over Bacalan. The Bordeaux port fire brigade were called in. What the Germans didn't know was that Raymond Brard, the man directing the port firemen, was himself the leader of a local Resistance group. When the Germans weren't looking, Brard ordered his men to reverse the direction of the pumps so that they sucked water into the stricken vessel instead of pumping it out, causing the *Cap Hadid* to settle gently on the Garonne mud, half submerged, alongside the quay.

At first the Germans, mystified, suspected local sabotage. But Italian divers called in during the morning confirmed that the explosions had come from the outside. As the day wore on, the true story began to emerge. It had been a daring commando raid carried out by ten Royal Marines in five canoes, who had disembarked near the mouth of the Gironde from a submarine five days previously. On the first night, two of the raiders had perished in treacherous tidal rips at the entrance of the Gironde and two more were wrecked, swiftly falling into German hands. The captured Marines were interrogated, using, Berlin insisted, 'all means necessary'.

From the information gathered and the materials found in the captured canoe, the Germans were quickly able to piece together the details of the operation and the fact that the target was shipping in Bordeaux harbour. Nevertheless, through overconfidence, complacency, or perhaps just in the belief that no one could make it in fragile canoes down the dangerous, heavily patrolled, densely defended 110 kilometres from the mouth of the Gironde to Bordeaux harbour, the German admiral in charge of the defence of the area concluded that the raid was over and the danger had passed. But it hadn't. Two of the raiders' canoes had managed to slip past the German defences undetected and reach the port, as planned. On the night before the final attack, as their colleagues lay hidden in the reeds outside the port observing their targets, the two captured Marines were taken to Souge and, under Hitler's infamous and illegal Commando Order, executed by firing squad.

Of the remaining six Marines on Operation Frankton (more famously known as the Cockleshell Heroes raid), four were captured afterwards. They were interrogated by, among others, Friedrich Dohse, who tried to find out the names of French people who had helped them. But the Marines gave nothing. They were eventually transferred to Paris where they too were subsequently shot. With the help of the French Resistance, the final pair, the raid commander Major Blondie Hasler and his canoe partner Marine Bill Sparks, made it home over the Pyrenees.

Hitler was furious, and sent a message through Field Marshal Wilhelm Keitel, the commander-in-chief of the German army, scolding local commanders for failures which were 'difficult to comprehend', and warning that 'the Führer expects [an end to] this carelessness which still appears to be widespread'.

De Baissac was furious too – and with almost equally good reason. Operation Frankton had been masterminded by Combined Operations, whose headquarters in Whitehall were closer to SOE in Baker Street than Dohse's office in Bouscat was to the Café des Chartrons. Yet neither had told the other what they were doing. 'At the critical moment ... the unfortunate Commando attack took place,' de Baissac commented sourly, 'charges were laid on seven ships, but the only result was that the ships, which were empty, settled one metre into the water and were immediately raised ... the Bordeaux Docks are now in a state of continuous alert ... the dock guards were increased to 200 men ... armed with grenades and automatic weapons [who] ... open fire at sight. As a result, Scientist has had to give up these targets.'

But this did not mean that the Scientist team was idle when it came to the business of 'crackers and bangs'. Vic Hayes (who soon earned the soubriquet 'Charles le Démolisseur' amongst his colleagues) and Jean Duboué assembled a team of forty or so saboteurs who they trained and led on a series of raids across southwestern France. This began just a few days after the Frankton raid with an attack on the rail network southeast of Bordeaux. Not long afterwards, railway lines were blown up at Dax, high-level pylons attacked at Facture and junction boxes demolished at Bayonne. The attacks caused a complete collapse of the electricity supply across the entire regional rail system. Following the sabotage, de Baissac's men (no doubt with technical advice from the ardently pro-British cheminots) took advantage of the disconnections to short-circuit the railway's electricity supply systems. The result was that, when the Germans turned on the supply again, there were more violent explosions and more serious damage. Rail traffic across the region was disrupted for days. Taken aback by the scale of the attacks coming so soon after the Frankton raid, the German authorities concluded that this was the prelude to an invasion. Panicky alerts were issued to all units, and trucks rushed to main headquarters, where they were swiftly loaded with the military archives and sent to dispersed locations outside the city.

This spate of attacks was followed over succeeding months by raids on Bordeaux's main power station at Pessac on the eastern outskirts of the city, on an electricity substation at Quatre Pavillons just 200 metres from the bungalow in Cenon where Roger Landes operated his wireless (Landes himself drew the sketch map for this raid), and on several small steamships in Pauillac harbour. Although Vic Hayes's demolition teams could not gain access to the Bordeaux dock area, they did manage to contaminate a consignment of battery acid with a special chemical sent out from London, causing serious damage to the accumulators on German and Italian U-boats operating from the Bordeaux pens.

On 22 November 1942, Landes signalled London informing them that de Baissac intended to appoint Léo Paillère (who had by now been released from jail) as Scientist's 'organiser-in-chief'. This meant that Scientist was now intimately connected, through Duboué and Paillère, with Grandclément's Organisation Civile et Militaire (OCM) – though de Baissac had not as yet met the head of the OCM in Bordeaux (probably because André Grandclément had been in Paris, at the bedside of his ailing father.)

Things were also now moving on the wider scale, as the balance of the war began to change in the Allies' favour. Following Operation Torch, the invasion of North Africa in November 1942, German, British and French minds turned to what everyone knew would happen next – the attempt by the Allies to gain a foothold on the mainland of occupied Europe. Torch had opened the way to the era of large-scale invasions, rather than small commando raids such as Operation Frankton. As 1942 drew to a close the idea began to take root in some circles in London (including Baker Street), in the high command in Berlin and amongst the people of France, that the long anticipated Allied landing on the French coast would take place sometime in the summer or early autumn of 1943.

SOE, meanwhile, were still under some criticism in London for how little they were delivering to the main war effort, measured against the resources they were employing – especially Halifax bombers which could, the RAF strenuously argued, be more gainfully deployed attacking German cities than dropping secret agents and arms into France. In an attempt to boost their record of success, Baker Street claimed in their December 1942 report to Churchill that the blockade-runners in Bordeaux harbour had been sunk by them (de Baissac's team), not Hasler's Royal Marines. Churchill, however, knew the truth from German signals, decrypted by Bletchley, which told him of Hasler's success little more than twenty-four hours after his limpet mines had exploded. It was now politically vital that SOE showed that it had a major role to play in the coming invasion – minor, random pinprick acts of sabotage would no longer do.

It was in this context that, in the second half of November 1942, de Baissac and Duboué travelled north to Poitiers for a meeting with the Paris-based leaders of the OCM. Among those present were André Grandclément's uncle, General Paul Jouffrault, and the overall OCM head, Colonel Touny. The main task of what would come to be known as the *conférence de Poitiers*, was to reorganise the entire underground OCM structure in Bordeaux and the Gironde, rather grandiosely, along the lines of a conventional division of the French army. But the secondary purpose was to reach an 'agreement' with de Baissac that Scientist would henceforth act as the channel through which SOE would arm the entire OCM network across occupied France, estimated by de Baissac to number 15,000–20,000 fighters. This was a huge logistic undertaking which would, over time, involve de Baissac having control of sixty parachute sites and a dozen or so Lysander landing grounds spread from Brittany in the north, to Paris and northern Burgundy in the east, to the foothills of the Pyrenees in the south.

When de Baissac put the Poitiers compact to London for approval, Baker Street agreed.

It was a crucial moment in Britain's secret war in France. For political reasons, which had more to do with increasing SOE's influence in London than having secure and effective networks in France, SOE ditched its policy of small self-contained networks in favour of the more tempting prospect of having a whole underground army under its control in the case of an invasion. From now on Scientist, which had been tightly targeted and secure in Bordeaux, would be vulnerable to infiltration and destruction through any weakness in the vast rambling, rickety structure of the OCM, which sprawled across the whole of northern and western France.

The OCM leaders in Paris wanted even more centralisation. At the end of 1942, Colonel Touny proposed to de Gaulle that he should have the command of the French Resistance in all of northern France. Although the OCM was clearly the largest Resistance organisation in the country, and despite the fact that the London French were at the time supporting it with a subvention of 1.5 million francs a month, the proposal was rejected by London on the grounds that the OCM was seen as too right-wing, too elitist and 'too' anti-Semitic.

At some point during the Christmas holiday period, de Baissac went to Paris where, over lunch, he met André Grandclément for the first time.

No doubt much of Grandclément's two months in Paris had been spent clearing up the old admiral's affairs and taking on his duties as the new head of the Grandclément family. But he had also been busy with politics – especially right-wing politics. At one meeting during this period he described his personal aims and those of the OCM in markedly ambitious terms: to create a force which would maintain internal order after the liberation of France so as '[to] establish a new system of civil, administrative and political government for the France of the future [which would be] anti-communist, anti-socialist ... and strongly opposed to further Jewish infiltration'.

Despite Grandclément's clear anti-Semitic leanings (and notwithstanding the fact that one of the key members of Scientist – Landes – was himself a Jew), the first meeting between the head of the most important British network in southwest France and the largest French Resistance organisation in the region was a success. A firm partnership – and friendship – were established between the two men, who agreed a merger between Scientist and the OCM in the southwest, with de Baissac in overall command and Grandclément (who was now equipped with the alias 'Bernard') acting as his deputy. De Baissac later assured Baker Street that he considered his new colleague 'very able and trustworthy' and suggested that Grandclément should be given 'an official status in the hierarchy of the organisation'. Baker Street gave their approval to the relationship and opened an SOE file for Grandclément – who would later claim that this moment had also been marked by SOE making him 'a major in the British Army'.

The scene was set for a new phase in the war against France's occupiers in the southwest.

For Dohse in his office in Bouscat a picture was beginning to emerge which he could no longer ignore. 'In the course of 1942 we knew the Resistance was forming, but we could not work out in what form,' he wrote later. 'Our local intelligence services were unable to give us a detailed picture of what was going on ... my job was to try to stick as close to the [newly forming] Resistance organisations as I could, so as to infiltrate my agents into the enemy networks ... but we lacked French agents capable of doing this.'

Meanwhile, sabotage attacks in the region were increasing, as was the frequency of the mysterious night flights over the Bordeaux area by British bombers. The threat against German lives and interests was growing. An invasion looked more and more likely. It would not be long before Berlin would be calling for action.

BUSINESSES, BROTHELS AND PLANS

In the first days of 1943, Churchill and Roosevelt met in the congenial surroundings of the Anfa Hotel, Casablanca, under a warm winter sun, to discuss the next phase of the war. Stalin was absent, saying he could not leave Moscow during the battle of Stalingrad. De Gaulle and his arch rival, General Henri Giraud, attended briefly for an awkward photograph meant to illustrate their 'unity'. It shows the two men – who enthusiastically hated each other – stiffly shaking hands from as far apart as possible, while Churchill smiles impishly at their discomfiture and Roosevelt looks on benignly, like an indulgent father watching his children behaving politely at a family gathering.

At Casablanca, Churchill and Roosevelt decided that the invasion of France would not take place until 1944. The French leaders were of course not informed. Neither, more controversially, was Baker Street. Both continued to act on the presumption that the invasion would happen – indeed was a certainty – by the early autumn of 1943. Colonel Buckmaster, the head of SOE, went so far as to claim after the war that '[in] 1943 we had a secret message telling us that the invasion might be closer than we thought' – a statement for which there is absolutely no supporting evidence.

In Bordeaux the early cold snap of November 1942 gave way to a mild winter of wind, rain and mud. Repeated squalls lashed the elegant frontages of the Quai des Chartrons and beat at the windows of Dohse's offices in Bouscat. The streets and alleys of the great port were empty, save for passers-by scurrying, collars up, to unavoidable destinations, a few cars sloshing through puddle-strewn streets and an occasional bedraggled horse pulling a bedraggled cart – and equally bedraggled carter – across wet cobblestones, under a leaden sky.

It was not good weather for parachuting.

In February, the weather at last turned, ushering in a long period of drought and unseasonable heat: in Bordeaux the temperature rose to twenty degrees. By the time April came, the ground was so dry that huge forest fires, driven by strong winds, consumed 100,000 hectares of conifer forest in the Landes region. It was whispered that the Germans had set the fires deliberately to destroy hidden Maquis camps and drive out the young men and women who had taken to the woods to escape being sent as compulsory labour to Germany.

But the fine weather had its advantages, too; Jean Duboué was now able to spend long days identifying and preparing parachute sites. This involved recruiting and training teams of men and women to act as reception parties who would mark the site with lights, collect the parachuted containers and spirit them away in lorries and carts to safe hiding places. He drew up sketch maps of each site with notable points, accurately established the location by latitude and longitude and agreed a special code-phrase for each dropping point, to be broadcast over the French service of the BBC when a drop was imminent. These were, in the main, utterly banal phrases such as 'the circle has become a square', 'artichokes have a hairy heart' and 'perhaps, perhaps and then'. In all, Duboué and his team established some sixty sites in and around Bordeaux and a further fifty across the rest of western France. These stretched from a water meadow near the village of Villedieu-les-Poêles, twenty-five kilometres from the Normandy coast, to a forest clearing close to the Burgundian village of Véron, southeast of Paris, to Scientist's most southern site, a field bounded on three sides by a river, near the town of Dax, in the shadow of the Pyrenees. The myriad details of all these sites were painstakingly encoded and sent to London in Morse code through Roger Landes's little radio set, perched on his kitchen table, in his bungalow beneath the German radio mast in Cenon. The strain on both man and machine was immense. London began to consider sending out a second radio operator.

Sometime towards the end of January, disaster struck when Landes's radio burnt out. London ordered him to take the defective wireless to Paris, where a radio engineer, who was a member of Francis Suttill's Prosper network, would either fix it or provide a replacement. Landes and Mary Herbert took the train north to the French capital, travelling as man and wife.

By now the Prosper circuit had become SOE's second-biggest network after Scientist in what had been the German occupied zone. During their week in Paris, Mary Herbert stayed at the flat of Andrée Borrel, Prosper's courier, close to where Landes had lived when he was at the École des Beaux-Arts before the war. Fearful of being recognised, Landes steered clear of the area and, security-conscious as ever, moved from address to address, never spending two consecutive nights in the same house.

Following this visit, the two British networks maintained close relations, with Borrel and Norman making several return visits to Bordeaux and staying in the rooms above the Café des Chartrons. It was friendly, fraternal and fun – but it was very bad security.

As was another event which took place at about the same time.

On 20 January, André Grandclément finally married his Lucette. A large reception was held afterwards at their apartment in the Cours de Verdun. It was all very grand, as one guest remembered: 'All André's friends were there, together with their neighbours and many of those in the Resistance who worked with him. It was a brilliant affair and André was in terrific form – very proud and full of self-confidence.' Another described the constant passage of Resistance leaders swirling in and out of the front door of number 34, directly opposite the gates of Pierre Poinsot's police headquarters on the other side of the road, as 'like a windmill'.

De Baissac was naturally among the guests invited to this grand occasion. And so too, at de Baissac's request, were Vic Hayes and Roger

Landes, who met Grandclément for the first time. The two English newcomers were deeply shocked by what they saw. Everyone referred to everyone else not by their aliases, but by their real names. There was no security of any sort, nor any attempt by the more than forty of André Grandclément's Resistance colleagues who attended to enter or leave discretely, or to hide who they were or what they did.

The two Englishmen were also taken aback at the right-wing views openly on display on all sides. The feeling was mutual. André Maleyran, one of Grandclément's key lieutenants, was also present that day. He described Landes in words which mix disdain with the unmistakeable undertows of anti-Semitism: 'At that time Landes was a little no-one – a tyke. He was the kind of person to whom you say "you stay there and keep quiet" – and he would do as he was told. He was just a small spoke in a big wheel. He was nothing.'

Landes responded to the event with alarm: 'I left the meeting immediately and told de Baissac that I never wanted to have anything to do with Grandclément again.' De Baissac, who was now spending much of his time with Grandclément, agreed that all future dealings with 'Bernard' and all liaison with the OCM would, in future, be handled by him. Landes and Hayes were given permission by London to team up with Duboué and Paillère and establish their own independent Resistance groups. There were ten of these in all, each with their own associated parachute drop sites, and all totally unconnected with Grandclément. From this small precaution would come, in due course, deliverance; but from the fissure it created would also grow an unbridgeable and deadly chasm of rivalry, suspicion and betrayal.

In fact, it may well have suited Claude de Baissac to be the sole point of contact with Grandclément. For by this time, the two friends were involved not just in Resistance affairs, but in business ones too.

Building up and arming the Resistance for the 'coming invasion' was an extremely expensive affair; Resistance leaders were regularly paid according to their responsibility. Even ordinary members of parachute reception parties received 500 francs every time they attended a drop. The guides across the Pyrenees received 5,000 francs for every escapee they delivered safely into Spain. To fund this expenditure, London provided huge sums of money to both Francis Suttill in Paris and Claude de Baissac in Bordeaux. When Landes dropped into the Loire valley in October 1942, he was carrying in his money belt 250,000 francs (about the equivalent of £50,000 today) to be shared between de Baissac and Suttill. Regular sums followed by parachute during the last months of that year and the early months of 1943.

Nevertheless, de Baissac was constantly short of ready cash and often had to resort to borrowing from local businessmen and bankers against promissory notes, or British government war bonds. These were to be paid back by the UK government after the war. One of these promissory notes was for 90,000 francs, lent to de Baissac by Grandclément on 10 March 1943. Money, however, was not changing hands in only one direction. Grandclément also received regular large subventions from de Baissac to cover the 'expenses' of his organisation, although in this case he showed a marked reluctance to provide either receipts or any account of his expenditure. One Resistance colleague complained that, quoting reasons of 'security', Grandclément resolutely 'refused to provide any monthly report accounting for his expenditure. He even refused to give the total numbers of people he was paying.' Sadly, Grandclément was not, in reality, being nearly as security-conscious as this might suggest. At the same time as claiming that keeping accounts was a security risk, he was meticulously recording the names and addresses of almost all his senior Resistance contacts, uncoded, in a special green file marked 'insurance customers', which he kept in an unlocked cupboard in his office at Cours de Verdun.

The local OCM chief was also known to have a number of other commercial activities. Some of these were straightforward and above board – for example, an investment which Grandclément had made in a local textile firm. Others were illegal – like a scam for creaming off the profits from the works canteen of a bank in Poitiers. Several more were closely connected with the black market.

In February 1943, de Baissac, the former film publicist, began to indulge in some of his own extracurricular business with his new

Resistance partner, setting up a small film distribution company, Sélections Cinématographiques du Sud-Ouest, in a narrow backstreet of Bordeaux. The company secretary was one of Grandclément's close friends, whose mistress was the company clerk. In due course de Baissac and Grandclément expanded their business by buying a cinema in Toulouse, no doubt making use of de Baissac's pre-war experience – and probably contacts – in the French movie business.

De Baissac's commercial activities did not end there. He also bought a brothel, though whether in this case Grandclément was a partner is not known. What exactly the British taxpayer would have thought of government money being used for such purposes is uncertain. But it was by no means uncommon for SOE agents to hold their meetings in what the French know as a *hôtel de passe*. Investing in brothels may also have been a useful way to launder the huge sums they were receiving from London. Though many prostitutes and pimps worked as spies for the Germans, there were, according to Landes, also 'a lot [of girls] working for the Resistance. The prostitutes would often give us shelter ... when we needed to spend the night somewhere safe so as not to be caught by the Germans.' The British habit of using brothels as meeting places was no secret in Bordeaux. One of Grandclément's lieutenants observed: 'I knew a pimp who had a brothel and a black-market restaurant. The English were often to be found there. Why do you think they liked to be there? Because they needed places where they felt protected and where it did not surprise people to see men coming and going.'

The full moon in February 1943 occurred in the third week of the month. With the weather still set fine, the parachuting of arms to Scientist could now begin in earnest. On the night of 21 February, London issued instructions for a drop of four containers and one agent at the edge of a wood close to Arcachon, fifty kilometres southwest of Bordeaux. A spate of parachute drops across the Bordeaux region and the west of France followed. In March the total for drops in France was 79; April and June saw 342 drops and between July and September the figure rose to 630. In the Bordeaux region alone, 121 successful drops took place between

January and August 1943, delivering 1,600 containers and 350 packages. These contained, among other stores, more than nine tons of explosive, 1,500 rifles, 300 Bren light machine guns and 17,200 grenades – enough, Landes estimated, 'to arm a Division'.

The Germans in Bouscat were, of course, fully aware that something big was happening. Hans Luther, Dohse's boss in KdS Bordeaux, noted: '[in 1943] the supply of weapons and sabotage materials by air reached a new level not seen before'.

Dohse too thought the matter was of 'great concern'. This new threat would have to be confronted – and quickly, if things were not to get out of hand when the imminently expected invasion came. 'I asked the Luftwaffe to set up a system of surveillance ... in order to map ... [the British bombers'] routes in and out and the dates and times of their drops, so we could work out where best to attack them. It was very clear that they were parachuting arms and explosives for sabotage and perhaps even setting up landing grounds for sabotage teams and to take agents back to England.'

The Luftwaffe responded with enthusiasm. Their new state-of-the-art radars, set up near the mouth of the Gironde, could now detect incoming British bombers while they were still far out at sea. They also had mobile sound-detector teams capable of tracking an aircraft which was flying too low for radar. It did not take long to bring the two systems together so as to provide comprehensive cover of an area stretching along the entire Aquitaine seaboard and extending south, well beyond Bordeaux.

Soon Dohse was receiving a full report every morning of the previous night's activity, accompanied by a 1:50,000-scale map showing the most likely drop sites. The ease with which he was able to plot the clandestine activity was very pleasing: 'We were able to establish without too much difficulty that after the [enemy] aircraft arrived, it circled and then slowly flew over an area, generally one which was isolated and wooded, before turning back to retrace its steps by the way it came ... We identified two areas of particular activity in Pissos and Le Temple [southeast and northeast of Arcachon respectively].'

Now Dohse could go further. By using this Luftwaffe information, a radio tuned to the BBC French Service, which he kept by his bedside, and daily reports from the German wireless interception service, he began to correlate the codewords broadcast by the BBC with local Halifax flights and their likely dropping points. It was painstaking and detailed work. But it soon began to bear fruit as, little by little, a remarkably accurate and comprehensive picture began to emerge of what the British were doing. Next, Dohse planned to infiltrate his agents into the Resistance reception committees.

The wolf was sharpening his claws. But he still did not know where to find his quarry.

10

'JE SUIS FORT –
JE SUIS MÊME TRÈS FORT'

On the evening of 17 March 1943, two unlit Lysander aircraft took off into the dusk from RAF Tangmere on the south coast of Britain and, like a pair of giant moths, disappeared into the night. Once clear of prying eyes, they swung south and began their long journey through the night to a water meadow near Marnay, twenty kilometres south of Poitiers. Tonight, as every night on these special Lysander operations, the two pilots, Flight Lieutenants 'Bunny' Rymills and Peter Vaughan-Williams, would fly singlehanded nearly a thousand kilometres across enemy-occupied France, unarmed and with no navigational aids beyond a compass and a folding map on their knees. When they arrived back – if they arrived back – they would have no fuel left in their tanks, for Marnay, 560 kilometres north of Bordeaux and 475 kilometres away from their home base, was close to the operational limit of the Lysander's range. The task they embarked on this early spring evening was to land four secret agents in France and bring four back. One of those returning to Britain to be debriefed was Claude de Baissac.

What no one involved knew was that the person organising the land-ing site at Marnay that night, a Frenchman by the name of Henri Déricourt, was already working under the control of Dohse's Gestapo spymaster in Paris, Karl Bömelburg.

It is probable that Mary Herbert had travelled north from Bordeaux a few days previously to prepare for de Baissac's departure, for that was

89

part of her job. She may even have been on the landing field to see him go. If so, she would almost certainly have been unware of the fact, as she waved her lover goodbye, that she was a few weeks' pregnant with his child.

Claude de Baissac arrived at 59 Wimpole Street, London, the house SOE set aside for debriefing returning agents, on the afternoon of 18 March. The subsequent debriefing report describes de Baissac laying 'claim to 3/4,000 men' covering 'a large and important area', and buoyantly summing up his six months' work in southwest France with the words: '*Je suis fort – je suis même très fort.*' His assessment of Grandclément seems to owe more to Dr Pangloss than reality: '*Extremely* intelligent ... very well understood our problems ... best left autonomous.' He added that Grandclément's 'organisation ... has been carefully built up ... and is ... excellently compartmentalised [so as to create] the minimum risk of any widespread trouble if something goes wrong.'

De Baissac's view that Scientist and the OCM in the Bordeaux region were *très forts* was shared by the London-based French. Three weeks before de Baissac left for London, Colonel André Dewavrin, the head of de Gaulle's Resistance directorate in London, parachuted into France to make an assessment of Resistance strengths and weaknesses. The report of his visit confirms that, in Dewavrin's view, the most solid of the OCM structures in all France (whose overall strength a few months later was estimated at 42,000) was its organisation in Bordeaux.

A second conviction enthusiastically shared by those, British and French, who directed the Resistance from London, was that the invasion would be launched by the end of September 1943. Apart from an urgent request from de Baissac for an extra radio operator in Bordeaux to support the overworked Landes, the only other matters of substance discussed during his four-week stay in London were money (de Baissac needed more); a proposal from de Baissac and Suttill that they should between them take over as in-country heads of the entire British secret effort in France (Buckmaster firmly rejected this: 'You have your own regions. You should work within those and not get involved with others outside your area'); and preparations for the coming invasion. De Baissac was instructed to be ready for a landing before the 1943 autumn equinox and given one codeword to alert him when the landings were imminent; another to tell him when they were actually happening; a list of targets to attack; a special course training him in the sabotage of railways and telephone exchanges (he was later described as a 'lazy student'); and instructions on what to do when Bordeaux was overrun by invading Allied troops. Francis Suttill, meanwhile, reported from Paris in March that the French capital was in a 'state of siege' because the Germans feared an Allied attack on the Channel coast in the course of May.

On the night of 14/15 April, de Baissac was parachuted back into France near Angoulême, fully briefed and prepared for an invasion that was, in reality, never going to happen.

Five weeks later, on the night of 20/21 May, Suttill was also taken out of France by Lysander for a briefing in London. Maurice Buckmaster would later claim that the purpose of Suttill's visit was to warn him that 'D-Day' was *not* imminent. But this seems as unlikely as Buckmaster's earlier claim to have received a 'secret message' saying that it was. Even allowing for the confusion that sometimes reigned in Baker Street, it is almost inconceivable that they would have briefed one agent in detail that the landings were coming soon and another, a month later, that they weren't. Some reports even claim that Suttill had a secret meeting with Churchill, who apparently left him in no doubt that the 'great event' would happen in the summer. But there is no evidence beyond conjecture for this and it seems highly unlikely.

De Gaulle's organisation in London also played their part in heightening the expectation of an invasion before the autumn of 1943 – and indeed that it might even take place on the Aquitaine coast. In the early months of that year they tasked one of their intelligence agents in the southwest to report on the suitability of the beaches at Mimizan, ninety kilometres southwest of Bordeaux, as a possible site for the landings. The spy's orders included providing information on the state of the beaches, beach gradients and composition, depths of water, location of pillboxes, barbed wire, minefields, key roads, and, 'as the invasion approaches, details on the tides around the port of Bayonne. We will be sending two volunteers through Bilbao [in Spain] who can act as guides for the British troops when they arrive.'

Some explanation for the deadly confusion about the date on which the second front would be opened up may lie in the fact that London was at the time engaged in a major deception operation designed to persuade the Germans that the invasion would indeed come during the summer or early autumn of 1943. Operation Cockade, a detailed and highly secret plan, was launched that year with the aim of implementing an 'elaborate camouflage and deception scheme extending over the whole summer with a view to pinning the enemy in the West of France [during 1943, when the Allied focus was actually on the Mediterranean] and keeping alive the expectation of large-scale cross channel operations in 1943'. The problem was that, since Baker Street was deliberately kept out of the highest councils of the war by 'the powers that be', the unwitting effect of Cockade was to deceive not so much the Germans, as SOE and the London French.

The fact that the Germans – or at least the Germans in France – might be taking the bait came to light sometime in the middle of 1943 when American codebreakers, who had cracked the Japanese diplomatic codes at the beginning of the war, deciphered a telegram from the Japanese ambassador in Paris reporting to his capital on a visit to Vichy. The ambassador informed Tokyo that the Gestapo had widely penetrated both the British and French networks in France and, 'in an attempt to anticipate a hypothetical D-Day which they feared might be imminent', had already started a 'heavy drive' to smash the Resistance before any invasion could happen.

The German high command in France also made other preparations for the event they were sure was coming. Roads and bridges around Poitiers were mined, so that they could be blown up quickly if needed, and Dohse was instructed to set up a stay-behind network of spies in Bordeaux whose task was to pass reports back to Germany on troop movements and political developments after the Allied assault. There were several of these 'fifth column' agents in the Bordeaux area. One was run by a Bordeaux midwife, who was recruited by Dohse and sent for training at the German wireless school in Paris. She was then set up in a safe house in Bordeaux and equipped with a captured SOE radio set, which worked to a German transmitter in Spain and another in Stuttgart. Dohse also recruited a network of local agents whose task would be to pass reports to her for onward transmission to Berlin through secret 'letterboxes' in four Bordeaux churches. The network remained dormant, waiting for an invasion which was, in fact, still more than a year away.

Back in Bordeaux, de Baissac spent April, May and June strengthening his organisation in the hinterland behind the Aquitaine coastline; this included setting up two escape lines to Spain, one over the Pyrenees and one from the Aquitaine port of Hendaye to San Sebastián. In a report sent back to London by Lysander on 17 June, de Baissac described how he was carrying out military training and creating a 21,000-strong quasi-military organisation 'capable of taking offensive action … to create a bridgehead … in the case of an invasion'. From de Baissac and Grandclément down, a lot of Resistance fighters were now risking all to assemble a large organisation under the Germans' noses, in the expectation that an Allied landing was imminent. They had placed themselves in considerable danger, even if the assault did come. And mortal danger, if it didn't.

SOE was well aware of the risk. One of their reports at this time, dated 29 July 1943, said: 'It is … undoubted that failure to invade this autumn will involve considerable losses (a) among our personnel (b) to morale among sympathisers.'

A spell of bad weather and storms interrupted parachute operations at the start of the May moon period. But this soon passed and parachuting continued apace throughout the remainder of the spring and into the early summer.

One of these drops took place on 13 May in a forest clearing four kilometres north of the little village of Marcheprime, midway as the crow flies between Arcachon and Bordeaux. 'The English at that time only parachuted on the nights of the full moon,' recalled one member of the Arcachon Resistance. 'I had bought a little radio receiver which I listened to at my friend Jeanne's house so as not to cause my parents worry. Every night we listened intently to the BBC *Messages Personnels* hoping to hear our secret code-phrase "Even heaven recoils with horror in the face of this monster"':

> The full moon period of April came and went – nothing. And then one night – there it was. My heart gave a jump at the impossible thought that an aeroplane could drop to us without attracting the attention of the Germans … at 9 o'clock the six of us took the train to Lamothe with our bikes and cycled north to the site … The wall of my tyre had worn very thin at one point and I prayed that it would last up … Finally we arrived at a large clearing in a pine forest which was covered in bushes as high as a man. Shortly afterwards Jean Duboué and Claude de Baissac arrived on motor-bikes. The plan was to line up three red lights in a row with a fourth, white light at the back. De Baissac stood to the right of this white light with a signal lamp to flash the agreed Morse code letter at the aircraft. Duboué instructed us to be sure to point our lamps at the aircraft as it turned so that the pilot could always see where we were. At midnight we took up our positions. Time passed. The night was silent. The moon shone brilliantly. I began to grow drowsy.

Earlier that night at 2122 hours, Pilot Officer Higgins took off from RAF Tempsford airfield in Halifax EB 129. He transited south over Selsey Bill, just east of Portsmouth, and turned his aircraft first west down the English Channel and then, when well clear of Finistère at the tip of Brittany, swung south across the Bay of Biscay. The gibbous moon, in its third quarter, had risen in the northeast in the early afternoon and was now arching from north to south above him during his long passage south, a lonely dot in an empty night sky. The weather had been fine across the English Channel, but there were heavy showers over the Bay of Biscay. Higgins could see the clouds piling up around the Pyrenees and over Bordeaux as he drew towards the Aquitaine coastline. By the time he crossed the French coast at a little after 0100 hours, the moon, now sinking fast towards the horizon, was shining almost directly into his cockpit, making it difficult to pick out the red and white lights and the code letter being flashed by de Baissac on the drop site. But then he saw it: 'Very good. White flashing letter A.'

'At around one o'clock we heard the distant hum of an aircraft. It was him!' described the Arcachon Maquisard:

> I felt a lurch of silent elation. The noise got closer and closer. It seemed to invade us. Then the black shape was above us – and then it was gone and we could no longer hear it. Suddenly we felt deflated. But Duboué explained that he was circling round so as to confuse the Germans about the exact location of the landing site. He was away so long that I began to wonder if it had just been a German plane returning to base. But the pessimism didn't last long, because suddenly there he was above us, his engines quiet now as he half glided in for the drop. The night was suddenly full of the clack of silk opening, as eight parachutes appeared above us. A few seconds later we heard the heavy thuds of the containers hitting the ground – and then the night was silent again – the aircraft had gone. In a few hours the pilot would be back on free soil again in England – how we all wished we could be there too!
>
> Duboué shouted after the departing aircraft: 'Those bloody cowardly pigs of Polish pilots – they've dropped all the containers in the bushes!' After some searching we found seven containers. But there should have been eight. I was sure that one of the parachutes had carried a man. I thought I could see his legs. But the night was now drawing on and our first task was to clear the site.

By the time Pilot Officer Higgins landed his Halifax back at Tempsford, a little after dawn, the parachutes had been gathered up, all tell-tale signs of the drop had been erased, the containers had been securely hidden in the forest and the reception team, having enjoyed an *al fresco* breakfast while waiting for the curfew to lift, had all safely returned on their bicycles to their homes.

There was indeed an eighth parachute dropped that night and it did indeed carry a man.

The new arrival was Marcel Eusèbe Défence, sent out at de Baissac's request to assist Roger Landes. Défence, noted for his calm and taciturn nature, had landed in the bushes, too. Hearing the sound of Duboué's men all around him and having been instructed before leaving London that he should on no account be seen by anyone on the ground on his arrival, he hid in a bush until morning and all was quiet. Emerging from his hiding place he bumped straight into a farmer from a nearby house:

'What are you doing on my land at this hour?'

'I'm out for a walk.'

'Don't give me that rubbish! You're a parachutist. I heard the aircraft circling last night.'

Défence pulled out his automatic and pointed it at the Frenchman's head.

'Don't worry, don't worry.' The farmer laughed. 'I am a good Frenchman. There are plenty more like me in France.'

'I smelled him out as an Englishman from two kilometres away,' the farmer claimed later. If so, then it seems more likely that he would have used his ears rather than his nose. For Défence, who had a French father and a Belgian mother, had been brought up in Glasgow and spoke French with the thickest of Sauchiehall accents.

The new arrival was led to the farmer's home, where he washed, shaved, breakfasted and was taken to Marcheprime station to be put on a train for Bordeaux.

On 17 May, shortly after Défence arrived in the city, thirty-four American B52 Flying Fortresses raided Bordeaux (the fourteenth time the port had been bombed since the start of the war). 'Direct hits burst the great lock gates ... a 480 yard pier ... collapsed completely ... two U-Boats vanished completely ... chemical works were hit ... damage to residential areas was negligible,' one of the US pilots exuberated afterwards, describing it as a 'sweet job'. In reality almost no damage was done to military installations. But 184 French civilians were killed, 276 injured and considerable destruction caused to residential quarters, especially the poor working-class area of Bacalan. The Bordeaux authorities produced a propaganda video criticising 'this revolting aggression by the Anglo-Saxon air-force', a sentiment widely shared in the city. Claude de Baissac, who had just returned from receiving another parachute drop near Arcachon, was in Bordeaux that day and having lunch on the Quai des Chartrons, where he had a ringside view of the raid. He sent a report and a sketch map back to London listing the places where the bombs struck and giving details of the damage done.

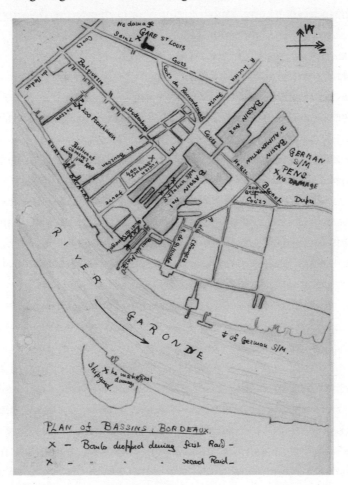

Marcel Défence had arrived at a critical time. Over the early months of 1943, Roger Landes's near-continuous hours of work, sending and receiving signals, had placed him at real risk of detection at Cenon. To make matters worse he had started to draw the attention of neighbours, many of whom were German. In April he decided to move his transmissions to a less populated area – the little community of L'Alouette at the southern edge of Bordeaux. After Landes's departure, the Germans took over the Cenon bungalow and used it to billet officers from the nearby anti-aircraft headquarters.

The move from Cenon did not solve all Landes's problems. With still only one radio, borrowed from Prosper – and therefore only one place to operate from – he remained highly vulnerable to the detector vans, which now patrolled day and night, with increasing regularity.

Défence's arrival with three new, more powerful radios enabled the two men, working turn and turn about, to vary their locations and change the frequencies of their transmissions constantly. Landes secreted the four wireless sets in different safe houses around Bordeaux, shifting them from time to time to other locations as the need arose. This meant that he and Défence were barely off their bicycles, riding in the spring sunshine along the cobbled backstreets and alleys of Bordeaux, from covert letterbox to letterbox, collecting and distributing messages – and from safe house to safe house, transmitting and receiving them. This intense activity also meant a lot of work for Scientist's two couriers, Mary Herbert and Ginette Corbin, who had to carry many of the messages, fill and empty letterboxes and move radios and crystals from place to place. It was not long before a working relationship deepened into a love affair between Défence and Ginette Corbin, who seems not to have noticed the affection that Roger Landes held for her.

About this time, Landes finally found permanent lodgings at 29 Rue Guynemer, the home of the Fagets, François and Marguerite, who ran a bicycle shop in Bordeaux. The couple were also active in the black market and had assiduously cultivated a reputation for being staunchly pro-Vichy in order to deflect the attention of the local authorities. For the neighbours and the inquisitive, the new arrival in the Faget house was described by Mme Faget as her long-absent 'nephew'. In reality, Marguerite Faget's relationship with the new arrival was soon to become much closer than that. Taller than Landes and twenty years his senior, Marguerite Faget, known affectionately as 'Mitou', had a generous mouth, eyes permanently inhabited by a twinkle, and a tumbling profusion of auburn hair arranged in the style of the Beverley Sisters. Sometime, probably not long after he moved in, Mitou Faget and her new lodger began an affair which would underpin their clandestine work together until the war ended. Given the closeness of the *ménage* at Rue Guynemer, it seems unlikely that Monsieur Faget was unaware of the relationship.

There was a curious ambivalence to Landes's attitude towards engagements with the opposite sex. He avoided (and indeed strongly disapproved of) genuine love affairs, but had no qualms at all about a little sex on the side, if he could get it. It seemed that it was not the sex he considered unprofessional, but any emotional entanglement which could affect the judgements of those involved. The first was just a little harmless fun; the second was dangerous unprofessionalism and a threat to security.

By now the 'heavy drive' against the Resistance, predicted in the Japanese ambassador's telegram, was well under way. In March alone, there were 6,200 arrests across France, of whom 500 were classified by the Germans as 'terrorists'; 160 of these were shot, thirteen hanged, and most of the rest were deported to Germany, never to be seen again. In late May, almost the entire Resistance leadership structure on the Vercors plateau above Grenoble had been arrested in a single morning. In June, a Gestapo sweep of the Vendée and Deux-Sèvres departments, north of Bordeaux, turned up a number of buried weapons dumps. The Germans concluded (wrongly) that these had been strategically placed in preparation for an imminent invasion.

In Bordeaux, however, Dohse remained stuck. He knew what was going on well enough. He could plot and measure the increased tempo of parachute drops from the morning reports he received from the Luftwaffe. And everyone could see their effect in the six major sabotage attacks which had been launched in and around Bordeaux in the months of April and May – two provocatively timed to coincide with Hitler's birthday on 20 May. But try as Dohse would – and despite reinforcements from Paris to help, and intelligence from his own spies in the local population – he could as yet find no way to break into his enemy's now substantial, fast-growing and increasingly threatening secret networks in and around Bordeaux.

11

A BIRTHDAY PRESENT FOR FRIEDRICH

The great unravelling began at 1 a.m. on the morning of 11 June 1943, with an explosion in a field 340 kilometres north of Bordeaux.

It had been a scorching June, with day after day of blue skies, burning sun and star-spangled nights heavy with the fragrance of new-mown hay and wild flowers. The long grass in the water meadows of the Loire turned light gold almost overnight and the strawberries were ripe, plentiful and succulent in little village plots and in the gardens of the great châteaux alike. The full moon, huge and luminous, fell on 7 June. It was perfect weather for parachuting.

Pierre Culioli and Yvonne Rudellat, finding it impossible to work with the ever-suspicious and increasingly panicky Raymond Flower, had set up their own network (known locally as 'Le Réseau Adolphe' after Culioli's mock Hitler moustache). This had been subsequently subsumed into Suttill's Prosper circuit. The couple, who were by now lovers, had taken up residence in a small farm worker's cottage close to Neuvy, east of Blois, and set up a number of parachute sites and reception committees in the area.

On the evening of 11 June the reception committee at Neuvy heard the BBC code-phrase they had been waiting for – '*Le chien éternue dans les draps*' ('the dog sneezes in the bedsheets'). The team gathered shortly after dark on the designated site, under the direction of Culioli. Not long after midnight a Halifax, starkly outlined against a three-quarters gibbous moon, appeared and, after two passes, glided in on feathered propellers to drop its load. Everything seemed to go well until, 'a few seconds after the containers landed, a blinding glare came up from the ground … Followed by a deafening bang. Thirty seconds later a second more violent bang shook the air.' The explosions must have been heard at the Wehrmacht base three kilometres away, for the following morning, German troops arrived to gather up the remains and detonate the unexploded ammunition.

Things might have rested there with little more damage done. But, even with the enemy so close and so clearly alerted, more drops of both agents and containers took place in the area on six of the following ten nights; one was even observed by a German night fighter. It was asking for trouble.

Trouble duly arrived in the form of a German encirclement of the whole Neuvy area on the night of 20/21 June. Fortunately the farm worker's cottage where Culioli and Rudellat were staying (along with two recently parachuted Canadian agents) lay just outside the area of the encirclement.

Early on the morning of 21 June, Culioli and Rudellat, together with the Canadians, crammed themselves into the Frenchman's battered little Citroën and set off to catch the train to Paris. Unaware of the overnight German operation, they blundered straight into a roadblock in the market town of Dhuizon. The four occupants of the Citroën were taken into Dhuizon *mairie* for questioning. Culioli managed to convince the Germans that he and Yvonne Rudellat were forestry officials. Released, they returned to their car and waited nervously for the Canadians, leaving the engine of the Citroën running for a prompt getaway.

A few moments later, a Gestapo officer came out of the building and ran towards them, shouting that they had to return. Culioli, concluding the game was up, slammed his foot to the floor and made a run for it. The Germans gave chase in two powerful French-made Fords. Drawing level with the Citroën they raked the little vehicle with machine-gun fire. Several bullets punctured Culioli's tyres, one smashed through his windscreen and another into his leg. Three more struck Yvonne Rudellat in the head, just above her left ear. She slumped against Culioli, pouring blood and apparently dead. Culioli, trying desperately to get away, charged at a sharp bend at speed but lost control of the car, which slewed off the wall of a house, crashed through a hedge and careered into a field, throwing its driver clear, before finally coming to a stop.

After arresting Culioli, the Germans searched his car and found his briefcase, stuffed full of compromising documents, including two messages for 'Archambaud' (the codename of Gilbert Norman, Suttill's radio operator) and one for 'Marie-Louise' (Mary Herbert). They also found the two Canadians' radios and frequency crystals – and Yvonne Rudellat, still breathing. In due course Avenue Foch would 'play back' the two radios to London, successfully fooling Baker Street into transmitting another treasure trove of secrets, straight into the hands of the Germans.

Altogether, Monday 21 June 1943 was a bumper day for German intelligence.

At 2.15 that afternoon in the northern Lyon suburb of Caluire-et-Cuire, a good-looking middle-aged man, wearing a trilby with the brim pulled down over his eyes, walked into the house of a local doctor. He was followed almost immediately by a Gestapo raiding party. Jean Moulin, sent to France by de Gaulle to unite the French 'civil' Resistance, was arrested together with seven other key Resistance chiefs. Moulin's arrest, coming just two weeks after the capture in Paris of General Charles Delestraint, who had been charged by de Gaulle with setting up the Armée Secrète to unite all military Resistance structures, was a triumph for German counter-intelligence and a disaster for the French Resistance, which was now effectively decapitated.

The Caluire arrests were the result of a long and complex German operation. So it was hardly surprising that the main Gestapo attention on that day and the next was on how to exploit their carefully planned harvest from Caluire, rather than the lucky finds they had stumbled on in Pierre Culioli's Citroën. It took the local Gestapo chief in the Blois area, Ludwig Bauer, a couple of days to get round to interrogating Culioli (at the time Yvonne Rudellat was lying unconscious in the local hospital, after an operation during which the surgeon tried but failed to remove a bullet from her head). It was only then that Bauer realised what he had uncovered: the major British network that the Germans had been looking for in Paris.

Police reports of the time confirm that, within days of Culioli's arrest, the Germans had concluded that the haul of documents retrieved from his briefcase was their most important intelligence coup in France since the start of the occupation. Hitler himself, who had previously been informed of the existence of a major British 'spy ring' in Paris connected to a possible invasion and had taken a close personal interest, now demanded immediate action. Berlin authorised Paris to offer a million francs for information leading to the capture of a British agent and ordered them to 'neglect all other matters' and concentrate on destroying this 'particularly dangerous' network, which 'must be rooted out as an over-riding task'. It may be that Berlin's change of emphasis from following up the Lyon arrests to exploiting the Neuvy windfall was the reason why, after being terribly tortured by Klaus Barbie, Jean Moulin was taken first to Paris (where he stayed briefly in Bömelburg's house) and then, instead of being exploited for his intelligence locally, packed off to Germany. He died of the injuries he had received under torture, en route, at Metz station.

There is uncertainty as to whether Ludwig Bauer obtained the addresses of Gilbert Norman and Andrée Borrel from Culioli personally, or from the documents found in his briefcase. But there is none about the fact that, shortly before midnight on 23 June, the Gestapo burst into the house where Norman normally stayed. They had struck lucky again: netting both Norman and Andrée Borrel, who were in bed together, and acquiring another priceless list of names and addresses from Borrel's briefcase.

The Gestapo now had a vast treasure trove of intelligence, including hundreds of names and addresses, to exploit at their leisure.

Six days after his arrest – and no doubt after physical coercion – Gilbert Norman agreed to use his radio to transmit to London under

Bordeaux in the 1930s: (*above*) the Port de la Lune and the
Quai des Chartrons and (*below*) the Pont de Pierre

The Quai des Chartrons in 1938, with the building that housed the Café des Chartrons marked

Jean Duboué

Marie-Louise and Suzanne Duboué

Gaston Hèches

Léonce Dussarrat

André Grandclément

Lucette

Grandclément
and his father,
the old Admiral

Karl Bömelburg, Friedrich Dohse and Josef Kieffer on their 1941 tour in Bömelburg's armour-plated Cadillac

The tour took them across occupied and Vichy France and into Italy. Left to right: Kieffer, Dohse, an unidentified man, and Bömelburg, possibly at Cannes

Roger Landes, c. 1944

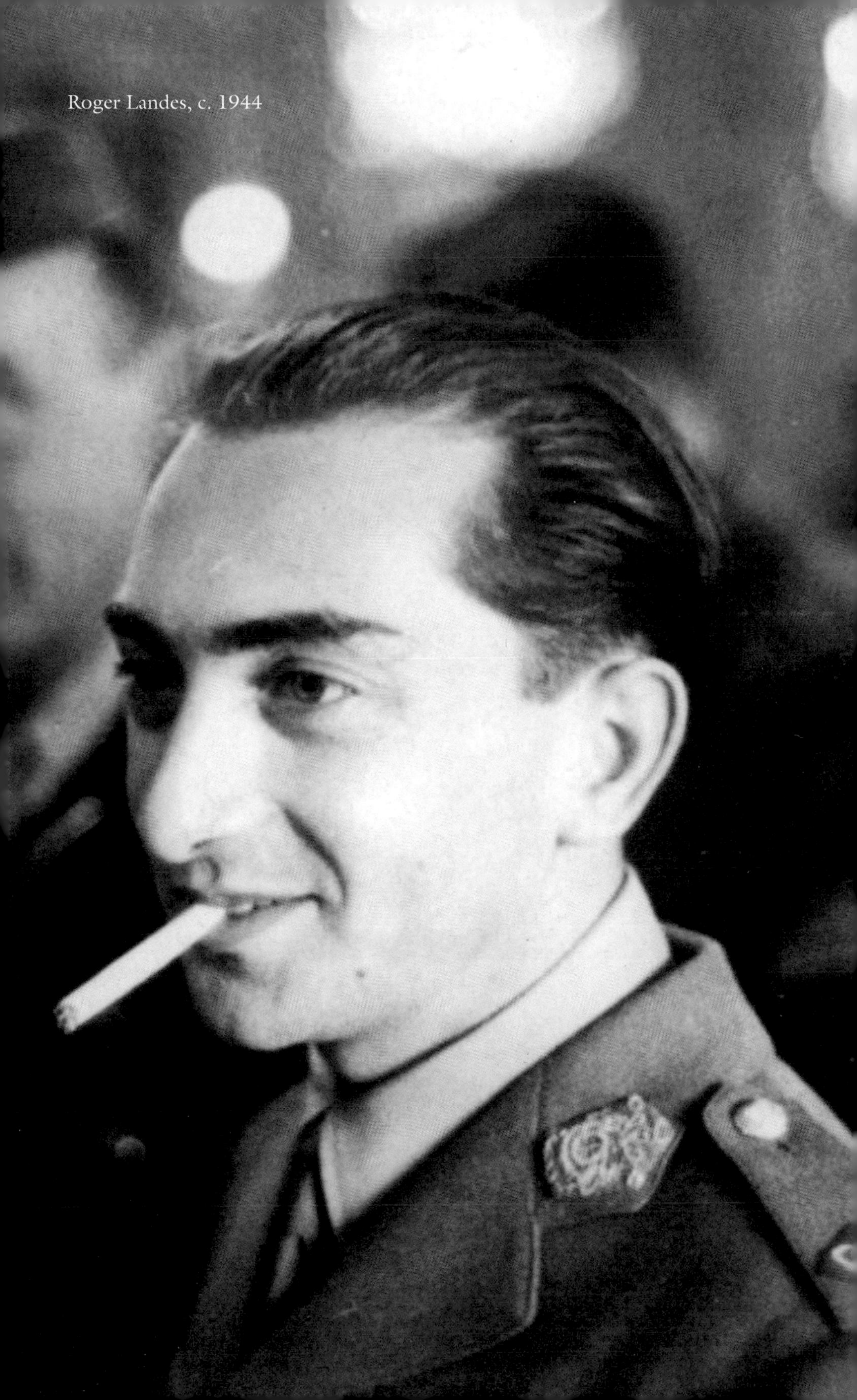

Wanborough Manor, Special Training
School No. 5, 1946

Claude de Baissac

Francis Suttill

Harry Peulevé

A Lysander of No. 161 (Special Duties) Squadron at RAF Tempsford, 1943

Charles Corbin

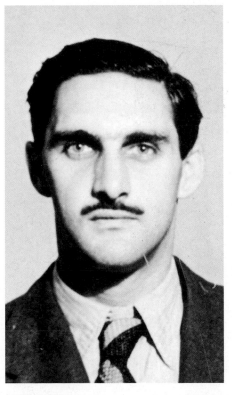

Gilbert Norman

Yvonne Rudellat

Andrée Borrel

Victor Hayes

Mary Herbert

Marcel Défence

German control. He tried to alert Baker Street of his predicament by ensuring that his first message did not contain the secret 'tell-tale' sign, whose absence was supposed to alert SOE that he was operating under duress. London, tragically, mistook Norman's mistake for an oversight – despite his reputation in SOE for near-flawless coding and for his meticulous use of the tell-tales in all previous transmissions. Baker Street also brushed aside the fact that Norman's transmission was noted by the operator who took his message at SOE's Grendon Hall wireless reception station in Northamptonshire as 'unusual, hesitant … the work of a flustered man doing his first transmission under protest'. To add insult to injury, Buckmaster sent Norman a strongly worded coded signal criticising him for omitting the 'tell-tale', describing this as 'a serious breach of security which must not, repeat must not be allowed to happen again'. For Norman, exhausted and on the edge even before his arrest, this must have been the last straw. His resistance collapsed and he started a period of active cooperation with the Germans, giving them, over time, almost everything they wanted.

On the morning after the arrest of Borrel and Norman, Francis Suttill, who had been inspecting parachute sites in the northwest, arrived back in Paris at the Gare Saint-Lazare for a 9 a.m. meeting with Grandclément's old school friend, Marc O'Neill, in the station café. Afterwards he returned to the backstreet hotel in which he was staying. Opening the door of his third-floor room, he was immediately surrounded, handcuffed, bundled into a car and taken to the Gestapo headquarters at Avenue Foch.

De Baissac, on London's instructions, had arrived in Paris the previous day to hand over Scientist's northern parachute grounds to Suttill and the Prosper network. In the evening, he had gone to Andrée Borrel's flat to arrange with Suttill where the handover would take place. Not finding Borrel in, he left a message proposing a 10.30 a.m. meeting the following morning at a local café.

When Suttill did not turn up the next morning, de Baissac returned to Borrel's flat. Arriving at 11.30, he found a terrified concierge who told him that the Gestapo had only just left, carrying a bundle of papers from

Borrel's room. De Baissac, close to panic now, departed in a hurry and spent the rest of the day checking that he was not being tailed.

Over the days which followed, the Germans mounted a huge operation to roll up the entire Prosper network, arresting hundreds in and around Paris and across the whole of northern France. As part of this, Norman was persuaded, no doubt still under terrible duress, to do a deal. He would lead the Gestapo to arms dumps in exchange for the release of some of those who had been arrested. Later, Roger Landes even claimed to have seen him – or someone very like him – being driven around Bordeaux in a Gestapo car, pointing out the places used as Scientist letterboxes and safe houses in the city.

London's 'played back' radio traffic with Norman almost immediately confirmed what Friedrich Dohse strongly suspected – that there was another powerful British network operating in Bordeaux. At this stage, the Germans did not know where it was or have the details of who was in it. But they did know that it was big, numbering four or five British agents, and they knew some of their aliases: 'Stanislas' (Roger Landes), 'David' (Claude de Baissac), 'Odile' (de Baissac's sister Lise), 'Charles' (Vic Hayes) and 'Marie-Louise' (Mary Herbert).

All of this, along with copies of London's exchanges with Norman and several of Suttill's reports, were sent to Dohse. These he would use as 'evidence' in future interrogations to persuade his subjects that the Germans had a 'mole' in Baker Street and that it was therefore 'pointless to resist', as they knew everything already.

De Baissac's precise movements after the collapse of Prosper are not known, though there are records of him seeking money from Resistance contacts in Paris in the days immediately following Suttill's arrest. He must at some stage have returned to Bordeaux, for at the end of June he and Grandclément signed a joint report to London claiming they had 50,000 men who could be mobilised for the invasion, but declaring that their organisation would collapse if the invasion was delayed beyond September 1943. No mention was made of the collapse of Prosper or its implications for Bordeaux.

* * *

The weather in the weeks following the collapse of Prosper was unbearably hot and oppressive in Bordeaux. In the city's narrow streets, the sun beat mercilessly off walls and cobbles alike, forcing the pavement-café-goers to huddle into what patches of shadow they could find and sweating pedestrians to seek the shadier sides of the streets. The public swimming pools were so full that the authorities tried to limit bathers to one hour each, including time for dressing and undressing. But these new restrictions made the crowds bad tempered and unruly and had to be quietly abandoned. A thick haze hung over the city, the air was foul and the river ran sluggish, flat and leaden under a burnished sky. Only the prisoners in the dank cellars below Dohse's offices on the Avenue du Maréchal Pétain, and the grapes contentedly fattening on their tresses in the vineyards of the Médoc, found the heat congenial. In the midst of all this discomfiture, nineteen trains and forty coaches filled with the seized personal possessions of the city's Jews – everything from furniture, to crockery, to luxury clothing and jewellery – left for Germany.

Thanks to the revelations from Paris, Dohse, sweltering in his office, now knew more about his enemy – but still not enough to find and break them. A period of frantic searches and raids across Bordeaux ensued, but all were fruitless. Meanwhile, the rolling programme of SOE parachute drops and sabotage raids in the area continued unabated.

Dohse's lack of success now began to have a material effect on his position in KdS Bordeaux. Criticised for his 'pro-French' attitude and 'soft' ways, he increasingly found himself squeezed out of active operations and confined to intelligence-gathering. More and more it was Kunesch who was in the driving seat.

But then, as so often at the most difficult moments of Dohse's time in Bordeaux, luck gave him a break.

On 17 July, Poinsot's SAP officers arrested a Bordeaux bicycle shop owner. He was, though Poinsot didn't know it, Roger Landes's chief fixer for safe houses in the city. Fortunately for Landes, the man, though tortured, said nothing. But his adopted twenty-two-year-old son, who was also arrested, was not so strong, and broke. The information he gave Poinsot provided the first detailed indication that he and Dohse were not dealing just with the British network identified by members of the Prosper network, but also with what Dohse described as 'an organised [French-run] Resistance movement [numbering 'several thousand'] which included a large number of arms depots' operating across the southwest from a headquarters in Bordeaux. This came as something of a shock to Dohse and his colleagues, who had previously been aware of individual Resistance groups, but completely oblivious of anything so large, organised, wide-ranging and well equipped.

But there was more.

Poinsot's young prisoner also turned out to be a member of a local Resistance group called 'Alouette', which was closely affiliated to the OCM. Though he did not know the name of the head of the OCM in the southwest, the young man did know his codename – 'Bernard' – and gave it to Poinsot. The French police chief also extracted the names of twenty or so others, who were swiftly arrested, before the whole operation was taken over by Dohse. Around two hundred further arrests followed, as the Alouette network was swiftly dismantled. In the third week of July the operation culminated with the arrest of the network's head (and a senior commander of de Gaulle's underground army, the Armée Secrète), Colonel Grandier-Vazeille.

Dohse's first interrogation of Grandier-Vazeille was courteous but fruitless. Eventually he warned his prisoner: 'If you will not talk then we have ways of forcing you. I am sure you are intelligent enough to know what I mean. I'll leave you until tomorrow morning to think about it.' Faced with the colonel's continued silence on the following day, Dohse handed him over to Kunesch and his team. Kunesch and Enzelsberger savagely beat their prisoner, breaking both his eardrums, whipping the soles of his feet and injuring him so badly that he could not stand and had to be carried to the toilet, covered in blood, by his fellow prisoners. Then he was brought back to Dohse's office: 'I hope you now understand how it works; if you don't, we can start again.'

Still refusing to talk, Grandier-Vazeille was thrown in the 'Action Chamber', where he was left for four days without food or drink. After this he was passed back to Kunesch's team who continued torturing him until the end of August, when they finally lost patience. Concluding that they could not make him talk, Grandier-Vazeille was shipped off to the death camps in Nazi Europe.

Thanks to the French Resistance habit of allowing their agents to belong to several organisations at the same time, Alouette gave the Germans sight of, and access into, the much larger OCM. It now became imperative to unravel the local OCM, and in particular to identify its head, the elusive Bernard.

But how?

The answer came on 22 July, Dohse's thirtieth birthday. The previous evening an eighteen-year-old student who lived with his parents in Bordeaux heard the BBC code-phrase he had been waiting for: '*La Saint-Félix tombe en juillet*' ('St Felix's Day falls in July'). Christian Fossard was young, eager, untried and impatient. While these are no doubt attributes common to many eighteen-year-olds, they are dangerous ones when it comes to participating in, let alone leading, clandestine operations against an efficient and cunning enemy. Fossard was not just a member of the Alouette network, he was also, despite his age and inexperience, the head of one of its newly established parachute reception committees. This team, mostly local students, were given responsibility for a drop site near the little village of Verteuil-d'Agenais, eighty-five kilometres south-west of Bordeaux.

The BBC code-phrase Fossard heard on the evening of 21 July was the warning which indicated that his team's first parachute reception was to be that night.

Eight containers packed with arms and explosives were dropped on schedule at 0130 hours the following morning from a Halifax. But no transport had been arranged, so the containers had to be hidden for later collection. Some were concealed in a hedge and the rest stocked in a nearby barn.

Dohse claimed that what happened next was an organised operation, resulting from his careful work to track British bombers. It was nothing of the sort. Like so much in spying and counter-espionage, it was pure luck.

Early on the morning following the drop, while gathering fallen fruit, an itinerant Italian worker called Longi spotted some of Fossard's containers poking out of a hedge. Not wishing to get into trouble, Longi called the local police. Fossard and his accomplices were swiftly found asleep in a barn, arrested and, in line with the orders of the time, delivered to Bouscat.

On the same day, Poinsot's policemen arrested and searched one of Grandclément's close contacts, acquiring a list of names and addresses, a suspicious-looking map and a curious policy taken out with André Grandclément's insurance business at 34 Cours de Verdun. Poinsot's men were sure they had something of importance, but, as yet, they didn't know what.

On arrival in Bouscat, Christian Fossard was brutally tortured by Kunesch's men. A prisoner being held at the same time remembers Fossard as being in 'a bloody mess, with his face covered in gore and his hands mangled from being crushed in a book press'. He was then handed over to Dohse for interrogation. Accompanied by his mistress and personal assistant Claire Keimer, Dohse interviewed Fossard, still bloodied and bruised and still in the shorts he had worn at the parachute drop. 'Armed not with a whip but with a bottle of white wine, I started to probe Fossard in the belief, built on past experience, that I would get more positive results from the soft approach than by any other interrogation tactic,' the Gestapo man recalled, with more than a hint of self-congratulation.

He was right. He soon discovered that there was indeed a deal to be done. If Dohse would ensure that Fossard's father and younger brother were released, then the young man would tell Dohse all that he knew. And for an eighteen-year-old student, he knew a lot.

There has always been some puzzlement as to why such a senior German official as Dohse paid so much attention to such a junior member of the Resistance. Dohse later claimed that he was following a 'premonition'. But here again, there is a more likely – and more prosaic – explanation: his interest in Fossard was probably due more to his skills as a police detective than to some kind of sixth sense. What he may have spotted (and what those who have subsequently tried to reconstruct the story have missed) was that the address of the building in which the Fossard family was living was the same as that of the parents of Henri Labit – the SOE agent and cousin of Ginette Corbin who had killed himself rather than be captured at Langon station. If this was what had sparked Dohse's interest in the young student, then he had, albeit unwittingly, struck a rich seam.

Fossard's extensive knowledge of matters way above his level may be explained by his connections. Through Henri Labit's parents he knew Charles Corbin (the ex-police inspector and father of Landes's courier, Ginette), who was now one of Grandclément's closest lieutenants.

Whether as a result of the Labit connection or because of the haphazard security which characterised all Grandclément's clandestine activities, or perhaps a combination of both, Christian Fossard knew enough to deliver to Dohse the breakthrough that he needed into the most senior ranks of the Resistance structures in Bordeaux.

By the time Dohse and Claire Keimer's all-night, white wine-assisted interrogation of Fossard was over, they knew that 'Bernard' was André Grandclément and where he could be found. But there was more – much more. Fossard also gave the names and addresses of a number of the key OCM leaders in the southwest; he informed Dohse that Grandclément's most important secret letterbox in Bordeaux was a modest house at 62 Rue du Palais Gallien, two kilometres from Dohse's office in Bouscat; he added to the information from Prosper in Paris by revealing the local name by which Stanislas (Landes) was known: 'René Pol'. And, most important of all, he identified that the head of the British network in Bordeaux – whose alias, 'David', Gilbert Norman had given the Germans – was Claude de Baissac.

Now at last Dohse could act.

As dawn broke he issued orders for the arrest of all the names he had been given by Fossard and for an around-the-clock watch to be placed on Rue du Palais Gallien.

Then he headed for 34 Cours de Verdun to arrest André Grandclément.

THE WOLF IN THE FOLD

In fact Dohse's 'victory' with Christian Fossard was not the great break-through he thought it was – and proudly proclaimed it to be afterwards. For what he didn't know – and perhaps never knew – was that Pierre Poinsot had beaten him to the punch. Sometime around the middle of the year Poinsot had himself recruited Grandclément as an informer, but decided to keep this secret from his German master. Poinsot's intention was to roll up the OCM network himself in order, according to a British report at the time: 'to show the Gestapo how effective he was'.

André Grandclément had originally come to Poinsot's attention when his name had been found in papers seized during a raid on the home of an ex-police inspector from Limoges. Subsequently questioned by one of Poinsot's men, Grandclément had confessed that he was indeed the head of a local Resistance organisation, though he had made no mention of his contact with de Baissac and the British. Poinsot offered to free him in return for his cooperation. Grandclément agreed, gave his interroga-tor 143 names (including that of the Bordeaux bicycle shop owner whose detention had sparked Poinsot's mid-July wave of arrests) and then promptly fled for Paris with Lucette.

On the morning of 24 July – the same day that Fossard was arrested – Poinsot discovered that Grandclément had flown (though not the fact that he had gone to Paris). Taking a dozen men with him, he headed out of the front gate of his headquarters and across the road to Grandclément's front door. It was opened by Lucette's cousin, who acted as Grandclément's secretary, and who was in the middle of writing a letter to Grandclément in Paris, reporting the recent wave of arrests. The woman was immediately placed under arrest and the flat searched. Opening a metal cabinet in Grandclément's office, Poinsot's men found, amongst other insurance dossiers, a green folder of 'policies' which looked very different from the others. For a start, there were no premiums shown against the list of names. Poinsot ordered the suspicious files to be taken away for further examination.

At some stage over the next few days Poinsot received intelligence that the Grandcléments would be returning to Bordeaux on 29 July. At seven that morning (and still without telling Dohse), the French police chief sent one of his surveillance teams to keep watch on arrivals at the Gare Saint-Jean. Another team, led by one of his key lieutenants, was sent to stake out the Grandcléments' home. At around 9 a.m. Friedrich Dohse, fresh from his 'triumph' with Fossard, turned up at 34 Cours de Verdun full of anticipation that he was about, at last, to ensnare his quarry. Instead he found Poinsot's stake-out team. Angry and disappointed, Dohse insisted that Poinsot's men should accompany him on a thorough search of the apartment. This, unsurprisingly, revealed nothing and they all went away empty handed (except for one of the search party, Poinsot's brother Jean, who helped himself to some of the Grandcléments' valuables and a collection of Lucette's silk dresses, which he slipped into his bicycle panniers. Challenged by one of his colleagues, he responded: 'Why shouldn't I? If we don't take this stuff, the Germans certainly will.')

It was either at this moment, or a little later, that Poinsot tried to cover his tracks by handing over the suspicious 'green dossier' – perhaps even claiming to have found it that morning. Dohse recognised immediately that the insurance documents were a cover. They were not the names and addresses of Grandclément's clients, but a list of his most senior lieutenants in the regional OCM.

Dohse immediately took personal charge of the Grandclément case. He now had the key, not just to arresting Grandclément himself, but to unravelling the whole of the OCM network in the southwest. The professional in him was also rather shocked at what he had found. Grandclément was clearly 'not someone emotionally equipped for secret work', he later reflected. 'All his friends knew exactly what he was up to … he trusted people who were far too young … his close [commercial] involvement with de Baissac was unpardonable in such secret matters … he was little more than a child when it came to this kind of work.'

The day after the second raid on the Grandcléments' apartment, Claude de Baissac left Bordeaux 'in a hurry' for Paris, saying he would be back in a week.

It has always been assumed that the Cours de Verdun raids were the cause of de Baissac's rushed flight to Paris. But there may have been another reason why he – and Grandclément – did not want to be in Bordeaux at that moment. At the same time as the Cours de Verdun raids were taking place, the Bordeaux tax authorities were preparing a case for submission to the Bordeaux commercial court against Sélections Cinématographiques du Sud-Ouest, the film distribution company run by de Baissac and Grandclément. This, as both men must have known, would be very likely to unmask not only any business impropriety they had committed, but also their Resistance activities. (The commercial court heard the case in early September 1944 and ruled that, in the absence of the company officers, the administration of the business should be handed over to a third party.)

For the Resistance in the Bordeaux region, the wolf was now well and truly in the fold. Dohse was in his element and, thanks to the information provided by Fossard and the treasure trove from Cours de Verdun, firmly back in operational charge of the main task now occupying KdS Bordeaux: the arrest of Grandclément and the destruction of OCM Southwest.

According to Dohse's assessment, the green dossier, combined with further information flowing in every day from interrogations and betrayals, led to the arrest of some 250 men and women, obliterating the entire middle-rank structures of the OCM network in southwest France. Bouscat's cellars soon overflowed and prisoners had to be chained in the huge cupboards lining the château's corridors, where they were incarcerated with little air and no light, sometimes for days, awaiting interrogation. All the other jails were also crammed full, most notably Bordeaux's main prison at the Fort du Hâ, an old fortress in the middle of the city.

As the round-up gathered pace, there was a rush of fugitives trying to flee to Spain. Dohse arranged for troops to strengthen patrols in the area around the Spanish frontier and many of the resistants were caught like birds driven into nets. In the first weeks of August 1943, more than forty escapees were picked up near the Spanish border. Despite Dohse's best attempts, however, even more made it to safety. According to German estimates, a total of 1,250 fugitives successfully crossed the Pyrenees into Spain between July and December 1943.

Back in Bouscat, Dohse's resources were now in danger of being over-whelmed as the vast, rickety, insecure structure of the OCM disinte-grated, dragging with it other, smaller, Resistance networks in the area.

Amidst all this success, however, Dohse still had two pressing problems.

First, he didn't actually have André Grandclément; indeed, he didn't even know where to look for him. Secondly, thanks to the earlier deci-sion taken by Roger Landes and Vic Hayes to operate independently, Dohse was still no closer to the British network in Bordeaux either.

As the summer heat intensified through July into August, invasion fever rose to a new pitch across France. In August, Operation Cockade, the Allies' deception plan to convince the Germans that the invasion would be launched in September 1943, reached its peak. Stories were deliber-ately planted in the BBC and international newspapers suggesting that an Allied attack on the coast of France was imminent. On 19 August the *New York Times* blared: 'Armies ready to go, says Eisenhower'. In that same week United Press carried a report from a 'source in London' that 'French underground leaders were revealed today to be confidently expecting an early invasion of France ... zero hour for the assault on Western Europe is approaching.'

The Germans didn't need to read the international press to know that something was afoot. They could read the signs from the rise in the number of sabotage attacks on German targets. These had increased from 337 incidents in January 1943 to 1,061 in August. The fact that, despite the turmoil all around them, Jean Duboué, Charles le

Démolisseur and their men were still able to keep up the pace of damage and disruption around Bordeaux was a constant reminder to Dohse (and Berlin) that, despite the spate of arrests, the task was very far from over.

The increasing tempo of SOE parachute drops told the same story. German figures for August record 977 containers dropped in ninety-nine successful operations across France.

Again, the figures for France as a whole were reflected in what was happening in and around Bordeaux. Twenty-two containers carrying almost four tons of arms were parachuted in from three aircraft at Pissos, southwest of Bordeaux, on the night after Poinsot's raid on 34 Cours de Verdun. And on the night after that, in one of the biggest multiple drops of the war so far, more than seventy containers were dropped in seven sorties across the Bordeaux area.

Dohse knew of all these drops from his morning Luftwaffe reports – but only after the event, when whatever had been parachuted would have been long ago spirited away into secret hiding places.

As the drums beat ever louder in favour of an early invasion, Friedrich Dohse was well aware that his successes against the lower ranks of the French-led Resistance were at best partial, if he was having little against their leadership and even less against the British. Unless he could lay his hands on the leaders and, above all, on the huge tonnage of arms dropped by the British, his enemies could very quickly reconstitute themselves.

Dohse might have been even more concerned if he had known that, in addition to weapons and explosives, London was now also dropping huge sums of money into the Bordeaux area. At this stage of the war, de Baissac's Scientist network was receiving more financial support than any other SOE network in France (2.1 million francs out of a total 7.2 million in the month of August 1943). The problem for de Baissac and Grandclément was that, while there may have been money aplenty in Bordeaux, they had no access to it, living an underground life in Paris with little or nothing to live on. On the day de Baissac left Bordeaux he negotiated a hurried loan of 200,000 francs – 'to be reimbursed at a rate of 250 francs to the pound' after the war – from two sympathetic local businessmen. One of these, Léonce Dussarrat, known locally as Léon des Landes, would become a key figure in the year ahead.

Two days later, on 27 July, one of Grandclément's business partners, Charles Artagnan – an occasional go-between for Germans operating on the black market – made the journey from Bordeaux to Paris to have lunch with Grandclément in a Paris café. Artagnan told his partner about the raids on 34 Cours de Verdun and warned that the Gestapo were watching for him at Bordeaux station. Grandclément took the opportunity to complain that he and Lucette were desperate for money to continue their clandestine existence in Paris. Artagnan agreed to advance him 90,000 francs to enable them to 'live in hiding'. The collateral for the loan was a receipt for the same sum which Grandclément had lent de Baissac back in March, which stipulated that it was to be repaid after the war by London.

Around the same time, Grandclément negotiated a second loan of 120,000 francs, on the same terms, from another business friend and partner in Angoulême.

Grandclément's next move was also about money – and it was a disastrous one. He was either so desperate for funds to live on, or so keen to pay back the loans he had received from his friends, that he took the very considerable risk of sending Lucette to Bordeaux, accompanied by Artagnan, to recover a million francs that he had deposited with a contact in Dax. The plan was for André to travel to Angoulême and wait there for news, before joining Lucette and Artagnan in Bordeaux, if the coast was clear.

Like most of André Grandclément's schemes, the hare-brained plan to send Lucette back to Bordeaux was born of self-interest, greed, impatience and a habitual love of taking risks, without making any attempt to distinguish between risks which were worth taking and those which were not.

Dohse was a much better gambler. After almost a week during which his watchers at the house on Rue du Palais Gallien had seen nothing, his superiors concluded that the surveillance was wasting precious resources. Dohse, however, insisted on extending the operation for a further twenty-four hours, however. Now André Grandclément played right into his hands.

Lucette and Artagnan arrived at the Gare Saint-Jean on the evening train from Paris on 29 July and went straight to 62 Rue du Palais Gallien. Early the next morning, the house was raided and Lucette and Artagnan – and two Portuguese women who happened to be staying in the house – were arrested. The presence of the two Portuguese nationals was an unexpected complication; Dohse did not want to risk a diplomatic incident. The Spanish consul, in his role as doyen of Bordeaux's diplomatic community, protested and demanded the women's release. Dohse, who had no firm evidence against either them or Artagnan, freed all three.

But not Lucette. She was taken to the Fort du Hâ, where she was interrogated by Poinsot. Although distressed and crying, she refused to talk. Next, Dohse ordered that she should be brought to him at Bouscat. A prisoner in a neighbouring cell overheard the ensuing interrogation and later confirmed that it was conducted without either threat or violence. Dohse first tried to use as leverage some potential charges related to black-market dealings in wine by Lucette's parents, and 'some cinema concern in which her husband was interested'. But Lucette, who was made of sterner stuff than her husband, steadfastly refused to say anything beyond the fact that André was in Paris, and that she had said goodbye to him at the Gare d'Austerlitz the previous afternoon. It was less than Dohse hoped for, but at least he now knew to focus his search on the French capital.

Dohse returned Lucette to the Fort du Hâ and waited to see what would happen. Charles Corbin – whose Resistance activities Dohse was still ignorant of – was permitted to take Lucette extra food and other luxuries and was secretly able to pass reassuring messages back to Landes and Duboué that she had said nothing.

For Dohse, it was now imperative that he find André Grandclément – and quickly, before he had the opportunity to disappear again. Fortunately, the search of Rue du Palais Gallien had yielded something of real value – a photograph of Grandclément. Dohse had this copied and sent to Bömelburg, with an urgent request that it be circulated to all

Gestapo units in Paris who should, he requested, be ordered to make finding the fugitive their top priority.

At about the same time that Lucette Grandclément was travelling south from Paris, Mary Herbert, now visibly pregnant with Claude de Baissac's child, was on a train travelling north on de Baissac's orders. She was lugging with her a suitcase containing Marcel Défence's wireless set. Défence himself was in a different carriage, so as not to be implicated if the radio was found.

Unknown to any of his colleagues in Bordeaux, on 17 July, a week before the Cours de Verdun raids, de Baissac had sent the first of what would be several messages urgently asking London for a Lysander to take him back to England. The reasons he gave for needing to return were varied according to his audience. London was told that he needed to return to escape imminent arrest. His friends in France were told that he wanted to press London for an early Allied invasion. Mary Herbert was told when she got to Paris that he had been urgently recalled to report to Baker Street. Roger Landes and Vic Hayes were told nothing at all.

Landes would later claim that the reason Défence and Herbert were ordered by de Baissac to make their late July trip to Paris with a radio, was to make it easier for de Baissac to arrange directly with London for a Lysander to take him out, without having to reveal his intentions to his colleagues in Bordeaux. When Mary Herbert left Paris to return to Bordeaux, de Baissac told her that he would be staying in the French capital until his Lysander 'was fixed', and instructed her that if any important messages arrived for him in Bordeaux, she should bring them to him immediately.

Dohse, of course, had no idea either of de Baissac's whereabouts, or of his intentions. But on or around 2 August he finally got a crucial breakthrough when Paris passed on to him the address of one of Landes's safe houses, which had been given to them by Gilbert Norman.

At last he could begin to break into the British network which had for so long, and so embarrassingly, eluded him.

August broke with another spell of furnace-hot weather in Bordeaux. Temperatures of more than forty degrees were recorded across the region. Life in the city once more became unbearable and most of its inhabitants retreated indoors to find what comfort they could behind thick walls and open windows. But not Roger Landes. He still had wireless schedules to keep.

In the early afternoon of Tuesday 3 August, Landes cycled across the cobblestones of the Avenue de la République, two kilometres from Dohse's office in Bouscat. The street, roasting under a pitiless sun, was shadeless and empty, save for a man lighting a cigarette opposite the house Landes was heading for: an art deco town villa at number 174, the home of a widow called Marcelle Caralp-Jardel. She had been introduced to Landes by Grandclément back in May and had offered her home as a safe house where Landes could hide a radio and transmit to London. There was a Gestapo officer already billeted on the second floor of the Caralp-Jardel house. But to Landes this only added to its attractions, for it meant he would be hiding in his favourite place – in plain sight, where the Germans would never think to look for him.

The house was one of four or five safe houses Landes had around the city, in each of which he had pre-positioned a radio in a suitcase so that he could constantly change the positions from which he transmitted to London. He hardly ever travelled armed in the city, believing that his ability to blend into the crowd was his best protection. Though he was never questioned at a checkpoint, and was only once asked for his papers during his entire time in France, Landes never took his luck for granted and always prepared for the worst, especially when making radio transmissions. In each suitcase where he had a radio, he hid a Colt automatic.

Of all his safe houses in Bordeaux, Roger Landes especially liked 174 Avenue de la République because it stood on a corner, had a number of entrances and could be approached from several directions. Best of all, the villa was served by two garages, one beneath the main house and the other below a neighbouring property, which Mme Caralp-Jardel had purchased and incorporated into her own house. To any outside observer, the second garage served not the Caralp-Jardel residence, but the house next door.

Landes paid little attention to the man opposite; he had been coming here once or twice a week for the last two months to work his radio from the maid's bedroom, next to the garage below the main house. The street was, in normal times, always busy and he had never attracted any attention. He unlocked the garage to one side of the villa and wheeled in his bicycle. The man on the other side of the street seemed to pay no heed.

Whatever comfort Landes may have felt on entering the cool of the garage was immediately dispelled by the look on the face of Marcelle Caralp-Jardel's sixteen-year-old daughter, who was waiting for him in the gloom. 'The Gestapo came this morning at 8.30,' she whispered urgently. 'They searched the house; every room; behind the furniture; behind the cupboards; they emptied the drawers; they even sounded out the walls. Then they took mother away.'

'Did they find the radio?'

'No. They searched the maid's room but never looked under the bed. They still have the house under surveillance. There is a man watching outside. I am sure they will be back to search again. I took the suitcase containing your radio out from under the bed and tried to throw it down the drain. But it was too big.'

Landes now had to act fast. He then reasoned that if there was a Gestapo watcher on this side of the house, then the other sides would be covered too. At least the man this side had not seemed to notice him going in. Or perhaps he had and had called for reinforcements?

There was only one thing to do. He would have to brave it by leaving the same way he came in – and quickly, before anyone else could arrive.

He took the Colt from the suitcase and put it in his pocket. Then, using an old piece of elastic rope, he strapped the case containing his wireless onto the carrier of his bicycle and told the girl to check from an upstairs window that the Gestapo watcher was still concentrating on the house, not the garage next door – and that the street was clear. She shouted down that all seemed okay.

Landes opened the garage door and pushed his bicycle out, coolly locking the door behind him. The German watcher, as before, paid no attention. But then, disaster! As Landes wheeled his bike over the cobbles the rope snapped, sending the case flying off its carrier and landing with a crash at the Gestapo man's feet. 'He bent down to pick up the suitcase. I put my hand [on the Colt] in my pocket, ready to shoot him. But instead he helped me put my suitcase back on the bicycle. He had been told to look out for a British officer and I didn't look like one at all,' Landes related later.

It was not the first time that Landes's cool nerves and quiet demeanour, coupled with his olive skin and short stature, had saved his life. And it would not be the last. Dohse admitted ruefully after the war that thanks to the stupidity of his Gestapo watcher, he had missed his most important quarry by a hair's breadth.

The following day, 4 August, news of Lucette Grandclément's arrest reached her husband in Paris, sending him spiralling into another deep depression. His friend and partner de Baissac was abandoning him for London; the organisation of which he had been head – and into which he had put so much hope and effort – had been dismembered; and the hope of an Allied invasion, which de Baissac had promised before the autumn equinox – and on which he had risked so much – was evaporating fast. To cap it all, his beloved wife was now in the hands of the Gestapo. Before leaving, de Baissac tried to persuade Grandclément to return to London with him, but the Frenchman insisted he would not leave without Lucette. He was separately ordered by the head of OCM Paris to leave France immediately for Algiers. But again he refused.

In mid-August, an urgent message arrived for de Baissac in Bordeaux. The redoubtable Mary Herbert, undaunted by the fact that she was now nearly six months pregnant with her first child, again took the train to Paris to deliver the message in person, as instructed. But when she got there she found de Baissac had just left.

On the night of 15/16 August 1943, a Lysander touched down on a field in the Loire valley, 170 kilometres southwest of Paris. It landed one passenger and collected three others, before heading back to its base in

Tangmere. The returning passengers were Claude de Baissac, his sister Lise and Jean Renaud-Dandicolle (known as 'Dandy'), who was the son of the Nicaraguan consul in Bordeaux and acted as a kind of secretary to de Baissac.

Landes was livid when he heard the news of de Baissac's departure in a signal from London, received on the day he left. In this, London instructed Landes to take charge of the Scientist network in his chief's absence, and informed him that he had been promoted to captain. Landes's anger stemmed not so much from de Baissac's unannounced flight as from the fact that he had chosen to take his sister and some minor player in the Bordeaux Resistance with him, and left poor Mary Herbert behind. 'This was a woman of 42 [sic] who was pregnant with his child, who he just dumped on us. He was afraid that, if he returned to London with her, they would know that he had made his own courier pregnant and this could have affected his career.'

Three months later, on 11 November 1943, Claude de Baissac received the DSO for his work in Bordeaux. He was amongst the first in SOE to receive this medal, Britain's second-highest decoration for valour in time of war, after the Victoria Cross.

13

THE TRAP CLOSES

Lucette's arrest, the imprisonment of most of his men and Claude de Baissac's departure for London marked the end of André Grandclément's dreams.

He is 'in a very unstable frame of mind', remarked Marcel Défence, who operated a radio for him in Paris during the weeks following Lucette's arrest. His Resistance friends also became increasingly worried about Grandclément's mood swings and unpredictability. He said to one: 'If I did anything strange in the future, do not be surprised. If I did anything against my country, what would you do?' The answer was swift, unequivocal – and visibly unsettling to Grandclément: 'Shoot you down without hesitation.'

Senior Resistance leaders lunching with him at a Paris restaurant in the first days of August found him racked with worry for the fate of his organisation in Bordeaux, and 'so obsessed by the sexual tortures that the Germans may be inflicting on his wife, that he was ready to do anything – including returning to Bordeaux to give himself up'.

Later in the month, however, Grandclément, ever hopeful about what was round the corner, seems to have briefly stabilised and begun to develop some sort of strategy for his future. He met with ex-members of the Vichy administration to see if they might be interested in incorporating his Bordeaux Maquis units into the anti-communist groupings which they were forming with the tacit support of the Germans. There is strong evidence that he also made overtures to senior members of the Vichy administration during this time. Some even suspect that he was trying to create a role for himself as an intermediary between those who supported de Gaulle and those who followed his arch-rival for control of the Free French, General Henri Giraud.

André Thinières, one of the Resistance leaders who met Grandclément in Paris at this time, recalls him in terms which, even allowing for hindsight, are excoriating:

> I was extremely suspicious of him, not just because I judged him susceptible to treason, but also because he seemed to me driven by ambition and a near desperate need for money. He appeared out of touch with reality and ready for anything … [he] systematically obstructed us getting in touch with his Resistance organisations in Bordeaux … he wanted to have command [of all Resistance units] between the Loire and the Pyrenees. He also insisted that he should have control of all the money coming from London and would pass on to us what he judged appropriate, after first reimbursing his own living expenses in Paris.

Speaking to another Paris contact, Grandclément's mood had swung again – this time to one of delusional *folie des grandeurs*. 'If there is no invasion this year, we will attack the Germans in the southwest directly – as Tito is doing in Yugoslavia.'

All hope of the early invasion for which Grandclément – and so many others across France – had taken such risks vanished on 9 September 1943, when Operation Cockade reached its conclusion with a mock invasion force setting out from Britain's southern ports, apparently heading for the beaches of Boulogne. The aim of the operation was twofold. To persuade the Germans to keep substantial forces in northern Europe, instead of deploying them to other fronts; and to draw the Luftwaffe into a major battle over the Channel where they could be destroyed.

It failed on both counts. Although some German commanders in France had convinced themselves an invasion was possible that September, the high command in Berlin had long concluded that Cockade was a deception. Between April and December 1943, they withdrew no less than twenty-seven divisions from France and sent them to

Italy, the Balkans and Russia. And on 9 September, when the Allies' fake invasion fleet set sail on their fake invasion, the Luftwaffe never budged from their airfields. Shortly afterwards the BBC announced that it had all been simply 'an invasion rehearsal'.

In the end those most deceived by this ill-considered deception plan were not the Germans, but the people of France in general and the Resistance in particular. French confidence in Britain plummeted, and those in the Resistance who had based all their actions on the prospects of an early invasion knew that they would have to face the consequences.

One of these was André Grandclément.

The image which emerges of Grandclément after Lucette's arrest, the departure of de Baissac and the end of the hopes of a 1943 invasion is of a desperate man who, having seen one future destroyed, frantically casts around to find another. Most of his actions seem motivated more by French politics than resisting foreign occupation. Whatever the truth, one thing is certain: Grandclément the chancer, the opportunist, the dreamer, had once again lost both his moorings and his sense of reality and was now seeking some new anchorage which would provide him with the kind of role and respect to which he believed himself entitled.

When de Baissac arrived back in London on 16 August 1943, he was closely debriefed and wrote several reports. The picture these give of the situation in Bordeaux is, once again, startlingly Panglossian. He congratulates himself on 'having obtained the confidence of everyone, who unquestionably regard him as their Chief – a great success'; he portrays Resistance morale in the southwest as being 'higher than it has ever been'; he claims his forces, numbering more than 20,000, are 'now in a position to prevent enemy interference' along the entire Aquitaine coast; he assures London that he controls 'all shades of Resistance in a very large area of France'. And he predicts that though Grandclément – 'a man of marked intelligence' – is 'in Paris lying low', he will shortly return 'to continue his work'.

De Baissac also brought back with him a report written by Grandclément. This too is swollen with self-congratulation and hyperbole, ending a list of 'achievements' with the ringing self-endorsement: 'All this has been achieved through exactly the kind of intelligent management and partnership [between himself and de Baissac] which ought to exist between all Allies on the field of battle.'

Nowhere in these reports is there any mention at all of the total dismemberment of the OCM, which, in a briefing note dated the day after his arrival, de Baissac describes disingenuously as 'among the most powerful' Resistance organisations in France. De Baissac also asserts that, had he not returned, increased Gestapo activity in Bordeaux would have resulted in him being 'lucky to survive another one or two months in the field'. He does not mention at all the equal, if not greater, risks now faced by those he had left behind, including Landes, Hayes and Herbert (whose pregnancy he also omits to mention).

As a result of de Baissac's reports, Baker Street decided to divide the vast area he had previously managed into three. In the last week of August 1943 they sent Landes new instructions ordering him to take charge of the area from Bordeaux to the Pyrenees; Vic Hayes was to be responsible for the Charente and Charente-Maritime departments to the east and north of Bordeaux. They also promised to send out further help in the form of Harry Peulevé, whose broken leg had healed sufficiently for him to get back over the Pyrenees on crutches the previous February. Peulevé's task would be to take over the Corrèze area, midway between Bordeaux and Clermont-Ferrand.

Hayes, however, rejected London's orders and insisted on staying in Bordeaux. He had fallen in love with Jean Duboué's nineteen-year-old daughter Suzanne, and flatly refused to leave her side. Though London objected, they had no option but to accept the situation.

Landes, on the other hand, was secretly delighted. He had been under immense pressure with the volume of work in Bordeaux and he needed all the help he could get if he was to keep pace with the weapons and explosives now flooding into his area (464 containers delivered in twenty-two sorties in the week ending 24 August alone – a larger number by far than to any other SOE circuit in France), to say nothing of the programme of sabotage which also continued at an unrelenting pace.

For Friedrich Dohse, too, these were busy weeks. KdS Bordeaux was now at full stretch interrogating the prisoners who filled the cellars of Bouscat and the city jails. Eventually all further arrests had to be suspended until the interrogations of those already arrested had been completed. The exception, of course, was André Grandclément, for news of whom Dohse waited daily and anxiously, but in vain. Dohse was also conscious that he had made no further progress in breaking the British network in Bordeaux: 'I was at an impasse,' he said later, 'and only a stroke of luck would get me out.'

As always with Dohse, luck duly arrived, this time in the form of a phone call from his mentor, Karl Bömelburg, on the afternoon of 18 September 1943.

The story the head of the Gestapo in France had to tell was a complex one, involving infiltration, a double agent and a carefully prepared ambush.

He explained that one of his star French double agents had managed to infiltrate a Paris Resistance group with connections to Bordeaux. After much careful cultivation, Bömelburg's man had persuaded Grandclément and Marc O'Neill to come to a meeting, which had taken place that very morning in Paris in the ornate gardens of the Palais-Royal. A further meeting had been fixed for the following day.

This was just the opportunity Dohse had been waiting for. Bömelburg advised him to get to Paris as fast as he could. Dohse spent the rest of the day trying to get hold of a plane to fly him to the French capital, but none was available. He rang Bömelburg that evening explaining his predicament and asking his old chief to take all necessary steps to arrest Grandclément at the meeting the following day.

Despite a premonition that he was walking into a trap, André Grandclément met Bömelburg's agent and another member of the Paris Maquis unit he had infiltrated, as agreed, at eleven on Sunday morning, 19 September, at the exit of the Étoile Métro station beneath the Arc de

Triomphe. It was a popular place for Resistance meetings, for the area was large and open, affording little cover for clandestine surveillance by Gestapo watchers. In warm sunshine, the three men shook hands and walked the short distance to the Restaurant Monte Carlo. Here they took a table on the terrace, which juts out onto the pavement of the Avenue Wagram and, like any three friends out on a pleasant afternoon, ordered some drinks.

The fine weather had brought Paris out in the closest imitation of pre-war style and joie de vivre that wartime exigencies would allow. The air was warm and the light crisp, though little drifts of fallen leaves presaging the arrival of autumn were already beginning to gather at the foot of trees and in the gutters. The clatter of passing traffic, diminished by pre-war levels, was still loud enough to cover the secret conversations of spies and lovers alike. The talk among the three men turned chiefly on the situation in the southwest and the urgent need for arms. After about half an hour, Bömelburg's agent pulled out a packet of cigarettes and offered them to his companions. It was the signal. Before the first cigarette could be lit, the table was surrounded by six men armed with revolvers. Grandclément and his young Maquis friend were bundled into a car and taken to the Gestapo interrogation centre at Rue des Saussaies.

In some things Grandclément may have been a naïve dreamer. But he was not without courage or poise in moments of crisis – as he had shown as a decorated soldier in the battle of France. This was the moment he half-dreaded, half-hoped for, as a man with a death wish waits for the event which will at last settle all uncertainties. Grandclément remained defiant, calm and self-possessed in the back of the Gestapo car. When accused by his captor, Hermann Gentzel, of being 'Bernard', he coolly replied: 'Yes. I am Bernard. But that's all you'll learn from me.' Frustrated, Gentzel turned to the second captured man: 'Then you must be the chief of the Resistance in the South West?' Grandclément jumped in to save his shocked companion, chiding the German for spending two months searching for the wrong man and informing him that the 'Chief of the Resistance in the South West' was not 'Bernard' as the Germans thought, but – inventing a name out of thin air – 'Marcel'.

None of this impudence improved the reception accorded to the Resistance men at the Rue des Saussaies. After some rough handling, Grandclément and his partner were thrown into separate cells. The next day, as he was led out from his first interrogation, already significantly bloodied, Grandclément bumped into his fellow prisoner and managed to pass him a whispered instruction to maintain the fiction about 'Marcel', which the young man duly did, despite considerable violence by the Gestapo.

In Bordeaux, a frustrated Dohse waited nervously for the results of the Paris interrogations. When, after three days, they had yielded nothing, he asked Bömelburg to have his quarry sent south to him in Bordeaux.

14

THE DEAL

Handcuffed and escorted by four Gestapo men, Grandclément arrived at Bordeaux station on the evening of 21 September 1943. He looked haggard and thin, having eaten only 'two meagre meals' since his arrest.

Dohse, dapper in civilian clothes, greeted his prisoner on the platform and led him to the Gestapo car, which took them to Bouscat. Normally a new prisoner would have been interrogated at length by Kunesch, and then passed to Dohse. But Dohse had obtained a special dispensation from Bömelburg, allowing him to take personal charge of the Grandclément case. The interview by Kunesch and his French interpreter, Pierre Esch, was therefore a brief formality. At around two in the morning, Dohse called in to see his new charge in his cell. To Grandclément's surprise, instead of continuing the questioning, Dohse told him to get some sleep: 'Tomorrow, we will see if we can get to the bottom of this matter.'

It is clear from what happened over the next few days that Dohse had given a great deal of thought as to how he was going to handle André Grandclément. The technique of the interrogator is to confuse and unbalance in order to keep his subject disoriented until he has what he wants. Some, like Kunesch, use fear and pain as the means of gaining control. Many use sleep deprivation. Dohse used psychological understanding and a close knowledge of his subjects' desires, fears and weaknesses to get inside their carapace of protection. First he would disarm, then charm and finally, when he had extracted all he needed, he would salve his victims' consciences by convincing them that they had done the right thing.

'One did not see the Gestapo officer,' said one of Dohse's interrogation subjects, 'he was not at all a brute.' Another commentator, in a passage that might have been applied specifically to Grandclément, said that being questioned by Dohse was less like an interrogation and 'more like a conversation with someone whose good company one might enjoy in more peaceful times – he didn't ask you to betray, he never demanded names or posed too brutal a question. He mostly just discussed your political views and hopes. If you truly, in your heart, hated the communists above all others, then he would scare the living daylights out of you with descriptions of the scale of their ambitions and terrify you with a picture of what France would be like if it was taken over by the Bolsheviks.'

The morning after Grandclément's arrival in Bouscat, a deep depression passed over the city, bringing with it low cloud, wind and squalls of heavy rain. Dohse personally collected his prisoner from the cells, escorted him to his office, installed him in a comfortable chair by the hearth, and, as the rain beat steadily against the windows, opened a long, friendly fireside discussion on politics – chatting as two new acquaintances might, having just met at their gentlemen's club. Dohse was later to claim that this was all in keeping with his 'human approach' to his job. It was of course nothing of the sort. It was just Dohse the hunter assessing the psychology of his prey and seeking out his weak points.

To Grandclément, hungry for recognition, Dohse's manner must have been beguiling in the extreme. Here was a German – not any German, the most important German in Bordeaux – who took him seriously and wanted to hear his views. Here was a man he enjoyed talking to. True, he was a Nazi and right-wing. But not really more right-wing than those in the Vichy regime and others on the French far right whom he had grown up with and whom he had recently met in Paris.

What Dohse discovered during these first sessions would prove vital to his strategy for using Grandclément to divide, destabilise and ultimately destroy the entire Resistance network in his area. There were many things that he and Grandclément had in common. They were both strongly anti-communist. They both believed in order and hierarchy.

And they both saw the greatest threat to Europe as coming from Bolshevism and Russia. There was solid common ground here for Dohse to build on.

Dohse, the master reader of characters, also spotted weaknesses and contradictions he could exploit. Though Grandclément was, at first sight, imposing – impressive, even – beneath the surface he was vain and needy. In many things he was a decent, if simple man, who loved Lucette and his two daughters, and was genuinely patriotic. But he was also weak, easily influenced: an 'ideological gigolo' who was prone to holding contradictory opinions when this was necessary to make sense of the situations in which he found himself. He supported Pétain's right-wing politics – but was opposed to Pétain's Vichy administration, who he regarded as a bunch of collaborators. He hated the German occupation – but he hated the French communists more. He was committed to liberation – but not if it handed France over to the Bolsheviks. Most surprising of all, given that Grandclément as head of the OCM was a self-declared Gaullist, he now described de Gaulle, to a startled Dohse, as 'a cunt' (even years later Dohse was very precise about the term used).

Dohse also discovered two other psychological keys to his interlocutor. To his surprise, he found Grandclément deeply concerned about the fate of 'his men'. This, Dohse mused, he could really work with, since the fate of more than 250 of Grandclément's resistants, and their families, now lay entirely in the German's hands.

But the master key to André Grandclément's personality – and the subject he returned to most frequently throughout his interrogation – was his beloved Lucette. Grandclément knew she had been arrested and that she was languishing in a cell in the Fort du Hâ. And he knew who had the key to open that cell door: Dohse did.

'Don't worry,' Dohse reassured him. 'It'll be fine. But first we have to make sure that we *understand* each other.'

The preliminaries over, Dohse attempted to break his prisoner's resistance by the old trick of persuading him that withholding information was pointless, since he knew everything already. He showed Grandclément the wireless traffic between Gilbert Norman and London;

he showed him the messages found in Pierre Culioli's briefcase, which were destined for members of the British network in Bordeaux; he gave his prisoner the names and aliases of Landes, Hayes, de Baissac and others in the Scientist network. And he showed him the Luftwaffe maps which identified the positions (albeit approximate) of all the main parachute drop sites, adding that, since he also knew the rough areas where the arms had been hidden, it would be only a matter of time before he identified these locations, too.

None of these revelations had the slightest effect. Grandclément remained voluble in general conversation, especially where it touched on politics; but silent when it came to giving specific information.

They talked all through that first day and deep into the following night. Slowly, charm and fatigue began to weaken the Frenchman's defences.

The crucial moment came in the very early hours of the second day when Dohse, taking a considerable risk, showed Grandclément a list of the names of his men who were in prison. Then he added to these a second list of 150 names and addresses of those under Grandclément's command, who were shortly to be arrested. Then he explained how he, Grandclément, could save them all. If he would cooperate by revealing some sites where the parachuted arms were hidden, Dohse, for his part, would try to persuade his superiors to stop further arrests and even perhaps do something to help free certain individuals already in prison.

Grandclément hesitated. Dohse, sensing a breakthrough, said: 'Go and get some sleep, think about it and we can talk again in the morning. Perhaps I can arrange for you to see Lucette then too.' Then a master stroke. Instead of returning Grandclément to his cell, he arranged to have the KdS duty drivers turned out of their attic rest room on the top floor of the château and had a bed installed there so that his prisoner could have good night's sleep in a temptingly comfortable, proper bed.

At a meeting the following morning, Dohse reported back on what had happened overnight to his boss Luther, Kunesch and a new man, 'Commandant John', who had recently been brought in to oversee

Dohse's department. They listened and expressed reservations – but in the end, agreed that he should continue.

Dohse, who had had almost no sleep for the last twenty-four hours, now took another risk. Around mid-morning he ordered Lucette to be brought to Bouscat. 'I told her that she would shortly meet her husband and, after giving her time to wash and prepare herself, took her to my office and asked her to wait.' Without any warning, Dohse led Grandclément into the room to find his beloved Lucette, safe and beautiful, waiting for him. 'There I found myself witness to a most touching and emotional scene when they were reunited ... I was so moved at the sight of the two of them that I indulged myself and told them that, apart from the periods when they were being questioned, I had decided that they should not be parted again,' Dohse recalled, once more cloaking cunning in righteousness. This was, in fact, nothing more than a perfectly targeted, carefully stage-managed and most subtle bribe.

Grandclément's insubstantial will was finally broken by his interrogator's kindnesses. Now for the coup de grâce. A question – simple, short and quick as a dart.

Had Grandclément thought about last night's proposition? Did they have a deal? Grandclément nodded.

Dohse knew better than to press the point. The deal was done. He gave orders for a second bed to be moved into the attic bedroom, which he also furnished with a writing table, a mirror, a radio capable of receiving the BBC, a well-stocked drinks cabinet and a constant supply of fresh flowers. 'Then I wished the couple all happiness and went off to a meeting with my superiors.'

Dohse was now far outside his terms of reference as a relatively junior officer. At the meeting with his superiors there was strong opposition to the way things were developing, especially from Kunesch, who did not relish the idea of freeing prisoners he was busily (and brutally) interrogating. But it was reluctantly decided that Dohse should be allowed to firm up the 'deal' with Grandclément and then, when a detailed plan had been assembled, there would be a second meeting, after which, if all went well, it might be necessary to put the plan to Paris for approval.

Later that day, when negotiations between the two men restarted, Grandclément redefined his position. He would not give Dohse any names and addresses. Nor would he betray any person. But if it helped save his men, he would show Dohse where some of the arms were hidden. He explained, however, that only his subordinates knew the exact locations of the weapons dumps. And anyway, he would not feel able to make a deal on the lines agreed with Dohse without first putting the matter to his two key lieutenants, André Maleyran and Roland Chazeau. To do this, Grandclément continued, he would need Dohse to give him a period of complete freedom on the basis of his word of honour that he would return; and Dohse's word of honour that he would not be followed. It was a startling suggestion. But Dohse did not reject it out of hand – after all, he knew that Grandclément would not go far without Lucette. She was the leash by which he could always pull his quarry back. As long as she was under his lock and key in Bordeaux, his prisoner would always be prepared to return to the prison.

Dohse now turned this verbal understanding between the two of them into a formal written agreement. The first clause stipulated that Grandclément would give Dohse the locations of all the arms depots 'under his control' (Dohse did not reveal that he had a checklist showing the total tonnage of all the arms in question, which had been found during one of the Cours de Verdun raids). Grandclément would also produce a full written statement of his activities in the Resistance, including his contact with the British in the region. In return, Dohse would begin the process of liberating all Grandclément's men currently held in detention in Bordeaux. This would not, Dohse insisted, include any prisoner who belonged to other Resistance groups; they would be outside the deal. To assist this process, Dohse would provide Grandclément with a complete list of all those in Gestapo hands and permit the Frenchman to nominate his own representative to oversee the process of release. The liberation of Grandclément's men would proceed on a stage-by-stage basis in line with the delivery of arms. He additionally undertook to take no further action against any resistant under Grandclément's command who had participated in receiving parachuted arms, or in hiding them afterwards. Finally, Grandclément would be allowed the period of free-dom he had requested, on the terms that he had asked for.

Even given the fact that Dohse still held the trump card, Lucette, this was still an astonishingly generous and risky agreement on his part. But the opportunity, he judged, was exceptional and it required exceptional means to get Grandclément finally over the Rubicon. After all, it was Grandclément who was the rider, while he, Dohse, was the tiger. In sum, Dohse understood what Grandclément did not. That true deals can only be made between parties who have equal freedom of manoeuvre. The relationship between prisoner and captor is so unequal that anything that looks or sounds like a deal is in reality just a prelude to betrayal, which, over time, becomes an excuse for it afterwards. Once Grandclément had crossed this line, he would have no other course but one which would take him further and deeper into his relationship with his Gestapo controller.

That evening André Grandclément sat down at the writing table in his attic bedroom and wrote out the statement of his Resistance activities which he had promised Dohse. He described in detail the full history of his involvement with the OCM, providing the strengths of all the Resistance units under his control. He also outlined his relationship with de Baissac and the Scientist network. The opening words of Grandclément's 'confession' give an interesting picture of the overlapping ambivalences with which he was wrestling at this moment:

The actions of the Resistance which we have been discussing were entirely initiated by me without any foreign influence. I am neither a Germanophobe, nor an Anglophile. I am a French patriot and that is all I need to be in order to understand the suffering of my country since it has been occupied by the Germans.

After the Armistice in 1940, I hoped that France and Germany would have been able to cooperate. But I now no longer believe this in view of what has occurred since, on the political front.

I am anti-Bolshevik and would [in 1940] have volunteered to coop-erate in a joint Franco/German fight against this menace, but it did not seem to me possible to cooperate later with an Army which was at the time occupying my country …

Dohse's next problem was not with Grandclément, but with the KdS command. He was under no illusion how difficult it would be to get their agreement to implementing the 'deal'.

The meeting which followed with his senior colleagues was a predictably stormy one. Luther understood the potential of the deal and listened attentively. But Kunesch was violently opposed, insisting that if there were to be any release of prisoners they should be confined to junior members of Grandclément's organisation only. 'Commandant John' went even further, threatening to place Dohse under arrest if he released Grandclément; it was obvious, he insisted, that the Frenchman had fooled him and would immediately escape. Dohse responded by insisting that Grandclément would return – not least because Dohse – lying – said he had made it plain that Lucette would be executed if he did not. Dohse, who was the most junior person in the room, was on the back foot. He would have liked to ring Bömelburg for support, but did not dare for fear he too would disapprove.

Eventually Luther closed the meeting by saying that the proposal was beyond his level of authority; he would have to take it to headquarters.

That afternoon Luther took the train to Paris for a late evening meeting with Helmut Knochen, who, as his superior, reported through the most senior German security official in France to Himmler's headquarters in Berlin. It took some persuasion but finally Knochen agreed that Dohse could continue, but cautiously. He made it abundantly clear, however, that if the slightest thing went wrong, it would be Dohse individually and personally who would pay the price.

Later that evening, Dohse went up to the attic and knocked on the bedroom door. The deal was on. André Grandclément could have his period of freedom. A bicycle would be waiting for him in the courtyard in the morning.

ARMS AND ALARMS

At a little after seven the following morning, 24 September, there was a knock on the door of the Corbins' tiny, single-storey terraced house in Rue Robert d'Ennery, in the Bordeaux suburb of Caudéran.

Opening it, Charles Corbin was taken aback to discover a thin, dishevelled and unshaven André Grandclément on his doorstep. Corbin motioned him in and wheeled his bicycle through the house into the back garden, away from the prying eyes of neighbours.

'You go into the bathroom and clean up. I'll make us some coffee,' Corbin said.

Just then Marcel Défence walked in. He had spent the night at the house, having arrived from Paris the previous evening to report Grandclément's disappearance. He was surprised, to say the least, to see the missing man standing before him in the Corbins' front room.

While Grandclément went to wash and shave, Corbin slipped out of the house and bicycled furiously to 29 Rue Guynemer where he alerted Roger Landes. Landes, in bed when Corbin arrived, dressed quickly, slipped his Colt automatic into his pocket and wrote out a note for Vic Hayes: 'Come immediately to Rue Guynemer. Speak to no one. Wait for my return.'

At the Corbin house, Landes burst into the bathroom and confronted Grandclément, demanding an explanation. The Frenchman, shaken by Landes's sudden appearance, briefly described his arrest in Paris and subsequent interrogation, adding that after some 'insignificant revelations' he had been allowed a short period of liberty to visit a friend.

'Do they know who you're visiting?'

'No. I just said a friend who had nothing to do with the Resistance.'

'Were you followed?'

'No. I left Bouscat in the dark and came by a roundabout way. I am sure I wasn't followed. Now please let me finish in here and we can talk in a minute.'

Landes went into the kitchen where the Corbin family were now gathered: Charles Corbin looked sombre; his wife Albertine fussed around the kitchen to hide her concern; Ginette, who had just woken up, stood tousle-haired and bleary-eyed alongside Marcel Défence, who looked bewildered and out of place. There was a hurried 'council of war'. Landes led off. He was furious and, in truth – though he tried not to show it – a bit taken aback by the turn of events. Grandclément's story just didn't add up; he must have betrayed them; he had gone over to the Germans. Landes had always distrusted him; he would have to be killed, Landes concluded, pulling the Colt out of his pocket and clicking off the safety catch.

Corbin gave him a warning look and shook his head; the message was unspoken, but unmistakeable – not here, in front of his family. And not when the Gestapo were almost certainly nearby and would hear the shot.

Landes hesitated for a moment before deciding that Corbin was right. He slid the safety catch back and returned the gun to his pocket, comforting himself with the thought that he would have better opportunities later. 'It was a decision I would be sorry for all my life,' he would write. 'If I had killed him then and there, it would have saved so much damage later.'

A few moments afterwards, a clean-shaven Grandclément, unaware that he had just escaped death by a whisker, came back into the kitchen. He had recovered his composure and was breezy and bombastic, justifying himself by saying that he had only come that morning to warn Landes and the others that the Germans were on to them. He repeated his claim that he had given only limited information to Dohse – and then only because of excessive physical duress. But it soon became clear to all that Dohse now knew almost everything about Scientist – including the local identities of de Baissac and his sister Lise, Vic Hayes, Roger Landes,

Marcel Défence and Mary Herbert, the address of Scientist's 'headquarters' at the Bertrands' café on the Quai des Chartrons and another address at which Landes kept a radio and a stash of arms, 43 Cours Portal. The climax came when Grandclément explained that he had agreed to hand over 'ten per cent' of Scientist's hidden arms in order, as he put it, to 'satisfy the Germans'.

Landes exploded: 'As a British officer I cannot allow you to deliver a single weapon to the Germans; if you did not know what to do [under the pressure of interrogation] then you should have committed suicide.' Even if this deal was acceptable to some French, Landes continued, it could only be regarded by the British as an act of 'treason'.

Grandclément replied that he did not take orders from Landes. If Landes did not have the confidence in him that de Baissac had, he would break off relations with 'the English' and go his own way.

With the meeting now effectively over, Grandclément turned to Corbin and asked him to find a car so that he could visit 'his men' out of the city. Corbin, seeming to acquiesce, left the room. He had realised, as had Landes, that they were now in a deadly race with Grandclément and his Gestapo handler. It was imperative that Landes got to Grandclément's Maquis first, to warn them of their commander's treachery. Corbin spent some time phoning around to find a vehicle, but for Landes, not Grandclément. In wartime Bordeaux, however, readily available cars were an extremely rare commodity. Corbin eventually returned to report that no one had a car to offer at such short notice.

Leaving, Grandclément turned to Défence and asked him to send two messages. The first was to de Baissac in London: 'In this very grave situation, I have had to lay down my responsibilities in order to limit wider damage. Do not lose confidence in me.' The second was to his old school friend in Paris, Marc O'Neill: 'I am doing my best in difficult circumstances – have confidence in me – keep open a means by which I can contact you in the next 24 hours.'

Then he collected his bicycle and rode off, leaving behind some clothes, which he said he would collect later.

Now Landes had to move fast.

He asked Corbin to pretend to side with Grandclément and Dohse, so that he could monitor and report back on the pair's activities. Corbin agreed without hesitation – though he knew that acting as Landes's 'double agent' with a man like Dohse would put him and his family in very grave danger. Perhaps Corbin believed that the strong anti-communist views he had expressed in the past and his connections with the right-wing Croix-de-Feu gave him 'cover' with Dohse and the German authorities.

Returning to Rue Guynemer, Landes met Vic Hayes and sent him, in haste, first to the café on the Quai des Chartrons to alert the Bertrands, and then to warn as many others as possible to go to ground until further orders. Afterwards Landes sent an emergency message to London reporting on what had happened and, picking up one of his key agents (a man called Nicolle) on the back of his motorbike, rode at full speed to warn his man at 43 Cours Portal. On arrival, Landes immediately spotted that the street was under surveillance by Poinsot's men, so he and Nicolle retreated to a café to watch the watchers. Eventually Poinsot's men got bored and left. Landes hurriedly collected his radio, while Nicolle and the owner of the safe house threw the cache of arms into a trailer hitched to a borrowed car and drove the hoard to another house in the city.

In the early afternoon Landes met again with Hayes, who reported that it had been impossible to reach any of their key contacts, except the Bertrands, who had decided to stay put rather than flee because they believed their cover was good enough.

As luck would have it, Landes had previously agreed to meet his old Wanborough Manor colleague, Harry Peulevé, off the train from Paris at six that evening. Peulevé, who was on his way to take up his new role as head of the Corrèze region, had planned to spend a couple of days with Landes in Bordeaux to get the feel of the area. Given that the Gare Saint-Jean was a very public place and would be full of Germans, meeting Peulevé was incredibly risky. But Landes could not let his colleague down.

Using the techniques he had learnt under SOE training, Landes now proceeded to completely alter his appearance. In the privacy of Rue Guynemer, and probably with Marguerite Faget's help, he changed his hairstyle, cutting it much shorter and dying it; he thinned his heavy eyebrows, borrowed a pair of glasses, adopted a new style of dress, adjusted his gait and – lastly – repainted his bicycle. By the time he had finished, even close friends could not recognise him.

Landes met Peulevé off the Paris train, as agreed, and whisked him back to Rue Guynemer. Here Peulevé lay low for the next few days, before travelling east to begin his mission in the Corrèze.

That night a Resistance council of war was held at the city centre offices of a local estate agent. Those present included Jean Duboué, Léo Paillère and his son Danny, Vic Hayes, Roger Landes and Grandclément's replacement as Resistance chief for the area, Eugène Camplan. After a brief discussion they unanimously agreed that André Grandclément must be killed without delay and by whatever means possible. Steps were also to be taken to warn his chief lieutenants, Maleyran and Chazeau, that they should reject Grandclément if he tried to persuade them to accept the deal with Dohse.

But it was too late. Grandclément kept his promise, arriving back in Bouscat within the appointed time. He briefed Dohse on his meeting at the Corbins', telling him that Landes had refused to cooperate. Dohse, also realising that he was now in a race with Landes, lent Grandclément a Gestapo car to take him that afternoon to Arcachon. There, via a local Resistance chief, Grandclément set up a meeting with Maleyran and Chazeau, who had fled Bordeaux after Lucette's arrest and taken refuge with one of the local Maquis units.

The following day Grandclément, again driven in a Gestapo car and with a Gestapo driver, met with his two lieutenants. He told them that delivering a number of arms caches to the Germans was the best way to avoid the complete destruction of their organisation and the imprisonment – if not worse – of all the men for whom they were responsible. Maleyran and Chazeau agreed, and promised to take Dohse to a hidden arms dump at Pissos, east of Arcachon.

The next afternoon, Sunday 26 September, Dohse's men, dressed as Maquisards, complete with berets and carrying British Sten guns, gathered on the forecourt of Gestapo headquarters. Dohse, never shy of drama, relished the fact that his Bouscat colleagues turned out to see the incongruous spectacle. After a short briefing, and with Grandclément and Kunesch in the back of his car and the rest of his men in a covered lorry, Dohse led his small convoy with appropriate flourish out of the gates of Bouscat and off for their rendezvous: 'For the first time, I was going to meet the Maquis on their own ground. I confess I felt somewhat nervous,' Dohse later wrote, embellishing the moment. 'Could I really trust Grandclément? The way that my Commander [Luther] and my colleagues came out to say their goodbyes seemed to suggest that they were not at all sure they would see me again … [Luther] had taken the precaution of asking one of the local Infantry Divisions to strengthen patrols in the area, telling them to be ready for anything. It was probably the least he could do – though I was not at all sure that it would be enough to prevent an attack on me personally.'

Despite the matter-of-fact, almost light-hearted tone of his account, Dohse was embarking on a dangerous and foolhardy operation, which would have been regarded by many of his Bouscat colleagues as a wild escapade brought about by his overly trusting attitude towards the French. It would not, some no doubt thought – even hoped – end well.

They were right to have their concerns. Roger Landes, too, had plans for that afternoon. 'From the moment we learned, through Corbin, of Grandclément's plan to deliver arms [to the Germans] we decided to ambush them and kill both Grandclément and Dohse. But in the end we were unable to carry the plan out because we couldn't find a car to take us to Pissos.'

Dohse's first stop that afternoon was the Boulevard du Président Wilson in Bordeaux where, in the middle of a torrential downpour, an anonymous young Maquisard who was to be their guide jumped into the front seat of the Gestapo chief's car, which then led the small convoy to the little country town of Liposthey, sixty kilometres southwest of Bordeaux. On the journey Grandclément chatted away while Dohse offered round a packet of Gauloises cigarettes, which their young Maquis guide refused. By the time they reached Liposthey the weather had cleared into a bright autumn day, scudded with clouds. They turned into a narrow earth track closely bordered by forest and thick undergrowth – an excellent place for an ambush.

Finally they came to a stop in the middle of a large clearing, where they all got down from their vehicles. Dohse ordered his men to stay behind with the lorry and, with Grandclément and Kunesch, his finger poised on the trigger of his Sten, followed the young Maquisard guide on foot down a forestry track and into the trees, which now seemed to cluster ever more closely around them. They could see the tyre marks of a heavy vehicle on the woodland path, still puddled after the morning's rain. A couple of hundred metres or so into the forest, the guide suddenly stopped and gave two low whistles.

A moment or so later, there was a movement in the trees. 'Two armed men appeared and made their way towards us,' Dohse later wrote. 'Instinctively, I flicked up the flap on my holster and put my hand on my 7.65 automatic.' Grandclément introduced the men as his lieutenants, Maleyran and Chazeau. 'We shook hands and I ... gave my word that they would be safe. They confirmed on their word of honour that they were acting on the orders and under the authority of Grandclément.'

The formal introductions over, Maleyran and Chazeau led the little party deeper into the woods to a spot where forty containers of arms waited for them, stacked up on the forest floor. Dohse called up the lorry and instructed his men to load up the spoils. They included dozens of weapons, substantial supplies of ammunition and around 400 kilos of explosives.

The booty safely loaded, Dohse drew Maleyran and Chazeau to one side and told them that their families, who were under arrest, could be released soon – provided they undertook to continue handing over arms. The two men nodded their agreement and there was a short discussion about where they would go next. A rendezvous was fixed for the following day at a restaurant at Captieux, southeast of Bordeaux. There, over lunch, they would agree a programme of future arms delivery.

His job done, Dohse bundled Grandclément back into his car, and led the convoy, laden with five tons of British arms, triumphantly back to Bouscat.

That evening Ginette Corbin met Landes in a backstreet café and told him that Grandclément was planning to return to the Corbin house the following day to collect his clothes. What should she say? Landes instructed her to tell the traitor that he had fled to Britain through Spain, adding that she should pass an urgent message to her father to get her and her mother out of Bordeaux as quickly as possible.

The birds of prey were circling. It was time to scatter.

16

PROGRESS AND PRECAUTIONS

On Monday 27 September, the morning of his lunch with the Maquisard lieutenants in Captieux, Dohse pulled another of his 'little tricks'.

The previous afternoon at Liposthey he had confirmed to the twenty-one-year-old Roland Chazeau that he would be releasing his mother and father, as a consequence of the successful recovery of arms, but not his fiancée, Suzanne. She was under arrest for a more serious offence.

It was a lie. Dohse had, in fact, nothing on the young woman. But he did have plans for her.

Before leaving for the lunch meeting, Dohse had Suzanne brought from her cell to his office and, using the same play as with Lucette Grandclément, informed her that she would shortly be reunited with her fiancé and should use his bathroom to make herself presentable.

Settled down at table at the restaurant in Captieux with Grandclément and his lieutenants, Dohse, with a flourish worthy of a Hollywood film director, ordered that the now 'fresh and beautiful' (Dohse's words) Suzanne should be brought in as 'a kind of hors d'oeuvres … [which] I had planned the night before, believing it would have a powerful psychological effect – and I wasn't wrong. By this little trick – which cost me nothing – I won the absolute confidence and sympathy of Chazeau and his fiancée.'

It was an 'absolute confidence' which would, before long, be paid for at a far higher price than a little make-up and a lunchtime surprise.

Over a pleasant meal the four men, with Suzanne looking on, planned their next steps. They would begin with the retrieval of arms buried among the vines of Château La Brède – the great medieval fortress where

Montesquieu had invented and perfected the art of the essay. The conspirators also agreed that, from now on, no German uniforms or lorries would be seen when recovering arms: all vehicles would be ordinary civilian ones and all Dohse's men would be dressed as Maquisards and carry only captured British weapons. This would excite less interest in the locality and enable the three French collaborators to explain, if asked, that the Resistance was moving weapons from one location to another for operational reasons.

The following day, accompanied by a team of men and a small fleet of unmarked lorries, the quartet descended on a farm near Château La Brède, where they recovered around 250 containers buried in several shallow holes among the vines. 'The day passed calmly without any disturbances,' Dohse wrote. One suspects the poor *vignerons* of La Brède were less sanguine at this sudden descent of soldiers and lorries with picks and shovels on their precious vines. The *vendanges* (harvest) for the best-quality Bordeaux had started just nine days previously.

That evening the first ten prisoners, including the parents of Roland Chazeau and André Maleyran, were released.

By now Friedrich Dohse was back as the undisputed ringmaster of all that happened in KdS Bouscat, orchestrating almost every major event which contributed to the chaos and collapse of the Resistance across the Bordeaux region. Recruiting Grandclément as his agent had been Bouscat's greatest counter-espionage coup in a summer of mixed results. Dohse was in his element and enjoying himself.

Towards the beginning of August, a schoolmaster and parachute reception committee chief from the seaside resort of Soulac-sur-Mer gave the names of his reception team to Rudolf Kunesch, along with the location of their drop site near the Médoc village of Queyrac, fifty kilometres north of Bordeaux, and the BBC codeword which would signal that a drop was imminent.

On 18 September (the day before Grandclément's arrest in Paris), Dohse was listening to the BBC 19.30 broadcast on the radio in his bedroom when he heard what he had been waiting for: '*Nous avons bon vent ce soir*' ('We have good wind tonight') – the signal for a parachute drop on the Queyrac site. Alerting his men, he waited expectantly for the final confirmation of the drop, which would be indicated by the repetition of the same code-phrase on the 21.30 broadcast. Two hours later, sure enough, there it was again:

> No doubt was possible … We left for the drop site at Queyrac. Arriving at the spot I posted my men at the four corners of the drop zone and waited. The summer night was clear and we were totally silent. After about an hour, we heard the noise of the approaching aircraft. We lit the lamps which we had laid out in the shape of an L … and, using a red torch, signalled the first letter of the second word of the BBC code-phrase – that is, the letter 'A' in Morse. The noise of the aircraft grew louder and louder. And then suddenly we could see it in the moonlight flying towards us … It flew over us at a height of 80 to 100 metres – and then flew on to the west without dropping anything! We were so disappointed. Then we thought, perhaps it would be back. But nothing. We waited an hour. Still nothing. We returned, crestfallen, to Bordeaux.

If Dohse had been at RAF Tempsford at 02.24 the following morning, the pilot of the Halifax he had seen, Flight Sergeant Lime of the Royal Australian Air Force, could have explained his disappointment. And it would have made him even more 'crestfallen'.

Flight Sergeant Lime had an agent and fifteen containers to drop into Dohse's arms that night. He'd taken off from Tempsford at 20.33 German time and arrived at a height of 600 feet over Queyrac at 23.40. The weather was good and the flashing of Dohse's torch, distinct. But, as Lime makes clear in his post-operational report, it was 'not flashing the correct letter'. In one crucial element, Dohse's intelligence had been wrong. The recognition signal, which had to be flashed from drop sites to show all was well, was changed for each drop and was not fixed as a given letter in the BBC code-phrase sequence, as Dohse had believed. Lime knew his orders. He dropped only on the right letter. He turned for home, no doubt somewhat disappointed himself –

though, had he known the truth, he would have realised he had far less reason to be.

Autumn came early in 1943, bringing a prolonged spell of cold weather, which began soon after the *vendanges* was gathered in and extended well into November. It presaged, some country folk said, another hard winter. By mid-October the vineyards of the Médoc and Charentes had already begun to turn russet and gold, and by the end of the month the first light hoar frosts lay white on unsheltered fields.

During these weeks, Dohse and Grandclément were out almost every day, emptying arms dumps across the region.

On one of these chilly autumn days, Roger Landes bumped into them – almost literally – on his way back to Rue Guynemer in Bordeaux. He was wheeling his newly liveried bicycle across a junction when a large black car stopped to let him cross. Turning instinctively to see who it was, Landes recognised with horror the number plate – DJ342951 – Dohse's Cadillac! Suddenly he found himself staring straight into the eyes of André Grandclément, who was sitting alongside the driver. The Frenchman stared back blankly, without even a flicker of recognition. Once again Landes's talent for becoming invisible when it mattered, assisted by a little disguise, saved him.

Others, too, were trying to keep their heads low.

Jean Duboué's Café des Marchands on the Bordeaux waterfront had been hit by an Allied bomb in 1940. (It was the only house on the quay which had been damaged in the raid, causing his friends to joke that this was his reward for helping 'the English!') Then, in mid-1942, the restaurant was taken over by the Germans. After Grandclément's arrest, Duboué decided not to tempt fate further and moved everything – including furniture, pictures, linen, crockery and his stock of wines, barrels of Cognac, bottles of aperitifs, boxes of cigars and tins and jars of conserves – to the Villa Roucoule, in Lestiac-sur-Garonne. Here the family took up permanent residence and tried to live as quietly as they could. Duboué cultivated a little garden for vegetables and even planted some vines. Vic Hayes, too, shifted his weekend base to Lestiac so that he could be closer to Suzanne. Landes decided he was safer remaining in the bustle of Bordeaux, even though he knew by now from Corbin that the Gestapo detection vans had picked up his signals and, recognising his Morse 'hand', knew he was still in the area. Every night he slept in a different place, often relying on the sympathy of the girls in the local brothels to provide him with a bed.

Marcel Défence, meanwhile, decided that it was time to leave for London. With Landes's agreement, he started to make plans to cross the Pyrenees into Spain.

Landes had an additional concern in these highly charged weeks: Mary Herbert, who was now into her seventh month of pregnancy. In late September, Vic Hayes warned her that 'there was trouble brewing' and advised her to go to ground. Landes arranged for her to travel north to Poitiers, where she spent the last weeks of her confinement with friends, celebrating her fortieth birthday on 1 October.

Meanwhile, Dohse too was having a 'handling' problem – with Lucette Grandclément. Knowing her influence on her weaker husband, Dohse spoke to Lucette almost every day. He soon discovered that, though she was keen to see the Maquisards freed from jail, she was vociferously opposed to relinquishing arms to the Germans in exchange, telling her husband that the weapons were not his to give away; only London or Paris could authorise it.

Dohse, fearing that her opposition would upset his delicately balanced apple cart, decided that, despite his promise to keep them together, he now needed to find a way to prise them apart. After some persuasion he finally convinced the couple that 'for operational reasons' Lucette should leave the city for a while, and move in with her mother, Mme Chastel, at Pompignac, ten kilometres to the east of Bordeaux.

In most other ways, things were going extraordinarily smoothly for Dohse. By the end of the first week of October he had emptied seven major caches, delivering up the astonishing total of 945 containers packed with 45,000 kilos of painstakingly parachuted British arms, including 2,000 Sten sub-machine guns, numerous pistols, rifles and light machine guns, millions of rounds of assorted ammunition, several radio sets and a mass of explosive and other sabotage material. The windfall was doubly pleasing, for not only did it deny British arms to the Resistance, it also provided a source of useful weapons for German troops, not least on the Russian front. One senior German officer welcomed the cornucopia, which included:

> Stens by the thousands, a marvellously efficient sturdy little gun that delighted its German users beyond description. It was the best machine gun they had ever seen – so primitive, so unpolished, welded in parts. What German workman would do something like that? Yet this ugly little thing would fire and fire while highly polished and refined German guns were jamming after very little firing. Ah! And the plastic explosive! This too, they had never seen ... and welcome indeed it was with the German Army running short of explosives. It was much favoured on the Eastern front where, mixed with some tarry substance, it was converted into a very effective anti-tank weapon.

Meanwhile, as the weapons flowed into the Germans' stocks, more and more prisoners flowed out of their jails, each personally selected by Grandclément. This boosted Grandclément's prestige and sense of self-importance, causing his friends to note a sudden change in his appearance. As if to underline his new gravitas, Grandclément began to wear spectacles and sport a neatly trimmed moustache.

The operation to hand over arms to Dohse went on until the end of October, when Grandclément, Maleyran and Chazeau told Dohse that they had now exhausted all the dumps. Dohse knew this to be a lie and could have proved it. He had so far tallied up forty-five tons of surrendered arms, but the crib sheet found at 34 Cours de Verdun showed that around eighty tons of weapons had been parachuted. For the moment Dohse decided not to press the matter. There would be time enough later.

With Grandclément busy persuading local Resistance units to join the 'deal', Dohse began to consider how he could extend the operation beyond the immediate Bordeaux area by making similar approaches to three other key Resistance leaders in the southwest region. One of these was the leader of the Resistance in the Landes area between Bordeaux and the Pyrenees. This was Léonce Dussarrat, one of the local business-men who had loaned de Baissac 100,000 francs when he fled Bordeaux, just thirteen weeks previously. Grandclément told Dohse that, in his opinion, this was the man who would be the most susceptible to an approach along the lines Dohse had made to him.

Known locally by his alias 'Léon des Landes', Dussarrat was an electri-cian by trade. Thirty-nine years old, he was unusually short in stature and had a frame almost as wide as it was tall, a pugnacious personality and a temper to match. Notorious in the region for his aggression and hard living, he ran an ironmonger's shop in the centre of the market town of Dax. He was also well known to Rudolf Kunesch, who had placed him under surveillance for Resistance activities ever since Christian Fossard identified him as the Maquis leader responsible for arms caches in the area. In late September, Dohse heard that Kunesch was about to arrest Dussarrat, and persuaded Luther that, given the success he had had with Grandclément, he should be the one to handle him. Neutralising the Resistance by sequestrating their arms, he explained, was far more effective than simply arresting their chief, who would soon be replaced by another. After all, Dohse argued, 'what threat was an enemy without weapons?' Luther agreed, and told the furious Kunesch to pull back and leave Dussarrat to Dohse.

The Gestapo man proposed that Grandclément should try to persuade Maleyran and Chazeau to act as intermediaries in negotiating the deal with Dussarrat. The plan was agreed by the two men, though not without some reluctance, which made Dohse briefly wonder whether the rela-tionship between the three Frenchmen and Dussarrat was as good as they claimed.

One reason why Dohse was so keen to press ahead with this some-what hare-brained scheme was to suck Grandclément deeper into collaboration with him. 'It was this [step], much more than delivering arms, which moved him [Grandclément] into the realm of treason [because now] he was becoming my instrument to sow mischief and instability within the ranks of the Resistance. In this he was, from the start, driven by pride, ambition and egotism. These pushed him to continue to seek a role of importance in a "double game" in which he thought himself the cunning master, when he was in fact no more than a pawn on my chessboard.'

On 29 September, Dohse, Grandclément, Maleyran, Chazeau and Kunesch drove to Dax, where they parked in front of the town gendarmerie, at a spot which commanded a clear view of the front door of Dussarrat's store. Maleyran and Chazeau went in first to see Dussarrat, who had just returned from the funeral of a friend. They told him that two Gestapo officers were outside with Grandclément and suggested that he should come down for a chat, stressing: 'If you give up your arms, you will be left at liberty.'

'You will have neither my arms, nor me,' Léon des Landes replied, flushing with anger.

'I think you will find it's too late.'

'Too late?' said Dussarrat, walking over to look out of the window; he saw a number of German policemen, a Gestapo car and Dohse standing talking to André Grandclément. Dussarrat, true to his reputation for temper and unpredictability, exploded into a rage, railing against Grandclément and his treachery.

'Your Resistance activities are over,' Maleyran announced. 'If you don't want to cooperate, you had better flee.'

'I told them to go to hell and barged through a secret door that led into my secretary's office, which I had to open with my shoulder. Then I fled down some stairs leading to my backyard,' Dussarrat, never a man to resist embellishing a good story, later related. From here the Maquis leader apparently leapt over the walls of his neighbours' back gardens, ran through the back door of a butcher's shop, out through the front, onto a backstreet – and away. Dohse's subsequent search of Dussarrat's shop and house produced nothing.

For the first time since the arrest of Lucette, Friedrich Dohse had been publicly outwitted. He had been made to look a fool and Kunesch did not let him forget it, reminding all and sundry that he didn't approve of these 'soft ways'. The only way with the French was speed, toughness and uncompromising repression. 'I lost a great deal of prestige with my superiors,' Dohse admitted later. 'I had to concede that Kunesch was right.'

Next time he would arrest first and negotiate afterwards.

THE BATTLE OF LESTIAC

As so often in the business of spying, it was the unravelling of a single tiny thread which led to the coup that, after the Dussarrat affair, restored Friedrich Dohse's reputation among his superiors in Berlin, Paris and Bordeaux.

It all began on 22 September with the arrest of a man caught in the act of clearing a secret letterbox. Louis Verhelst, a Belgian, was taken to Bouscat and handed over to Kunesch's men, who alternately beat him and roasted him in front of two braziers for the best part of thirty-six hours. Then, covered in blood, with a broken eardrum, severely swollen knees and a burnt and lacerated back, he was 'interviewed' by Kunesch. At some point over the course of his torture he gave the name of Pierre Edmond Desbouillons, a colleague in the Resistance.

Desbouillons, who lived only a few hundred metres from the back of Dohse's office, was arrested on 11 October. Already well known as a docker and a communist, he had been originally detained in the round-up which had followed the discovery of the body of a German officer, Lieutenant Reimers, in Bordeaux harbour in October 1941. He would probably have been one of the hostages executed at Souge in reprisal, had it not been for his wife's intervention with a French Gestapo agent she knew, who managed to get him released.

Since then Desbouillons had been involved with several Resistance organisations, including Scientist. In September 1943 he made contact with Jean Duboué and offered to put together a team to assassinate Pierre Poinsot, if Duboué would supply the weapons. Duboué provided Desbouillons and his team with four Colt automatics, forty-five rounds of ammunition, five hand grenades, an SOE commando knife and 20,000 francs. When nothing had happened by early October, Duboué considered breaking contact with Desbouillons, but had not yet done so.

Pierre Desbouillons was not, however, the only member of the family who was well known to the Germans at Bouscat. His wife Raymonde was too – though for different reasons. She had, it seems, been involved with various men from the occupying forces, and was at the time having an affair with the German editor of the Axis forces' local daily, *Soldat am Atlantik*. Relations between the Desbouillons were, to say the least, strained, with Pierre unchivalrously responding to his wife's serial infidelity by letting all and sundry know that he no longer risked marital relations with her because she had venereal disease.

It may have been that Pierre Desbouillons' arrest presented his wife with an opportunity to get her husband out of the way for good, for on Tuesday 12 October 1943, not long after Kunesch started his interrogation of Desbouillons, she delivered a letter to Bouscat denouncing her husband and giving full details to support her accusations. In the face of this final betrayal by his wife, Pierre Desbouillons's resolve collapsed and he gave all to Kunesch – including information about Duboué, Léo Paillère, Vic Hayes, and Duboué's headquarters at Villa Roucoule in Lestiac. He even offered to lead his captors to the house.

That evening, Lucette Grandclément, hearing from her husband that Desbouillons had been arrested and that Léo Paillère was now at risk, rushed to her friend Jean Paillère's home in Bordeaux to warn her. Mme Paillère immediately rang her husband, who was dining with their three sons, Jean Duboué and Vic Hayes at a local restaurant. Duboué took the news calmly; Hayes, who had worked on the docks with Desbouillons, was confident he wouldn't talk. But Paillère, not wishing to serve another term in jail, fled to a friend's house in a suburb of eastern Bordeaux, where he went to ground.

The following morning, 13 October, Hayes met with Roger Landes at one of their regular meeting places, a run-down café in a working-class area of Bastide on the east bank of the Garonne. The two men discussed Desbouillons's arrest. Landes was not, at this stage, overly concerned; 'It wasn't the first time one of our men had been arrested,' he commented later. Hayes told Landes that Jean Duboué had heard from one of his men that Poinsot was now searching for him by name, and had concluded that the time had come to leave Lestiac until things calmed down. The two of them were going to the Villa Roucoule later, Hayes added, to collect Mme Duboué and Suzanne, and to clean out the house. Landes strongly advised his colleague to stay away from Lestiac. But Hayes insisted – Duboué needed him and he had to protect Suzanne. They parted company, arranging to meet again at the same time and place forty-eight hours later.

That evening Duboué and Hayes set off for Lestiac, picking up two Sten guns on the way and arriving at the villa at around eight. Over dinner Duboué calmly brought Suzanne Duboué and his wife, Marie-Louise, up to speed on what had happened and told them to gather together their belongings. They would be leaving for Brittany before dawn.

While the two women packed suitcases, Duboué and Hayes checked their weapons and filled magazines, placing some at strategic points around the house in case of trouble during the night. The family finally got to bed just after midnight struck on the Lestiac church clock. The night was moonless, cloud-covered and unusually dark.

About ninety minutes later, in the very early hours of Thursday 14 October, a small convoy of three vehicles snaked quietly out of the main gate of the headquarters at Bouscat, led by a large black Cadillac. Dohse sat in the back seat with Desbouillons, while behind were two other cars containing three of Dohse's officers and four or five of his men. All were in civilian clothes and heavily armed.

A little before 3 a.m. the convoy, its lights extinguished, slipped quietly down the narrow main street of Lestiac and glided to a halt outside the Villa Roucoule. Dohse, making as little noise as possible, posted his men around the property.

It was Marie-Louise who heard them first, alerting her husband. Suzanne, in her bedroom on the ground floor, was woken by the sound of her father's footsteps tumbling down the stairs. He burst into her room, Sten gun in hand. 'It's them! The Gestapo's here!' he whispered urgently: 'Mother heard the sound of brakes in the road outside. Get ready as fast as you can.' Then he called up to his wife: 'Wake Charles [Hayes] and tell him to get to the window with his gun!'

Outside, Dohse had quietly opened the garden gate and was now at the front door. Banging loudly, he shouted: 'Police! Open up!'

Hayes, already awake, grabbed his Sten and dashed to the window of his first-floor bedroom. In the rush to arm his weapon, he accidentally let one shot fly, sending the bullet careering into the wall of his bedroom. Cursing at the carelessly loosed-off bullet and flinging open the shutters, he unleashed a full magazine from his Sten at the dark shadow below. A furious German fusillade crashed around the window, while Dohse, miraculously unharmed, dashed back to behind a garden wall to take cover with his men.

And so began what was to become known locally as the battle of Lestiac.

Inside, Jean Duboué, taking charge, ordered his wife and Suzanne to stay downstairs and shouted to Hayes that the two of them should dash from window to window on the first floor firing into the darkness to give the impression that there were numerous defenders. Perhaps, Duboué thought to himself, Dohse's men would spread themselves so thinly around the house that, sooner or later, he and Hayes would find a weak spot and be able to slip away.

After an hour or so Hayes suddenly shouted out in pain. He had been hit in the right arm. Duboué shouted angrily at him: 'Do you know nothing about combat? You need to protect yourself!' Suzanne bandaged his arm with her scarf, and then, with her father's help, tucked the butt of Hayes's Sten under his wounded arm so he could go on firing. At some stage during the night, perhaps at this point, Hayes and Suzanne declared their love to each other and promised that whatever happened, they would get back together after the war. These were the last private words they would ever exchange.

A little later, Suzanne suggested that she and her mother should walk out the front door and surrender, hoping that the distraction would give the men the opportunity to slip away through the back. But Duboué rejected this as too dangerous. Instead, at around five in the morning, as the sky began to lighten with smudges of grey, Hayes and Duboué decided to make a run for it from the back door. They got as far as a lime tree in the garden when Hayes changed his mind, saying: 'We can't leave the women,' and dashed back, with Duboué following under heavy fire. Just as he reached the rear of the house, Hayes took a second bullet in the leg.

By now Dohse had called up reinforcements, including machine guns and more hand grenades. The streets of Lestiac were now full of German soldiers who blocked the entry and exit points from the village and took up vantage points in neighbouring houses. The defenders began to fear that, when daylight came, the Germans would use flame-throwers or blow up the house.

Not long before dawn there was a mighty crash in the room where Suzanne and her mother were sheltering, blasting the window open and causing Mme Duboué to scream loudly. She had been hit twice, in the stomach, probably by shrapnel from a grenade.

'You bandits! You are shooting women,' Duboué yelled into the night. 'Let the women at least come out!'

A voice from behind the garden wall, almost certainly that of Dohse, shouted back: 'We are soldiers. If you let the women out, we won't shoot and we'll take care of them.' Duboué's response was another burst of fire from his Sten.

Suzanne, seizing the moment, ran upstairs and jumped from the first-floor balcony. Landing heavily, she found herself face to face with a German soldier's machine gun. 'How many men are there? How many?' the soldier demanded.

'I – I don't know, there's my father …' she stammered, stealing a glance at the family bicycles propped against the garden fence. As she did so, the soldier turned to listen to the voice of someone (again, almost certainly Dohse) exchanging shouted words in French with Duboué, calling on him to surrender. Suzanne didn't wait; her mother needed a doctor. She grabbed a bicycle and pedalled furiously off into the darkness.

Up to now Dohse had been content for his men to stay back under cover and leave the defenders to waste their ammunition, knowing that in due course it would run out. Now, however, it was coming up to 7 a.m. and, with full daylight fast approaching, he knew he had to bring things to a close. He ordered all the weapons around the house, including the newly arrived machine guns, to direct a simultaneous, concentrated storm of fire against all the doors and windows. When the firing died down, Dohse, standing at the front of the house, called through a loudhailer that the wounded should be brought out to safety so that they could be properly tended to. Suddenly there was a shout from the back door. It was Duboué, his Sten in his hand and spare magazines sticking out of his belt, calling for urgent medical attention for his wife.

As the firing stopped, Duboué moved forward, still fully armed, to find himself face to face with an unarmed Dohse, who took a step back in alarm.

Duboué calmed him: 'You have nothing to fear,' and put his Sten down on top of a nearby barrel.

'It's a pleasure to deal with real soldiers. I respect your courage and your patriotism,' Dohse replied. 'Go and fetch your wife and we will see she gets the attention she needs. Then we can talk again.'

Duboué re-emerged with Marie-Louise in his arms, wrapped in a bed cover. He brought her a dozen paces beyond the back door and laid her gently on a large wooden board in the garden. According to local legend, Marie-Louise, slipping in and out of consciousness, looked up and murmured to her husband: 'I am so proud of you – you defend your home as fiercely as you do your country.' Duboué instructed her: 'Make sure you don't cry in front of these people.'

As Duboué turned to return to the house, Dohse called him back. 'It's time to call a halt,' the German said, as his men took Marie-Louise away. 'You have fought bravely, but it's useless to continue. Better to finish it now than risk more blood … I know there is a British officer in there with you. If you surrender now I promise you will be treated as prisoners of war.'

Duboué replied that he would have to consult his comrade. Initially Hayes wanted to fight to the bitter end – but after a few minutes the two men came out with their hands in the air. Hayes walked up to Dohse and, reversing his pistol in the classic sign of surrender, handed it to the German. Dohse pulled out a packet of Lucky Strike taken from a recovered container and, offering a cigarette to each man, lit them in turn, before taking one for himself. Duboué and Hayes, misinterpreting the gesture, concluded that they were about to be shot. Dohse reassured them and chatted to the pair for a while, as his car was brought up.

It was a little past eight now and fully light. The battle had gone on for more than four hours. The Germans were astounded to find that they had been in furious combat not with seven or eight fighters, as they had imagined, but with just two. Dohse commented wryly that if he had known there were only a couple of combatants, he would have stormed the house.

While Dohse, with Duboué in the rear seat of his car, drove back to his headquarters at Bouscat, Marie-Louise Duboué and Hayes were taken to separate hospitals in Bordeaux.

After the Germans had ransacked and pillaged the Villa Roucoule, they burnt it, leaving a blackened shell as a warning to others. A little time later, Suzanne Duboué, returning with the doctor, saw the house burning from a distance and presumed that Vic and her parents had all been killed. She too was quickly taken into custody.

At Bouscat, Jean Duboué's name, address and details were recorded. Then he was escorted by two men with machine guns to a first-floor room where he found Dohse seated at his desk, surrounded by members of his staff, including Kunesch, Poinsot and some of his men, the interpreter Pierre Esch, and two secretaries with typewriters ready to take a record. Duboué was pushed into a chair facing Dohse on the other side of his desk, handcuffed, chained by the feet and thoroughly searched by Kunesch, who removed his wallet, identity documents and 135,000 francs.

'I am aware that I have in my hands two of the most important members of SOE's "French Section" in London,' Dohse began, portentously. 'I am aware also that one of your colleagues has already left for London' – a reference to Claude de Baissac – 'leaving only your radio operator "Stanislas" still at liberty … it is in your interest to tell me where he is in order to avoid him being killed, because there is no way now that he can escape.'

Duboué responded that he did not know where Landes was; each agent's whereabouts were known only to them. Communication was exclusively through secret letterboxes.

'Very well,' Dohse responded. 'We'll see about that later. You will recall that I said I respected you as a soldier. But the fact remains that you are fighting against your country, which has signed an armistice. You are therefore a rebel and a terrorist.'

'I never signed that armistice. As a true Frenchman I fight the enemy wherever I find him.'

Dohse took a paper from Esch and read it out. It was Desbouillons's deposition confirming that Duboué was a British agent, had organised parachute drops, had attended clandestine meetings at the Café des Chartrons and had been involved in sabotage attacks with Claude de Baissac, Vic Hayes and Roger Landes. He had also worked with Robert Leroy to gather intelligence on the German submarine base, which had been passed to the enemy in London. 'You see, not all Frenchmen are like you,' he said. 'This one for instance' – referring to Desbouillons – 'is a coward.'

At this stage Pierre Poinsot approached Duboué, the brim of his hat dramatically pulled down over his eyes. 'You also tried to have me assassinated,' he said menacingly to the restaurateur. 'Here is a list of people, with me at the head, which contains the names, addresses, car number plates of my men – everything is here. You gave this list to Desbouillons when you met him at a public place in Bacalan. For what reason?'

Duboué denied ever having written the paper and said he could prove it. Dohse took out Desbouillons's deposition and read from it again. 'The paper which was found on me at my arrest was given to me by Duboué.'

Poinsot continued: 'I am well aware of what was planned against me and I am not afraid … you are a traitor … I am surrounded by traitors … but I serve my country and my conscience is clear.'

'I serve my country, too,' said Duboué. 'Not from under the skirts of the enemy, but fighting them for the liberation of France.'

'But legally we are not your enemy. You are the rebel and the terrorist,' Dohse interjected.

Kunesch, concluding that menace was not working, tried Dohse-style theatricals instead. He unlocked one of the prisoner's handcuffs and, with a flourish, produced a box of cigars and offered him one. 'Good God!' Duboué exclaimed to general merriment in the room. 'Those are MY cigars. You took them from my house!' Then he was handcuffed again and led down to the cells in chains.

Hayes, whose wounds were declared by a German doctor not to be serious, was interrogated later that day. But the Germans got nothing from him either.

The search of the Villa Roucoule yielded a number of pistols and Stens. But Dohse's men did not find a hidden cellar in which Duboué had stashed a wireless and more weapons. These lay undiscovered until nearly nine months later, when they would again see the light of day and be used to arm Maquis units after D-Day.

On several occasions over the next few weeks, Dohse, who repeatedly insisted that he had a high respect for the courage of Duboué and Hayes, entertained them both to dinner and 'conversation' at his table in Bouscat. He was never able to persuade either to collaborate, though Hayes did reveal two small arms dumps, while Duboué let slip the existence of another in a Bordeaux townhouse. These revelations produced, among other things, eighteen hand grenades complete with detonators, ten Sten guns, ten Colt automatics, several boxes of explosive, 240,000 francs, one gold watch, a suitcase containing a British wireless set and thousands of rounds of ammunition of various calibres. Faced with Dohse's repeated questions about the whereabouts of Roger Landes, Hayes repeatedly lied, saying he had gone to Spain.

On one occasion Dohse brought André Grandclément and Maleyran to meet the two prisoners, who, believing these to be the pair who had betrayed them, refused to shake their hands. It was only when Dohse brought Desbouillons into the room that they were convinced otherwise – though both made clear that they still regarded Grandclément and Maleyran as traitors and would have nothing to do with them.

In the course of a conversation with Dohse around this time, Grandclément revealed that Duboué and Hayes had been personally implicated in the recent wave of sabotage, which had severely damaged installations in Bordeaux port. This immediately changed the nature of the charges against the two men. Acts of sabotage meant that they would be regarded by the authorities no longer as soldiers, but as 'saboteur-terrorists' and therefore beyond the reach of the Geneva Convention. The death penalty was now mandatory.

When Gestapo headquarters Paris decreed that Duboué and Hayes were to be shot within twenty-four hours of their trial, Dohse took an urgent train to Paris to plead for their lives. He explained to his superiors at Avenue Foch that he would have a much better chance of persuading other Resistance fighters to work for him if it was known that his 'word of honour' would be respected. Extraordinarily, he got his way. It was agreed that after a trial in Bordeaux the two men, instead of being immediately executed, would be transferred first to the infamous Fresnes prison in Paris, where they would be placed 'at the disposition of the German authorities'.

Roger Landes had spent the day after the battle of Lestiac looking for new safe houses outside Bordeaux. Unaware of what had happened to his comrades, he returned to Marguerite Faget's house late that evening. The next day, a Friday, he left for his agreed rendezvous with Vic Hayes, but there was no sign of him. Hayes never missed a meeting. Landes wasn't too worried at first, presuming he would make their meeting at the same time and place the following day.

Next day – still no Hayes. But there was news of alarming developments: the Germans had raided the Café des Chartrons and arrested

Marcel Bertrand and his wife. 'For only the second time since I came to Bordeaux, I didn't sleep that night,' Landes recalled.

The following day there was again no sign of Hayes. Worse, a check of Hayes's main contacts confirmed that no one else had seen him either.

The blow fell the following day when one of Landes's men, distraught and scared, told him that he had overheard the driver of the Bordeaux-to-Cadillac bus regaling colleagues in a local café about the 'battle of Lestiac'.

Landes knew what it meant. Hayes and Duboué had been captured.

Now he was completely alone and in the very gravest danger. A hunted man, he would now be pursued by all Dohse's formidable resources. Gestapo agents and collaborators would, even now, be scouring Bordeaux to find him.

Landes went immediately to ground, shutting down his radios and once more changing the place he slept every night – no doubt depending again on his network of sympathetic brothels for refuge. Unable to transmit (and perhaps also trying to convince Dohse that he had fled), he sent a courier to Harry Peulevé in the Corrèze asking him to tell London what had happened. And so it was that, two weeks after the event, a coded signal reporting the battle of Lestiac finally arrived in Baker Street:

FROM PEULEVÉ – 31 OCTOBER 1943

    HAYES REPEAT HAYES ARRESTED AFTER THREE HOUR GUN BATTLE WITH GESTAPO STOP WOUNDED ARM AND LEG STOP NOW IN MILITARY HOSPITAL LE BÉQUET BORDEAUX STOP HAVE SENT MAP STOP INVESTI-GATING MEANS OF ESCAPE STOP LANDES COMPLETELY BURNT STOP MUST RETURN URGENTLY STOP VITAL YOU SEND INSTRUCTIONS NOW … STOP THIS IS DOUBLE IMPORTANT ENDS.

His SOS message sent, Peulevé dashed immediately to Bordeaux to assist in the rescue of his colleague.

Conditions for Hayes at Le Béquet were markedly more relaxed than in the cells at Bouscat. His wounds were being tended by a Czech doctor sympathetic to the Resistance and Léo Paillère's sons were even able to smuggle clothes and food in to the prisoner and information about his condition and location out to the rescuers. A plan was swiftly hatched and a rescue team assembled. They were actually in the van and about to leave for the hospital when one of the nursing staff dashed in to report that Dohse had moved his prisoner to an unknown location. The attempt to free Hayes was abandoned. There would be no other.

Nine weeks after the battle of Lestiac, on 17 January 1944, Jean Duboué, Suzanne Duboué and Victor Hayes appeared before the German military tribunal in Bordeaux. Suzanne and Vic exchanged their last lovers' signals across the courtroom. All three were sentenced to transportation: Hayes to Fresnes; Suzanne to the concentration camp for women at Ravensbrück; Jean Duboué to Buchenwald. They left Bordeaux from Saint-Jean station that same evening.

18

MAQUIS OFFICIELS

SOE had now lost its two largest and most important networks in the occupied zone of France: Prosper and Scientist. Extraordinarily Baker Street, instead of learning lessons, attempted to gloss their losses as evidence of effectiveness and success. SOE's regular six-monthly assessment to Churchill, for the period April to September 1943, began: 'The institution by the enemy of violent Gestapo drives against Resistance organisations has been the principal feature during the period under review. Despite increased repression however [we] have made progress and it is probably for this very reason that the enemy have intensified their counter measures ...'

The report continued by speculating what might have been if the invasion which had never been planned had happened and their networks, instead of being destroyed, had survived: 'If a landing had been possible [in 1943]', it claimed, 'the assistance invading troops would have received would have been tremendous.'

Finally, they blamed the French: 'Resistance is still conditioned by the unwillingness of a large part of the population – and particularly [French] Army circles – to take any action before D-Day ... Denunciations have become more frequent owing ... [to] neglect on the part of the people to "do their duty".'

Another Baker Street report of the same date took a different approach, lauding SOE's results and euphemising their losses: '[There have been] so many acts of sabotage ... in France that [we] no longer enumerate them individually ... Continued Gestapo activity arising out of the special drive against Resistance groups in June caused setbacks especially in the Paris and Bordeaux areas ... [we have] altogether lost four British officers [actually they had lost five: Suttill, Norman, Borrel, Rudellat and Hayes] and four not very important leaders of Resistance groups.'

In reality Baker Street realised only too well that, with the invasion fast approaching, they would have to rebuild these networks as a matter of urgency – especially in Bordeaux.

But their first priority was to clear up the wreckage.

In the last days of October, Landes sent a signal to London, probably also through Harry Peulevé, asking them to cease *all* parachute drops. Baker Street agreed and ordered Landes to return to London as soon as possible. Landes, who had decided that he could not leave until he had cleared up loose ends and put his networks into hibernation, told Baker Street that he would not be able to return to England until the second half of November at the earliest.

On 19 October, five days after the battle of Lestiac, André Grandclément passed on an unexpected invitation to police inspector Charles Corbin, Landes's 'double agent'. Would he care to join Dohse for lunch at the Vidal (Grandclément's favourite restaurant) the next day? Fearing a trap, Corbin asked Landes what he should do. Landes tried to think of a pretext for Corbin to refuse. But eventually the two men decided that Corbin would have to brazen it out. Though dangerous, the meeting could even be useful, if Corbin could succeed in probing Dohse's intentions.

The following day Corbin was picked up by a Gestapo car and dropped under the art deco iron-and-glass awning of the Vidal restaurant, on the Boulevard du Président Wilson. He was the first to arrive and chose a corner table, which gave him good sight of the room and all its exits.

What followed was classic Dohse – part fishing expedition, part theatre, part cheerful bonhomie, part cat-and-mouse – all dished up with a large dose of peppery, if subtle, persuasion to encourage Corbin to choose the right side. Apart from Dohse and Corbin, Grandclément, Maleyran and another young man (probably Chazeau) were also at the lunch. Dohse, who strongly suspected Corbin of playing a double game, was, as ever, charming and courteous – but utterly deadly. He first brought to the table the police officer whom Dohse had tasked with investigating Corbin. The officer laid out in precise, policemanly manner all he had against Corbin: he had given information to assist in the plan to assassinate Poinsot; he had sheltered British agents on the run; he was active in the Gaullist cause. All the evidence, the police officer concluded, pointed in one direction: Corbin was either sympathetic to 'the terrorists' or was himself one. Corbin, well used to police interrogation techniques, coolly denied everything. Dohse, possibly fooled by Corbin's former right-wing credentials, or perhaps simply affecting politesse, appeared to accept the denials. His purpose at this stage was not to arrest Corbin, but to make him understand that he was firmly in the Gestapo's crosswires and why, therefore, it was in his interests to cooperate. The mailed fist having been clearly exposed, Dohse returned it to the velvet glove and they all had a pleasant meal together chatting about politics and the war just like any group of friends out for a comradely lunch. Then they went their separate ways.

Corbin, deeply shaken, contacted Landes afterwards, who suggested that his friend should take himself out of circulation by feigning sickness. Albertine and Ginette were already safely in the country, so at least Corbin knew that his family was safe.

In fact, for all his subtlety and intelligence, Dohse had this time misjudged his man. 'I thought he agreed with us … I should have immediately arrested him,' Dohse admitted later. He had hoped to play Charles Corbin. But instead Corbin was the only Frenchman successfully to play Dohse, staying resolutely loyal to Roger Landes while successfully convincing Dohse that he supported Grandclément.

On the day that Dohse had lunch with Corbin, a new chief of KdS Bordeaux arrived to take over from Hans Luther.

Walter Machule, tall, corpulent, with a livid duelling scar on his cheek, was a forty-seven-year-old doctor of philosophy. Devoted to the good life, he was an accomplished pianist, notoriously corrupt and an energetic sexual adventurer who did not take long to acquire himself a local mistress. As far as Dohse was concerned, he shared one useful charac-teristic with his predecessor Luther – indolence. Machule had been keen to be posted to Bordeaux because it was regarded as a quiet backwater. Few if any German VIPs visited; life was good and the danger level low. If there was trouble then he had the experienced Dohse to deal with it. So, provided Dohse continued to deliver successes and not problems, Machule would support his approach over Kunesch's more brutal meth-ods. Which was just as well, because Friedrich Dohse's plans were about to get even more ambitious.

On the face of it, André Grandclément's importance to Dohse remained just as it was. Dohse allowed the Frenchman to hold court with Resistance colleagues in the attic bedroom (he had seen Louis Verhelst there before the battle of Lestiac) and gave him free rein to wander at liberty around his headquarters. Maleyran and Chazeau were also frequent visitors to the Bouscat attic and, together with Grandclément, dined with Dohse at local restaurants, usually once a week.

But appearances were deceptive. In reality, with the end of the current phase of arms recovery, Grandclément's usefulness to Dohse was dimin-ishing fast. In late October, someone came up with a solution: Dohse claimed it was Machule, who took a close interest in the Grandclément affair, but there is evidence that it could easily have been Grandclément himself. The suggestion was that Grandclément and Dohse should set up their own official – that is, German-sponsored – Maquis. The French would christen them *Maquis officiels*, or, on occasion, *Maquis blancs*.

André Grandclément would be allowed to form the core of a new *Maquis officiel* from the 250 prisoners the Germans had liberated, plus the 150 who they had refrained from arresting under the Grandclément–Dohse 'deal'. The purpose of these *Maquis officiels* was to create a force capable of 'saving' France from communist takeover once the German occupation had ended. Provided the *officiels* stuck strictly to this purpose and did not in any way or at any time attack or harass German forces, they would be given back their weapons – with the exception of the explosive, detonators and grenades – and would be free from any further German harassment.

At first sight, his was an extremely radical proposal, since it was based on the premise that Nazi Germany's occupation of France would eventually end. At the time, any such admission was regarded by Berlin as defeatism, punishable by death. In fact, the formation of the *Maquis officiels* was not as radical as it seemed, either for Grandclément or for the Germans. As far as Grandclément was concerned, it was almost identical to the proposal he had made to the Vichy authorities in Paris before his arrest: to hand over his Bordeaux organisation to the anti-communist Maquis formations which had already, with the tacit agreement of the German occupiers, formed within Vichy circles. For Berlin, it was very similar to their policy in Yugoslavia, where they had backed General Mihailovic's Serbian royalist Chetniks against Tito's communist partisans.

The proposal also had specific attractions for both Grandclément and Dohse personally. For Dohse, this was the perfect way to neutralise the Resistance and bring it under German control, while at the same time providing a means to rebuild André Grandclément's flagging influence among his French friends and Resistance colleagues.

The appeal to Grandclément was that he would once more be in charge of a regional force which would, in due course, play a historic role in shaping the post-war destiny of his country. Dohse, playing shamefully to Grandclément's ego, explained in detail what an important role this would be. Always quick to provide a cunning ruse with a cloak of respectability, he backed his proposition with a visionary thought. When the war was over, he predicted, the biggest threat to the West would not be Germany, but the Soviet Union. To face this threat, there would need to be a united Europe built around a Franco-German axis. Grandclément's *Maquis officiels* was merely the first step towards this end, making Grandclément, he suggested, a pioneer in the creation of a united Europe, in the interest of both France and Germany. Dohse had, with deadly purpose, carefully taken Grandclément up the mountain and laid out before him all the land that would be his, stretching as far away as the eye could see and as far into the future as any man seeking glory could possibly hope for.

For Grandclément the dreamer, it was all irresistible, since it played perfectly to his sense of self-worth. For Maleyran and Chazeau, a German-sponsored *Maquis officiel* had more practical attractions. With winter coming, they had no idea how they could provide food and shelter for their young Maquisards – and especially those who had been released from German prisons under the Grandclément deal. This would solve their problem.

For Dohse, all the evidence suggests that this was, in fact, more than just a short-term artificial confection cooked up to cover a treachery. He really believed in the idea. It was exactly what he had worked on when, at Bömelburg's request, he had acted as the secretary to the Paris-based Cercle Européen, the Franco-German body which proposed a united Europe, dominated by the French and the Germans after Nazi Germany had won the war.

Sometime in the second half of October, Dohse called an extraordinary conference in the casino-cum-officers' mess housed in one of the KdS buildings in Bouscat. The purpose of the meeting was to discuss and agree the basic premise of the *Maquis officiels*. All Dohse's senior colleagues were present, as were Machule and Grandclément.

After the meeting, Dohse took Grandclément to one side and informed him that he knew of the existence of the missing thirty-five tons of arms, which should have been delivered up under their deal. He insisted that these should now be surrendered so they could be used to arm the *Maquis officiels*. Grandclément prevaricated, claiming that the arms could not be recovered as they had already been distributed; but, to compensate, he would now actively contact *all* Maquis units outside his immediate control and try to persuade them to join the new *Maquis officiels* under his command. Dohse saw no purpose in pushing the matter and accepted the compromise.

What no one knew, either at this meeting or amongst Dohse's superiors in Bordeaux and Paris, was that Dohse's fertile mind was already ranging onto even more dangerous ground. He was beginning to assemble a plan which, if discovered, would have been seen by his masters 'as an act of treason resulting in my execution by firing squad'. Dohse reasoned that the total collapse of Scientist had put the British in a very weak position in southwest France. Furthermore, it was obvious to him (if no one else) that an invasion across the beaches of the Aquitaine coast was not – and never would be – an option for the Allies. The supply lines from Britain necessary to keep an invasion force in operation in south-west France would be just too long and too exposed. He concluded, therefore, that the British might be willing to consider renouncing their plans for resistance in the southwest in favour of supporting armed *Maquis officiels*, which would stop France falling to communism after the defeat of Germany. This led Dohse to the even more startling conclusion that there might – just might – be a basis for a Grandclément-style deal with London:

> It seemed to me very likely that the English would be interested in establishing a strong anti-communist force in France, now that it was clear that we Germans were going to lose … I was thinking about a meeting in Spain with Claude de Baissac and Grandclément to discuss the British renouncing their organisation in the southwest and providing instead moral and material support [weapons], so as to turn Grandclément's '*Maquis Officiels*' into a credible military organisation.

For those who find such an idea fanciful, it is worth remembering that Churchill, at the Tehran tripartite conference just a month later, also wondered aloud whether, with German defeat now inevitable, the real threat to the Europe of the future would come not from Hitler, but from Stalin.

Dohse's final thought was the most dangerous one of all: 'A meeting [with de Baissac] would also enable me to establish direct contact with the British, which could provide me with a line of escape, if my plans came to light, causing my superiors to take severe sanctions against me.' This was extremely dangerous stuff – and made even more so by the fact that in early 1944 an Abwehr officer would do exactly what Dohse was considering he himself might have to do – defect to the British.

As Dohse's thinking ranged ahead on the next stage of his journey, André Grandclément, though he probably wasn't aware of it, was reaching the end of his. He had begun his relationship with Dohse as a misguided 'patriot'; now he was a fully fledged traitor. He had started by handing over some weapons to save his men – and ended as a wholehearted and committed agent of influence for the Gestapo. Dohse had achieved his objective. The tiger had eaten his rider.

And so it was that as Dohse's influence beyond Bordeaux grew, Grandclément's began to dwindle. And as the Frenchman's position weakened, he became more vulnerable to his many enemies. During the first half of October 1943, local Resistance leaders meeting in a council of war at a secret location confirmed the sentence of death on André Grandclément and ordered that he should be executed immediately.

This death sentence was confirmed by London on 28 October, when an official order was sent from the French counter-espionage service in the British capital to France. It instructed one of the French assassination teams in the Charente to kill not only André Grandclément, but also Lucette, without delay.

19

LENCOUACQ

Friedrich Dohse did not have to wait long for the opportunity to test out his plan to establish *Maquis officiels* in his area.

In the second half of October 1943, the Wehrmacht commander of the region south of Bordeaux contacted him to pass on some intelligence from a captured prisoner about a Maquis unit in the wild area of marshland and forest near the small village of Lencouacq. A few days later, Dohse, on his way to Spain with Claire Keimer, called at the German officer's headquarters where he was shown a map with the exact location of the old farmhouse in which the men were based. They were mostly fugitives from the Service du Travail Obligatoire (STO) programme, under which young Frenchmen (and some women) were sent to Germany to work. When the German commander explained that he intended to mount a full-scale attack, with heavy artillery, on the Maquis hideout, Dohse asked him to suspend the operation while he investigated alternatives.

Dohse was later to claim that this was to avoid bloodshed. Perhaps he did have such scruples. If so, they chimed most conveniently with his plan to launch *Maquis officiels*.

Returning to Bordeaux a few days later, Dohse called in Grandclément to discuss the possibility of persuading the young men at Lencouacq to become his first *Maquis officiel*. It was only then that Grandclément blushingly admitted that he was, in fact, in contact with the young Maquisards, who were already 'under his command'. He promised to visit the young men, explain the danger they were in and suggest that if they cooperated and re-formed as a German-sponsored *Maquis officiel* unit, then they could all remain free and safe. Dohse agreed, suggesting that it might even be possible for him to visit the camp in person to seal the deal.

The sixteen or so men who made up the Maquis de Lencouacq included both Paul Salles, the 'anonymous' young man who had, a month earlier, guided Dohse to the first arms cache, and Guy Bertrand, the son of the owners of the Café des Chartrons. The group had started off as a small unit under the control of André Grandclément in the Sabres forest, close to where Grandclément had handed over the first arms dump. On the day after that earlier handover, Grandclément had met the young Maquisards in a local café to try to persuade them to join his original deal with Dohse. They had promised to think about it, and get back to him. But before they could, one of them was arrested and the group decided to flee to somewhere more remote.

Their new hideout was an isolated derelict house called Sescons Farm, which had been abandoned forty years previously. It lay in the shelter of two large oak trees in a forest clearing, twelve kilometres north of Lencouacq, where a small unit of Wehrmacht soldiers also had their base. There were several other small Maquis groups scattered throughout the area; a dozen or so fierce Spanish Republican communists lived in another old farmhouse a couple of kilometres away, and beyond that, deeper into the woods, two more groups had also taken up residence in some abandoned forestry huts. There were even clandestine 'bistros' established in local farmhouses to serve the young fugitives.

On 28 October, Grandclément, accompanied by Maleyran, Chazeau and one other – all unarmed – visited Sescons farmhouse and gathered the young fighters together.

'Grandclément explained to them that, since they were not communists, the Germans had a high respect for their patriotic fight [to free their country],' one of those involved remembered; 'they [the Germans] would, if necessary, be ready to help the young men [with money and food] if they undertook to confine their activities to maintaining order after the Germans left and refrained from attacking them while they were still here.' Grandclément then made his pitch: they could either accept the condition not to attack the Germans, in which case they could keep their weapons and remain as a unit under his command, or they could give up their weapons and be free to return to their homes without any ensuing consequences or reprisals; or they could, of course, do neither and be wiped out in a German attack. Finally, Grandclément made an offer. In four days' time – at 10 a.m. on 1 November – Grandclément would bring Dohse to their base, unarmed; and after they had presented arms to him, the Gestapo chief would confirm in person the conditions which Grandclément had just laid out.

Having little choice, the young Maquisards agreed to hear what Dohse had to say.

After Grandclément left, the head of the Lencouacq Maquis contacted his commander and explained all. The senior man was horrified, insisting that any 'surrender' to the Germans along the lines suggested by Grandclément would be treachery, and ordered them to ambush Dohse's convoy instead.

On the day fixed for Dohse's visit, there was a furious debate within the group. Most agreed that Dohse and his party should be ambushed and killed; but one, a close friend of Maleyran and Grandclément and the son of the famous Resistance leader Colonel Rollot, insisted that they should welcome Dohse and accept his proposals. Tempers flared and there was some kind of council of war at which the young dissenter was condemned to death as a traitor. He was swiftly executed with a bullet in the back of the head and buried in a shallow grave near the farmhouse.

Back at Bouscat, Dohse had been forced to delay his departure by some minor personal indisposition. He finally left his headquarters around midday, accompanied by Kunesch, Grandclément, Maleyran and Chazeau. In accordance with the agreement with Grandclément, none of the visiting party were armed. Dohse, overconfident after the success of the past weeks, had not even taken the precaution of warning the local Wehrmacht units, including the one stationed at Lencouacq, of his intentions.

At some point on the journey to Lencouacq, Dohse's Cadillac broke down, causing a further delay of an hour or so.

The hold-ups saved Friedrich Dohse's life.

'We put the ambush in place from 0800 that Monday,' Paul Salles later recalled: '[Our chief] visited us shortly afterwards to check that all was in order, bringing two extra men with him. But for some reason, the Gestapo didn't arrive when they said they would and, when 1300 came and went without any sign of them, we all returned to the camp, leaving one sentry on watch.'

Arriving at Lencouacq, Dohse's Cadillac with its five passengers turned onto the twelve-kilometre-long unmade, potholed track leading to the farmhouse. They were travelling now under an overcast sky through flat marshy country relieved only by patches of scrub, scattered tall firs and occasional clumps of marsh oaks, whose leaves were already beginning to turn with the approach of autumn. At around 1600 hours, the group finally arrived at a small house set amongst pine trees. Maleyran explained that this was the house of a local muleteer who was away at the time. It was as far as they could go by vehicle.

The five set off on foot for the final kilometre, walking through sparse woodland and heath and skirting a small field of maze. About 200 metres from their destination they stopped, while Chazeau, at Grandclément's suggestion, went ahead to warn the Maquisards so they would not be taken by surprise. Grandclément's thoughtfulness saved his life and that of three of his companions. The sentry at the ambush site had seen the Cadillac arrive and dashed back to alert his colleagues. Paul Salles grabbed a machine gun and moved forward to ambush the party at the perimeter of the forest clearing.

Roland Chazeau had vanished from sight only for a few moments when the stillness was shattered by the rattle of machine-gun fire. A cautious reconnaissance revealed Chazeau lying dead in a pool of blood. Dohse and his party beat a hasty retreat to the Cadillac and returned at full speed to the refuge of the nearby Wehrmacht camp at Lencouacq.

The following day the Wehrmacht attacked Sescons Farm with infantry and artillery. Finding the Maquisards long gone, the soldiers razed the farmhouse to the ground and returned to their base empty-handed, save for the recovered corpse of Roland Chazeau.

Once again, luck had saved Dohse's life. He boasted that this was 'Stanislas's' second failed attempt to kill him. (In fact, though Landes was later to claim, along with several others, that he was involved in the decision to ambush Dohse, there is no hard evidence to support this.) The reality was that, through his failure to take any precautions, Dohse had acted unforgivably rashly and now bore the main responsibility for the unnecessary death of Chazeau, a valued collaborator, and for risking the lives of Kunesch and the others.

For Dohse's rivals in KdS Bordeaux the Lencouacq episode was confirmation of their view that he was 'half-French' and 'too soft'. Now he also gained a reputation amongst his superiors in Bordeaux and in Paris as an impetuous adventurer who was not to be trusted.

Dohse, however, true to form, simply ignored the criticisms and, instead of retreating to lick his wounds, set his sights even higher. In anyone else such an appetite for pushing the boundaries, both with the French and with his superiors, could have been viewed as some kind of death wish. But in Dohse it was just the product of his addiction to thinking outside the box and taking risks.

20

OF MISSIONS AND MACHINATIONS

The Lencouacq debacle convinced Dohse that using André Grandclément to create a network of *Maquis officiels* under indirect German control would not work. He would have to find other ways to extend his 'deal' to a wider stage.

Even before Lencouacq, Dohse had intended to bring other influential Resistance leaders, well beyond the likes of Grandclément, into his circle. He had his sights set especially on one man: Louis Joubert.

Joubert was a history teacher at Bordeaux's prestigious Lycée Michel Montaigne, a leader of the Protestant community in southwest France, a disciple of non-violence, a respected left-wing thinker on social matters and a resistant of the first hour. He was active in the OCM, had worked with de Baissac and been one of the group who had met in early October to condemn Grandclément to death for his treachery (though Joubert himself had voted against the death sentence).

Privately Dohse claimed to have considerable respect for Joubert. 'He was one of the outstanding examples of Bordeaux Protestantism,' Dohse reflected. 'When it came to the principles for which he struggled, he was utterly immovable and could not be shaken by either flattery or torture … non-violent but without the inflexibility of an idealist, he chose to fight his war without the use of arms.'

It was precisely these attributes and especially the fact that Joubert was so respected that made him such a desirable acquisition. Dohse's approach to Joubert was long, patient and cunning.

He first tried to ensnare him indirectly through Charles Corbin, using threat sugar-coated with self-interest. Corbin met Joubert and passed on a 'friendly warning' to him that had come from Grandclément (at the instigation of Dohse) that the Gestapo knew all about his pro-Resistance activities and that it might be helpful if Joubert and Grandclément could meet over lunch to discuss the situation. Joubert was understandably suspicious and reluctant. He asked the local Bordeaux Resistance command for guidance. They agreed that the lunch should go ahead.

Over the meal Grandclément tried to recruit Joubert to his 'deal' with Dohse. When Joubert rejected this out of hand, Grandclément moved on to what was probably the main purpose of the meeting: would Joubert himself be prepared to meet Dohse? Joubert did not reject the idea, but said (as he nearly always did, for he was a cautious man) that he would seek advice and get back to him.

A week later, Grandclément was given an emphatic answer: 'Impossible,' Joubert insisted. 'There is only one word for your actions – treason. Anyone who touches you is immediately suspect and is to be shunned,' adding bitterly 'and that now, it appears, includes me.'

Joubert's rejection was not, however, as definitive as it sounded. Informally, the dialogue between the two old friends, quietly continued. Dohse knew that Joubert's courtship couldn't be hurried and was happy to wait. He had other irons in the fire.

During October 1943, Dohse sent Grandclément to Paris to make contact with senior Resistance leaders in the capital and try to persuade them to meet with the Bordeaux Gestapo chief. Grandclément returned after a few days with several suggestions. The most interesting of these was a man well known to the Gestapo in Paris and to Dohse as well. His alias in Resistance circles was 'Père Lefèvre', but his real name was the Reverend Father Michel Riquet SJ. The forty-five-year-old Jesuit priest was highly influential in Catholic circles, a close personal friend of the Jesuit-educated Grandclément, and had been active in the Resistance from the very start.

In late October a message from Riquet was passed to Dohse through Grandclément. The Reverend Father was prepared to meet the Gestapo officer. But only if this was arranged through Grandclément and if Dohse came to the meeting alone, blindfolded, unarmed and in a car provided by the Resistance. Dohse agreed, no doubt relishing once again the element of cloak-and-dagger involved. Significantly, he did not inform his superiors what he was about to do.

In the early evening of 4 November 1943, just three days after his brush with death at Lencouacq, Dohse allowed himself to be taken, blindfolded, in the back of a car driven by Grandclément, with Lucette (who had joined her husband in Paris for the meeting) in the front passenger seat. They drove through the darkened streets of the city, pulling up outside an apartment in the Rue de Bourgogne, close to the French Assemblée Nationale. Here, Dohse, still blindfolded, was led upstairs to an apartment where he met Father Riquet and one of the priest's German-speaking academic friends. The meeting lasted three or four hours and covered many topics, including the position of the Jews, the Resistance in France, the state of the war and, of course, Dohse's 'deal' with Grandclément: 'He told me,' Riquet said later, 'that he wished to make the war more humane and had, at Grandclément's request, freed many prisoners. He added that he had no wish to fight the French people, only the communists … to this end he had made an agreement with Grandclément and his Resistance friends which he hoped would be comprehensive – even chivalrous – and would enable Grandclément's young men to [have the food and shelter they needed] to survive [the coming winter].'

Dohse's version of the meeting goes somewhat further: '[He] assured me of his moral support for Grandclément on the question of the exchange of [our] prisoners for [their] arms, saying to me: "You have acted like a good Christian."'

Either way, this was a major win for Dohse. While reaching out to a key Protestant figure (Joubert) he could now also claim to have, at the very least, the tacit moral acquiescence of one of the most influential figures in the French Catholic Church too. Even allowing for the fact that in the Gestapo, as in much of the German hierarchy, who you knew was more important than your rank, this was an extraordinary achievement for someone who still only held the rank of *Oberscharführer* (equivalent in the British army to a company sergeant major).

Friedrich Dohse's sense of self-satisfaction might have been some-what less had he known that André Grandclément was also using Riquet to play a double game, whose purpose he would definitely not have approved of. At the same time that Grandclément was persuading Riquet to meet Dohse, he was also pressuring the priest to help him rebuild his relationship with London by writing a long personal apologia for Grandclément's actions to date.

The insurance agent was secretly reinsuring himself with the other side.

The Reverend Father's intercession with London on behalf of his errant 'brother' (it would eventually be hand-delivered to Baker Street by Marcel Défence) is dated the very day of his meeting with Dohse and includes the following paragraph, which attempts to exculpate his friend for cooperating with the Germans: 'Grandclément believed that, since he was a prisoner and since his organisation was, to all intents and purposes, condemned to perish, his duty was to save what could be saved and that, in doing so, [he had no option] but to betray the cause he had meant to serve – that of a strong France … It is Grandclément's intention to take no part in fresh activities.'

The promise contained in the last sentence was, of course, one which Grandclément had neither the power, nor the nature, to fulfil.

Back in Bordeaux, Dohse turned his attention once more to Louis Joubert, who, following a number of meetings with Grandclément, local Resistance leaders and the national OCM leadership in Paris, finally agreed to meet with him.

Dohse and Joubert met face to face on the afternoon of 22 November 1943. The event took place not in Bouscat, but in the more agreeable surroundings of Dohse's villa on the Route du Médoc. Grandclément was there as well, but Joubert coolly ignored him. A return meeting followed at Joubert's house, this time without Grandclément.

Dohse's patient combination of manipulation, charm and persuasion paid off when Joubert was finally inveigled into the Gestapo headquarters in Bouscat to meet with Dohse and his chief, Machule. Also present were Claire Keimer, one of Dohse's other senior colleagues and, once more in the background, Grandclément, who remained silent throughout. Over these three meetings a two-clause proposition was drawn up: the French Resistance in the Bordeaux region would cease all attacks on non-combatant Germans (such as hospital staff and trains carrying soldiers on leave). In return, the German authorities would undertake to cease all activities against French non-combatants (in particular, women and young men) and end the practice of taking civilian hostages.

Dohse initially wanted this arrangement to be applicable to all Resistance elements, except the communists. But Joubert insisted that the agreement and its accompanying ceasefire could be successful only if it was accepted first by the leadership of the OCM in Paris. In the end, Joubert's view prevailed; the proposition would be taken by Joubert to his OCM superiors in the French capital for their approval. Simultaneously, Dohse and Machule would also travel to Paris to seek the sanction of the Gestapo chief and Himmler's representative in France, Helmut Knochen. While these parallel consultations were in progress, a temporary ceasefire would exist between the German military and the Resistance in the southwest.

Dohse's carefully choreographed minuet was now drawing to its close. Towards the end of November, Joubert, Dohse and Machule travelled on the same train, but in separate carriages, to Paris to liaise with their respective superiors.

Joubert's meeting with the OCM leadership was inconclusive but encouraging. They listened to the German proposal, but decided that the matter was beyond their competence and had to be put to de Gaulle, in Algiers. The mood, however, was positive. At the very least, they argued, the 'ceasefire' proposed by the Germans would give the Resistance in Bordeaux time to regroup and rebuild during what otherwise would be a very tough winter, under constant German pressure. Moreover – and joining the now growing queue of those tempted to believe they could 'play' Dohse – they hoped to string the Bordeaux Gestapo chief along and in the process gain some intelligence of his true intentions. In a letter written after the war, Joubert described the attitude of his seniors in

Paris: 'You people [in Bordeaux] are bust. Accept [Dohse's] proposition. Play with him for as long as you can. While he is occupied, you will have the space to rebuild the organisation and save the movement.'

Not far away, while Joubert's meeting was in progress, Machule and Dohse were at the Gestapo headquarters in Avenue Foch, where they were briefing Helmut Knochen.

Knochen too was cautious, but finally agreed, remarking, according to Dohse, 'that the protocol implicitly recognised de Gaulle's government, which he very well knew could cause difficulty with the German Foreign Minister [Joachim von Ribbentrop, who was not to be informed]'. Knochen also made it explicitly clear that the agreement should be for the southwest region only and that, in the case of any difficulties, 'I [Dohse] was the person who would be solely responsible.'

After both meetings were over, Dohse met Joubert alone for lunch in the Hungaria restaurant in the Champs Élysées. It was getting cold now. The Arc de Triomphe, grey and brooding under a November mist, stood out gloomily above bare trees and glistening pavements, almost deserted of people. The Hungaria, famous before the war for its wild Tzigane music and Gypsy singers, was full. The menu tried, for old time's sake, to suggest that even wartime food could be made to have a Magyar flavour, while in a corner a small sad orchestra did its best to play Gypsy-free Hungarian music, providing useful cover for private conversation. Over lunch, Dohse reported – no doubt with a touch of triumph – that Knochen had given him the go-ahead. Joubert said that his bosses had been more cautious; while interested in the proposal, they had concluded that the issue could only be decided by de Gaulle in Algiers.

'Then you'll have to go to North Africa,' Dohse, seeing the opening, darted. 'Are you ready to do that?' Joubert nodded.

It was, by any measure, an extraordinary moment. Thanks to Dohse's patient play he had, in effect, persuaded the French to send one of their most respected Resistance leaders to see the head of their government-in-exile, carrying a Gestapo proposition for a ceasefire which would make it safer and easier for German troops to occupy southwest France.

There was, however, one more hurdle to cross: Berlin. Over the next few days Knochen reported the proposal to the high command in the German capital and sought their permission to proceed. Berlin said no. But Dohse had gone too far now and unilaterally decided to press ahead anyway. Bömelburg was shocked when he heard: 'You are going far, far outside the limits now,' he warned Dohse. 'If you get yourself into trouble, I won't be able to help you.'

In fact, the issue of Bömelburg's ability to provide top-level cover for Dohse, even if he had wanted to, soon became an academic one. In the spring of 1944 Dohse's protector was sent to Vichy as head of the Gestapo in the southern zone, apparently because of some corruption scandal involving Bömelburg's son. The new regime in Gestapo headquarters in Paris was now much more hard line and much less interested in the subtleties of counter-intelligence at which both Bömelburg and his young protégé in Bordeaux excelled. With his influence in Paris diminished and a new climate in Gestapo headquarters in the French capital, this was not a good time for Dohse to be taking risks. In his memoirs he muses at length that, if things went wrong, he knew he would end up on the Eastern front as an ordinary soldier – or perhaps even before a firing squad.

Maybe it was this nervousness that lay behind a curious cat-and-mouse conversation which took place not long after Dohse's lunch with Joubert in Paris.

In early December, Dohse was chatting with Jean-Philippe Larrose, the official French interpreter used by the Germans, who was also an academic at Bordeaux University and a close friend of Joubert. At the time, Larrose knew nothing of either the Paris talks or the plans Joubert and Dohse had concocted between them.

In a seemingly casual turn of the conversation, Dohse said to Larrose: 'What do you think of Joubert?'

'In what context?' Larrose asked, cautiously.

'He's a big man in the Resistance – isn't he?' Dohse said, as though it was a genuine question.

'I wouldn't know.'

'I can show you the proof if you like – I have everything I need to arrest him,' he said, knowing very well that Joubert would soon hear of the implied threat.

'You wouldn't do that,' Larrose responded, followed by a short pause. 'He's a great Professor you know ...'

'Of course I know that. But what do you think of him as a man?' Dohse insisted.

'He's a very fine man, a superb teacher, and a good Protestant ... you are wrong to think he hates the Germans. What his Christian philosophy finds repugnant is National Socialism, not the Germans.'

Dohse poured them both a large brandy, pulled a document from a locked cupboard as a conjurer might a rabbit from a hat, and continued: 'Read this and breathe not a word about it ... it is highly confidential. You must tell no one that you have seen it, especially your friend Helmut Knochen [Larrose had studied with Knochen at university in Germany before the war]. When you have read it you will realise that there are Germans who are thinking in very imaginative ways.'

Larrose read the document with growing astonishment: it was, in outline, the plan which Joubert had agreed to take to de Gaulle in Algiers. Larrose was especially struck by the fact that Dohse's proposition amounted to a tacit German acknowledgement that de Gaulle, and not Pétain, was the French leader.

'Your friend Joubert is a very important man,' Dohse purred, 'with huge influence and contacts in the higher circles of the Resistance – and of course amongst Protestants in the southwest ...' Here Dohse trailed off. He didn't need to say more. He had laid his bait and knew what would happen next.

And it did. That evening Larrose met Joubert at the faculty of letters at Bordeaux University and told him of Dohse's document. Joubert confirmed that he had indeed – with the agreement of the OCM Paris – been involved in an extended and secret dialogue with Dohse.

Dohse now began to put the finishing touches to Joubert's trip to Algiers. He was especially concerned that a proposition for a ceasefire coming from Joubert, an academic well known for his non-violent principles, would carry little weight in the military circles that dominated General de Gaulle's government-in-exile. It did not take him long to come up with a solution.

Around this time he learnt that the OCM leaders in Paris had ordered a senior Resistance commander with a respected army background, Colonel André Thinières, to leave France for Algiers immediately in order to avoid arrest. Thinières's wife had been arrested in October, after her husband had been sentenced to death in his absence by a German tribunal. Dohse also knew that Thinières had tried in vain to flee for Spain three times and was currently in hiding south of Bordeaux, waiting for a fourth opportunity. Without telling either Machule or his superiors in Paris, Dohse sent a message to Thinières offering the release of his wife from prison and a safe passage to Spain, if he would accompany Joubert on his mission. Thinières agreed and, coming out of hiding, travelled to Bordeaux, where he was reunited with his wife – whose release Dohse had arranged 'in order to illustrate my humanity'. The couple moved into the Joubert house in Bordeaux, where they spent the ten days prior to the departure for Algiers.

Dohse was, as ever, very proud of his work. 'Being a respected soldier,' he recalled, 'I knew he [Thinières] would add huge weight to [Joubert and] the proposition we were making, whilst at the same time providing concrete proof of my sincerity in making it.'

It is worth pointing out at this point that Friedrich Dohse did not for a moment believe that the 'mission to Algiers' would actually produce an agreement with de Gaulle. Nor, for all his talk, was this about 'humanising the war'. Dohse's task was to keep German troops and assets free from Resistance attack, and the ceasefire did just that, while at the same time preventing Resistance forces from regrouping after the grievous blows they had suffered as a result of Dohse's successes over the last few months. 'Our chief aim was to prevent the Resistance getting back on its feet,' Dohse explained.

Dohse's scheme also had a second, deeper purpose: to spread the infection of suspicion and instability from southwest France into the heart of de Gaulle's government in Algiers. German intelligence was well aware of the often fiery tensions which had been flaring up between de Gaulle on the one hand and Roosevelt and Churchill on the other – especially over Roosevelt's refusal to recognise de Gaulle's government-in-exile. By proposing an alternative 'deal' with the Germans which implicitly recognised de Gaulle, at a time when Roosevelt explicitly refused to do so, Dohse's 'play' with Joubert and Thinières had the useful by-product of insinuating even more poison into the already fraught relations between de Gaulle and his Anglo-Saxon allies.

For Louis Joubert, the Protestant peacemaker and dedicated man of non-violence, his mission was serious and sincerely undertaken; for French Resistance leaders it was an opportunity, they thought, to relieve intolerable German pressure in the southwest at a critical time; for Thinières it was a means to rescue his wife and get safely away from France. For Dohse it was just another play – a miniature version of the First World War German intelligence coup in which Lenin was smuggled into Russia in a sealed train to foment the revolution.

Roger Landes, meanwhile, also had his eyes on Spain during these late October, early November weeks of 1943. Soon he would have to make his way back to London. But first, as he had told London, he needed to 'put his networks to sleep', so that his men wouldn't think he was abandoning them.

This was an unusual thing for a 'blown' SOE agent hotly pursued by the Gestapo to do. Ordered home by Baker Street, he could (perhaps even should) have left immediately. With the invasion still six months away, his resistants could simply have melted back into their communities or taken refuge in the forests, ready to come out again when the moment was right. But Landes, like Grandclément, felt a genuine sense of responsibility for his men and for the maintenance of his organisation as an effective force which he could return to command in the future.

In mid-October, with many of his other identities 'burnt', Charles Corbin managed to obtain from police sources a new set of documents for Landes in the name of 'Roger Lalande'. Even so, with the Gestapo hot on his trail and checkpoints to pass on a daily basis, Landes was at almost constant risk, travelling around the region either by train or motorbike in order to visit each of his units. Most of his rendezvous during this period took place at night, which was safer, but meant breaking the curfew. It was also difficult to find places to meet his group leaders. Houses, though they had to be used from time to time, were always dangerous, so many of his meetings were held in the open countryside. As before in difficult times, he slept in a different location every night. 'We were at the end of our tether,' he wrote, 'and thought it just a matter of time before Corbin and I were arrested.'

With Corbin now in as much danger as himself, Landes requested that the two men be returned together. London agreed and planned to send a Lysander for them both. But bad weather prevented this. There was now no option. Landes and Corbin would have to do it the hard way – over the Pyrenees. (Landes was secretly pleased: he hated the fragile little Lysanders – too many of them got shot down.)

On 29 October, Landes signalled London: 'HAVE TRIED TO SAVE WHAT I CAN OF MY ORGANISATION STOP WILL RETURN TO LONDON THROUGH SPAIN WITH CORBIN STOP WARN MILITARY ATTACHÉ [MADRID] TO EXPECT US THROUGH PAMPLONA ENDS. [STANISLAS]'

London replied by return: 'WHEN IN SPAIN YOUR NEW COVER IDENTITY WILL BE WILLIAM CURTIS, CANADIAN COMMANDO ESCAPED FROM A GERMAN POW CAMP STOP BRITISH MILITARY ATTACHÉ'S CAR WILL MEET YOU AT 2000 ON 3 NOVEMBER, REPEAT 3 NOVEMBER, IN ARIZCUN, WHERE PAMPLONA RAILWAY CROSSES IRAQUIL RIVER STOP GOOD LUCK ENDS.'

In a subsequent signal, Baker Street added that Corbin's cover identity in Spain would be 'Peter Andrews', also an 'escaped Canadian Commando'.

London's hope was that, by posing as escaped Allied POWs, the two men could avoid the Spanish law that required all escaping French citizens to spend a long period of incarceration in the infamous Francoist internment camp of Miranda de Ebro before being released.

On 9 November, London sent a signal to Landes congratulating him on being awarded the Military Cross, though it is doubtful that this would have seemed of imperial significance to him at the time, in the midst of his other burdens and dangers.

Landes still had one more loose end to tie up: Marcel Défence.

Some weeks previously Défence had left Bordeaux intending to cross the Pyrenees but had become stranded in France. On 18 November, Charles Corbin eventually found him in the city of Pau, 170 kilometres south of Bordeaux. He was in a terrible state. Exhausted, ill and depressed, he attempted to cross the frontier but was forced to turn back by bad weather and treacherous guides. Landes had hoped to take his old radio colleague back with him to London, but now had to conclude that Défence was too weak and unwell to attempt the Pyrenees again. He would have to be left behind to recuperate.

Two days later, on 20 November, Roger Landes had a meeting with de Gaulle's newly arrived military delegate for the southwest region, Claude Bonnier, to brief him on the contingencies he had put in place and to report that he was leaving for London in the very near future. On that same day Corbin resigned from the Bordeaux police force on 'health grounds'. Dohse, finally exasperated, responded to Corbin's prevarication with an ultimatum: give up Landes in the next twenty-four hours, or be arrested.

Landes and Corbin could delay no longer. It was time to go.

On 22 November, 'Stanislas' signalled London telling them that he would now be crossing the Pyrenees with Corbin between 30 November and 3 December, and asking for a British embassy car to meet him at the railway station in the little Basque border town of Elizondo. It was the last signal sent by the Scientist network. Since arriving in France a year previously, Landes, despite constant German surveillance and being hunted by the Gestapo at every turn, had sent a total of 321 signals to London and received 221.

His last duty done, Landes burnt his radio codes and crystals in the cellar of the Faget house and caught the train with Charles Corbin and Marguerite Faget to the village of Parentis on the shores of Lake Biscarrosse, south of Arcachon. Here, in the substantial surroundings of the Hôtel du Lac, lying midway between the railway station and Parentis church, he said his goodbyes to Mitou Faget and a few of his most loyal men. He gave each of his group leaders 25,000 francs to tide them over until he returned, and instructed them to listen to the BBC each night. When they heard the phrase '*Roger reviendra manger des cèpes*' ('Roger will return to eat Boletus mushrooms'), they would know he was coming back.

CROSSING THE FRONTIER

No wartime clandestine crossing of the Pyrenees was ever easy. Success depended on luck, good guides and considerable endurance.

Landes and Corbin were fortunate compared with some. Nineteen forty-three ended with a spell of unusually mild weather, which meant more wind and rain, but no snow. Secondly, the point at which they were to cross was at the lower western end of the Pyrenees, where the great ridge finally dips through the Basque country into the Bay of Biscay. The highest point of the Pyrenean range is the Pico d'Aneto at 3,404 metres. The Izpegui pass, through which the two escapees would have to thread their way, was only 690 metres.

The height they had to climb may not have been great, but the terrain here is inhospitable and tough. At this point the Pyrenees rise like a great wave which swells up from Spain, breaks at the crest and crashes down a steep escarpment, rugged, rock-strewn and rough-grassed, into France. For two men used to the comforts of city life, this was not going to be an easy passage, particularly since, being in relatively populated country-side, the main crossing would have to be made at night.

Landes and Corbin stayed for two days in the area of Lake Biscarrosse before being driven south along the Route des Lacs, a little country road which skips from lake to lake just behind the long ribbon of beach and sand dunes that marks the southern end of the Aquitaine coast. On the night of 24 November they reached the home of Fernande and André Bouillar in Tarnos, five kilometres north of the ancient Basque port of Bayonne. It was the first time that Landes had met André Bouillar – known locally as 'Dédé le Basque' – and he was impressed by the twenty-six-year-old police inspector-cum-Resistance leader. 'He immediately inspired my confidence,' Landes said later. Bouillar was a much-respected figure of courage and resourcefulness who ran a number of escape routes over the Pyrenees. His original intention had been to deliver Landes and Corbin directly to Michael Cresswell's MI9 escape route, which had an undercover existence in the British consulate in San Sebastián. He probably planned to use a local fisherman who specialised (for a price) in taking escapees off the Aquitaine beaches at night, landing them on the Spanish side of the border. But sometime before their arrival, Bouillar received intelligence warning him not to use this route, but to cross by the Izpegui pass and deliver the two men to the station at Elizondo instead.

Landes, Corbin and Bouillar met their guides in a safe house between Biarritz and St Jean de Luz, finding to their surprise that three other escapees had been added to their party: a Catholic priest, a young woman and an eighteen-year-old 'deserter'. They stayed in the safe house until, on 26 November, they were driven in an 'ambulance' and dropped off just outside the little frontier town of St Étienne-de-Baïgorry. Here they began their ascent of the Pyrenean escarpment, which at this point marks the Franco-Spanish border.

The night was particularly dark and overcast and swept with curtains of heavy, cold rain. Landes's anorak, recently purchased on the black market, coped reasonably well with the deluges. But Corbin wore a flannel greatcoat, which soon became heavy and sodden. Both had real trouble with their soft city feet and tried to relieve their pain by frequently swapping shoes with Bouillar to ease their blisters. To add to their trials, they had to make a long detour from their intended route to avoid a German patrol. Crossing a bridge just before they started the climb, the guides (known as *passeurs*) suddenly stopped and refused to go further without more money. The escapees had no choice but to pay up.

The blackness of the night forced the group to snake along in crocodile, holding each other's clothes to keep in contact. It was normal practice amongst the *passeurs* to give their escapees white-painted espadrilles so as to be seen better on nights such as this. But, having their own stout walking shoes, Landes and Corbin had no need of these.

At night, and especially on such a night as this, hearing is a far more useful sense than sight. There were regular stops when all had to be totally silent, listening for hostile sounds in the darkness. This was just as well, for between the stops the guides pushed ahead at a strong pace, making little allowance for the Stygian darkness and the unfitness of their charges. Now, at last, they were on the final ascent to the crest. The going was rough and steep. It was hard, lung-bursting, muscle-aching work, but eventually they arrived at the narrow defile of the Izpegui pass.

Here they were met by a fierce wind blowing up from Navarre. Heads down now, as the incessant rain lashed their faces, they skirted along the crest above the pass in order to give a wide berth to the red-tiled, single-storey building which served as the frontier checkpoint, manned jointly by German police and Spanish guards. Its lights shone blearily, flickering through scudding clouds and the unrelenting downpour. Blundering across the steep hillside in single file through the darkness, the party loosed stones which tumbled down the hillside like little avalanches, causing a rattling that seemed loud enough to wake the dead.

Around six in the morning they were finally through, over the border and on their long descent into Navarre and Spain. As the first signs of dawn began to lighten a leaden sky, the *passeurs* stopped again, demanding yet more money if the group wanted a farmhouse for shelter. Again they paid up. After sixteen hours' solid walking they finally found refuge in a hay barn and a little comfort in a rough meal of milk, bread, sheep's cheese and dried meat.

Landes took Bouillar to one side and asked him if he would like to return to England with them. The Basque leader replied that his place was with his men. He would return to France with the guides. He told Landes and Corbin to get some sleep and press on the following day. He had been assured that the way was clear to Elizondo, fifteen kilometres away. Before parting, Landes gave Bouillar the BBC signal which would announce his safe arrival in England ('*Le beurre est cuit*' – 'The butter is done') and the phrase which would indicate his return to France ('*Roger reviendra manger des cèpes*'). He added that any messenger he sent to Bouillar after his return would say that he came 'on behalf of Stanislas' and show him a gold sovereign identical to the one Landes gave Bouillar before they parted. It was only after Bouillar left that Landes discovered he was still wearing his Basque friend's shoes – and would now have to wear them all the way back to London. If he made it.

The next morning the little group of fugitives woke to find that their rucksacks had been rifled and their valuables stolen while they slept. They didn't know whether the thieves were the rapacious *passeurs*, or their hard-pressed Spanish hosts trying to eke out a living from meagre ground which was difficult enough to live on even in peacetime. Fortunately, all of Landes's and Corbin's funds were in money belts safely secured around their bodies.

At three that afternoon, they set off through drizzle on the last leg to the small Basque town of Elizondo – neat, with its cream-fronted, ornate iron-balconied houses, magnificent church adorned with twin cupola-topped towers, and its wide square boasting a magnificent old traveller's inn. The town was, at the time, the terminus for a small single-tracked mountain railway which connected with Madrid, making Elizondo a destination of choice for those fleeing France.

That evening, as dusk was falling, the little party, bedraggled, footsore and weary, walked up the hill from the centre of Elizondo to the station. To their delight they saw the embassy car waiting for them, as planned, outside the station café. But to get to it they had to pass a Guardia Civil post in the station square. Here, several Spanish policemen lounged, smoking cigarettes. One of them stopped the travellers and asked, in Spanish, where they came from. The young deserter replied in French, accompanied by energetic hand gestures. They were swiftly arrested.

As they were led off, the British embassy car pulled quietly away and disappeared into the distance.

Under questioning, Landes and Corbin stuck to their cover story: they were French-Canadian commandos who had escaped from captivity. But the fact that Landes was carrying 32,620 French francs and Corbin 30,000 and six gold sovereigns in their money belts did not enhance their credibility. The five escapees were placed under guard in the attic of a local hotel that night and sent to Pamplona, the capital of

Navarre, the following morning. Before they left Elizondo, Landes managed to bribe a guard to slip a postcard into the town letterbox informing the British consulate in San Sebastián of their arrival and arrest, the details of which were also reported back to the Madrid embassy by the military attaché on his return from Elizondo.

Landes and Corbin were processed in Pamplona and then incarcerated in a single small room, where they spent almost two weeks 'under house arrest'. On 8 December, they were moved into a cramped cell in a military prison, which they shared with six other captured escapees of various nationalities and an uncertain regard for personal hygiene. The following day they were dispatched by train to the infamous internment camp of Miranda de Ebro.

While Landes and Corbin rattled across Spain to their new captivity, tied together with rope, Mary Herbert was giving birth to a baby girl in a nursing home in Bordeaux. She called her daughter Claudine, after her own *nom de guerre*.

On 20 December, three weeks after Landes and Corbin's arduous journey across the Spanish frontier, and thirty kilometres to the northwest, Friedrich Dohse, Louis Joubert and Colonel André Thinières also crossed into Spain, but by a far more congenial route.

At around eleven that day, Joubert and Thinières stepped down from the Bordeaux train at Hendaye, the French seaside resort and rail terminus on the Franco-Spanish border. Outside the station entrance, they found Dohse, Claire Keimer and Kunesch waiting for them in Dohse's black Cadillac. After the Germans were introduced to Thinières – who they had never met before – the party drove into the Basque hills and up to the picturesque hilltop town of Biriatou, where they lunched at the ancient wooden-beamed, flagstone-floored inn, the Auberge Hiribarren. Looking down from the dining room, they could see the turbulent white water of the Bidasoa river marking the frontier. Beyond, the hills of Spain, covered in oak woods and dotted with little farms and open pastures, rolled away into the distance under a cold December sky.

After lunch the group drove a little way down the hill to a quiet spot. Here Joubert and Thinières were taken out of Dohse's Cadillac and locked into the boot of a second Gestapo car, which was waiting for them. The convoy then snaked its way down the hill to the outskirts of Hendaye. Here they turned left and crossed a rickety bridge perched on concrete pylons which led over the Bidasoa river, to the checkpoints on the Spanish border.

This was a moment of high danger for Dohse, for though his superiors in Paris were aware of his plans to approach de Gaulle's government through Joubert, they knew nothing of his decision to send Colonel Thinières with him. The Bordeaux Gestapo chief was, in short, illegally smuggling two men – one of them a senior member of the French Resistance under sentence of death – out of France in the boot of a Gestapo car. 'At this moment I was taking a very great risk,' Dohse said later. 'If the Spanish customs men had arrested me that would have been it. No one in Paris knew what I was doing – not even [Machule in Bordeaux] … If anything had gone wrong it would have been straight to the Russian front for me.'

Normally, at this point, German officials without diplomatic papers, such as Dohse, would have been stopped and questioned – and, on occasion, even searched. But Dohse had previously arranged for a friend and colleague, who was the local German–Spanish liaison officer, to be engaged in deep conversation with the Spanish frontier guards as the illicit convoy approached. Distracted, the guards waved the cars through.

From Irun, Dohse led off along the back roads towards San Sebastián. Once in open countryside the two Frenchmen were released and transferred, in pouring rain, to the comfort of the Cadillac, where they joined Dohse in the back seat, chatting amiably with him for the rest of the journey. At San Sebastián, Joubert and Thinières were handed a couple of hundred pesetas – which Dohse insisted on exchanging for francs – and dropped at a café in the centre of the city. Here Dohse said his farewells, instructing his emissaries to send him a message ('*Louis et Charles sont bien arrivés*') through the BBC French service when they arrived in Algeria.

Suddenly out of occupied France and alone in a strange city, the two Frenchmen felt uncomfortable and exposed. 'In our heavy boots and rucksacks, we felt very out of place amongst all the fine buildings and décor,' Joubert noted in his diary. They caught a taxi to the British consulate, where, just as Dohse had predicted, they were welcomed as French fugitives by the MI9 escape organisation, who passed them on to the French section in the consulate, charged with getting escaped French citizens out of Spain. Joubert later complained that the resources of the French section were 'very limited and their contacts almost non-existent … too much bureaucracy and too little secrecy', adding in a tone of mild disapproval: 'they sent us in a taxi to a travellers' hostel [back] in Irun'.

Here they were told they would have to wait in the company of assorted other impecunious and desperate refugees of all nationalities, until further notice. After the heady drama of lunch with the Gestapo and a clandestine passage of the Franco-Spanish frontier in the boot of a Gestapo car, it was all rather an anticlimax.

What followed was a nervous and uncomfortable period full of bureaucratic problems, worrying rumours and inexplicable delays. Christmas came and went without movement or merriment, or prospect of anything different. Finally, on 27 December, Joubert and Thinières, now equipped with the necessary identity cards and travel documents, took the Southern Express for Madrid, where they reported to the French mission in the Spanish capital. The following day, at Malaga, they boarded a French ship which was waiting to take them to Casablanca. On board they were made a fuss of and invited to dine with the ship's officers. 'The talk was full of tales of the Resistance; the eyes were full of emotion; the conversation was full of politics, the Allies and the rivalries of French power … this is indeed the age of adventurers!' Joubert exuberated to his diary.

On New Year's Eve 1943, Joubert and Thinières landed at Casablanca.

The following day, as the two men were preparing for their journey to de Gaulle's headquarters in Algiers, Dohse got the news he had been waiting for. Reading the morning summary of the local German radio surveillance section, he saw, among the messages sent by BBC Algiers the previous night: '*Louis et Charles sont bien arrivés.*'

Roger Landes and Charles Corbin also had a New Year's present that day. They had their first hot baths since leaving France, more than a month previously.

Whatever the Christmas discomforts suffered by Thinières and Joubert at the travellers' hostel in Irun, they were nothing to what Landes and Corbin had to endure at Miranda de Ebro. Filthy, lice-ridden and riddled with corruption, Miranda was a byword for casual neglect by the Spanish authorities, disease and hopelessness for its inmates and violence perpetrated by criminals, desperadoes and the intelligence services of all the main wartime combatants. The camp had its own brothel, a casino run by some Chinese inmates, an active black market from which anything could be bought for the right money, 200 more prisoners than it could accommodate (or would feed), its own currency-exchange market, the foulest kitchen in Spain, untouchable food (except for the bread), very little running water, a sewage system 'which would have been inadequate for a cat's toilet', and a highly active spy ring made up of so-called 'German deserters'.

It took the British authorities in Madrid three weeks (which included Christmas) to get their two secret agents released from the camp. Finally, Landes and Corbin were allowed to travel on to the British embassy in Madrid, arriving in the early evening of 31 December 1943, the day after Joubert and Thinières had left the city.

The following morning, after completing administrative procedures, Corbin and Landes were moved into the Morar Hotel (it must have struck Landes as ironic to have escaped France, only to be put up in a hotel named after the Scottish loch at which he had done his SOE training!). The Morar was the British embassy's hotel of choice for those bound for London, and its delights, even under wartime constraints, were almost too much for the two escapees. '[The bath] was truly delicious, but the bed was so soft and the room so overheated that neither of us could catch a wink of sleep,' Landes complained after the war.

Over the next ten days, Landes and Corbin wrote lengthy debriefing reports, which they were required to leave behind in the embassy when, eventually, they left Madrid for the sixteen-hour journey to the British fortress island of Gibraltar.

Entering Gibraltar, Landes got into some difficulty with a British customs official because a magazine he was taking back to Baker Street, as an example of Nazi propaganda, was misconstrued as evidence that he was a smuggler of pro-German literature. It was not his only problem. For reasons he would not understand until later, an MI5 security officer at his first interrogation seemed highly suspicious of a gold watch he was wearing, which was taken away for examination.

Finally, on 16 January 1944, Corbin and Landes left Gibraltar by separate planes, arriving at RAF St Mawgan in Cornwall in the middle of a violent storm. From here, after more difficulties with a disbelieving immigration officer which had to be resolved by a call to Baker Street, the pair took a plane to Swindon, where they were met by Maurice Buckmaster and the SOE operations officer, Gerry Morel. They spent that night in Morel's Kensington flat before reporting to Orchard Court the following morning, to begin their proper debriefing.

That night, André Bouillar, listening to the *Messages personnels* on the BBC French Service, heard the words '*Le beurre est cuit*' – and knew that the two footsore friends he had helped over the Pyrenees that rainy night six weeks earlier had made it (along with the pair of shoes he had forgotten to retrieve before bidding them farewell).

Many of Landes's erstwhile colleagues in the Scientist network were not so lucky. Between July 1943, when the great unravelling began, and the end of that year, seventy-eight Scientist agents were arrested. Four of them were shot and the remainder deported to the concentration camps of Nazi Europe. Forty-seven never saw France, or their loved ones, again.

CYANIDE AND EXECUTION

By mid-October 1943, the Resistance of southwest France lay in tatters. The tidal wave of arrests towards the end of the summer, the emptying of arms dumps in September and the divisive effect of the *Maquis officiels* in October had left the organisation fractured, its units leaderless, and its individual members extremely wary of each other. Who would betray whom next? When would one of their leaders next turn up sitting alongside a Gestapo officer in the back seat of a Gestapo car? Where could they flee to?

The situation was made considerably worse by the fact that Resistance leaders seemed to come and go, almost on a weekly basis, and those sent in by Paris and London were either inappropriate, unpopular, or so badly briefed that they didn't seem to know what they were supposed to do – or worse, got involved in personality-fuelled turf wars with others who thought they themselves were doing the same thing. Between July and the end of 1943, no less that ten of the most senior leaders of the Resistance in the Bordeaux region had either fled, taken refuge, or been arrested. On 8 August, André Grandclément's replacement as regional OCM leader, Colonel Rollot, believing that he was 'blown', abruptly resigned and left for Algiers. He was briefly replaced by Colonel Thinières, who, sensing with some justification that the Germans were on to him, nominated the fifty-four-year-old Eugène Camplan as his successor. On 7 October, Camplan took over command of the main Resistance units in the southwest.

This should have solved the leadership problem. But Camplan was a man whose awkward personality made him less than universally popular.

Despite a prestigious First World War career as a fighter pilot, with seven kills to his name and a number of wounds which bore witness to his battles, Camplan was a man of implacably stoic disposition whom it was not easy to like – or, indeed, to look at. He had a slashing scar across his face and a wound in his leg, which made him limp with a markedly crooked gait. Austere and fiercely Protestant, he made few allowances for the feelings of others and none at all for his own discomforts, which he regarded not as badges of honour, but as personal tests of his ability to endure.

One of his chief problems was a complete inability to make up his mind on Grandclément.

In early September, just before Grandclément's arrest, Camplan had sworn to Marc O'Neill that he 'would bring [the 'traitor'] down'. Subsequently, Camplan had been among those who had condemned Grandclément to death on 24 September 1943. But, a month later, when Joubert asked Camplan if he should meet Grandclément to discuss opening talks with Dohse, Camplan had agreed. From this moment on, Eugène Camplan, for all his seeming intractability, shifted his position several times and, in the process, got slowly dragged into the outer orbit of Friedrich Dohse's plans, eventually supporting the Joubert mission to Algiers. On 4 November, at a meeting in Bordeaux called to discuss Grandclément's role in the Lencouaq incident, Camplan voted (unsuccessfully) to reprieve 'the traitor' from the death penalty which he had previously so strongly supported.

Camplan's ambivalent attitude to Grandclément created a deep and enduring split in the Bordeaux Resistance. One group pursued a policy which sought to accommodate Dohse's plans in an attempt to play him. Another, made up of 'hardliners', rejected Camplan's authority outright and remained implacably opposed to Grandclément, Joubert, Thinières, Dohse and all their works. These divisions soon began to spread throughout the entire structure of the regional Resistance, infecting it with a climate of suspicion and rivalry which would, over time, develop, into deadly enmity.

Politics was added to this already fractious and explosive mix when a young ex-aeronautical engineer was landed in France by Lysander on the night of 14/15 November 1943. Claude Bonnier was part of a nationwide network of senior officials parachuted in from London with the aim of giving de Gaulle control of the Resistance ahead of the coming invasion. As one of twelve 'military delegates', he was vested with 'unique authority over all the military forces in the region', on behalf of the French government-in-exile. He seems to have been blissfully unaware that the substance of the job he was being asked to do was, in fact, already being done by someone else: Eugène Camplan.

It is scarcely possible to imagine two personalities more different than the dour, unapproachable military professional Eugène Camplan and the bespectacled forty-six-year-old, brilliant, highly educated, sophisticated and well-connected Claude Bonnier. Like Camplan, Bonnier had had an impressive First War, rising through the ranks from an ordinary soldier to a lieutenant and Chevalier de la Légion d'Honneur, with a Croix de Guerre (and four bars) to his credit. But here the similarities ended. Between the wars, Bonnier had left the military and, graduating as a civil engineer, subsequently enjoyed a meteoric career in aeronautics. His closest Second World War colleague remembers him as 'very young-looking, with square-set shoulders, short-cut hair, kindly eyes and an intelligence which shone out behind his steel-rimmed glasses'. A friend of Jean Moulin, 'he was a natural leader whose ability to command derived from an impression which combined both physical and moral strength'.

Bonnier arrived in France equipped with de Gaulle's personal authority, an explosives expert and military instructor called Jacques Nancy, a self-destructing briefcase containing a lot of vital papers and almost nothing else. He had no wireless set, little information and even less idea of how he was to go about his job. Even the Bordeaux addresses he had been given as contacts for the local Resistance were out of date, having already been blown to the Gestapo.

After several attempts (one of them near-fatal when Bonnier called at Thinières's home to find it full of Germans), contact was finally made with Camplan and a meeting fixed between the two commanders for 20 November 1943.

It all went as badly as might have been expected. Camplan, who had heard rumours of the new arrival, but had received no official word of it from either Paris or London, demanded proof of Bonnier's authority. The newly arrived military delegate showed Camplan a letter signed by General de Gaulle himself. Bonnier then opened the substantive conversation by passing on the best wishes of Colonel Rollot, whom he had met in London – not knowing that Camplan hated Rollot with a passion, and vice versa. From then on it all went steadily downhill.

It was not just that the two men's personalities were different; their politics were too. Camplan was right-wing, a militarist and a supporter of General Giraud, de Gaulle's rival; Bonnier was an ardent socialist and an even more ardent Gaullist.

Their strategies were also mutually incompatible. Camplan was what was referred to at the time as an 'attentist' – that is, his policy was, as far as possible, to remain as invisible as possible for as long as possible. No attacks, no sabotage, no drawing attention to themselves. This, Camplan believed (along with the OCM and most other French military professionals), was the best way to improve the effectiveness of underground forces, while keeping them intact, so that they could emerge at maximum strength and effectiveness after the Allied invasion.

Bonnier on the other hand was an 'activist' – believing that attacking the Germans now, and with all means at his disposal, was the best way to draw more recruits to the cause. He wanted to start a wave of sabotage immediately.

Being in favour of waiting, Eugène Camplan was also in favour of the temporising 'truce' afforded by Joubert's mission to Algiers. This, for precisely the contrary reasons, Claude Bonnier strongly opposed, even going so far as to instruct Joubert to break off relations with Dohse – an order which Joubert seems simply to have ignored.

As for Grandclément, Camplan was, ultimately, prepared to tolerate him; whereas Bonnier insisted that he should immediately be killed as a traitor.

By the end of the meeting on 20 November, the only common ground between the two men was that each believed the other to be suspicious and probably tainted. Bonnier considered Camplan and his organisation unreliable at best and proto-collaborators at worst. Camplan thought Bonnier was probably a Gestapo agent provocateur. The one apparent act of fraternity between them occurred when Camplan lent his personal radio operator to the new arrival. But even this was not what it seemed, for as Camplan admitted later, he only lent his radio man to Bonnier, the better to keep an eye on him.

Things came to a head on 20 December (the day Joubert and Thinières were spirited over the Spanish frontier in the boot of Dohse's car), when Bonnier sent an exasperated telegram to London. This, according to one of Bonnier's closest lieutenants, demanded that London should send an urgent message to Camplan making it clear that Bonnier was in overall charge of the co-ordination of the Resistance throughout the region and instructing Camplan to break off relations with Grandclément immediately, 'failing which' Bonnier concluded, 'the only way to deal with the issue would be to kill him'.

On Christmas Day 1943, Jacques Nancy met with two of Camplan's men in a café in Bordeaux to ask them to join him in a sabotage attack ordered by London on a local rubber factory. Camplan refused to allow his young men to participate on the grounds that the 'truce' agreed with the Germans while the Joubert mission was underway was still in place. Nancy and Bonnier regarded this as nothing short of treason.

Early in the new year, after a brief passage of bitterly cold weather over Christmas, wet winds blew in over the Gironde, bringing with them drizzle and scudding low clouds which lit halos around evening street lamps and laid a thin film of moisture on the white limestone frontages of the Quai des Chartrons. As if to match the weather, a final stormy meeting took place between Bonnier and Camplan. This, according to some witnesses, ended with death threats being traded on both sides.

Things may, however, not have been quite as bad as they appeared on the surface. Shortly after the meeting, Camplan, perhaps at last prepared to accept Bonnier's command, sent a message to Algiers asking Resistance headquarters in the North African capital to confirm that the interloper was who he said he was. If he was, then Algiers should send Camplan a coded confirmation message ('*Chez Dupont, tout est bon*') and he would behave accordingly.

Camplan and his men waited nervously for the answer over several days, but none came. The delay was caused by yet another administrative mix-up between London and Algiers: the message which Camplan sent to Algiers identified Bonnier by his alias 'Bordin'. But since London had omitted to inform the French government-in-exile that this was Bonnier's alias, no one in Algiers had any idea who Camplan was referring to. The mystery was finally solved, and, on 19 January, a message was sent to Camplan confirming, '*Chez Dupont, tout est bon*'.

But it was too late.

On 18 January, having met his sister for lunch in Bordeaux, Camplan caught the evening train to Paris. At Angoulême, two men, probably Bonnier supporters, boarded the train and removed Camplan. He was driven under armed guard to a remote farm near Ruffec, northeast of Bordeaux. The following morning he was taken to an isolated wood, where a Colt .45 automatic was placed against his temple and he was executed.

The corpse of Eugène Émile Camplan, the First World War air ace whose scarred body and misshapen personality bore equal witness to the trials he had faced on behalf of his country, was stripped naked to obstruct identification and left lying among the damp, blood-soaked leaves where he fell.

On 20 January, Claude Bonnier sent a telegram to London reporting: 'Camplan has been "disappeared" by order of the Central Committee ... this is a great comfort to me.' That same day, following several signals from both the French and the British in London to break off all contact with Grandclément, de Gaulle's military chief in France sent a message to London confirming that he had ordered one of his agents to execute the 'traitor'.

Of these events and characters, Friedrich Dohse, all-seeing and all-manipulating at the centre of his web of informants and collaborators, knew everything. He also knew that the defining and dividing issues which Resistance leaders had to decide on were the incubi he had planted in their midst: the Grandclément 'deal' and the Joubert mission to Algiers.

Dohse, who hoped to turn Camplan through Grandclément, heard the news of his disappearance and suspected the worst. He cannot have been displeased, however. With the Resistance now doing his job for him, he could switch his full attention to catching Claude Bonnier.

These early weeks of 1944 should have been good ones for Friedrich Dohse. His promotion to *Untersturmführer* (the German equivalent of second lieutenant) at the turn of the year meant he now had full officer status in KdS Bordeaux. At regional level his strategy seemed to be working admirably, as the poison which he had filtered into the Resistance in the southwest began working its way through its structures with deadly effect.

But if inside France things were going well for Dohse, outside they were about to go seriously awry.

Joubert and Thinières finally got a meeting with de Gaulle on the morning of 8 January. 'He is intelligent, decisive, fully knowledgeable of all the difficulties, lively of spirit, able swiftly to find solutions and fully confident that France will rise above her present difficulties, both now and in the future. He is a great man,' enthused Joubert to his diary. The general was also – though Joubert entirely failed to spot it in the hour-and-a-half meeting – fully, decisively and in a lively manner, totally opposed to what Joubert was suggesting. Perhaps Thinières had seen the signs that Joubert missed, for that evening he went down with a bout of 'flu', which prevented him saying another word for several days.

The axe fell definitively four days later when, on 12 January 1944, the two men ('who were causing too much interest in Algiers' according to de Gaulle's most trusted lieutenant, Jacques Soustelle) were invited to fly to Laghouat, an isolated French air station 300 kilometres into the desert south of Algiers. Here Joubert and Thinières found they had been placed in what was effectively 'indefinite protective detention'.

Dohse heard of the failure of the Joubert mission in early February, first through a German spy ring in Algiers and then through

Grandclément. The effect on Dohse's position was immediate and potentially extremely serious: 'I was ordered by my commander in Paris to abandon my plans immediately … they were regarded as compromised and too "soft". There was talk of me being recalled to Paris … It was probably only the fact that they could not find anyone who could do my job as well as I could, that stopped me being sent to the Russian front.'

This time the order to be tougher came right from the very top. Hitler had himself decreed that all negotiation with the Resistance should cease forthwith and be replaced by a policy of uncompromising repression.

Shortly after the failure of the Joubert mission, Dohse was sent home on leave to his wife and two daughters in Elmshorn. Nine months later his third child, Heine, was born. The official reason for his absence was 'urgent family reasons', but it is difficult not to suspect that his chief, Machule, was getting him out of the way until the dust settled.

Returning to Bordeaux at the end of his leave, Dohse discovered that, in his absence, and despite his past successes and recent promotion to officer rank, he had been sidelined within the KdS. All operations were now closely scrutinised by Machule and invariably commanded by Kunesch. Dohse found himself restricted to the gathering and exploitation of intelligence only. Despite this he managed to remain influential in KdS decisions, not least through 'the Lioness of the Gestapo', Marcelle Sommer, whom he had originally appointed to manage his French agent network, but who was now running most of KdS's network of secret agents. Nevertheless, Dohse felt the blow of his reduced status keenly. 'He became more withdrawn into himself,' noted Sommer.

As so often in the past, Dohse was saved from a more substantial demotion, and a train ticket to the Eastern front, when luck once again played her hand in his favour.

On 14 January, a German customs inspector conducting a spot-check at Arcachon station found a number of typed documents of a clearly military nature on a young man who was en route to Bordeaux. A deeper search revealed a hoard of cigarette papers hidden in the prisoner's hat band on which were written coded notes and secret diagrams. The man, François Lespine, was one of those who had been prohibited by Camplan from joining Jacques Nancy's sabotage party before Christmas. He had been in Arcachon on a spying mission for Yves Toussaint, Camplan's deputy and head of intelligence.

Like Christian Fossard before him, twenty-three-year-old Lespine was a junior member of the Resistance with a lot more information than he should have had. Interrogated by Kunesch, he almost immediately, and without duress, agreed to cooperate, giving the names and addresses of nearly all his colleagues. Soon, like many converts, Lespine would become a most enthusiastic, energetic and ruthless anti-Resistance fighter for the Germans. For the moment, however, Dohse released him with a small but deadly task to accomplish: deliver Toussaint and his senior Resistance colleague, Pierre Grolleau.

On 8 February, Grolleau was duly arrested coming out of a café in Bordeaux and taken to Bouscat, where he found Toussaint, his own brother and several of his other colleagues – including the wireless operator lent to Bonnier by Camplan – already in the cells. During his interrogation of the radio operator, Kunesch suggested that his boss, Bonnier, had made Camplan 'disappear'. The prisoner denied this, but revealed that a senior (unnamed) Resistance leader would be coming to his house for a meeting the following morning. Shortly after breakfast the next day, Claude Bonnier arrived at his radio man's home and was swiftly arrested and taken to Bouscat.

Kunesch interviewed Bonnier first, but got nowhere and handed him on to Dohse – who did no better. The Frenchman would say nothing beyond 'I am a French officer …'

After ten or fifteen minutes Dohse called a halt and ordered that Bonnier be manacled and taken to his cell to think things over. Dohse then went to lunch: 'Ten or so minutes after I had arrived in our canteen, one of the cell guards rushed in and, in an excited state, reported that he had heard strange noises coming from Bonnier's cell. I dashed down to find that the man in charge had already opened the cell door. Bonnier was lying on the floor. He was dead and his mouth was covered in foam which smelled of potassium cyanide.'

Brave, brilliant, committed, loyal, Claude Bonnier, father of two young daughters, had committed suicide by swallowing his cyanide pill rather than falling into the hands of his enemy and risking the information he carried. Dohse agreed to a request from his French colleagues that a small ceremonial guard be mounted on Bonnier's body in the cell and, the following morning, led the gathering of flowers from Bouscat's gardens to be placed around it. It was typical Dohse, the showman and romantic, who knew that when it comes to establishing a reputation, a small gesture is often as important as a heavyweight action.

Two days later one of Bonnier's close lieutenants was arrested in a bar and followed the example of his commander by swallowing his cyanide tablet before he could be questioned.

Sadly, the terrible sacrifice made by the two men was wasted. Bonnier's briefcase, a special SOE production designed to explode if opened by an unauthorised person, didn't. Instead it yielded 4.5 million francs and a veritable cornucopia of documents, including operational orders, details of parachute sites and lists of Bonnier's networks. These the Germans were now able to exploit – and spend – at will.

To make matters worse, Toussaint, Grolleau and one of their senior Resistance colleagues now embarked on a full-scale collaboration with the Germans, which culminated in a six-page exposé, signed by all three men on 20 March 1944. This gave comprehensive details of all Camplan's units, including their strengths, locations and the names of their leaders, complete with addresses. The document ended: 'Following meetings [between ourselves] and Grandclément, which have been kindly accorded to us by Monsieur Dohse, we ask that we should be able, as soon as possible, to become active again under the orders of André Grandclément in order to restore France to its legitimate place. It is only with Grandclément that we can now take our place in the struggle against Judeo-Bolshevism ...'

It was to be the last time that Dohse would be able to use Grandclément's name as an instrument to encourage compliance. In January 1944 a BBC broadcast had named André Grandclément as a traitor and warned against any contact with him. Grandclément was now effectively a pariah to all except his most loyal followers.

As Grandclément's usefulness diminished, the problem of keeping him safe increased. With Dohse's encouragement, Grandclément spent most of the period from January to March 1944 in Paris, returning to Bordeaux only once every week or so. Sometime in February, however, Grandclément declared his intention to move back to Bordeaux permanently. Dohse, alarmed for his safety, suggested that Grandclément should instead take up a job in Germany, and undertook to arrange this. But the Frenchman once again refused. Eventually it was agreed that Grandclément should join Lucette at her mother's house in Pompignac. André Grandclément, once the Gestapo's most important agent in Bordeaux and the indispensable instrument of all of Dohse's successes, was now effectively abandoned to his own devices, with the single proviso that he should always keep Dohse informed of his whereabouts.

For Dohse the game now moved on to the exploitation of his successes. He estimated that, with the contents of Bonnier's briefcase and the treasons of Toussaint and his two colleagues, he now had the names of more than a thousand people who could be arrested immediately. In reality, there were too many for him to cope with.

For the second time in less than a year, the Resistance in southwest France lay in ruins. One report estimated that, of the 30,000 fighters armed with around 150 tons of weapons which the OCM claimed it could mobilise in the late summer of 1943, there remained only two surviving elements: the German-sponsored *Maquis officiels*, numbering around 3,000 and armed with some twenty-five tons of light weapons; and a further 3,000 Maquis who had managed to escape arrest by the Gestapo and were now scattered, mostly leaderless, demoralised and without arms, in places of refuge across southwest France.

It was against this background of disarray and desolation that, on the evening of 2 March 1944, Marguerite Faget, listening out on the BBC French Service's *Messages personnels*, heard the radio announcer say in his deadpan voice: '*Roger reviendra manger des cèpes ce soir.*'

ARISTIDE RETURNS

Roger Landes's problem was his gold watch. At about the same time as he arrived in Gibraltar, an MI5 source had warned that the Germans were about to infiltrate onto the Rock a male agent 'in his twenties' who spoke good English but with a strong French accent. The warning specified that the agent would be wearing a Swiss gold watch specially adapted to conceal microfilm. Landes seemed to fit the bill precisely. Responding to questions about his watch, the new arrival had been, according to his MI5 interrogator in Gibraltar, 'evasive and contradictory'. The suspicion that the gold watch indicated that Landes may have been 'turned' was reinforced by the fact that he had miraculously escaped from a catastrophe in which so many of his colleagues had been arrested. Alarm bells began to ring in both Baker Street and MI5.

When Landes arrived at Orchard Court at 9.30 on the morning of 17 January 1944, Buckmaster was waiting for him. He presented Landes with the ribbon for his MC, the three pips he was now entitled to wear as a captain, the clothes he had left behind when he had parachuted into France, and the mail that had accumulated during his absence. The ceremonies over, Landes was abruptly packed off to a special camp near Guildford where he was kept in strict isolation and subjected to three days of intensive interrogation, including one non-stop session lasting twenty-three hours.

Before his interrogation started in earnest, Landes was asked to write a full report on his activities in France. He explained he had already done this and left it at the embassy in Madrid. It had got lost, they claimed. But when his interrogation began, Landes noted that his interrogator had the two reports on his desk and was referring to each in turn and questioning discrepancies and contradictions between the two. Eventually the interrogator concluded that there were 'no important divergences between them'. As a secret agent, one of Landes's most useful attributes was a prodigious memory. Asked about the Swiss gold watch, Landes explained that Vic Hayes had bought four of them on the black market to use as potential bribes in the case of trouble. One, Hayes kept for himself, giving Landes and de Baissac a watch each and leaving the last with Duboué (it was among the items found by the Germans after the battle of Lestiac). MI5 immediately contacted de Baissac, who confirmed Landes's story.

Finally, on Saturday 24 January, Landes's MI5 interrogator formally cleared his subject of all suspicion, while commenting rather sniffily: '[He is] not a very impressive young man externally, but has done good work – steady temperament.'

SOE were kinder: 'As far as can be judged, Landes's behaviour throughout has been exemplary … he has shown wisdom beyond his years and a very developed sense of duty … The report received from Spain that he was suspicious rests on a triviality which MI5 have dismissed without further ado.'

On the day Landes was cleared by MI5, Marcel Défence finally arrived back in Britain. The Glaswegian had had an eventful journey which had taken him first back to Bordeaux (where he had proposed marriage to Ginette Corbin and been accepted), then to a rendezvous with a Lysander which failed, then to Paris (where he was given the letter of mitigation written by Père Riquet on behalf of Grandclément to take back to Baker Street) and finally to Brittany. Here, after several failed attempts to escape, he got away in a stolen fishing boat and finally made it across the Channel to Falmouth.

After his interrogation, Landes had a further meeting with Maurice Buckmaster, who questioned him closely about Mary Herbert. She had been ordered home. Why had she stayed in France? It was only at this stage that Baker Street learnt that Mary Herbert had been left behind because she was having Claude de Baissac's child.

Landes pressed his chief for permission to return to Bordeaux as soon as possible, pointing out that he had put five separate Resistance organisations into hibernation across the region. All were independent from each other, he explained, and none had been contaminated by contact with Grandclément. Each had a leader, 25,000 francs and its own parachute site, which could be activated as soon as he returned. He had promised them that he would go back and they were waiting for him. He had to honour that promise, he insisted. But Buckmaster peremptorily vetoed any question of Landes's return. He was completely blown to the Germans, and SOE never sent blown agents back to their original area – it was just too dangerous. Besides, Buckmaster explained, the French in London had already sent their own man (Bonnier) to head up the Resistance in southwest France. Landes would be more useful training new agents in England than risking his life as a blown one in Bordeaux.

After a week's leave and a brief refresher course in codes and security, Landes, to his disgust, was assigned to SOE's training team where he gave lectures on the pitfalls and trials of being an agent in occupied France.

In mid-February, returning from a lecture session at the SOE finishing school at Beaulieu, he was called in to see Buckmaster, who had just heard of Claude Bonnier's arrest and suicide and the second collapse of Resistance in the southwest. Desperate times needed desperate measures. With D-Day fast approaching, Baker Street had to take whatever risks were necessary to rebuild an effective Resistance in southwest France. Landes was their best hope of doing this in time – indeed probably their only one.

SOE had changed their mind, Buckmaster explained: 'Do you still want to go to Bordeaux? If you are still willing, we'll send you with our blessing.' Landes leapt at the chance.

On 18 February, at about the same time Buckmaster agreed to Landes returning to France, Mary Herbert was sitting up in bed feeding her ten-week-old daughter, Claudine, in Lise de Baissac's empty flat in Poitiers, when suddenly there was a loud banging on the door. It was the Gestapo. They arrested Mary Herbert and handed Claudine over to the maid, who, believing Mary was unlikely ever to be seen again, promptly put the baby girl in the local orphanage. The last traces of SOE's greatest network in occupied France were now obliterated.

Roger Landes's briefing for his new mission was specific and tightly targeted. He was given a new codename, 'Aristide', up-to-date documents in the name of 'Roger Lalande' and a cover story saying he was a surveyor from Agen, near Bordeaux, working (as in his first mission) for the German defence construction operation, Organisation Todt.

Landes, who was warned that D-Day was 'very, very near', was tasked to 'bring together under SOE command, those elements of the Resistance who had escaped German suppression and form them into operational units in preparation for the coming invasion'. When D-Day came, his Maquis were to be ready to come out into the open to sabotage German lines of communication. One specific job in his mission orders was to identify a possible site for a large-scale airborne landing. But this was secondary to his main task, which was to impede all attempts by Axis forces to move their units north in order to reinforce the defenders on the invasion beaches. His sabotage targets were to include all rail links to and from Bordeaux, the enemy's telecommunications networks, the chief German headquarters across the region and the two main roads running directly north to Angoulême and Poitiers. (Landes later claimed that, though he was not told where the landings would be, the special emphasis given to these two roads led him to conclude that D-Day would be in Normandy.)

To do this Landes would have to reactivate and grow the organisations he had left behind, make arrangements to receive the large number of parachute drops which would be necessary to rearm and re-equip his units, train his teams as a fighting force and prepare them for a detailed programme of sabotage to be initiated by coded signals sent from London just before the invasion. And all this under the watchful eye of Friedrich Dohse, whose command of almost everything that moved in his area was by now near universal, and against a backdrop of demoralisation, suspicion and betrayal amongst what remained of the Resistance in the region. It was a very tall order, and it is not hard to imagine that in sending Landes back to Bordeaux, SOE were only too aware that they were making a desperate last throw before the invasion – and that the chances of Landes returning alive were slim.

Quite a lot had changed since Landes's first mission, eighteen months previously.

To start with, Landes himself had changed. He was, of course, more battle-hardened and experienced. But Roger Landes Mark II was more than that.

During his first mission he had been surrounded by betrayal – immersed in it – and it had made him constantly, unsleepingly, alert. Ever watchful, ever suspicious, always on his guard, he was instinctively mistrusting, save to those closest to him. The Grandclément betrayals had also left him with a scepticism bordering on dislike of sophisticated Bordeaux society – people who were, in his words, 'so rich they had too much to lose' – and of the officer class, which he thought contained far too many quasi-collaborators and Johnny-cum-lately ex-Vichy supporters (known sardonically as *les Naphtalinards* because of the smell of naphthalene on uniforms only recently exhumed from the mothballed interiors of attic trunks in which they had so far spent the war). For friends, fighters and sanctuary, Landes preferred the sturdier 'peasant' virtues (the word does not have the same pejorative overtones in French as it does in English) of what he referred to as the 'the ordinary ... working-class people' of the rural hinterlands of Bordeaux, and especially the Médoc to the north and the Landes to the southeast.

Landes's role in his second mission was different too. Before, he had been a radio operator serving Claude de Baissac's Scientist network. Now, he was a soldier and a soldiers' leader. He had orders to carry out; an enemy to defeat; obstacles to overcome. He had to be more focussed, more able to calculate threat, more ruthless in dealing with anyone who, in his opinion, added to the risks which he and his men faced, even if this involved an element of rough soldier's justice. Above all, Roger Landes, still only twenty-seven years old, had developed an uncanny sixth sense for danger matched by an almost animal instinct for survival.

He was probably not much loved, for he was not that kind of man. But he was much trusted by those who followed him – many of them much older. They knew there was nothing he would not do to ensure their survival, just as much as his own. In a telling passage in which it is possible to detect both admiration and bewilderment, the consummate, dedicated, specially chosen, meticulously trained professional, Friedrich Dohse, commended his more 'amateur' adversary in these terms: 'The manner in which Roger Landes conducted his affairs created great confidence and respect amongst his companions. In London he had only been an architect. Nothing (in his previous life) had in any way predestined him for the extremely dangerous role that he now played so well.'

Baker Street had also changed. In early 1942, when Landes joined, SOE was small, freelance, amateur, piratical, romantic and a sideshow to the main war effort. It was enough just to be in France taking the fight to the enemy, even if this was only in the form of tiny pinpricks against the Leviathan. Now, however, in 1944, SOE was an integrated part of the greatest war enterprise the world had ever known – the Allied invasion of mainland Europe. During the early months of 1944, French Resistance forces commanded by de Gaulle's organisation in London were also changing, as they were brought under a single entity – Forces Françaises de l'Intérieur (FFI). Along with SOE, FFI would in due course become embedded within Supreme Headquarters Allied Expeditionary Forces (SHAEF). Their joint task would be singular and stark: to make it easier for Allied troops to cross the hundred metres or so of the invasion beaches, in order to gain, and successfully defend, a foothold on mainland Europe. Though he was still three months and hundreds of kilometres away from the invasion, from the moment Roger Landes's feet touched the soil of France, everything he and his fighters did would be directed to that gigantic enterprise, in which they would be just small cogs.

During the last week of February, while Landes made the final preparations for his mission, Dohse delivered the coup de grâce to what remained of the Resistance – and the OCM in particular – in southwest France. Around 300 of the 1,000 named individuals Dohse had harvested from Bonnier's briefcase and the treachery of Toussaint and his colleagues were rounded up. Almost all were deported to the death camps. Few would ever be seen alive again.

On 25 February the Gestapo arrested the OCM head Colonel Touny at his home in Paris, followed by most of Touny's 'general staff'. In order to create further mischief and mistrust Dohse spread the rumour that de Gaulle had ordered Joubert to be shot in Algiers. He also arranged, through Grandclément, to leak certain details of the documents he had found (or, where necessary, pretended he had found) in Bonnier's briefcase, generating more division, dissension and panic among what remained of the senior ranks of the Resistance in the southwest and in Paris.

With the effective end of the OCM, André Grandclément's circumstances became more secure. He and Lucette moved back to Bordeaux in February, renting furnished accommodation in a modest two-storey townhouse with a balcony overlooking the Parc Bordelais. He was now spending most of his time not on Resistance matters, but on his businesses, including trying to regain control of the film distribution company he and Claude de Baissac had set up. Dohse kept a watchful eye on his erstwhile collaborator, but contact between the two men was irregular and Grandclément's visits to Gestapo headquarters in Bouscat ceased altogether. The truth, though Dohse took care to hide it, was that André Grandclément was, for the moment at least, of no further use.

Parachute operations into southwest France were severely disrupted during the second half of February 1944 when a late spell of very cold weather swept in: temperatures fell to minus five, bringing scattered snow scurries borne on a blustery north wind. On the night of 27 February 1944, ten days after Mary Herbert's arrest, Landes and a Canadian called Allyre Sirois, who was on his way to join a neighbouring SOE circuit as their radio operator, boarded a Halifax at Tempsford and flew south, buffeted by bitterly cold winds, to a field close to Auch, 160 kilometres southeast of Bordeaux. But the drop was aborted because heavy cloud obscured the reception committee's lights. Once again Landes had to endure the long, cold, boring flight back to base.

The next night they tried again. This time the pilot had no difficulty finding the spot. But the winds were still strong enough to make parachuting marginal. Nevertheless, after three passes, Landes and Sirois jumped. As Landes approached the ground a strong gust caught his parachute and dumped him onto the ground fast and on one leg. He tried to get up, but the pain from his left ankle was too great. He lay helplessly waiting until the reception committee found him.

One of the reception team carried him by piggyback to a nearby deserted house, where he and Sirois were given a light meal and Landes was reunited with his suitcase and radio, which, dropped separately, had fallen into the only pond in the area. Taking off his left boot, Landes found his ankle black with bruising and so severely swollen that he could not walk. By now the moon had vanished and it was inky dark. Landes was again hoisted onto the back of one of his rescuers and carried four jarring kilometres across rutted fields to the village of Marsan and the home of a member of the reception committee, Renée Daubèze. Here Landes was tenderly put to bed.

But which bed?

Renée Daubèze, whose husband was in a German POW camp, lived with her two children and mother-in-law. According to Landes's post-mission report, he and Mme Daubèze quickly agreed that none of the other occupants of the house could be trusted to keep silent and therefore could not know of the wounded, bedbound visitor who must be kept out of sight at all times. So they needed a cover story which would work in the case of discovery by either the Germans, or the children, or the mother-in-law. They came up with an ingenious – and very French – solution. If discovered, the couple would pretend that Landes was Mme Daubèze's secret lover, who had injured his ankle in a fall while attempting a nocturnal entry through her bedroom window.

All this is plainly related in Landes's after-mission report.

But it begs a question: how did the pair keep Landes's existence secret from the other three occupants of what was a modest family house? Even if there was a spare bedroom, why would it suddenly be locked and out of bounds to the others? There seems only one likely solution to this puzzle: Landes was not just the virtual lover of the hospitable Mme Daubèze; he actually shared her bed. After all, if he really was her lover, why would he be sleeping anywhere else? And what better reason could there be to explain why her bedroom was out of bounds to the others? Landes is not explicit on this in any of his post-war accounts, perhaps because he wanted to protect the reputation of his redoubtable hostess – but it seems a more than reasonable conjecture. Landes's cover story for his presence in Renée Daubèze's bed may well have been believed, if he had been discovered. But it would have landed his generous hostess in real trouble – and not just with her mother-in-law. At this stage of the war it was punishable under law for a Frenchwoman to have an affair while her husband was away in the army or in captivity.

Meanwhile, there were other, more immediate, threats to deal with.

At the time Landes jumped, the Wehrmacht was already in the area conducting an operation to round up Gaullist sympathisers. Renée Daubèze's own brother-in-law was one of those who had been arrested. The repeated passes, over two successive nights, made by the Halifax trying to drop Landes and Sirois alerted the Germans that something new was afoot. At dawn on the day after Landes's arrival, German soldiers surrounded the neighbouring villages and began a detailed house-to-house search, eventually arriving at the property opposite the Daubèze's house. Landes hobbled to the bedroom window and, peering between the shutters, watched as the Germans made a thorough search of the neighbour's house. 'When they had finished, I knew they would come to us next,' Landes wrote later. He loaded his Colt and waited. 'The Germans came out of the neighbour's house looking disappointed and stopped in front of ours. They hesitated for a few moments, chatting amongst themselves … and then left.'

When all was quiet, Renée Daubèze slipped out to the nearby village of Gimont to fetch the local Resistance doctor for Landes's leg. The patient, presumably lying in Renée Daubèze's bed, explained his predicament, using the cover story which the two of them had already concocted. Assuming Landes to be a local peasant, the doctor addressed him using the familiar *tu* form of address. But on examining the injured ankle, he suddenly realised that he was in fact dealing with a parachutist and swiftly changed to the more respectful *vous*. The doctor declared the ankle severely sprained and prescribed three weeks' complete immobility.

The next day the doctor was arrested. For a moment it looked as though someone close to the Daubèze household was a traitor. But it soon transpired that the doctor's arrest was not related to Landes, but to an informer who told the Germans that he had previously treated escaping US airmen.

Landes's next problem was to get a message to Marguerite Faget in Bordeaux, explaining that he had been delayed and indicating when she should expect him. Again he and Renée Daubèze came up with the solution. Hidden in a very long letter to M. and Mme Faget, Landes included the information about his likely arrival date in coded language that he and Mitou Faget had used on his previous mission. Mme Daubèze took the letter to the post office and persuaded the local postmistress to ensure that the franking mark was so illegible that no one could tell from where it had been posted.

Over the next week Landes followed a regime of complete rest for his ankle by day and, with Renée Daubèze's help, 'light exercises after dark' (Landes's words). By 13 March 1944, keen not to expose his hostess to further risk, Landes felt well enough to leave. He offered to pay for his lodgings, but Renée Daubèze refused. The following morning she arranged for him to be taken in a lorry to the station at Agen, sixty kilometres north, where he caught the train to Bordeaux.

At the station at Langon (where Henri Labit had died) a German officer and two soldiers entered Landes's carriage and demanded papers. The man sitting next to him was thoroughly searched and his baggage opened for inspection. 'Then he came to me,' Landes wrote. 'I handed him my identity card. He looked at me closely and, without looking at my card, said: "Thank you. Is this your suitcase?" "Yes," I replied. He nodded and moved on.'

Landes's luck had held again. Like Henri Labit before him, his suitcase contained a radio and – hidden in a tin of peas – a set of crystals.

Arriving in Bordeaux, Landes went straight to Rue Guynemer. Cautious as ever, he first dropped in to see a neighbour to confirm that all was well and nothing untoward had happened to M. and Mme Faget while he had been away. He explained both his three months' absence and his injured ankle by saying that he had been away working in Germany, where his leg had been badly injured in an Allied air raid (which he described in compelling detail).

That night Marguerite Faget cooked as sumptuous a welcome-home meal as wartime exigencies would permit for her newly returned 'nephew'. Meanwhile Landes, somewhat overplaying his injury, signalled Baker Street: 'ARRIVED SAFELY IN BORDEAUX STOP FOOT BROKEN ON LANDING DUE TO STRONG WIND STOP SUITCASES FELL INTO POOLS ENDS.'

He was back. But the news was not good.

Before he had left France, Landes had asked Marguerite Faget to keep in contact with six of his key Resistance leaders. One, the man who had driven him on the first part of his journey to Spain in November, had died in a flu epidemic the previous winter. Rumour had it that the second, André Noël, had joined Grandclément not long after Landes had left; two more had fled France to escape imminent arrest, and Bouillar, his guide over the Pyrenees, had been forced into hiding. Only one of the key contacts around whom he had hoped to reconstruct his forces was still active and in touch with Marguerite Faget.

To make matters worse, the Grandclément affair and the catastrophes which had ensued had made people afraid of having anything to do with the Resistance. The general mood in France had changed, too. 'Most Frenchmen are anti-German and pro-British,' Charles Corbin reported to SOE at the time, but 'they have lost … confidence in the British since their disappointment that the invasion did not take place in September … [this] has been strongly fostered by the Germans'.

Landes had no alternative. He would have to start again, from scratch, and – given the prevailing climate of despondency among the local population and a savage new wave of repression sweeping in from Berlin – this was not going to be easy.

24

'I COME ON BEHALF OF STANISLAS'

In March 1944 Friedrich Dohse climbed another step up the officer's promotion ladder when he was promoted to *Obersturmführer* (full lieutenant). Dohse, however was not one to take the trappings of rank seriously (perhaps because he spent most of his time in civilian clothes). When the head of the Gestapo in France, Helmut Knochen, visited Bouscat around the middle of March 1944, Dohse appeared before him in a uniform which still bore the insignia of a company sergeant major. Knochen was furious and ordered the improperly dressed lieutenant to parade before him in his office in Paris, in his correct uniform, within twenty-four hours.

It must have been with some satisfaction and relief that Dohse now found himself, at last, the same rank as his KdS rival, Rudolf Kunesch. Despite his promotion, however, he still found that, thanks to the new repressive policy set by Hitler, his power within KdS Bordeaux continued to diminish, while that of Kunesch continued to grow.

A year before, the task of German counter-intelligence in France was to infiltrate, undermine and decapitate the Resistance to prevent it from growing. Now in the spring of 1944, with an invasion imminent, their task was to destroy established, trained and armed Resistance units. In this effort, so the German commanders thought, the more violent skills of people such as Kunesch and his assistant, 'Tony the boxer' Enzelsberger, backed by the brute force of the Wehrmacht, would have a larger part to play than the subtler techniques of persuasion and seduction which Dohse, with his reputation for being 'pro-French', had spent the last two years perfecting.

On 3 February 1944, the German Deputy Supreme Commander West, Luftwaffe Field Marshal Hugo Sperrle, set out the new policy with chilling clarity:

1. We are not in the occupied western territories to allow our troops to be shot at and abducted by saboteurs who go unpunished ...
2. If troops are attacked ... countermeasures [must be taken] immediately. These include an ... immediate return of fire. If innocent persons are hit, this is regrettable but entirely the fault of the terrorists.
3. The surroundings of any such incident are to be sealed off ... and all the civilians in the locality, regardless of rank and person, are to be taken into custody. Houses from which shots have been fired are to be burnt down ...
4. ... A slack and indecisive troop commander deserves to be severely punished because he endangers the lives of his troops ... and produces a lack of respect for German armed forces. Measures [taken by German commanders] that may subsequently be regarded as too severe cannot, in view of the present situation, provide cause for punishment.

A week later, on 12 February, the German military commander of France, General Carl-Heinrich von Stülpnagel, reinforced the point by laying out his priorities: '*The main task in the coming weeks and months is ... fully to repacify areas which are contaminated by bandits, in order to break up the secret Resistance organisations and to seize their weapons ... In areas where gang centres form, these must be combated with a concentrated use of all available forces ... The objective must be to break up all* terrorist and Resistance groups even before the enemy landing.'

It was the wrong policy, at the wrong time.

The wave of German excesses which ensued had the effect of alienating the French opinion which Dohse had so sedulously cultivated. Before long, his flow of intelligence began to dry up. For Landes, however, busily engaged in recruiting fighters and local support networks, the new wave of German brutality acted as a fresh recruiting sergeant for his cause.

In the third week of April a massive German operation was launched against a concentration of Maquis units in the forests and wildernesses of the Roquefort area, ninety kilometres southeast of Bordeaux. Machule instructed Dohse to plan this operation, which involved more than 2,000 men and included two regiments of the Wehrmacht and a large number of French police and auxiliary units under the overall command of a local Wehrmacht colonel. The operation produced swift results, harvesting some 2,000 young men, rounded up from various camps and Resistance bases in the area. A minority of these (some 400 or so) were genuine Maquisards, captured with weapons or incriminating documents in their possession. Others were just ordinary civilians whose papers were not in order. Others still were hiding in the forests to escape compulsory labour in Germany. Some were even from youth labour camps set up by the local French administration. One German commander on the operation offered the view that: 'The French workmen are innocent boys who were very surprised when rough German warriors suddenly got them out of their beds.'

All those rounded up were herded together into a hastily constructed barbed-wire prison camp near the town of Bazas. In a report written after the operation, the Wehrmacht commanders criticised Dohse for heavy-handedness in this operation. In his own account, however, Dohse blamed the Wehrmacht's plan to transport all the prisoners, lock, stock and barrel, back to Germany for causing uproar amongst the local population and claimed to have petitioned Machule, pointing out the folly of such a self-defeating policy. Eventually, thanks, Dohse asserts, to his personal intervention, only around fifty of the 2,000 rounded up (and these mostly from outside the region) were transported to labour camps in Nazi Europe. Hostility among the local population, which had risen to dangerous levels, gradually subsided.

Other similar operations did not have such relatively happy outcomes. In one, Kunesch summarily executed six young men; in others brutality, killings and torture were commonplace.

For Roger Landes, too, the spring of 1944 was a busy time.

In the days and weeks following his arrival in Bordeaux he gradually picked up the threads of what was left of his old organisations and made contact with the scattered remains of his old units, most of whom had been forced into hiding to avoid arrest. With the Germans south of Bordeaux busy conducting raids and round-ups, Landes turned his attention to contacting the Resistance leaders north of the city who had survived the purges of the early part of the year. The burden on his shoulders soon began to grow. He decided that he needed a second-in-command to spread the load. His first choice very soon proved inadequate – the man drank to cope with his fear and invented units to cover up his inability to find new recruits. Before Landes could start looking for a replacement, he was approached by twenty-three-year-old Louis Christian Campet, who offered to help. Campet was a police inspector in the Arcachon area who had been active in the local Resistance from the early days. Landes quickly recognised the young man's courage, loyalty and ability as an organiser and, despite his youth, appointed him as his second-in-command.

Campet's first act was to put Landes in contact with the commander of what had been a strong Resistance organisation in the Arcachon area, Commandant Édouard de Luze, who agreed to join forces with the new arrival from London. Campet also managed to track down André Bouillar. A messenger was sent to Bouillar, equipped with the code-phrase 'I come on behalf of Stanislas', and the gold sovereign which Landes had promised when the two men had parted that rainy night in Navarre, five months previously. 'Dédé le Basque' immediately came out of hiding, gathered his men and joined his old companion, soon proving himself to be one of Landes's most reliable, fearless and able commanders.

By the end of May, Landes had assembled a rough skeleton organisation from which he could rebuild his forces. Based on the initial reports he received (he was later to discover these were exaggerated), Landes signalled to SOE in mid-May that his forces consisted of six separate units with an overall strength of around 1,400 men. These were composed of de Luze's Maquis unit in Arcachon (numbering some 300); some groups in various suburbs of Bordeaux (numbering in all nearly 600); a small organisation in the port of Bordeaux (fifteen fighters); and another at Mérignac airport (fifty). In addition Landes developed good relations with the *cheminots*, the workers on the local railways, who could always be relied on to provide help and assistance when called on. A group of these under their chief Roger Schmaltz, the communist-leaning *cheminot* leader at the Gare Saint-Jean, also joined Landes as an organised Maquis unit. Sometime during May, the fiery Léonce Dussarrat, who had gone into hiding after his narrow escape through the back of his ironmonger's shop in Dax, added to these numbers by placing his 300 men under Landes's command.

Now Landes needed to start arming his new force.

His first weapons drop took place on 1 April 1944. Codenamed 'Prince', the site was an open and flat waterlogged field near the village of Saugnacq-et-Muret, southeast of Arcachon. Christian Campet was in charge of the reception. The arms were transported, half to the home of the area Resistance chief, Franck Cazenave, the son of a notable local factory owner, and half to a back street bar in Bordeaux. This was the beginning of what would become an avalanche of arms and explosives dropped over the next six months to over 135 individual reception operations, covering the whole of the area which Landes controlled.

Paradoxically, the fact that Dohse had previously seized many of the OCM's arms dumps now helped Landes in his task. The surviving Resistance groups urgently needed weapons. For those who wanted arms, Landes was the sole means of getting them: he was the only one who could command the appearance in the skies of the British Halifaxes with their precious cargos. As Dussarrat put it in a letter to Landes after the war: between them they had the power to decide who, among the Resistance leaders in the area, would be an armed king and who would remain a weaponless pauper. The echo here of a system built on local 'war lords' is probably accurate – especially in the case of Dussarrat himself. More than one visitor from London with close personal knowledge of Landes's networks at this time commented that they were 'run on gangster lines'. The film script which many in the Resistance had running in their heads was that of the American gangster movie, complete with tommy guns, Colt automatics, street assassinations, turned-up collars and soft-brimmed felt hats.

One element, however, was not left to hazard, or to the whims of a local commander: security. Landes himself trained his own team of bodyguards and personal staff (all of whom were armed with pistols), and insisted that similar training should be given by commanders to new Maquisards very soon after they were recruited.

This training included how to spot when they were being followed, what to do to shake off a pursuer, how to deal with an agent provocateur and, if captured, how to resist interrogation. New fighters were also taught the difference between a 'live letterbox' (run by a person and usually located in a place where comings and goings did not attract attention, such as a shop or a public facility) and a 'dead letterbox' (unmanned; a place to leave a message which could be collected later – such as a crack in a wall, or under a rock).

Landes, punctilious as ever, also insisted on strict security rules for his men. No one should go on a mission, even a minor one, without a prepared cover story for what they were doing. No one was allowed to know the home address of their commander. No one should ever try to make contact with his or her commander, unless asked to do so. No one should ever give his addresses to a fellow resistant, unless ordered by their commander. No one should ever try to approach a colleague who ignored them in the street. The signal to abort a street meeting because of danger was to pretend to study a nearby shop window for a short period and then walk away. Anything abnormal about the setting of the shutters on a house indicated danger. Punctuality at meetings was vital; no one should wait more than five minutes at a rendezvous before abandoning the meet. Cafés were out of bounds for meetings. Arms were not to be carried unless there was a realistic prospect of danger. If a meeting was arranged with someone who was unknown, then at the first attempt the meeting should be allowed deliberately to fail. In this way the person in question could be followed and the rendezvous observed for traps or ambushes.

Some rough-and-ready rules of discipline were established, enforced by an even rougher system of sanctions. There were only two punishments, depending on the offence. Landes described them as: 'dismissal from the organisation and dismissal from this life'. He claimed to have used 'both methods with success'.

Landes took care to pass on to his new recruits the tricks of the trade which he had learned on his first mission. Two of his favourites involved flowers. If a password had not been prearranged, then an ad hoc one could be established on the spot by the first person using the name of a flower (e.g. 'Marguerite') in the opening few sentences of the conversation. His interlocutor would then respond incorporating the number of petals of the flower in the reply. (Landes describes using this system, but it seems to presume a rather high level of instant horticultural recall from his Maquisards.) His other favourite trick was employed to find out whether someone still lived at a given contact address. A bunch of flowers would be sent to the address from a Resistance-friendly flower shop. If the flowers were returned, then the person could be presumed to have either moved or been arrested. If the flowers were not returned, then it was safe to visit.

With the swell of new recruits now joining his Maquis units, it soon became obvious to Landes that, if his men were to be ready for D-Day, he needed professional assistance. In the first week of April, he signalled London urgently requesting someone qualified to help train his men in tactics, explosives and the use of weapons. Baker Street said they were intending to send someone 'with a slight Greek accent'. Landes, only too conscious of the dangers of anyone who didn't easily fit in, replied sardonically that he would 'much prefer someone with a slight French accent'.

Baker Street's answer came in the form of not one, but two assistants with foreign accents, who were dropped into France on 9 April: a Canadian called Pierre Charles Meunier (who spoke French with a strong Canadian accent) and John Manolitsakis (the original strongly accented Greek). Manolitsakis's local alias, 'Cyriel', was swiftly transmuted by the French into 'Cyriel le Grec'.

It would be difficult to find two more unsuitable emissaries to parachute into a delicate and dangerous operation. Manolitsakis was a forty-year-old ex-merchant seaman, described in his SOE file as a 'combination of boy-scout, cum Kipling hero cum political anarchist'. Immediately on landing, Manolitsakis (roaring drunk and wearing a silk cravat proudly proclaiming it was 'made in Piccadilly') took refuge, with his hip flask, in a nearby bush. It took some time for the reception committee to find him and coax him out.

The following morning, Manolitsakis, Christian Campet and Pierre Meunier were cycling to the nearest station to catch the train to Bordeaux when they met a German convoy coming in the opposite direction. This sent Manolitsakis into a paroxysm of fear from which he emerged only rarely for the rest of his time in France.

During the eight days he had to spend in a safe house waiting for his papers to be put in order, Cyriel le Grec refused to speak to anyone or emerge from his bedroom, day or night. Even his meals had to be left outside his bedroom door for collection. Eventually he was installed in a café on the Bordeaux quayside to begin his task of organising marine sabotage at which he was said to be an expert (like his equally bibulous fellow merchant seaman, Robert Leroy). His subsidiary task was to prepare plans to save the port in case the Germans tried to blow it up when they retreated. But in the end, he stayed at the waterfront café for only forty-eight hours before (at the owners' insistence) Landes had him transferred back to the safe house. Here he again took refuge in his room, hiding under the bed whenever his hosts tuned in to the BBC. Eventually Landes signalled London that Cyriel le Grec's behaviour was having such a terrible effect on the morale and security of his teams that he proposed to have him killed. London replied that he was to do no such thing, ordering him instead to send the Greek back home over the Pyrenees. Manolitsakis finally left France by one of Bouillar's escape lines on 7 August 1944. It took him four months to make it back to London.

Perhaps SOE could not reasonably have foreseen that Manolitsakis would have a problem with courage. But no such excuses can be made for the deficiencies of Pierre Meunier. The Canadian's SOE personal reports include: 'impetuous, highly strung and apt to become excited and flustered'; 'more concerned with his own importance than the importance of security'; 'temperamental and ... easily depressed'; 'boastful and vain', 'self-centred'; 'tactless and with little intelligence'; 'not to be trusted in a tight corner [or] to keep his mouth shut'; 'unreliable ... unpleasant ... sycophantic and sly' and 'the worst student to have passed through the school for many months'.

The twenty-six-year-old Meunier was tall and strikingly handsome, with a flourish of hair swept back in the style of Rasputin (whose enthusiasm for sexual adventure he also shared). His local alias was 'Édouard', but, because of his height and expansive personality, he quickly became known as 'Édouard le Grand', or simply 'Le Grandiose'. Where Cyriel le Grec hid from danger, Le Grandiose actively courted it. He relished taking unnecessary risks which endangered not just himself, but also his French colleagues, such as insisting on dining in restaurants frequented by Germans, rather than in the quieter ones in the backstreets.

Landes sent Meunier first to train his Maquis units in Lormont, just to the north of Bordeaux on the east bank of the Garonne, and then to Arcachon. In both cases he did good work. But it was not long before Meunier's taste for amorous escapades began to get in the way of his mission and threaten the security of those around him. Landes warned him more than once to behave more discreetly, but it was to no avail. Discretion, especially when it came to sex, was simply beyond Le Grandiose's nature. Meunier committed other serious breaches of security too, such as giving shelter to four escaping Russians in one of Landes's safe houses. Worse, Landes learnt that Meunier had, without telling him, started to meet people known or suspected to have contacts with Grandclément and therefore, possibly, with the German authorities. He even shared a mistress – a Madame Plante – with a Russian called André Basilio, who was known to be close to Grandclément. When Landes questioned the Canadian about the affair – explaining that he suspected La Plante was just that, a 'Gestapo plant', Meunier at first denied any connection with her, and then promised not to see her again. But he just could not help himself. Far from ending the relationship with the eponymous Madame Plante, Meunier next spent an amorous afternoon with her at one of Landes's Bordeaux safe houses.

Landes took swift and brutal action to limit the damage. He disbanded all the Maquis units with whom Meunier had worked, paid off or closed down all of Meunier's contacts, and ordered the execution of the Russian, Basilio, in case he had discovered the locations of any of his safe houses. Finally, with Basilio 'neutralised', he dispatched Meunier back to London through Spain. One suspects, given Landes's utterly focused operational ruthlessness at this point in his mission, that he must have given at least a passing thought to killing Pierre Meunier, too.

Either way, it would not be the last time that Landes would deem it necessary to order an execution because he judged that to let a suspect live would entail taking too great a risk with the security of his men. With D-Day approaching and betrayal all around, the mere whiff of treachery was now enough to have a man killed.

This callousness was probably necessary. It was certainly welcomed by Landes's Maquisards, who trusted him because it showed that he put their security first. But it was also perfect for Friedrich Dohse, the arch-manipulator, sower of mischief and reaper of havoc. If anyone knew how to fish in waters poisoned by suspicion, doubt and fear, he did.

25

'FOREWARNED IS FOREARMED'

Sometime in late March or early April 1944, Friedrich Dohse began to hear rumours that a new SOE agent codenamed 'Aristide' had arrived in the area to direct Resistance operations. The Luftwaffe's reports flowing into his office confirmed what Bordeaux rumour suggested. The huge increase in night-time parachute drops indicated that the British were rearming the Resistance and, Dohse reasoned, they would not be doing that unless they had a new agent in place or on his way. 'This was (for me) the turning point of the war – and by no means a good one,' Dohse would write later. 'The coming invasion and the arrival of a new SOE agent effectively put an end to my plans [to persuade London to neutralise its Resistance activities in the southwest].'

What was happening in Bordeaux was being replicated all across France. A quarter of all the arms dropped to the French Resistance during the entire war were parachuted in during the single month of May 1944 – a sure sign, if any were needed, that an Allied invasion was fast approaching. In contemplating his next move, Dohse knew that, however successful he had been, the main threat he now faced, if he was successfully to minimise the threat to German troops, was the new arrival from London. Finding and capturing the elusive Aristide was now Dohse's first priority.

Landes, meanwhile, had his problems, too.

On 6 May, Jean-Baptiste Morraglia – a new Forces Françaises de l'Intérieur (FFI) commander of the seven departments of the southwest – had arrived in secret in Bordeaux.

Fifty-four-year-old Morraglia, the son of domestic servants, had risen to the rank of colonel in the French army before the war. He was well known as a supporter of de Gaulle's rival, Giraud, and struggled to impose his authority on the divided loyalties of his new command, many of whom saw him as a *parvenu* and a *naphtalinard* who had played no previous part in the Resistance. Nor did his service upbringing prepare him well for the informal, fluid nature of guerrilla warfare. Set in his ways, rigid in his outlook, Morraglia was above all a patriot and nationalist who hated all foreign interference in his country, and did not greatly distinguish in this matter between the Germans and the British.

He was also, in almost every regard, the polar opposite of Roger Landes. He was nearing retirement age and a career soldier; Landes was in his twenties and an amateur. Morraglia was a proud French nationalist; Landes appeared to him as a French Jew who had thrown his lot in with the British. Morraglia was a soldier trained in the art of formal war; Landes was mostly self-taught in the irregularities of the guerrilla. Morraglia was right-wing and hierarchical; Landes disliked politics and hated rigid hierarchies if they got in the way of effective action. Morraglia took his orders from the French line of command; Landes took his from the British-run SOE in Baker Street. Morraglia believed he was appointed to be in charge; Landes *was* in charge, and was not about to relinquish this position without orders to do so from above – especially to someone who, he suspected, didn't know what he was doing.

Given the chasms that existed between the two men, it was perhaps inevitable that their first encounter would be awkward.

But it was far worse than that.

The meeting between the two leaders took place on a park bench at the southern end of the ornamental lake in the Parc Bordelais, not far from (and probably within sight of) the balcony of the Grandcléments' new home on the Rue du Bocage. Thanks to Landes's obsession with security, General Morraglia and his party at first thought they had walked into an ambush. 'There were men watching from all sides and we thought that the Gestapo would arrest us at any moment. But we had no option so we just walked on,' remembered one of Morraglia's team. Suddenly, 'Christian Campet walked up to us to check who we were and then vanished into a clump of bushes, emerging accompanied by Landes. It was only then that we realised that the armed men skulking behind the bushes and trees all around us were his bodyguards. Landes's first words were not appealing: "Don't move. I am fully prepared for trouble. If there is the slightest difficulty my men will take you down instantly." We responded: "If we had done the same there would have been a bloodbath by now."'

The testosterone-fuelled stand-off between the two men continued in this manner for an hour and a half. In the version recorded by a Morraglia aide, the encounter came to a head when an exasperated Landes demanded: 'You should not forget that I am an officer in the British Army. I am highly decorated by His Majesty and I should be obeyed by all the French wherever and whoever they are.' A more flagrant red rag could not have been waved before a more predictable bull. 'And I am a general,' Morraglia expostulated, 'a Commandeur de la Légion d'Honneur, with ten other French decorations, all of which I consider to be greatly superior to anything you may have.'

There was little more to say. The two leaders parted and went their separate ways, each claiming to be in charge of the southwest.

The deadly rift which had started with the Grandclément 'betrayal' had been widened with the execution of Camplan in January, and widened further with the assassination of André Basilio. It now took on the dimensions of a running fratricidal conflict. What ensued was a struggle not just between the French and their German occupiers, but also between Frenchman and Frenchman (and in some cases French women). With Grandclément effectively 'retired', those who had supported him now gradually shifted their loyalties to Morraglia, whom they now regarded as the true leader of the right-wing, anti-communist, authentically 'French' forces of patriotic nationalism.

As the local representative of the 'English'-run Resistance, Landes was increasingly viewed by those who supported Morraglia with deep suspicion. 'We had to be very watchful of the English,' said one commentator on Bordeaux affairs at this time. 'They would always grab what they could for themselves and turn every operation to their advantage … in the maps in Allied headquarters in London there were very few French flags planted in the Bordeaux area, almost no American ones and many, many British ones … The English had all the radios and they used this fact to their profit so as to fly the English flag over Bordeaux.' Anti-Semitism was not far below the surface of these increasingly bitter and turbulent waters. Morraglia, commenting on Landes to a colleague, said that he 'refused to work with that dirty little English Jew who is an obstacle to the liberation of France'. There were even some who went so far as to summon up the ghosts of the Hundred Years' War, claiming that Landes was the modern instrument of the centuries-old English strategy to win back the Black Prince's lost lands in the Aquitaine.

The depth of the antagonism between the groups led by Landes and Morraglia at this time may have been unusual, but inter-Resistance feuding, some of it equally deadly, was not.

As D-Day approached, Resistance movements across France became increasingly infused with politics and personal rivalry as all began to manoeuvre for power, influence and position after the Liberation. Open conflict between rival groups was common, sometimes even involving loss of life, especially where the communists were involved. Landes did his best to ensure that his Maquisards were not drawn into this by making it a strict rule to accept individual recruits of all political persuasions and none, but to refuse any alliances with groups which had declared political affiliations.

With internal French political tensions rising, the number of assassinations in Bordeaux started to increase. The city was again becoming more dangerous by the day for the Grandcléments. On 18 May, following a number of threats to the 'traitor's' life, Dohse advised his charge to give up the lease on his house overlooking the Parc Bordelais and move out of the city. He tried to persuade Grandclément to go to Spain or Portugal, but, again, the Frenchman refused to leave his family. So Dohse moved him first to Saint-Germain-en-Laye, near Paris, and then to a villa overlooking the sea at Moulleau, on the outskirts of Arcachon. Here Lucette and André were placed under the protection of one of Dohse's friends who commanded the Wehrmacht detachment in the area.

With Grandclément safe, Friedrich Dohse, master of the dark arts of counter-intelligence, could now turn his attention to what he did best – stirring the pot of French division, suspicion and conspiracy by sowing disinformation wherever he could, and then leaving it to local rivalry and mistrust to do his work for him.

Which is what may well have happened in the case of one of Landes's erstwhile friends and a one-time trusted colleague.

On 20 May, Landes was crossing Bordeaux's famous Pont de Pierre when he saw, with a jolt, that among the crowds coming towards him was a face he recognised. It was André Noël, one of those names he had left with Marguerite Faget before he escaped over the Pyrenees. Landes had hoped that Noël would help him resurrect his resistance organisations when he returned. But in his absence, Noël had, according to Mitou Faget, betrayed him and 'joined Grandclément'.

Noël was as surprised to see Landes as Landes was to see him. In Landes's account of the incident he claims that Noël would have killed him on the spot, but for the fact that he feared that his old colleague might have hidden bodyguards in the crowd. The two exchanged a few words, in which Noël sarcastically welcomed the new arrival back to Bordeaux, promising that he 'wouldn't last long'.

Landes's suspicion of his old colleague, already deep as a result of Mitou Faget's condemnations, had been deepened further by the arrest of his old friend Harry Peulevé earlier that year. Noël reputedly had a hand in this, having worked with Peulevé until the two had parted in bad blood. Landes subsequently learned that Noël had also been close to Basilio and had met with the Canadian agent, Pierre Meunier. This, Landes concluded, placed it almost beyond doubt that André Noël was a Gestapo agent.

In fact, Landes's suspicions about the treachery of Noël were entirely unfounded. Dohse had indeed tried to recruit Noël, even inviting him to his home after turning André Grandclément. But Noël had firmly rebuffed the approach: 'In my view your work with Grandclément may be a great success for the Gestapo but it is betrayal for the Resistance. I do not share Grandclément's views and I will fight you to the end, my weapons in my hand … I could kill you now. I have my pistol on me. But I will not. Because I am not an assassin.' Dohse's interview with Noël had been held under an assurance of safe passage, so the German had no option but to let him go. Afterwards, however, he launched a series of determined attempts to arrest Noël, in one of which, in the middle of March 1944, his quarry escaped only by the narrowest of margins.

It seems, therefore, more than likely that Dohse would have done all he could to leak information which would encourage Landes in his belief that Noël was indeed a traitor. If so, it worked perfectly. Following the Pont de Pierre encounter, Landes planned an ambush to assassinate Noël. The ambush failed. But Landes's death sentence on Noël remained in place for another time.

None of the distractions with Meunier, Manolistakis, Morraglia or Noël disrupted Roger Landes's main efforts during the months of April and May, which were to lay the ground for the Allied invasion. As his units became trained, Landes tested them out in a series of minor sabotage attacks, beginning in early May with the destruction of sixteen railway engines at Morcenx station, north of Dax. Later in the month Bouillar's men destroyed a number of electricity transformers near Bayonne and, with the help of Schmaltz's *cheminots*, mounted a sabotage attack on the Gare Saint-Jean. The main telephone cable from the German control centre in the port of Bordeaux was cut in seventeen places and then 'repaired' in such a fashion that it was impossible to detect the damage. The cable remained out of action for the rest of the war.

The month of April was exceptionally dry across the whole of southern France and the May weeks which followed were gloriously sunny,

Quai des Chartrons, December 1942, at the time of the Cockleshell Heroes raid

The *Tannenfels* on the morning after the Cockleshell Heroes raid

The Fort du Hâ

197 Avenue du Maréchal Pétain, Dohse's headquarters in Bouscat

Roger Schmaltz (front, centre) and his *cheminots*

26 September 1943: Dohse's men dressed as Maquisards before their first recovery of arms

Post-Liberation military review of Resistance fighters in Bordeaux

Marc O'Neill on a Liberation Day parade

A copy of Landes's note taking responsibility for Grandclément's execution, signed 'In the field' on 27 July 1944

Landes and Charles Gaillard's Order No. 2, calling all FFI forces into Bordeaux to help maintain the public peace

Gaillard, Dussarrat and Landes in Dax

De Gaulle in Bordeaux, September 1944

Marie-Louise, Jean and Suzanne Duboué outside the Café des Marchands after the war – note Jean's false leg

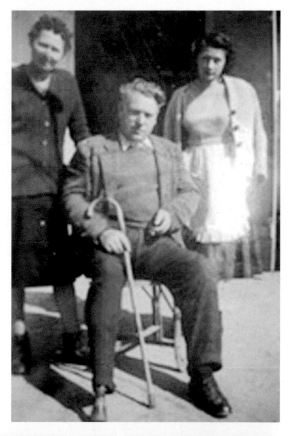

Dohse (right) on trial

Roger and Ginette on their wedding day, 29 July 1947

Roger Landes in the 1960s

with an unusual sharp, vertical quality to the light which seemed to exaggerate the blue of the Garonne, lapping placidly against the Bordeaux quays. It was perfect weather for lovers strolling in the city's boulevards and for *vignerons* watching their grape flowers turn into fattening buds, which swelled by the day under a benevolent sun. But the farmers of the region complained about the lack of rain.

During these brilliant weeks, Roger Landes put the finishing touches to building his fighting organisation. He set up his headquarters in Marguerite Faget's house in Rue Guynemer and arranged his forces in three elements, which he called 'echelons'. The first of these was a head-quarters echelon, commanded by Landes himself. This consisted of a communications section (wireless, couriers and letterboxes – including one in Spain which was used to pass documents, maps and plans back to Britain) and a local liaison and intelligence section which had agents in the police and local administration. At one stage Landes was 'running' both the chief of police and the head of the gendarmerie as agents, with-out either knowing the other was working for him. The headquarters echelon also had access to a small arms and supplies depot in a private house in Bordeaux, a car belonging to François Faget (whose reputation as a 'strong Vichy supporter' entitled him to keep a vehicle), twenty safe houses, two 'dead' letterboxes and four 'live' ones (in a butcher's shop, a grocer's, a wine merchant's and a clothing store).

In addition to Landes's headquarters, there was also a sabotage and guerrilla echelon commanded by Christian Campet. This was made up of a transport and logistics section, responsible for finding arms depots and obtaining lorries and cars as required; a section which undertook the reception of parachute drops; a number of independent sabotage teams; an escape section with its own evasion line to Spain; a courier section served by fifteen couriers, postboxes and safe houses; and even a medical section complete with doctors, other trained medical staff and two rudimentary clandestine 'house hospitals' in Bordeaux.

The third 'echelon' of Landes's force consisted of eight fighting units each with their own commander, transport and parachute recep-tion teams. These consisted in total of a hundred individual fighting groups of ten men (called *dizaines*) which could be combined into five larger units which Landes called *corps-francs* (free-standing fighting units).

Keeping this fast-growing and heterodox organisation together and paying its key members was a considerable administrative task – and an expensive one. At the height of his operations Landes had a budget of 3 million francs a month, which London parachuted to him on a regular basis. This enabled Landes to replace a haphazard system of payment and reimbursements with something more structured and formal. Ordinary Maquisards were not paid, though clothes and living expenses were provided for. Landes's key leaders, together with those who under-took special tasks, did however receive regular stipends. Campet received 10,000 francs a month, rising to 15,000 in August 1944. Bouillar and Dussarrat were paid rather less. Wireless operators were also entitled to payment as were those on parachute reception teams, who received 500 francs a night whether the drop was successful or not. The dependants of those killed, deported, under arrest, or sent away from home on duty were paid (usually by postal order) up to 5,000 francs a month, accord-ing to need.

The burden and responsibilities of managing all this fell almost entirely on Landes's shoulders. He organised and attended hundreds of individual clandestine meetings, every one fraught with danger. These were often held in people's houses, but also in woods and open fields (one favourite meeting place was a field known as the 'goat field' after the solitary goat which grazed contentedly in one corner). During these early months of his Aristide mission, Landes was regularly working twenty hours in twenty-four, sustained by Benzedrine sent from London and his habitual sixty cigarettes a day.

By the end of May, it was done. In just two months, starting from almost nothing, despite all the rigours, dangers and distractions of a clandestine life, despite being hotly pursued by the Gestapo and despite risking daily betrayal by his colleagues, Landes had assembled a lightly armed and rudimentarily trained fighting force of more than 5,000 Maquisards, who were intensely loyal to him and ready for action. As one close observer described: 'Dohse had succeeded in dismantling all the [Resistance] movements, and made Bordeaux little more than a city of hostages. The only exception to this was the group led by Landes.'

Landes's preparation was completed just in time. On 1 June, the announcement section of the BBC French Service programme 'Les Français parlent aux Français', included the phrase: 'forewarned is forearmed'. It was the alert code to warn the Resistance in the southwest that they should listen out carefully to their radios over the next few days; something big was about to happen. Everyone knew that D Day was now very near.

Three more messages were broadcast by the BBC that night. Each was an SOE code indicating which pre-set programmes of sabotage Aristide should prepare to launch in the early hours of D-Day, with the purpose of sowing chaos in the German transport and communications system and holding up German reinforcements moving north to the invasion beaches. The messages – all on a classical theme – were: 'Jupiter met Mercury and the flood began' (prepare attacks on the rail network); 'Venus, you magnificent and heroic woman!' (prepare guerrilla attacks on German headquarters); and 'Cupid fires his arrow and love begins' (prepare to sabotage the enemy's telecommunications infrastructure).

On the afternoon of 3 June, Landes called his Maquis commanders to a meeting in a modest two-storey townhouse at 30 Rue de Méry, a narrow Bordeaux backstreet just a kilometre and a half from Dohse's office in Bouscat. Here over the next twelve hours, the former architect's clerk laid out his plans and briefed his commanders on their tasks for D-Day.

Among those present were Christian Campet; Marguerite and François Faget; Landes's radio operator Michel Expert; Roger Schmaltz (the head of the St Jean cheminots); Pierre Capdepont (cheminot leader in the Gironde), André Bouillar; Léonce Dussarrat's representative; a representative of de Luze's men from Arcachon; and Pierre Chatenet, the leader of a group of fighters at Mérignac. It was not until the early hours of the following morning, 4 June, that the meeting broke up, leaving each leader to slip away into the darkness and begin preparing their forces for the great day when, at last, the liberation of their homeland could begin.

'THIS POISONED ARROW CAUSES DEATH'

Friedrich Dohse had long ago given up hope that his successes would mean a quiet D-Day in the Bordeaux region. But the scale of sabotage Aristide was able to achieve on the morning of 6 June 1944 must have come to him as a shock.

At 23.15 on the evening of Monday 5 June the BBC French Service broadcast 187 messages to Resistance groups across the whole of France. They were all different – but they all meant the same thing: 'D-Day is this morning. You have your tasks. Strike!'

Among these messages were three 'strike' signals for Roger Landes. Each instructed him to launch his prepared sabotage plans immediately: 'The flood team does its work' (rail sabotage); 'Don't be tempted by Venus' (guerrilla attacks on German command centres); and 'This poisoned arrow causes death' (attack communications installations). Landes passed the orders swiftly to each of his groups. They all knew what they had to do.

That night, while Allied landing craft made their way through darkness and choppy seas to the Normandy beaches, the towns and villages across France were alive with flitting shadows and the sound of muffled knocks on doors and whispered orders. Weapons were slid from secret places to be checked and loaded; young men and women pulled on boots, hitched up rucksacks and said goodbye to their loved ones;

country roads resonated with the quiet rumble of unlit cars and lorries bearing dark shadows to their appointed targets.

Though the weather on the beaches of Normandy was blustery and cold for June, in southwest France, thanks to approaching high pressure, the morning broke bright, clear and cloudless. A thin mist hung over the marshes of the Gironde and the sea lapped, quiet and azure, against the beaches of the Aquitaine coast. In the sunlit forests of the Landes, insects buzzed among tall pines standing as lonely sentinels on the black earth. The grape buds in the ancient vineyards of the Gironde hung content-edly in anticipation of another day of ripening sun. And in Bordeaux, under its habitual summer haze, people stirred in their beds and contem-plated another Tuesday.

Since the very smallest hours of that morning, Landes's men had been busy on railway cuttings, under bridges and beneath road culverts, prepar-ing ambushes and planting charges. Over the next two days, seventy-six successful sabotage operations would be carried out. The detonations were heard in every corner and community of the region – and everyone knew what they meant. France's hour of liberation had at last arrived.

From now on, the pace of life for Landes's Maquis began to quicken as his fighters came out into the open. Increasingly, speed and aggression became more important than cover and security. Attacks by Landes's forces on 6 and 7 June included ambushing a German convoy heading north along the Route Nationale 137 for the Normandy beaches; cutting all the main rail lines out of Bordeaux; dynamiting eleven locomotives in the Bordeaux suburb of Pessac; blowing up the main telecommunica-tions cables running north from the city; attacking the headquarters for the port; severing fifteen high-tension electricity cables across the region and cutting the main telephone line serving the château which acted as the headquarters of the German First Army, under General von der Chevallerie. Chevallerie sent a panicky (and wildly exaggerated) message to Army Group G headquarters in Toulouse: 'The Departments of Dordogne and Corrèze are held by terrorists.'

Landes spent most of the period immediately following D-Day at his headquarters in Rue Guynemer sending regular situation reports to

London, based on the messages he was receiving by courier from his commanders. On 8 June, he sent to Baker Street:

GERMAN TROOP TRANSPORTS DERAILED NEAR PONS STOP CONSIDERABLE GERMAN LOSSES STOP GOODS TRAIN ALSO DERAILED NEAR PONS STOP DESTRUCTION OF THE RAILWAY BRIDGE NEAR FLÉAC STOP DERAILED GERMAN TROOP TRANSPORT IN COLLISION WITH A TRAIN CARRYING FUEL NEAR BORDEAUX STOP HUGE EXPLOSION AND FIRE ON THE LINE STOP SERIOUS GERMAN LOSSES INCLUDING A CAPTAIN AND A SERGEANT STOP 33-TON CRANE DYNAMITED FALLING ON A STEAM ENGINE STOP LINE BLOCKED STOP BOTH NOW OUT OF ACTION STOP THE RAILWAY LINE TO SOULAC CUT ENDS.

Even allowing for the fact that some of these reports from the front line were the overstated accounts of those who had never seen war before, the picture of widespread activity against key German installations is probably accurate enough.

It is easy in retrospect to overlook the extraordinary courage and determination of the young men and women of the Resistance during the days which followed 6 June 1944. They too were part of the invasion. Many had never seen a shot fired in anger. Yet, in the Bordeaux area, as across the rest of France, they took on the might of the German army with only Sten guns and plastic explosive. Eisenhower later said that the outcome on the Normandy beaches may well have been different without 'the action taken by the French Resistance whose results exceeded my hopes'.

On the 7th, Hitler, who had been slow to react, fearing that the Normandy landings were a feint, finally gave the order to General Johannes Blaskowitz, the commander of Army Group G in southwest France, to move his main battle units north and join in the defence of Normandy. As Blaskowitz's divisions, the infamous SS Panzer division Das Reich amongst them, began their long, blood-soaked journey north, Bordeaux and the region began to empty of frontline troops and equipment, leaving behind mostly second-rate troops and administrative units. This was followed two weeks later by the withdrawal of all non-essential German female staff from the city.

The effect on the morale of German troops in the area was sharply compounded by widespread shortages. Lack of petrol and scarcity of vehicles meant that, instead of riding in comfort, the German troops had to march almost everywhere – or – perhaps more humiliatingly – use horse-drawn transport. 'Morale ... is very low ... [they are] extremely nervous and never go anywhere alone. Their uniform and equipment is poor ... they have a lot of rifles and submachine guns [which] they take everywhere – even to the cinema. The Milice always carry two grenades and a machine gun [and are] very nervous; there are many desertions,' reported the Canadian Pierre Meunier on his return to London. The wave of sabotage had an effect on the lives of ordinary citizens in Bordeaux, too. 'Numerous sabotage attacks on the railways. Following an explosion in the Labour Exchange ... we had curfew from 10.00pm for several days ... there are constant stoppages in electricity supply and very few trams. Those that there are, break down all the time,' one young resistant wrote in his diary.

Despite their diminished numbers, however, the occupiers could still hit back. On 11 June, a 500-strong force of Wehrmacht soldiers mounted an attack on Léonce Dussarrat's headquarters near Dax, which, at the time, housed more than ten tons of arms and explosive. Forced to retreat, Léon des Landes blew the whole place up, causing an explosion which could be heard forty kilometres away and which, according to Dussarrat (who was famous for exaggerated reports), killed forty-two German soldiers.

Not all of the actions of Landes's men were 'glorious'. The rudimentary nature of his hastily assembled units began to show in breakdowns of discipline. On 11 June, André Bouillar's men raided and quickly overran a Milice base in Bordeaux. According to one (uncorroborated) source, what followed was an exercise in unbridled and ferocious vengeance. Some of the Milice were beaten to death. Others were first chained up and then eviscerated. One teenage *Milicien* was strung up by his heels and, his throat cut, left hanging, bleeding to death, like an animal in an abattoir. Another was knifed to death in front of his comrades. Bouillar did his best to intervene and stop the carnage, telling the assailants: 'These are our prisoners! … behave like proper soldiers! Stop this massacre!' There was a brief lull, but then, when someone reported that German reinforcements were approaching, the remaining prisoners were machine-gunned to death.

Landes was furious with Bouillar's men. 'What you have done has poisoned the sacred cause for which you fight,' he told them. 'I know how much you hate these people, but we must not act as they themselves have done to their prisoners … [now] the Germans will have cause when they treat our captured men, not as soldiers, but as terrorists.'

But not all Landes's problems were with his ordinary Maquisards. By 13 June, a week after D-Day, Commandant de Luze, the head of the Arcachon Maquis, had failed to carry out a single one of his sabotage attacks. Landes sent him a note drawing attention to the failure and threatening a report to Supreme Allied Headquarters in London. De Luze's reply was as swift as it was furious: he did not take orders from a 'mere sabotage chief' and would henceforth take instructions only from Morraglia's local FFI representative, Georges Julien. At least Julien 'has the advantage of being a Frenchman', de Luze ended pointedly. De Luze's volte-face was the first step along a road that would, in due course, lead to the death of the man whose command he now accepted – Georges Julien.

The defection of de Luze was a clear illustration of one of Landes's biggest difficulties: some of his guerrilla bands had attached themselves to him not because they accepted his leadership, but because it was the only way to get access to the arms from parachute drops.

The loss of Édouard de Luze's 350 men was not as serious as it might seem at first sight, for by now new recruits were joining Landes's Maquis bands in large numbers. The rate of parachute drops was also increasing apace. By the end of June, Landes estimated that, despite casualties and some defections to other Resistance groups, he could still call on some 4,000 men under arms.

The flow of messages to and from London was growing, too. By the middle of June, Landes had finished training a locally recruited second radio operator and had a third in operation by early August. Coding and decoding of messages was carried out by François and Mitou Faget, whose home by now resonated with the comings and goings of a full-scale guerrilla headquarters. Copies of communications traffic with London were kept for two days and then burnt. Fortunately Landes had an uncanny ability to recall previous messages almost verbatim, and even from weeks previously. Sometime around the end of July or early August, Landes managed to obtain – or had parachuted to him – a Morse-compatible teleprinter, which greatly speeded up the transmission and reception of messages.

Landes's biggest problem now was not his men or their arms, but the vexed and seemingly insoluble problem of command and control in the Bordeaux area. On 18 June, London sent out messages to all its SOE networks, instructing them that henceforth they were to come under the command of the FFI, whose overall head, the London-based French general Marie-Joseph Koenig, had now been incorporated into Eisenhower's SHAEF headquarters. Landes, remembering that his mission orders stipulated that he was in sole charge – and not having been given any instructions to the contrary – presumed 'in good faith' that this order meant he was Koenig's senior representative in Bordeaux. Morraglia, on the other hand, took London's signal to be confirmation that he was the person in charge – and so the deadly confusion deepened.

The problem should have been resolved when, three weeks later, a new regional military delegate, Lieutenant-Colonel Charles Gaillard, arrived in Bordeaux. But for some reason, the thirty-one-year-old wine merchant, whose love of good company was, by some measure, greater than his natural ability to command, did not manage to meet Landes until almost a month after his arrival. By this time the fratricidal conflict paralysing the Bordeaux Resistance had reached unstoppable proportions.

While most of Landes's concerns in the weeks after D-Day were the problems of success, most of Dohse's difficulties were those of impending defeat. Even though the Allies would not finally break out from the Normandy beachhead for another two months, it was plain to most

Frenchmen, and all but the most diehard Germans, that the Nazis could not now win the war. As Landes's numbers swelled, Dohse's sources of intelligence and support began to dry up. Although German forces retained a tight grip over the main arteries of communication and the chief centres of population, the withdrawal of troops from country areas meant that control in many rural districts now slipped into the hands of the Resistance. Meanwhile, the Gestapo, also now on the back foot, had to substitute desperate short-term measures for long-term strategy. Before D-Day, a captured Resistance fighter would be patiently interrogated and then released on a promise to collaborate. After D-Day, they were given one chance to talk, followed by immediate torture and a swift execution if they did not.

On 20 June, Dohse moved André and Lucette Grandclément out of the seaside villa at Moulleau and back to Bordeaux. Under the surname 'Gonthier', they took a rented apartment in a city-centre backstreet two kilometres from the KdS headquarters.

Ten days later, on the night of 30 June, German forces launched one of their last major anti-Resistance operations, arresting more than forty Maquisards in and around Arcachon (Grandclément's move to Bordeaux may have been arranged in order to avoid the consequences of this sweep). The raid was planned and commanded by Kunesch, while Dohse, reduced to the status of a mere observer, stood idly watching from the steps of the Arcachon war memorial, dressed – most unusually – in the full uniform of a Gestapo lieutenant.

With German forces now being pounded into submission in Normandy and diminishing resources available to him in Bordeaux, Dohse knew that he didn't have the means to influence the course of events in his region. The best he could do was to diminish their effect. He understood that soon – in the next few weeks – German forces would have to withdraw. His job now was to reduce, as far as he could, the dangers they would face when doing so.

Fortunately, he could always rely on a divided Resistance to help him where he could not help himself.

*　*　*

A week after the defection of de Luze's Arcachon units to General Morraglia's man Georges Julien, the forty-nine-year-old Julien detected, or thought he did, that he was under surveillance. He shaved his beard, moved address and changed his name. His suspicion may have been well founded for it was believed by some at the time (wrongly) that de Gaulle's government in London had appointed Julien as the future *préfet* of the Gironde. The perceived appointment was not popular with some (such as Landes, who suspected Julien's closeness to Morraglia) and excited jealousy and enmity in many others.

The precise course of events which ensued is confused and contested. But what happened as a result of them is not.

On 25 June, Georges Julien was sitting on the terrace of a café in the centre of Bordeaux with colleagues (including André Noël, the man who had threatened Landes on the Pont de Pierre in April) when André Bouillar – Dédé le Basque – walked by. A brief conversation followed, in which Julien and Bouillar agreed to meet the following day to try to resolve the antagonism between Landes and Morraglia. The rendezvous was fixed for 1100 hours on the corner of the Rue Élie Gintrac, a narrow cobbled backstreet close by.

The next morning at 10.30, Bouillar, accompanied by four men, arrived on the Rue Élie Gintrac and started making his way to the meeting point. There was as yet no sign of Julien. Instead 'the whole place was infected with the "flics" [police],' one of his group recalled. Bouillar 'pointed at two of them and said: "I'll [pretend I am still an inspector and] ask them for their papers." He came back a moment later and whispered: "Yes. One is French and the other is German. We'd better beat it."'

Bouillar turned and vanished down a sidestreet. The others, too, made to leave. But, 'then, just as we turned to go, I felt the muzzle of a pistol in my side accompanied by an order barked in a German accent, to raise my hands. I looked round. They had rounded up all the rest of us.' The four men were herded through the front door of a nearby cheese shop, put up against a wall and searched. Pistols and grenades were found. The officer in charge ordered one of his men to ask the French policeman watching outside on the pavement to order up some transport and take the prisoners away. The 'French policeman' at the window was in fact Dédé le Basque, who had returned to find his men. Bouillar entered the cheese shop, and, while exclaiming 'Ah! You have them,' pulled out his pistol and, firing several shots in succession, killed two of the policemen and wounded others, including the Gestapo's official interpreter, Pierre Esch. In the ensuing confusion, Bouillar and his four companions made good a hasty escape.

Georges Julien finally turned up at the rendezvous at around 11.15, claiming that his tram had broken down. Post-war evidence would reveal that he was telling the truth. But the damage was done: the suspicion was planted that his absence was deliberate and that he had betrayed Bouillar and his men to the Gestapo.

Two days later, a council of war was convened at a Resistance safe house not far from the Bordeaux waterfront. There was a long discussion and some disagreement. Julien's fate was finally swung by the evidence of Josette Lassalle who, though only nineteen, had become one of the most influential women in the Bordeaux Resistance movement. Julien and André Noël were condemned to death. The council also reaffirmed a sentence of execution on André Grandclément for good measure.

The following day after lunch, Josette Lassalle met Julien outside the Palais de Justice, where he had been conducting some private business. The two took a stroll along the boulevards in the June sunshine. 'He didn't ask any questions about where we were heading,' Josette said afterwards. 'We chatted about nothing in particular … I was nervous, but he didn't seem to notice and appeared very relaxed and at ease. I was very conscious that I was walking alongside a man who was about to die and knew nothing of it. As we walked down the steps of the Palais I pulled my handkerchief out of my blouse pocket. It was the signal.' Julien noticed neither the gesture nor the two men who slipped quietly out of the shadows and started following them. Lassalle led her prey out of the open space of the Place de la République and down a narrow sidestreet.

Suddenly and seemingly from nowhere, one of the assassins was in front of Julien, his pistol pointing at the condemned man. 'Don't shoot,'

Julien pleaded, as his assailant fired his weapon. 'Next thing there were two other men running up behind us,' Lassalle continued.

The new arrivals on the scene were two police auxiliaries who happened to be in the area. The wounded Julien cried to them for help as he lay bleeding on the pavement.

A 'lively exchange of fire' ensued as Lassalle fled the scene on a bicycle which had been left there by her cousin. 'It was only afterwards,' she wrote, 'that I heard that Julien had been killed. That night the BBC announced that Georges Julien, the traitor, had been killed by the Bordeaux Resistance.' Later she heard that one of the assassins had also been seriously wounded and was now in the hands of the Gestapo.

The next day, 30 June, André and Lucette Grandclément once more packed up their things and moved back to Moulleau and their Gestapo villa by the sea. The city was becoming too dangerous for anyone under suspicion as a traitor.

On 11 July, less than a week after the incident on the Rue Élie Gintrac, Landes, putting aside his suspicions, agreed to meet Morraglia again in a last bid to heal the rift between them.

As before, the two men held their meeting on a bench in the Parc Bordelais. And as before, it ended not by resolving their divisions, but by widening them. Both men were obdurate, each asserting that they alone were in charge: 'I am the only Resistance leader in this region,' Landes stated flatly. 'I do not recognise any authority except that of the inter-Allied headquarters in London … I know nothing of the FFI headquarters in London. I have been in this region for two years now and I do not accept the authority of others who come here on Resistance business, unless if I have received orders from London to do so.'

With the Resistance squabbling over who was in charge and the German grip loosening, Bordeaux began to descend into a vortex of disorder and gangsterism driven by suspicion, rivalry and the settlement of old scores. Soon another motivation would be thrown into this witches' brew – the desire to extract as much money as possible in rewards from the Germans, before they left and the well dried up.

A DEADLY CHARADE

On 4 July 1944, as Bordeaux hummed with the news of the plain-daylight execution of Georges Julien, the BBC programme *Les Français parlent aux Français* took the unusual step of transmitting a message that did not contain *any* codewords and could be understood by all who heard it:

> Important information for the FFI in the Departments of the Gironde, the Landes and the Basses-Pyrénées: the Gestapo are creating Maquis groups who are passing themselves off as members of the Resistance. At the head of this organisation is an individual who calls himself 'Grandclément' and is well known for his activities in support of the enemy. [The Gestapo] have threatened that 100 hostages will be executed if any harm comes to Grandclément. André Noël and Georges Julien are his lieutenants. Julien has already been executed. All FFI forces should be prudent in the face of these tricks.

The message was then repeated on subsequent BBC broadcasts, over several days.

André Noël – the man who had bravely rebuffed Dohse's approaches – heard of the broadcast at a friend's house, where he had gone into hiding following Georges Julien's murder. Learning from a colleague that he had been named a traitor and Grandclément's lieutenant, 'he picked up his revolver to kill himself'. He soon had second thoughts, however, and instead locked himself in his office and, to occasional sounds of weeping, refused to come out for three days.

The broadcast was received with no less horror by Grandclément himself. On Saturday 8 July, one of his Resistance friends travelled to Moulleau to tell him in person. The news sent him into a flood of tears, triggering an impassioned third-person-singular outburst. 'Grandclément is NOT a traitor!' he cried.

Desperate to find a way to rehabilitate himself with the Allies and to escape death, Grandclément met with colleagues to discuss his options. If he could persuade Baker Street to send a Lysander to pick him up, he could justify himself personally in London, he reasoned. He started to write a long explanation of his activities and why it was so wrong to condemn him as a traitor. This document can still be found in Grandclément's SOE file in London. It reads like a last appeal for his life:

Moulleau 10 July 1944

I am writing this account because now I have nothing to do but wait for your judgement. I have nothing to save but the honour of a family name, which is not mine alone …

It is not important any more to respond to the accusations which have been made against me. The history of our struggle is not the thing that matters now because of the lack of understanding and seriousness shown by those [in London] who should have been our friends.

I could have abandoned my work many times. Then I would not have been subject to the terrible publicity and even worse accusations made by the BBC, which I heard about last Saturday. I need hardly say that I regard this as a repudiation of all that I have done for you.

I swear that no Frenchman has been arrested because of me … and that I am not, as you claim, an enemy agent.

In the fourteen-page, closely typed document, which was written over the next few weeks, Grandclément lists his actions in great detail and attempts to explain why he should still be considered a true and committed French patriot.

Of all this, Roger Landes, still unaware of Grandclément's whereabouts, knew nothing. For the moment, he had other matters to deal with.

In the first ten days of July, a serious dispute broke out in the area controlled by Léonce Dussarrat when an ex-army FFI colonel tried by force to take over two of Dussarrat's parachute sites. Dussarrat's men had to open fire to beat off the intruders. When a furious Landes asked for an explanation, the colonel – described by Landes as 'a Vichy supporter often seen in photos alongside Marshall Pétain' – said he had been operating on orders from Morraglia. Another reason, Landes concluded, for suspecting Morraglia's intentions.

On 14 July, Bastille day, under a sun so hot it seemed to scorch the earth, the great, wounded, lumbering beast of the Wehrmacht lashed out for one last last time. The target of all their iron-clad, mobilised might was a group of fifteen students, aged between seventeen and twenty-one, who had taken up residence at a ramshackle farm in the midst of a pine forest at Saucats, twenty kilometres south of Bordeaux. Attacked by a mixed force of Pierre Poinsot's police, French auxiliaries and Wehrmacht, the youngsters tried to defend themselves with a few light arms. The Germans brought up a 105mm cannon and, in short order, reduced the building to rubble, killing all its occupants. Dohse later claimed that he had no part in the massacre; Kunesch was in charge of the operation. But the planning had been done by Dohse, who was almost certainly present in his role as 'observer'.

Three days after Saucats, on 17 July, Grandclément, more nervous than ever about his security in Arcachon, decided that he should move again. Accompanied by Lucette and a friend, he called on the parents of twenty-two-year-old Marc Duluguet, who, at some point after meeting Grandclément at Lencouacq, had subsequently become his 'bodyguard'.

'A couple came to our restaurant in Biganos and asked to see my son,' Duluguet's mother, Augustine, later related. 'They were introduced as M. and Mme Bernard Lefrançois. They chatted for a while, before my son left with them for Arcachon in a lorry.'

Four days later, on 21 July, 'M. and Mme Lefrançois' returned, this time with two suitcases, and asked Mme Duluguet if she could 'put them up for forty-eight hours?' The reason, Grandclément explained, was that 'They [the Resistance] now know where I am in Arcachon.' Augustine Duluguet agreed and the couple moved in.

The following morning, a Saturday, André Grandclément and Marc Duluguet left to catch the train to Bordeaux, where Grandclément had two important appointments to keep: the first with a Resistance colleague, Jean Charlin, who had promised to fix a Lysander flight to London for him and Lucette; the second meeting, later that afternoon, was with Dohse. That day, however, all trains were cancelled, almost certainly because of sabotage on the line. The two men hitched a lift instead on a milk lorry. Arriving in the city shortly before two o'clock, they went straight to the restaurant Le Volant d'Or, where Grandclément had arranged to meet Charlin.

It was a trap. André Grandclément thought he was about to have lunch. He was, in fact, about to be arrested by Charlin, the head of a Resistance 'fast response team' that had been sent to detain him, by force if necessary, and take him to a Bordeaux safe house for interrogation.

The man behind this carefully laid ambush was the new Regional Military Delegate, Charles Gaillard, who had arrived in Bordeaux on 10 July with instructions to find Grandclément and have him killed. It was he who had fixed the false lunch invitation and it was he who had proposed the promise of a Lysander flight to London, as bait, knowing all along that no such flight was possible; Bordeaux was well beyond the range of Lysanders flying from London.

Some days previously, Gaillard had met Morraglia and one of his senior lieutenants to discuss the Grandclément question. They decided that before Grandclément's execution, he should be questioned to establish the full facts of his 'treachery'. 'We had as yet not decided that he should be executed,' said one of those present at the meeting, 'because first we wanted to find out exactly what had happened. Though I have to say that in my view his guilt was inescapable ... One thing we needed to avoid, if we could, was an execution on a public street – we had to respect some standards.'

Grandclément put up no struggle when he was taken. 'Neither he nor his bodyguard made any aggressive or defensive moves,' Charlin wrote in the report to his superiors later that day.

There was, however, Charlin soon discovered, a problem. What was to be done about Grandclément's meeting with Dohse later that afternoon? After a discussion, the prisoner was escorted to the restaurant telephone and made to ring Dohse and tell him that he was going to Toulouse on business for a fortnight. Finding Dohse out, Grandclément left a message.

While Duluguet remained at the restaurant, Grandclément was driven through the city to a safe house, just 150 metres from Dohse's office. Here the 'prisoner' was handed over to three of Gaillard's men. They were under instructions first to interrogate Grandclément and then, when they had extracted all the information they needed, to decide whether he was to be executed or not.

A period of intensive questioning followed in which Grandclément seems to have given a convincing account of himself. Late in the afternoon, his interrogators, now increasingly uncertain about their prisoner's fate, took him back to the Volant d'Or, where, reunited with Duluguet, they had further discussions over a light meal. Finally, with Grandclément believing that the Lysander flight was still on, the group returned to the Duluguet house to collect Lucette and move all three prisoners to another safe house in Bordeaux.

The party arrived in Biganos at 19.30, just as the Duluguet family were preparing for their evening meal. According to Augustine Duluguet's witness statement, Grandclément said: 'We have to leave now. But don't be worried. Nothing bad will happen because of what you are about to see. I am about to be "kidnapped". Please wait an hour and then contact the police and report that a "Bernard Lefrançois" has been kidnapped. Leave the rest to them. If, after forty-eight hours, you are getting trouble from the Germans, then you can tell them that you have reason to believe that "Lefrançois" was in fact André Grandclément.' Mme Duluguet was given a script to use with the police when they arrived. She was to claim that 'a group of armed men broke into our house shouting "Hands up".

They seized the two "Lefrançois" and my son, bundled them into an open-topped Citroën and drove off at speed.'

In reality, the Grandcléments had ample time to collect their suitcases (including one packed full of Lucette's dresses and shoes), and a leather briefcase containing André Grandclément's papers, some gold coins, and Lucette's favourite items of jewellery (which had been brought to the Duluguet house the day before by Lucette's mother, who thought they might be 'useful in England'). At this stage, all three 'prisoners' were still armed; the men with automatic pistols and Lucette with a 'ladies' 6.35 mm revolver which she kept in her handbag. All had Gestapo certificates (issued by Dohse) entitling them to carry arms.

When everything was set for their departure, the charade was acted out for the benefit of the neighbours.

At 2300 hours that evening, the local police station sent a report to their headquarters in Bordeaux giving the descriptions of a '*Monsieur et Madame Lefrançois*', who that evening at 20.30 had been abducted in a Citroën car from the Duluguet restaurant in Biganos.

The 'kidnappers' and their 'prisoners', meanwhile, returned to the safe house in Bouscat where they spent the night. The following day, 23 July 1944, Grandclément wrote the final pages of his apologia. His last words were 'That's all'. Lucette, meanwhile, wrote a letter to her mother, telling her: 'If André lies low, we'll be fine.' Marc Duluguet also wrote a letter that day – to his parents: 'After a short journey, my morale is high and my health excellent. Don't worry about me, my dear parents. More news soon. I embrace you both. With much love. Marc.'

Despite this appearance of normality, Grandclément's captors were now getting worried: their prisoners were, they reported, beginning to 'show signs of nervousness'. That evening, it was decided that the three should be moved again, this time to the village of Macau in the midst of the vineyards of Margaux, sixteen kilometres north of Bordeaux. Here they spent the next two days and nights. Then their increasingly jumpy captors again heard a rumour of German units on their way. There was another hurried departure to another safe location in a western suburb of Bordeaux – at 73 Allée des Pins, a substantial townhouse with a high-fenced garden. Further questioning, spread out over three days, ensued. Once again Grandclément's interrogators found his account and his passionate declarations of innocence convincing. Slowly, the interrogators began to wonder whether, after all, an execution was justified.

Back in Bouscat, Dohse, unaware that Grandclément had been held within yards of his office, began to smell a rat. On 25 July, he called in for questioning Grandclément's chief lieutenant, André Maleyran, plus Lucette's mother and cousin. None of them had any idea of the where-abouts of the fugitives.

Dohse started to spread the word that if anything happened to the Grandcléments, fifty hostages would be shot. He ordered his men to find the couple as a matter of urgency.

On 27 July the Grandcléments' captors received yet more warnings that the German authorities were on to them. Under the pretext that the 'Lysander to London' was due to arrive that evening, the party left in a hurry in two cars, heading for a 'Lysander landing site', close to the remote village of Saugnacq-et-Muret, southeast of Arcachon. But when they arrived in the area, the Grandcléments were told that the plans had changed again, this time because the flight had been 'delayed'. They would now have to spend the night in a nearby barn to avoid 'German patrols in the area'. In the evening, one of the bodyguards returned to Bordeaux to pick up a packed meal from a restaurant.

It seems that at about this time the executioners, faced with the task of killing their prisoners – especially Lucette – lost their nerve and began to think of alternatives.

One alternative was Roger Landes. If he could be made aware that the Grandcléments had been found, he might take the burdensome prison-ers off their hands. If this was indeed their plan, then they judged their man perfectly.

Late in the morning of 27 July, one of Landes's key lieutenants, a man named Alban Bordes, burst into his room on the Rue Guynemer with dramatic news. 'We have Grandclément!' he exclaimed.

Landes immediately instructed Bordes to meet with Grandclément's captors and insist that they hand over the 'prisoner' and his companions. Bordes should then deliver the captive, and anyone with him, to the home of his parachute reception chief in the area, Franck Cazenave. Landes would join them later at Cazenave's house on the outskirts of Belin-Béliet, not far from the Prince drop site at Saugnacq-et-Muret where, back in April, Landes and Campet had taken their first parachute drop of weapons, after Landes's return to France. If Grandclément tried to escape, he was to be shot, ordered Landes. Writing out a note on the spot, Roger Landes took full responsibility for the execution: 'Consistent with the powers vested in me,' began Landes, who had been promoted to full major the day before:

> I have ordered the execution of Grandclément.
>
> The blood of numerous Frenchmen, which has been spilt for their country, demands no less.
>
> Grandclément is an agent of the Gestapo [and] his actions prove it. His staged kidnapping by patriots is only a ruse to draw us into a trap, which could put the future of our clandestine struggle in jeopardy.
>
> On my word of honour, I judge that this is no more or less than an act of justice and I take full responsibility for this action.
>
> [signed] In the field
> the 27th of July 1944
> Aristide
> [Military Delegate of the War Office]

Meanwhile in the barn at Saugnacq-et-Muret, the kidnappers had decided to move their prisoners yet again, this time to a nearby wood. It was here at around four in the afternoon that Bordes, accompanied by some of Landes's men in two cars, found them. The captors seemed content, even eager, to hand over their charges – though, for form's sake, they demanded a signed undertaking that the Grandcléments would be 'sent back to London'.

The handover procedures completed, Bordes disarmed the three prisoners, bundled them into one of his cars and drove them to the Cazenave
villa. During the journey Bordes sat in the front, his body twisted round
so that he could point his pistol at Grandclément, who sat in the back
with Duluguet and one of Bordes's men. There was no seat for Lucette,
who had to perch on her husband's knee.

That night the prisoners were accommodated in the cellars of
Cazenave's house on the pretext that they needed to be kept out of sight
until the Lysander arrived from London.

The following afternoon, 28 July, Landes, Christian Campet and
André Bouillar, together with Landes's driver/bodyguard, Max Faye,
arrived at the Cazenave villa and walked into the cellar. André
Grandclément, horrified, cried out: 'It's a trap!'

Landes was later to describe what happened next as a 'court martial'.
It was, in reality, nothing of the sort. There had already been several
orders, not least those broadcast by the BBC, that André Grandclément
was to be executed. The sentence had been passed. Landes's duty as a
soldier was now to carry it out. The purpose of the ensuing interrogation
in the cellars of the villa was not to determine guilt or innocence, but to
extract as much information from the condemned man as possible.
However, in order to keep the prisoners calm, Landes went to some
lengths to continue the fiction that they were being prepared for a return
to England by Lysander, which would land on the Prince drop site that
night. As part of this deception, Landes gave the trio some time to
prepare for the flight. Lucette washed and put on a green dress and some
wooden-soled sandals with slingbacks, which she had brought with her
specially for London. Marc Duluguet, who was already wearing a brown
suit and a blue tartan shirt, was carrying 10,000 francs in his wallet.
Grandclément put on a dark city suit and well-polished shoes.

At one stage Grandclément asked Landes to guarantee on his honour
that he, Lucette and Duluguet were going to London. Landes replied,
ambiguously: 'I give you my word that you will be leaving here.'

During the afternoon, Mitou Faget arrived on her bicycle from
Bordeaux. She had taken a huge risk, cycling forty-five kilometres

through the German roadblocks which were now covering the area. And she did not have good news. A German unit was heading for the villa. They had to move fast. The group had already worked out who would do what. No one wanted to kill the woman, so Landes agreed that, as their chief, he would have to. Bouillar would shoot André Grandclément and Campet would kill Marc Duluguet.

Landes placed a small magnetic clam mine, normally used to sabotage railway lines, under the petrol tank of Faye's car. It was primed with a time pencil set to go off in half an hour. This Landes could quickly initiate so that the car would blow up if they were forced to flee in the face of an ambush or a roadblock. Landes himself travelled with André Grandclément and Campet in the front vehicle, while Marc Duluguet and Lucette, accompanied by Bouillar, and Bordes were in the second. Marguerite Faget and Franck Cazenave stayed behind at the villa.

At 16.30 the little convoy swung right out of the villa's stout wooden gates and dropped down a sharp escarpment onto the marshy plain below. The late afternoon sun shone, dappled, through the trees lining the first part of their journey. André and Lucette seemed relaxed and confident that they were soon to be picked up for the flight to London. But Marc Duluguet was visibly nervous.

After ten minutes or so, they passed through Saugnacq-et-Muret, taking the last turning right at the end of the village and driving 500 metres along a rough track, past some farm labourers' cottages and on until they were on open, deserted ground. They were now only 150 metres from the Prince parachute site.

Faye drew the front car to a halt in the shadow of a large oak. They all got out and walked towards the 'landing site'. After seventy-five metres they arrived at a junction, where the party halted. It was moving towards dusk now. The air was still and the sky luminous with evening colours. Little birds flitted in and out of bushes, chasing a cloud of flies hatching from a small stream running in a deep drainage ditch, half hidden in grasses and ferns at the side of the track.

André Bouillar proposed that he, Campet, Duluguet and Grandclément should walk a little distance up the left-hand fork to check that all was clear, while Landes, Faye and Lucette should go up the right-hand side leading to the landing site.

They had parted company only for a couple of minutes or so when a loud shout – almost a scream – followed by an explosion of repeated shots shattered the evening air. Landes, walking slightly behind Lucette, pulled out his Colt, put it to her head and pulled the trigger. But the safety catch was still on. In the moment it took him to push it off, 'she felt the cold of the muzzle on the back of her head, and began to turn to look at me. But at that moment the shot went off. The bullet entered at the back of her head and exited from her forehead with a jet of blood … more than a metre long.' Lucette Grandclément, who had tried to dissuade her husband from his foolishness with the Germans, fell to the track in a crumple of shimmering green, splattered with wet blood. Landes and Faye dragged her body to the edge of the ditch at the side of the track and rolled it in. Her blood billowed in the clear water, staining the ferns and grasses as it flowed.

Bouillar, who was used to the business of assassination, dispatched André Grandclément cleanly. But Christian Campet's nerve failed him at the last moment, leaving Duluguet on the ground wounded and screaming for mercy. Marc Duluguet, whose only sin was to be in the wrong place at the wrong time, was finished off with two further shots from Bouillar's pistol. The two bodies were dragged to the ditch and rolled in on top of Lucette's, followed by their luggage (except for Grandclément's briefcase, which Landes took away for examination). The executioners did their best to cover the corpses with ferns and branches, working as fast as they could. The shots would have been heard in the houses nearby, so they could not delay long. Landes had previously made arrangements for a team to collect and dispose of the cadavers in the morning.

With night falling, the team transferred machine guns and grenades out of the boot of Landes's car into the interior, in case of trouble, and left for Bordeaux, taking the long way back to avoid roadblocks. They had to be very careful now. It would be late by the time they got to the city and the countryside was crawling with German soldiers and French police.

Near Bordeaux, turning a corner, they bumped into a Milice checkpoint on a level crossing. They had no choice but to risk it. They pushed the safety catches off their machine guns, ready to fire. But, drawing level to the barrier, they were suddenly waved through with salutes and an order for the guards to present arms. Campet, realising that the Milice had mistaken their large black car for a Gestapo vehicle, wound down the window, stuck out his hand in the Nazi salute and shouted '*Heil Hitler!*' as they sped away.

Arriving back at 29 Rue Guynemer, Landes examined the contents of Grandclément's briefcase, finding a bundle of blank receipts signed by Claude de Baissac and other evidence that Grandclément had been in close touch with Jean-Baptiste Morraglia. That night there was a bonfire in Mitou Faget's back garden, accompanied by the acrid smell of burning leather, as Landes destroyed Grandclément's briefcase and all its contents.

THE VIPER'S NEST

It was not until the day of the execution of André Grandclément that Roger Landes learned that three days previously, on 25 July, one of his key Resistance leaders in the city, Lucien Nouaux, had walked into a trap and been captured. Nouaux was taken back to Bouscat, where he was guarded by two Gestapo agents while waiting to be interrogated by 'Tony the Boxer' Enzelsberger. As his interrogator walked into Nouaux's cell, the Frenchman pulled a concealed pistol. In the firefight which ensued, Enzelsberger was wounded and Nouaux killed outright.

Nouaux had been betrayed by one of his men, who had been arrested and promised his freedom by Dohse if he gave away his chief. Landes, however, suspected Morraglia was behind it somewhere. Two days later, the driver who had taken Bordes and Grandclément to the Cazenave villa in Belin-Béliet, was also arrested in circumstances which seemed to cast suspicion on Morraglia. Now Landes was certain: Morraglia *was* a traitor.

A wave of further arrests followed. Landes told his men to lie low until the dust settled and ignored repeated urgent requests to meet with Morraglia and the Regional Military Delegate, Charles Gaillard.

On 1 August, fifty hostages were taken to the military camp at Souge and shot. The executions – seen at the time as Dohse carrying out his threat to shoot hostages if anything happened to the Grandcléments – deepened the climate of recrimination, suspicion and fear in the city. A post-war investigation would clear Dohse of any involvement in the executions, concluding that they were probably unconnected with the death of the Grandcléments. But by then the damage had been done.

A week after the Souge executions, on 7 August, having taken elaborate precautions, Landes finally met Lieutenant-Colonel Gaillard, de Gaulle's newly arrived Regional Military Delegate, in the Parc Bordelais. As when Landes had met Morraglia for the first time, the two men sat on a park bench amongst the ornamental flower beds, surrounded at some distance by two circles of armed bodyguards, each regarding the other with hair-trigger suspicion. This time, however, the meeting was a success. The two men hit it off immediately. Gaillard undertook to deliver Grandclément's fellow 'traitor', André Noël, to Landes, and agreed to join forces and create a single unified headquarters under the overall command of the FFI. General Morraglia was now left isolated and even more disgruntled.

That same day, Gaillard sent a message to one of his men: 'I have received instructions for the departure of André Noël. Place him under the care of one of my agents who will look after him until his departure.'

The following day Gaillard's man found Noël at the home of a colleague and showed him a letter of authority from London demanding his return to the British capital. A car would take him to a landing site near Montendre, forty kilometres northeast of Bordeaux, where a Lysander would pick him up and take him to England. 'Perhaps you will be going back with André and Lucette Grandclément and young Duluguet,' Noël was told, disingenuously. As with Grandclément, assurances were sought by and given to Noël that he would indeed be delivered 'as a free man' to London.

On 10 August, Noël was lunching and playing cards at a restaurant with his mistress and an acquaintance when the telephone rang to say that his Lysander would be leaving that evening. After making his excuses to his cards partner – 'Please give my apologies to your wife and tell her that I shall not be able to come to dinner with you both tonight' – Noël returned home with his lover to wait for the call. Later that afternoon, he rang a lifelong friend to say goodbye. 'Have confidence in me,' Noël said. 'I am not a shit.'

At five that evening, wearing a lightly striped blue suit, a white shirt, carrying a raincoat for the London weather and papers in the name of

'Louis Boudet', Noël was collected by a Resistance contact and taken to wait in the garden of a nearby restaurant. Half an hour later he was picked up and, under an escort of five of Landes's men, including, once again, Bordes, taken to the ruined eighteenth-century Château Grattequina on the west bank of the Garonne.

Here, after a brief interrogation, André Noël, the supposed 'Gestapo agent' who had refused all of Dohse's advances, was executed with a bullet to the back of his head and another through his temple. Stripping his corpse of identifying items and valuables, one of his assassins took Noël's gold watch chain, while another helped himself to the dead man's wallet and a small suitcase. Noël's body was then weighted down with a large stone, carried the few yards from the château to the bank of the Garonne and thrown in.

Three days later, on 13 August, the BBC announced that 'André of Bordeaux has arrived in London'. That same day a decomposing body popped to the surface alongside a fishing jetty two kilometres downstream from Château Grattequina. It was not until a year later that the corpse was identified as that of André Noël. London knew exactly who it was, however. They had sent a message to Landes the day before the body's discovery: 'BRAVO! STOP YOU HAVE DONE VERY WELL ON THE SUBJECT OF ANDRÉ NOËL ENDS.'

As Bordeaux approached its last days under German occupation, the city sank deeper and deeper into a viper's nest of betrayal, score-settling and manoeuvring for advantage. Those who had power vied for ascendancy after the German departure. Those who had grudges found whatever means they could to settle them. Those who were venal strenuously applied themselves to extracting as much money as possible from the Nazi golden goose, before it flew away home.

In the first days of August, an anonymous letter dropped onto the desk of Walter Machule, the head of KdS Bordeaux:

I suppose that you may be interested in American, British and Canadian pilots who have been shot down? I can deliver a number of these pilots who are at the moment attempting to cross the frontier into Spain. If you want to see what I can do, send a car driven by someone in civilian clothes at 0700 tomorrow morning to the Boulevard du Médoc, outside the Rex Cinema. Four pilots will get into the vehicle. You can do what you like with them. I will need 500,000 francs and a permission to drive anywhere in France for my troubles. The password will be 'Philippe Henriot's revenge'.

Dohse persuaded Machule to let him take charge of the operation. The Rex was, after all, less than 500 metres from his office.

When the car, driven by one of Dohse's agents, arrived at the rendez-vous, two British pilots emerged from the cinema and got in. Without waiting further, the chauffeur drove off and, just around the corner, delivered them into the hands of Dohse's men. An hour later, at eight, Dohse received a phone call. It was from 'Philippe Henriot':

'Did you get the four pilots?'

'No. I only got two.'

'That's because your driver drove off too quickly.'

Henriot promised he would ring back with instructions to pick up the missing two pilots. Sure enough, a few minutes afterwards the phone rang again: 'Send a car to the bar in the Place des Quinconces as quick as you can.'

Once more, as soon as the car arrived outside the bar, the pilots – two Americans – emerged, got in the car and were whisked away to captivity.

The transactions completed, Dohse handed over not the 500,000 francs that had been demanded (which he regarded as excessive), but 50,000 francs. Over the following days, some fifty further escapees were delivered to Dohse at an average cost of 10,000 francs each. They included two Royal Navy officers and several more airmen.

It did not take long for Dohse to identify his benefactor as François Charles Cominetti, one of Landes's men, who was also rumoured to be close to Morraglia. On 10 August, Cominetti, under the guise of 'Philippe Henriot', contacted Dohse again – would he like Landes as well? If so, it would cost him 500,000 francs. Dohse jumped at the possibility. This was the first time, after two years of hunting for first Stanislas and then Aristide, that Dohse had been offered a betrayal by someone so close to his quarry. Cominetti explained that he was going to Arcachon to meet Landes and would contact Dohse again on his return.

A few days later, before the deal could be finalised, the order was received for KdS to pack up, destroy all their files and prepare to pull out of Bordeaux. It seems highly unlikely that Landes would have allowed himself to be betrayed by Cominetti. Nevertheless, it must have been galling in the extreme for Dohse to have to leave Bordeaux before he could take advantage of such an apparently tempting offer.

Everyone knew that the German occupation of the city was now drawing to a close. On 10 August a German commander told the mayor of Bordeaux that the city would be defended against the Allies at all costs. The entire population of the working-class suburb of Bacalan was moved out to make way for concrete barricades and a new line of trenches. Vast amounts of explosives were shipped into the quays area and all the major installations were mined, ready for the planned destruction of the entire port at 12.30 on 25 August.

This time, however, the Resistance was a jump ahead. Ten days previously a young German staff sergeant, Heinz Stahlschmidt, who was involved in preparing the demolition charges, asked a docker friend to put him in contact with the Resistance. Stahlschmidt handed over the entire German demolition plan and offered to help avoid the disaster. Plans were laid for a Resistance raid to blow the explosives before they could be planted. But in the event, it was Stahlschmidt himself who, on 22 August – three days before the planned destruction – dynamited the main German warehouse containing all the detonators and much of the explosives which were to be used to obliterate the ancient port. Fifty German soldiers were killed in the blast, which rocked the whole city. But the port was saved. Stahlschmidt immediately went into hiding under an alias and French protection.

On 16 August, Landes returned from a tour of his units around the region and, for the first and only time since he arrived in France, promptly took to his bed. He had been working impossible hours, eating rarely and always in rush. He spent the next few days being nursed by Mitou Faget for what he self-diagnosed as a 'liver complaint' (doctors later diagnosed gallstones).

Gaillard came to visit Landes on his sickbed in Rue Guynemer two days later. He had some worrying news. In an attempt to strengthen their hand in advance of the liberation, Morraglia and three of his men (including Cominetti) were planning to kidnap Landes and force him to use his radio to fool London into dropping arms to them. Gaillard, who did not have any men beyond his personal staff, asked Landes if he would arrest Morraglia and his conspirators. Landes agreed, pointing out that, since he had no secure facilities, the prisoners would have to be killed. Gaillard agreed and promised to inform his FFI superiors.

Landes signalled London and reported his intention to execute Morraglia and his co-conspirators. London replied by return: 'WE AWAIT YOUR REPORT ON THE SUBJECT OF MORRAGLIA AND HIS THREE ACCOMPLICES AND ADVISE YOU TO CONSIDER VERY CAREFULLY BEFORE PROCEEDING WITH THEIR EXECUTION STOP ... DEEPEN YOUR ENQUIRIES AND DO NOT PROCEED UNLESS YOU ARE ABSOLUTELY CERTAIN ENDS.'

In the event, the arrest of Morraglia and his plotters was overtaken by events. There were still substantial German forces in the Bordeaux area and these were now the priority.

On 19 August, while Landes was still recuperating, Dohse was busy tying up loose ends before quitting France. This included activating the stay-behind spy network run by the Bordeaux midwife-cum-secret-radio-operator which, back in 1943, Dohse had recruited, trained, equipped and tasked to feed information to Berlin on Allied troop movements and political developments in the city. That same day Walter Machule sent him to the city prison at Fort du Hâ to deal with the 230 prisoners still held in German custody there. The Wehrmacht planned to give them all a quick trial and then shoot them. Instead, Dohse moved them to the French part of the prison from where, two days later, they were all released.

A story about Dohse, widely circulated during these last days of the German occupation, describes him – in full Gestapo uniform and protected against Maquis ambush by a large contingent of bodyguards – driving one day through the countryside. Rounding a bend, he suddenly encountered a young man, with a pack on his back and an old French Army helmet on his head, standing at the side of the road.

The Gestapo officer stepped down from his car: 'What's this? Are you on your way to join the Maquis?'

'Who's going to stop me?' the young man responded, with more courage than sense.

'Don't be a fool,' Dohse said. 'We are leaving soon and you shouldn't be an idiot and risk your life for nothing.'

The young man hesitated.

'Tell you what. I'll do you a deal,' Dohse continued. 'Go away and think about it. I will be coming back this way this evening. If you are still here, I'll give you a lift back to Bordeaux.'

That evening, finding the young man back at the same spot, Dohse picked him up and took him home to his parents.

The fact that this story is probably apocryphal is less important than the fact that it was believed, reflecting the legend Friedrich Dohse had skilfully spun around himself as a man not only of cunning, but also compassion.

On 26 August, in a long winding convoy of eighty-four vehicles, KdS Bordeaux left the Avenue du Maréchal Pétain and began the journey back to Germany. It was the start of a total withdrawal from France ordered by Hitler. In all there were more than 300 men and women in the KdS convoy. They comprised not just the German staff at Bouscat – including Dohse himself – but also many of their French and Spanish local agents who had asked to flee with their Nazi masters.

Despite minor skirmishes and ambushes along the way, the convoy made good progress, reaching Angoulême by the end of the day. Here, Walter Machule (who had changed his name to Walter Fischer in an attempt to avoid detection) appears to have had a breakdown, ordering the entire convoy to capitulate to the French in order to avoid further casualties. Dohse and his fellow officers arrested their erstwhile chief, placed him in chains and continued their journey north through Tours, Bourges, Beaune, Dôle, Besançon, Belfort, Mulhouse and Colmar. Passing through France they were constantly harried by Resistance attacks and ambushes, especially in the Vosges mountains, where Dohse once more narrowly escaped death in an ambush. Altogether the convoy lost some forty killed before they finally crossed into the relative safety of German territory at Strasbourg, after a non-stop journey of four days and three nights.

But there was little rest for Dohse and his men. By now Germany was collapsing and all available troops were sent to the Eastern front. After a brief period of respite Dohse and his team set off again, this time for Danzig where he joined a Wehrmacht unit fighting Russian and Polish partisans. Forced to retreat, he led his men, under constant air attack, south to new defensive positions on the frontiers of Germany.

Landès spent these last days of the German occupation coordinating attacks by his Maquis units and calling in RAF bombers to attack the remaining German fortifications and shipping gathering at the mouth of the Gironde to evacuate German troops.

On 21 August, Léonce Dussarrat's men liberated both Mont de Marsan, a hundred kilometres south of Bordeaux, and Arcachon. The liberation of the towns of Bayonne, Biarritz and Hendaye, lying between Bordeaux and the Spanish border, followed in quick succession.

Bordeaux itself was finally liberated on 28 August 1944.

The longed-for moment of freedom was followed by an extended period of disorder, chaos, revenge and excess. After Dussarrat occupied Dax, he set himself up in some luxury with his mistress, Mlle Gouyètes, in the Hôtel Splendid. Here Léon des Landes and his men proceeded to terrorise the staff and carry out reprisals, especially against women accused of consorting with the Germans. Dussarrat, declaring himself 'the barber of the Landes', joined his men in a public event in which the heads of seventy-two women 'collaborators' were shaved in three hours. Gouyètes added to the grim spectacle by stripping naked many of the 'guilty' women and personally shaving their private parts.

On 26 or 27 August, Dussarrat visited the prison in Mont de Marsan where he relieved prisoners of their valuables, while Gouyètes, half drunk, ordered a number of male prisoners to be stripped naked so that she could whip their genitals, remarking for all to hear: 'I like to see blood running.'

The following day, in a dispatch to the British embassy, the head of MI9 in northern Spain, Michael Cresswell, reported that Dussarrat had set himself up 'as a kind of dictator in an area where there is a conspicuous lack of responsible authority', adding that it was proving 'extremely difficult to curb the activities of armed scallywags who are at present claiming to exercise authority in the area'. A similar report from a British observer at the time related that 'the most picturesque [of the local warlords is an] ironmonger [Dussarrat] who has mysteriously become a Brigadier General in command of perhaps a thousand followers and has set up a petty dictatorship at Dax'.

In an attempt to curb the disorder, Landes and Gaillard issued Order No. 1, which was posted around Bordeaux and its hinterland on the evening of 27 August: 'At the moment of our liberation we draw to your attention the fact that we are the sole channel for the issuing of orders from General Koenig [the overall head of the FFI in France]. We require all FFI forces to remain calm and not to undertake premature actions. Our success depends on your discipline.'

The following morning at 4.30, the last German troops left Bordeaux – though substantial pockets of troops still remained around Royan. Two hours later, 1,500 Maquisards, mostly from the Dordogne area, entered the city. On the same day Landes and Gaillard were forced to issue Order No. 2, calling all FFI forces into Bordeaux to help maintain the public peace. But the instruction was frustrated by General Morraglia, who arranged for Landes's units to be waylaid outside the city for three days. Landes suspected that the delay was to enable Morraglia to seize control of Bordeaux before his Maquisards arrived.

Now the twenty-seven-year-old Landes and the thirty-one-year-old Gaillard found themselves swamped, not just with mopping up the last remnants of German forces in the area, but also with a myriad of other administrative problems in newly liberated Bordeaux.

On the 31st, Landes signalled London: 'HUNDREDS OF PEOPLE CLAIMING BRITISH PROTECTION HAVE ARRIVED BORDEAUX STOP SEND A CIVIL OFFICER TO DEAL WITH THEM ENDS.'

The next day he followed this up with: 'NEARLY 1K PRISONERS RELEASED BY THE AMERICANS HAVE ARRIVED BORDEAUX STOP INSTRUCTIONS PLEASE ENDS.'

By 3 September, the problem was further complicated by a flood of German prisoners of war for whom there were no facilities. London instructed Landes to incarcerate them in the old German internment camp at Mérignac. Two days later Landes found himself organising the pursuit of German war criminals and French collaborators trying to escape across the Pyrenees. On 6 September he appealed to London again, this time to send him more money, fuel for vehicles and an Allied officer senior enough to accept the surrender of a German general in Royan. In the days which followed, food supplies in the city began to run out and order showed alarming signs of breaking down altogether.

On 15 September, Landes signalled Baker Street with more disturbing news: '(COMMUNIST FORCES) HAVE ARRIVED IN GREAT NUMBERS FROM ALL OVER FRANCE STOP DISORDER AND LOOTING EVERYWHERE STOP THE SITUATION HAS BECOME CRITICAL IN THE CITY AS THEY HAVE MORE FORCES THAN I HAVE STOP I CANNOT ANY LONGER GUARANTEE THE MAINTENANCE OF ORDER STOP PLEASE ASSIST ENDS'

Not content with looting, the new arrivals also set up their own prisons and tribunals and started to try those they regarded as 'traitors and Milice'. In many cases the accused were simply those who were politically opposed to Bordeaux's new occupiers. Kangaroo courts dispensing justice based on revenge and political partiality sprang up in many parts of the city.

Fortunately, on the same day that Landes signalled London about his concerns over the influx of communists, Colonel Rollot, the one-time commander of the OCM in the southwest whose son had been executed by his Resistance comrades in Lencouacq, arrived from Paris to organise French army units in the area.

Over the next few days, order slowly began to be restored. At a dinner for the new arrival on the evening of 15 September, attended by Landes, it was announced to great excitement that, in two days' time, General de Gaulle himself would pay an official visit to newly liberated Bordeaux.

Though Roger Landes could not have anticipated it, he was about to become a pawn in de Gaulle's campaign to erase – with malice if necessary – all recognition of the role played by British agents in France's struggle and all record of those French men and women who worked with them.

TWO HOURS TO LEAVE FRANCE

On 16 September 1944, the day before de Gaulle arrived in Bordeaux, the senior French civilian representative of his government, Commissioner of the Republic Gaston Cusin, held a planning meeting to work out the details of the general's visit. Those present were Landes, Gaillard (in his role as de Gaulle's Regional Military Delegate), the newly announced interim mayor of Bordeaux, the new commissioner for police and the recently appointed commander of the FFI units in the area. After much discussion they agreed that there would be an address by the general from the balcony of the Hôtel de Ville, the home of the city administration. This would be followed by a reception and lunch, followed by a review of troops, rounded off by a gala dinner in the evening to which all the notables of the city would be invited, including of course Landes and Gaillard.

On the morning of de Gaulle's arrival, Landes, Dussarrat and Gaillard were involved in an incident near the Médoc town of Verdon-sur-Mer, guarding the mouth of the Gironde estuary, where arrangements had been made to celebrate de Gaulle's visit by receiving the surrender of a small pocket of German troops under the command of a Colonel Fritz Meyer.

At 13.30, Colonel Meyer and his staff travelled, unarmed, to meet the French officers who were to take their surrender in the nearby village of Queyrac. The surrender ceremony was proceeding with due solemnity and with the customary respect being shown to the German forces, when Dussarrat (whose men had been doing much of the actual fighting around Verdon), accompanied by Landes, Gaillard and a number of

Dussarrat's fighters, all bristling with sub-machine guns and grenades, burst into the room. Dussarrat made it clear that he was having none of these foppish military practices and proceeded to bang his fist on the table and shout abuse at the German commander, accusing him of being a war criminal. Unsurprisingly, the negotiations ended abruptly, with the German colonel getting up from the table and stalking out in disgust. The French military professionals, too, were scandalised at this breach of military etiquette, only to find themselves being abused by Dussarrat in their turn. It took a lot more delicate negotiations and a lot more time before the German officers would finally be persuaded to return to the surrender table.

It was not a good beginning to what was supposed to be an auspicious day.

That afternoon, Landes drove to meet de Gaulle in Bordeaux in his jeep, with its outsize Union Jack flanked by two smaller ones fluttering from the bonnet and a notice proclaiming he was the representative of the 'British Military Headquarters'. This was not a very diplomatic thing to do, bearing in mind that he was on his way to meet France's proudest Frenchman, who regarded the 'English' in France with no affection whatsoever. De Gaulle's attitude was driven not so much by personal animus, as by reasons of state. The only way he could reconstruct his nation's sense of pride after the humiliation of defeat was by promoting the legend – however flawed – of 'the Resistance' and the sacrifices France had made to liberate herself through her own efforts. The idea that the 'English' had any significant part in the liberation of France was anathema to what de Gaulle was trying to achieve.

De Gaulle's visit began, as planned, with a walk through the city flanked by a crowd of officials (including Landes, whose diminutive figure in battledress and wearing a pistol holster is just recognisable a few paces behind the general's lofty figure in the newsreels of the day). After the procession, de Gaulle appeared on the balcony of the Hôtel de Ville, accompanied by city dignitaries, including the new mayor, resplendent in his mayoral sash, Commissioner of the Republic Gaston Cusin and the French Minister for War. Below him in the square was gathered a large polyglot crowd of Bordeaux's citizens who had come to hear their new head of state. By no means all were de Gaulle supporters and some had already made their discontent known to the city authorities.

Most reports indicate that the general was listened to attentively by a huge and respectful crowd – though one observer, strongly sympathetic to Landes, wrote: 'de Gaulle made a very poor impression in the southwest and especially in Bordeaux, Cognac and the Charente. He is no doubt a very good soldier. But as a diplomat and psychologist, he lacks the finesse to fulfil his functions [as head of state]. After his visit the situation [between the various competing armed groups in Bordeaux] became, not more stable, but more critical and troubling.'

The general, never short of a sonorous phrase to match the moment, ended: 'It is with deep joy and emotion that I have the honour today in the name of France, to salute free Bordeaux.'

The dreadful nightmare which engulfed your city and all of France these last four years has at last blown away. The nightmare of invasion, of capitulation, of servitude has gone ... leaving behind a France once again free, once again indomitable, once again proud ... During these terrible and hopeless months it was not just our tears, our suffering, and our rage which motivated us, but also our courage, our sacrifices, our passion ...

To see us now, to see what we have become – to see each other with clear eyes, this is all that is necessary to understand that, henceforth our unity can never be broken. Let us, then sing those words which mean more than a thousand speeches – let us sing together the great hymn of our nation *La Marseillaise*.

After the thunder of the voices in the square had died away, de Gaulle turned and left the balcony. The municipal party followed him into the formal reception rooms of the Hôtel de Ville, where Landes joined them. The mayor made a short speech which transformed the last four years into an indomitable, heroic and unwavering struggle for victory over Bordeaux's occupiers.

... I hope, *mon Général*, that you will take away from your visit here
the indelible memory of our patriotic pride which never dimmed; of
our unshakeable belief in victory which never died and of the deep
conviction with which we, along with the brave soldiers who fight for
our liberty in every corner of France, follow you on the path of honour
to fulfil the sacred Republican motto of a France once again made
great by its humanity: Liberty, Equality and Fraternity.

After a lunch at which Landes and Gaillard were notably absent, the
general went outside to review the troops.

Here Gaillard introduced him to Landes, dressed in his homemade
British battledress, complete with the shoulder insignia of a British
major.

What followed was brief and brutal.

The general drew himself up to his considerable height and looked
down at the diminutive twenty-seven-year-old British agent with undisguised contempt: 'You are English. Your place is not here. You are to
return to England in the next twenty-four hours.'

Landes replied: 'Pardon me, *mon Général*, but I am a British officer
and I obey only orders from my headquarters in London. I will leave
France when I am ordered to leave.'

De Gaulle made no reply, but swung on his heels and coldly continued
his progress down the line of troops paraded for his inspection.

There was worse to come. After the parade, Landes received instructions to go to the city *préfecture*. Here, walking up the ceremonial marble
staircase to the first floor with his driver and bodyguard Max Faye, he
was confronted by two men in civilian clothes whom he did not recognise. One of them, his voice raised, told Landes he had 'two hours to
leave France'. Max Faye stepped forward and, poking his machine gun in
the Frenchman's stomach, said quietly: 'If you don't shut up I'll pull the
trigger.'

The man turned pale. 'Do you know who I am?' he demanded.

'No,' Landes replied.

'I am the Minister for War, Monsieur Diethelm.'

'Well Monsieur Diethelm,' Landes replied, coolly, 'First, you should introduce yourself – and second, if you want to talk with me it would be better to do it in private, not in public.'

There, unsurprisingly, the interview ended.

According to a British Embassy report on the incident, Landes's crime was 'that he was English, that he had taken too much on himself and that he had made himself too much loved by his men', who, when they heard what had happened – the report continued – were 'highly indignant. Four thousand of them demonstrated that evening outside Landes's and Gaillard's headquarters ... ready to mount a putsch'. Tension mounted, as the angry crowd outside the headquarters shouted '*Aristide au balcon*'. Eventually, Landes appeared on the balcony and, in the words of the embassy report, 'managed to keep them in check'.

That evening, to add insult to injury, Landes and Gaillard's names were conspicuously removed from the guest list for the gala dinner at the Hôtel de Ville. 'Neither you or I are welcome here any longer,' Gaillard observed tartly.

On 20 September, a dinner was given in honour of both Landes and Gaillard by the Bordeaux authorities. According to Landes, the event was held as a form of apology to both men for the way they had been treated by de Gaulle. The following day Landes left Bordeaux for Dax, where he took three weeks' leave doing, in his own words, 'absolutely nothing'.

That same day, Gaillard was ordered to Paris, where he was told to report to the French headquarters at Les Invalides. Here he appears to have been put through some kind of court martial which stripped him of the title of Regional Military Delegate and sentenced him to sixty days' house arrest for what a British diplomat sarcastically described, in a report to the ambassador in Madrid, as 'the hideous crime of cooperating with a British officer'. The diplomat's report ends in superior tone: '[And so,] the political career of this rather pathetic little couple [Landes and Gaillard] is cut short.'

But that was by no means the end of the matter. The day after Landes left Bordeaux, Duff Cooper, Britain's ambassador in Paris, received an official call from Minister of Defence Diethelm's private secretary – 'a personal friend', as Duff Cooper was at pains to point out. This was not, however, a social visit. Monsieur Diethelm wished to lodge an official complaint that Major Landes had 'refused to obey the Minister's orders'. At this stage, the old rule of who you know, rather than what happened, took over. Duff Cooper wrote an excoriating report to London, commenting grandly that Landes and Gaillard were 'in no way equipped to act as military advisors', adding, without reference to the inconvenient fact that there was no one else available to take charge when the Germans left the city, that the two men should never have been allowed to be 'even temporary administrators of places like Bordeaux'. Cooper ended his report in high ambassadorial mode: 'I would submit that [Landes's] immediate recall to London is urgently necessary.'

The effect of Cooper's intervention was immediate. On 21 September, London signalled Landes: 'YOU HAVE ALREADY RECEIVED INSTRUCTIONS TO RETURN UK STOP … CRYSTALS SHOULD BE TAKEN TO PARIS AND WIRELESS EQUIPMENT … SHOULD BE STORED SAFELY FOR COLLECTION LATER ENDS.'

Landes responded the same day, pleading illness: 'MY STATE OF HEALTH AND THE EVENTS OF LAST SUNDAY [THE INTERVIEW WITH DE GAULLE AND DIETHELM] DO NOT PERMIT ME TO RETURN BY WAY OF PARIS STOP VERY SICK AT THE MOMENT STOP DOCTORS BELIEVE MAY NEED SURGERY STOP NEED TO TAKE A REST STOP … WILL STAY HERE IN DAX WAITING FOR FURTHER INSTRUCTIONS ENDS.'

London replied the following day: 'IF STATE OF HEALTH DOES NOT PERMIT A RETURN YET THEN STAY WHERE YOU ARE AND REST STOP BUT YOU MUST SUSPEND ALL, REPEAT ALL, ACTIVITIES IMMEDIATELY ENDS.'

On 24 September, in his last signal to London, Landes tetchily demanded an aircraft to fly him back to Britain: 'KEEN TO RETURN TO LONDON AS SOON AS POSSIBLE, BUT CANNOT GO VIA PARIS BECAUSE OF HEALTH STOP … AM INFORMED THAT A PLANE CAN LAND AT BAYONNE AIRPORT STOP PLEASE GIVE INSTRUCTIONS FOR AN AIRCRAFT TO COME AND COLLECT ME STOP … YOU PUT AN AIRCRAFT AT MY DISPOSAL TO GET ME INTO FRANCE, YOU CAN NOW PROVIDE ME WITH ONE TO GET ME BACK TO ENGLAND ENDS.'

Landes's demands were in vain. After another week in Dax doing 'absolutely nothing', except being fêted nightly by his old comrades, he drove to Bordeaux on 4 October in a sumptuous black limousine 'requisitioned' from a local collaborator. Here Landes had what a British embassy report described as 'secret meetings' with old friends, before, the following day, proceeding at a leisurely pace in his limousine to Paris, where he received instructions for his return to Britain.

Roger Landes finally reached London on 10 October 1944. Despite the brief time off in Dax, he was still in a bad way physically, due to stress, overwork and irregular hours. In just three months he had lost ten kilogrammes in weight from his already slender frame. SOE sent him to Shenley Military Hospital near Watford to recuperate.

Friedrich Dohse, meanwhile, having survived his time on the Eastern front, was passing through a bleak midwinter Berlin, now little more than one vast snow-covered bombsite, on his way to a new marine counter-espionage post in Copenhagen. Dohse called in at Gestapo headquarters in the German capital for a briefing and to pick up the latest news. He was surprised to learn that the stay-behind spy network, led by the French midwife he had trained as a clandestine radio operator and equipped with one of Roger Landes's radios, was still passing detailed information to Berlin on the political developments and the movement of Allied troops in Bordeaux.

Meanwhile, forty-five kilometres southwest of Bordeaux, in shallow water-filled graves near an abandoned shepherd's hut, the body of André Grandclément, together with those of his beloved Lucette and the faithful Marc Duluguet, would lie for another two months before being discovered – and they would remain there for a further two years beyond that, before finally being exhumed and given proper burials.

*

The secrets of the interwoven lives of these three men, one British, one French and one German, who fought a deadly duel for survival during the most crucial years of the Second World War, would take even longer to uncover. At the time, what each did involved great personal danger and was a matter of high secrecy for their comrades and their countries. Today, using official papers, personal accounts and testimonies, we can piece together their actions and reactions to events and to each other, almost by the day.

These individuals' lives were extraordinary – but they were not unusual. Across France and in all the occupied countries of Europe, similar tales of courage, cruelty and cunning – of espionage and counter-espionage – can probably be found.

Neither did what happened to these three make much difference to the fate of France – or even southwest France – in the Second World War.

The importance of this story does not lie in its effect on great events, but rather in the light it throws on how individuals act in the moments of turbulence and danger which are the products of great events. What matters here is not the sweep of history, but what happens when history sweeps ordinary people up and challenges them to become extraordinary and to do extraordinary things.

What we see here, sharply etched and tightly compressed in three lives, lived over just two dramatic years, is what we should be able to see in ourselves, but indistinctly, as through a glass, darkly: the good, the bad; the noble, the shameful; the wise, the stupid; the vain, the selfless; courage and cowardice; loyalty and treachery; the drives of high principle and of low cunning; the instincts both of mercy and of vengeance.

We know how they reacted.

How we might have acted in their place, we may only guess at.

30

NUNC DIMITTIS

From August 1941 – when the two neighbours Jean Duboué and Léo Paillère placed their small Resistance network under the control of SOE in London – until liberation three years later, almost a thousand secret agents worked for the SOE-run networks in and around the Bordeaux area; 293 of these were arrested, of whom twenty-three were shot or hanged, fourteen jailed and 256 deported to the death camps. Among those deported, 156 never saw France again. In addition to these losses, Roger Landes's fighting units also suffered appreciable casualties in the actions fought between D-Day and the surrender of the last German pocket at the mouth of the Gironde, which did not occur until April 1945 – seven months after the liberation of Bordeaux. Among the many killed was the brave and loyal André Bouillar. In the summer of 1944, leading his men as always from the front, Bouillar took a full burst of German machine-gun fire in the chest during an ambush on an armoured column near Montendre. He died of his wounds in hospital on 23 August 1944.

Extraordinarily, Jean Duboué did see France again. After being sent by the German military tribunal to Buchenwald, he was moved to Mittelbau-Dora, the infamous underground slave labour camp in the Hertz mountains where the Nazis secretly constructed their V-weapons. Here, Duboué was shot and wounded trying to escape. Later a runaway rail wagon full of stones ran over his leg, which had to be amputated without anaesthetic. Despite his injuries Jean Duboué survived and made it back to France, reaching Bordeaux in May 1945. He was in such a bad condition that he had to spend several weeks in hospital. Eventually he was able to return to his restaurant on the Quai des Chartrons and his life as one of Bordeaux's most noted restaurateurs.

After the war the French government gave pensions or emoluments to all who could prove they had fought for the liberty of France by serving in the French-run Resistance – including those in SOE's RF Section. But Jean Duboué, as a member of Scientist, had been in the British-controlled F Section and was thus not accepted by the French as their responsibility. His SOE file contains a protracted correspondence between SOE and the British Treasury in which Baker Street argued for the payment of a pension equivalent to the rank of a lieutenant in the British Army. Despite a promise given to Duboué (recorded in his file on 7 May 1943) that he would be eligible for a post-war pension and 'disability or pension rights in relation to casualties incurred in our service', the Treasury refused either a regular or a disability pension, insisting that this was 'a liability of the French government and not of SOE or any other British government department'. But they did grant him a single ex-gratia payment of 75,000 francs.

Whitehall did, however, graciously consent to Duboué being awarded the King's Medal for Courage, which no doubt cost considerably less than the pension to which he was entitled. The French government appointed him a member of the Légion d'Honneur and awarded him the Croix de Guerre and the Médaille de la Résistance. The Belgian government honoured him with the Ordre de Léopold II. But, although the local school at Lestiac is now named in his honour, the city of Bordeaux has erected neither plaque, nor monument, nor memorial to Duboué, or to his family, or to any of his extraordinary colleagues in the Scientist and Actor networks who fought for the liberation of their country through a British, rather than a French Resistance network.

Despite the injuries and depredations he had suffered, Duboué lived until the age of ninety, dying at Lestiac-sur-Garonne on the eve of the forty-second anniversary of the battle of Lestiac, on 13 October 1986.

Jean Duboué's wife, Marie-Louise, who sustained shrapnel wounds to her stomach in the battle of Lestiac, recovered enough to escape from Saint-André hospital and return to the Lestiac area. Afraid of being betrayed by her neighbours, she hid in the vines and was looked after by the local *curé* until the end of the war. Claude de Baissac sought her out when he returned to Bordeaux on a British mission later in 1944. Finding Marie-Louise 'in great need', he arranged for the British government to give her an ex-gratia payment of 25,000 francs. This meagre subvention tided her over until her husband returned (and was subsequently deducted from the 75,000 francs awarded to him). Marie-Louise died just two months before her beloved Jean.

Duboué's fellow restaurateurs, M. and Mme Bertrand, who ran Scientist's headquarters at the Café des Chartrons, were deported. Marcel was never seen again. The café was razed to the ground by the Germans in 1943 as an example to others.

After being sentenced by the Bordeaux military tribunal in January 1944, Suzanne Duboué ('Mouton') spent the rest of the war in Ravensbrück concentration camp. She too survived. The former courier who had, from the age of sixteen, carried clandestine messages hundreds of kilometres through occupied territory in her shopping basket, made her own way back from Ravensbrück to Bordeaux on foot. She subsequently married Robert Léglise, spent much of her married life in the Congo and had a son, whom she named Yves – after the nom de guerre of her former lover, Vic Hayes. Suzanne lost the stability of her mind in the last years of her life, which she spent near Yves and his wife and children, who live in a village close to Nice. In the summer of 2011, she went missing from her home and has not been seen since. Her family believe that her body lies undiscovered somewhere in the ravines and rough country in the area.

Sadly, there is no firm evidence of the fate of Vic Hayes. Some sources claim that he died of his wounds, but given that he was seen with Dohse only days after his capture, this seems unlikely. Others, confusing him with another Hayes in SOE, wrongly suggest that he survived, was released by the Germans and fought in Normandy. His SOE file records that he was executed and suggests that he was killed at Gross-Rosen concentration camp in Poland. This conclusion was based on evidence given by the Gross-Rosen guards after the war, who claimed to identify

Hayes from a photograph as one of those executed in July/August 1944. However, in the course of research, I stumbled across a document containing evidence from one Otto Bernau, a German cook who was in prison in Paris awaiting execution for firing three shots, while drunk, at a portrait of Hitler. Bernau describes sharing a cell with a British captain who precisely fits Hayes's description (wounds to the arm and leg, same height, of medium build, about forty years old, bald, and married before the war to a French wife who had drowned on her way back to Britain). Bernau continues: 'On 6th February 1944, the Captain was taken out of the cell for questioning. When he returned he had been beaten and ill-treated so much that he was unable to stand, eat or even sleep. On 16th February 1944 at 4 o'clock in the morning he was removed from the cell and did not return. This was the usual time that prisoners who were to be shot were taken from their cells.'

After the war, Hayes was awarded a posthumous Military Cross.

Marcel Défence, who joined Scientist to help Landes as a second radio operator and became engaged to Ginette Corbin before escaping to Britain in late 1943, was parachuted back to France on a second mission in the same week in 1944 that Landes returned. He was betrayed shortly after his arrival and sent, it is believed, to Gross-Rosen, where he was executed in the summer of 1944.

Harry Peulevé was sent to Buchenwald concentration camp but managed to escape execution at the last minute by swapping identities with a typhus victim. On his return to Britain he received counselling to help him overcome his experiences. Awarded a DSO, an MC and the Croix de Guerre, and made a Chevalier de la Légion d'Honneur for his services, he pursued a post-war career working for Shell Oil, and died in Spain in 1963.

Pierre Culioli, whose briefcase contained the papers which gave the Germans their breakthrough on the Prosper network in Paris, was deported to Buchenwald, but survived. Tried for treachery after the war, he was acquitted of the major charge, but found guilty of passing information to the enemy. Culioli challenged the verdict and was acquitted of all charges on appeal.

Having survived the car crash with Culioli and, miraculously, three bullets to the head, Yvonne Rudellat was hospitalised and then, still suffering from brain injuries, sent to the concentration camps. She was in Bergen-Belsen when it was liberated in April 1945, but died shortly afterwards from typhus and dysentery. After the war the French government awarded Rudellat the Croix de Guerre. She was never honoured by the British government.

None of the other British agents in the Prosper network survived.

After her arrest in June 1943, the ex-Paris 'street urchin' Andrée Borrel, who became Francis Suttill's courier, was sent to the Natzweiler-Struthof concentration camp along with three other SOE women agents. They were all given a lethal injection of phenol to render them unconscious and then burnt in the camp ovens in July 1944. According to evidence gathered by SOE after the war, Andrée Borrel recovered consciousness and fought for her life before being put, alive, into the ovens.

In September of that year Borrel's lover, Gilbert Norman, the radio operator who parachuted into France with Roger Landes in 1941, was hanged at Mauthausen.

Francis Suttill was shot six months later, in March 1945, at Sachsenhausen concentration camp near Berlin.

Claude and Lise de Baissac were parachuted back into northern France in 1944 and did exceptional work behind the German lines during the battle of Normandy. For this de Baissac was awarded a bar to his DSO. The French government also appointed de Baissac a Chevalier de la Légion d'Honneur and awarded him the Croix de Guerre with Palm.

Lise de Baissac, in conformity with SOE's habit of awarding SOE women only lower-rank decorations, received an MBE from the British (the lowest military order for those who show courage in time of war) and the Croix de Guerre from the French, who also made her a Chevalier de la Légion d'Honneur. Parachute wings were awarded to SOE agents only after six training jumps. But women SOE agents did only five training jumps and so never got their 'wings' – irrespective of how many operational jumps they did later. In 2003, the year before her death at the age of ninety-one, Lise de Baissac was finally presented with the parachute wings she was denied during the war at the annual remembrance service at the SOE F Section memorial in Valençay, south of Orléans.

De Baissac, who had given Mary Herbert a written undertaking to marry her before leaving France in August 1943, travelled back to the Bordeaux area with the commission investigating what had happened to missing SOE agents after liberation. He was reunited with Mary and met his daughter Claudine for the first time. The couple were married at Corpus Christi Church in London on 11 November 1944, but lived separately and divorced in 1960. In the mid-1950s, French intelligence suspected that de Baissac, at the time working for a Paris perfume house, was an MI6 agent. In 1964, he married a second time, settling in Aix-en-Provence, where he died aged sixty-seven in 1974.

After her arrest, Mary Herbert had managed, extraordinarily, to persuade her German interrogators she was not connected with Scientist at all, but a married woman from Alexandria whose husband had abandoned her with his child. She was released by the Germans at Easter 1944 and was able, after some searching, to find her child Claudine, who was being cared for in a local orphanage. The two took refuge in a small country house near Poitiers, where Claude de Baissac found them at the end of the war. Mary Herbert received a Croix de Guerre from the French but was never recognised by the British for her work in France. After her divorce from de Baissac she returned to Britain with Claudine, bought a cottage in Frant, Sussex, and gave French lessons. Claudine emigrated to the United States, marrying an airline pilot and settling in Los Angeles. She was at her mother's bedside when she passed way in 1983, three months after her seventy-ninth birthday.

Marguerite Faget divorced her husband in 1952. She died in 1989, aged ninety.

Renée Daubèze, the woman who had lent her bed to Roger Landes after he was injured parachuting back to France in March 1944, died in 1990, aged ninety-one. She had kept the bedroom in which Landes had recuperated exactly as it was when he left, as a shrine to her unusual guest.

Having crossed the Pyrenees, Bordeaux police inspector Charles Corbin reached London with Landes in early 1944. He was then sent to an SOE training school and landed back in France by Lysander that April, with orders to work in the La Rochelle area. He survived the war and was awarded a Military Cross by the British and made a Chevalier de la Légion d'Honneur for his bravery. After the war he returned to his first profession, becoming a salesman in the pharmaceutical industry. He died in 1972, aged seventy-eight.

Léonce Dussarrat was made a Chevalier de la Légion d'Honneur and awarded the Croix de Guerre by the French and the King's Medal for Courage by the British. He returned to his hardware shop in Dax, expanded his businesses, acquired a number of properties and became one of the most prosperous businessmen in the area. He died in August 1976 aged seventy-two.

Christian Campet ended up as a Commandeur de la Légion d'Honneur, and was awarded the Croix de Guerre with four citations and the Médaille de la Résistance by the French. The British also awarded him the Military Cross. After the war he resumed his career in the police, rising to the rank of police commissioner in Bordeaux, before retiring in 1981.

Professor Louis Joubert, who had led the 'mission to Algiers' after being smuggled into Spain in the boot of Dohse's car, was released from house arrest in Algeria in July 1945. He went on to become a *pasteur*, France's National Inspector of Education, and an Officier de la Légion d'Honneur.

Roger Landes's troublesome rival in Bordeaux, Jean-Baptiste Morraglia, commanded a brigade in the French air force after the war, before retiring to the reserves. He died, aged seventy-five, in the Charente-Maritime, in 1965.

After his recall to Paris to be disciplined for 'the hideous crime of working with the British', Roger Landes's colleague, Charles Gaillard, the ex-wine merchant from Mâcon, vanishes completely from view. No readily available public record appears to exist chronicling his life after the war.

John Manolitsakis, 'Cyriel le Grec', relinquished his commission on leaving SOE in late 1945. He died two years later in Nairobi, aged forty-four.

In the last days of the war, Pierre Meunier, whose love of risk was only exceeded by his enthusiasm for the opposite sex, parachuted into the Malayan jungle to join Force 136, a British clandestine unit operating with local tribesmen behind Japanese lines. But the war ended before he saw serious action. On his return to Canada, he was feted as a hero.

Most of the main French collaborators in Bordeaux were tried according to French law after the war. Sentences ranged from imprisonment, through penal servitude, to death. Almost all sentences of death were subsequently commuted to life imprisonment, or penal servitude. But this was not the case for Friedrich Dohse's chief agent and the head of the Vichy police in Bordeaux, Pierre Poinsot, who was executed by firing squad on 12 July 1945. On condemning him to death, the judge said: 'The most terrible of the charges laid against him is the list of the 900 names written in blood on his account, who were shot because of him.'

François Charles ('Charly') Cominetti, who sold Dohse escaped pilots at 10,000 francs a piece and offered to sell Landes himself for 500,000, was arrested in December 1947 and tried before a military tribunal. Found guilty, the court stripped him of all military rank, confiscated his private property and goods and sentenced him to fifteen years' imprisonment with hard labour.

Rudolf Kunesch, Dohse's rival in KdS, was posted to Danzig after his return to Germany and was either killed or committed suicide in the final months of the war.

In August 1944, Karl Bömelburg masterminded Marshal Pétain's escape from Vichy – and then promptly disappeared by adopting the identity of a Sergeant Bergman who had been killed in an Allied bombing raid. It has subsequently come to light that he secretly returned to Germany and took a job first as a gardener and then as the librarian in a grand house in Munich. On New Year's Eve 1946, he slipped on some ice, suffering a severe head injury from which he died shortly afterwards.

* * *

On 16 December 1944, Friedrich Dohse arrived in Copenhagen to head a unit combating marine sabotage in the harbour. Five weeks later, on 22 January 1945, he was re-posted to the Danish port of Odense to head up a Gestapo unit dealing with intelligence on resistance forces (the same job he had done in Bordeaux). When the German troops in Denmark capitulated on 8 May 1945, Dohse left the city with his men in a small convoy and made a dash for Germany. But he was captured by the British before reaching the frontier and placed in a prisoner of war camp. Here he was soon identified as a Gestapo officer and subjected to an extensive interrogation which began on 3 July 1945. During this time, Dohse was approached several times by the British Secret Service (SIS), who tried to persuade him that, to avoid being hanged, he should work for them. Well aware of the danger of making deals while in captivity, he refused. 'They wanted information on my countrymen – they wanted me to betray my colleagues. I was just not interested in that kind of thing.'

In late 1946, Dohse, still in a British POW camp in Denmark, heard that key people in KdS Bordeaux were being transferred to the city for trial. He wrote to the French ambassador in Copenhagen asking to join his former colleagues in Bordeaux so that he could be with his men and personally account for his actions to the French authorities. Dohse had heard that Jean Duboué had returned and, perhaps fearful of the testimony that could be given in his absence, felt: 'It was important for me to justify myself before the French authorities … I was not afraid of being accused of being a war criminal because I did not believe that I had done anything which contravened the laws either of war, or of common humanity.'

On 22 November 1946, Dohse wrote to the French military commander in Bordeaux. 'Sir, you will no doubt be astonished to receive this letter from me, but I have had permission from the Danish authorities to be in contact with ex-members of the French Resistance.' Dohse lists his various actions to 'humanise the conflict', ending: 'After all I have done for the resistance in France, I do not believe it is right to treat me like the others, as a war criminal. I did my duty as a German patriot in accordance with the rules of war and of humanity, always respecting the patriotism of the French [who fought us] – I hope they will now respect mine.'

Friedrich Dohse, who was to prove a formidable lobbyist in his own cause, got his way. In June 1947 he was sent to Bordeaux along with some 250 other prisoners – German soldiers and French collaborators – who were to stand trial for their actions in the city during the war years. In Bordeaux, he joined a mass of other prisoners awaiting judgement in the notorious Fort du Hâ, where he had imprisoned so many others in his time.

There followed a long period of investigation by French *juges d'in-struction*, during which, for the first time, Dohse came face to face with Roger Landes. For three hours the two discussed, among other matters, what happened in 1943, when the Gestapo 'watcher' outside Madame Jardel's house helped Landes put his radio back on his bicycle instead of arresting him.

Dohse used his years in Fort du Hâ to write his memoirs – in French. Although these were almost certainly penned by Dohse as part of the case for his defence in a trial that was yet to begin, they remain the only memoirs written by any Gestapo officer in France. In 1988, Dohse's book was prepared for publication by a Swiss publishing house (Favre). But in the end, it never saw the light of day.

On 28 April 1953, six years after arriving in the Fort du Hâ, Dohse was finally put on trial with, among others, Hans Luther, Walter Machule, Marcelle Sommer and Anton Enzelsberger. On 4 May, Jean Duboué was called to the bar of the court to give evidence against the man who had been responsible for his arrest, and therefore (albeit despite Dohse's efforts) the almost unimaginable horrors of Dora labour camp. Taking the witness stand, Jean Duboué, looking steadily at Dohse, stunned the court with one of the most remarkable testaments of any post-war trial of war criminals: 'You treated us as soldiers. It is my duty to say it … I regret that you were not on our side. You are a skilful and clever man and you destroyed the resistance in our region.'

Dohse interjected: 'I did no more than was my duty as a German soldier.'

'I do not forget,' Duboué continued, 'those who were killed by the Gestapo … But it is my opinion that you were not one of the torturers.'

Dohse interrupted again: 'May I ask Commandant Duboué if, in his opinion, I acted according to the [established] rules governing special [police] forces?'

'I would say that you did,' Duboué concluded.

At this point the judge intervened: 'It is not our purpose here to treat our enemies with vengeance because they were our enemies. It is our job to deliver justice and punishment to those who went beyond what was necessary and legal in the proper conduct of their mission.'

On the morning of 6 May 1953, the Bordeaux tribunal announced its verdict. Hans Luther was sentenced to five years in prison and Enzelsberger to four years. Friedrich Dohse was given seven years of forced labour, but because he had already been interned for eight years, he was immediately released and left a free man.

In the years that followed, Dohse used his contacts in Bordeaux to set up a small business importing fine wines and champagnes from France and meat from Denmark. He retired with his wife Erika to a shutter-board bungalow on the shores of the Baltic near Kiel, where he kept a small sailing boat. Here, supported by a library full of books and a well-stocked cellar, he spent a comfortable old age, bald and plump, indulging his passions for painting, reading, music and baking. He died quietly in his bed in 1995, aged eighty-two.

Early on the morning after the executions of André Grandclément, Lucette and Marc Duluguet, a team of Roger Landes's men arrived at the site with a small lorry. After cleaning up as best they could, they took the three bodies further into the marshy area west of the village of Saugnacq-et-Muret and disposed of them at the edges of the Prince parachute site. André Grandclément's corpse was dropped vertically into a deep hole under the overhanging roof of a ruined shepherd's hut on one side of the site. The other two bodies were thrown, one on top of the other, into a woodland grave on the opposite side.

There they lay until just after Christmas 1944, when a small delegation consisting of three policemen and a captain from the French secret service visited the site to identify the corpses. Because of the waterlogged ground and the fact that the grave refilled with water as fast as they dug it, they were able to expose only André Grandclément's head. The captain, who seemed to know Grandclément, bent down to examine the face, declaring: 'It's definitely Grandclément.' All further efforts to extract the cadaver failed, leaving the investigating party with no alternative but to leave it in situ, covering it as best they could with earth, branches and undergrowth.

Then the party moved to the other side of the parachute site, where, in a deep hole, they found two bodies, one male and one female, lying one on top of the other. After a brief examination the captain declared that the top body was that of Lucette Grandclément. They also found the remains of Lucette's suitcase. Again they tried to extract the bodies but, even with the help of two local woodsmen, were unable to 'without the aid of a hydraulic pump to empty the water from the hole'. They took photographs and left. One of the original members of Landes's team who had disposed of the bodies later confirmed that the second cadaver must have been that of Marc Duluguet.

There the three corpses lay for almost two more years until, on 5 September 1946, they were retrieved by a police team and temporarily buried in the cemetery at Saugnacq-et-Muret. At the time of her interment, Lucette was still wearing the green dress and sandals she had put on specially for London on the afternoon of her execution. She also wore a gold ring on her wedding finger, on the inside of which was engraved '24.9.39 A.L.' – the day that André and Lucette first met.

In the spring of 1947, the body of Marc Duluguet was disinterred by his family and reburied in his home town of Biganos.

Later, Lucette's mother, Mme Jeanne Chastel, had the remains of André and her daughter moved and reinterred in the Chastel family crypt at Pompignac. The coffins were draped with a tricolour and André Maleyran fired a single shot from his revolver in lonely salute over the sarcophagus. In time, a plaque was erected: 'To the memory of Lucette and André Grandclément. Martyrs of the Resistance. Assassinated by cowards. 28 July 1944.'

Not long after Roger Landes arrived at Shenley Military Hospital in October 1944, he was sent for an x-ray. This revealed that his gall bladder needed to be removed. The operation was eventually carried out on 15 December, but the surgeon could find nothing wrong and so – not wishing to waste the opportunity of an open body – removed his appendix instead, on general principles.

Shortly after Christmas 1944, Landes, still languishing in his hospital sickbed, was visited by the F Section head, Maurice Buckmaster. It was not a seasonal call. He told Landes that he had received a high-level complaint from the French who had issued an arrest warrant for Landes and accused SOE of allowing him to smuggle himself back to Paris, where he had been seen recently in a nightclub. Buckmaster, furious, asked him what was going on. Landes assured him that the French were wrong: for the last six weeks he had been here in Shenley, recuperating. Nevertheless, Buckmaster ordered that he was not to return to France for at least two years.

A few days later, a French delegation visited Shenley hospital to confirm that the man who had a reputation for being everywhere and nowhere at the same time was indeed firmly tucked up in a British hospital bed.

Landes left Shenley in January 1945 to spend two months at a convalescent home in the New Forest. In late February, Landes, now fit, reported to SOE headquarters in Baker Street and offered himself for another mission. Buckmaster's first proposal was that he should be dropped into Germany to raise a fighting unit from French workers who had been compulsorily deported to work in the German factories. Not speaking a word of German, Landes declined. SOE's second offer was that he should be parachuted behind Japanese lines into the jungles of Malaya to join Force 136. Landes agreed.

On 20 April 1945, Landes was flown to Colombo, where he was sent on a three-week jungle training course. In early June he was put in charge of a four-man team and dropped into the jungle close to the town of Grik on the Malay–Thai border. His orders were to raise, train and arm a fighting force from the local communist Chinese, and then lead them in attacks on road and rail communications, with the aim of impeding the Japanese retreat from General Slim's Fourteenth Army, which was storming south from Burma. In the event, the atomic bomb was dropped and the war ended before Landes's group could become operational. Despite rising hostility to the British amongst the communist Chinese, Landes and his team made it south down the Malayan peninsula to Singapore, where they were immediately put on a troop ship heading back to Colombo and carrying over 400 nurses. Landes later described the voyage as 'exhausting'.

Arriving in Ceylon in November 1945, Landes was debriefed, during which he accurately predicted that the Malayan Chinese communists would lead an uprising against the British in Malaya (what would be known as the Malayan Emergency), using the troops he had trained and the arms Britain had dropped to them.

By January 1946, Landes was back in Britain where he was discharged from SOE two months later. In a final comment, which betrays all the sense of superiority and snobbishness for which SOE was famous, Buckmaster wrote of the man who had served him so well, won an MC and bar, wore the ribbon of Commandeur de la Légion d'Honneur and was arguably one of the most successful agents SOE ever sent into France: 'As a man he is not awfully attractive and I think his friends are as a whole most unpleasing. I wish he would not wear exotic uniforms. Thank God he doesn't wear much scent. But if you want a brave man for a lost venture, choose Landes.'

Roger Landes did not take easily to life after SOE. He applied to join the army and was given a permanent commission and a job working on photographic interpretation for the RAF. But he found his fellow officers, all of whom had spent their war safely behind Whitehall desks, irksome and snobbish.

His two-year banishment from France over, Landes returned to Bordeaux in 1946, seeing old friends and visiting old haunts. Quite by chance he bumped into Charles Corbin's wife in Biarritz (she was estranged from her husband by then). She invited him to visit her and Ginette in Bordeaux. It was only at this point that Landes, who had kept his feelings for Ginette hidden all through the war, felt able to reveal his love for her. The couple were married on 29 July 1947 in Paris. On the marriage certificate Roger described himself as a jeweller living in Paris. They moved to London and in 1949 had a son – whom they christened Alain Henri Léon (after Ginette's late fiancé, Henri Labit, and their friend Léonce Dussarrat).

In 1949 Landes returned to his old employers, the LCC, employing his architectural skills in the vast task of rebuilding London. He was happy there, but the pay was poor. The following year, he was persuaded by his father, on grounds of filial duty, to leave the London County Council and become chief buyer in Landes senior's jewellery firm. Roger and Ginette rented a flat next to Landes's parents in Stamford Hill so as to be closer to the business.

It was not a happy move. Barnet Landes was, by all accounts, a most unpleasant man. Domineering and mean, he spent most of the firm's profits on himself – and especially on gambling, expensive cars and even more expensive women. When the family firm did not generate enough to keep him in the style to which he considered himself entitled, he demanded that his sons contribute to his living expenses. Barnet Landes had neither respect for, nor interest in, what Roger had done in France, always favouring his elder son, Marcel, with a greater share of the profits and with more status and responsibility in the firm. Landes put up with the humiliation and bullying until, sometime around 1954, there was a blazing row and he left to set up on his own as a wholesale jeweller.

Landes did not have an easy time launching his business, not least because his father energetically blackened his name with both customers and suppliers. He spent most of his days lugging heavy suitcases full of jewellery from shop to shop across London. He was attacked several times by criminal gangs, on one occasion suffering a broken arm.

To make ends meet Ginette took two jobs, teaching French in a local school and working in a ladies' outfitters. The couple's one treat, when they could afford it, was an annual holiday to Bordeaux. When he was old enough, their son Alain was sent to southwest France every summer, staying with his godfathers – whose names read like a Gestapo 'Wanted' list from 1944: Léonce Dussarrat, Christian Campet, Roger Schmaltz and Robert Angelaud. At the end of every summer his godfathers would club together to send him back to England with a new set of clothes – which always included a blazer and a pair of grey flannels.

There is a strange ambivalence in the way Roger Landes lived his life in these post-war years. In the Bordeaux region he was feted as a hero. In England he was no more than a curious little anonymous Frenchman who spoke with a music hall accent. In southwest France there were always dinners in his honour and old comrades who never tired of telling and retelling the tales of their past glories. At home his war record was little known of and even less spoken about. Landes was quintessentially French and only skin-deep British by an accident of history. Though he attended Armistice Day parades and SOE reunions regularly, he was always an outsider in the post-war SOE community – not really 'one of them'. Yet, unlike his brother Marcel, who remained proudly French, Landes insisted on retaining his British identity. Behind Roger and Ginette's front door, only French was spoken; only French habits and customs were followed and nothing but French cuisine was served at the table. But beyond his front door, Landes's life was run exclusively by the strange rhythms and norms of the English.

It was as though Landes, unable to relinquish the habit of the secret agent of living two existences at the same time, never allowed himself to be trapped in one identity without having the option of taking refuge in another.

Eventually, in the mid-1960s, Landes's business generated enough money for him to buy a between-the-wars semi in Stanmore. Shortly afterwards his firm was bought out by a long-established firm of London jewellers, for whom he became the chief buyer. It looked as though Roger and Ginette had finally sailed into more settled waters. But then tragedy struck. Ginette was diagnosed with cancer and died aged sixty-one in 1983. Landes, who had never spent a night away from his beloved wife since their marriage, was bereft. He retreated into himself, living only for his dog, his weekly game of bridge and twice-weekly lunches with his son Alain.

Seven years after Ginette's death, however, he met and married his second wife, Margaret. She was devoted to him and immensely proud of his war record. The couple bought a modest little chalet bungalow in Liphook, Hampshire, which they called 'Aristide'. Here, Roger Landes, who from 1942 to 1944 had been the most important man in southwest France, lived out a quiet existence. He was once again where he felt most comfortable, invisible in plain sight, just as he had been at the bungalow with its walled garden at Cenon, hiding beneath the radio masts of the Germans.

As Landes reached his ninth decade (despite his undiminished habit of smoking sixty a day), he started to develop dementia. On one occasion he locked Margaret in a bedroom for several days, denouncing her as a Gestapo officer. On another, he tried to bundle her hurriedly out of the house because, he said, Ginette might come back at any moment and find them together. After treatment at Basingstoke hospital, Landes was moved to a retirement home in Surrey. Here, lovingly nursed by Margaret, he lived out his last days.

Unlike most of his SOE colleagues who settled in France after the war, Landes resolutely declined to do so. Later in life, after his retirement, his son Alain suggested he should return to Bordeaux. Landes replied that it was all too difficult and too much of a risk: he had, he said, lost the habit of living in his homeland and found its routines and bureaucracy alien and disconcerting.

There is a plangent sadness, tinged with paradox, about the unfulfilled nature of Roger Landes's post-war life. In France, he had been decisive, courageous and resourceful. In England he was dominated by his father and his family. During the war Landes had been a shaper of events. After the peace he seemed to submit himself to them. It was as though the cautious secret agent with an uncanny ability to vanish into the crowd had simply been emptied of adventure by the war and, uncomfortable with notoriety in his own country, was attempting one last vanishing trick, disappearing into the humdrum and the ordinary in his adopted land.

On 16 July 2008, death finally found Roger Landes, the man the Gestapo could not find, and took him quietly in his sleep, at a nursing home in Hindhead, in his ninety-second year.

EPILOGUE

POST HOC PROPTER HOC

The execution of André and Lucette Grandclément and Marc Duluguet attracted neither attention nor comment in the years immediately after the war. In August 1948, five years before Dohse's trial in Bordeaux, a series of accounts of Roger Landes's story, including the execution of Grandclément, appeared in a local newspaper. These were clearly based on interviews with Landes himself and, though heavily dramatised, were straightforward and broadly adhered to the accounts given by Landes on his return to Britain.

Three years later a different story began to emerge. On 21 May 1951, Marcelle Caralp-Jardel, the woman who had been arrested on the morning that Landes was nearly caught operating his radio from her house, gave evidence as part of the preparations for Dohse's trial. 'I am convinced, even though there is no absolute proof of it, that Landes's motive [for the execution of Grandclément] was financial,' she stated. 'He spent a very great deal of money during the time of the Occupation in luxury living and the high life and I strongly doubt that the sums necessary to pursue this lifestyle were obtained in a regular manner. I am sure that Grandclément was aware of this and that there were full records of these transactions which would have been extremely compromising after the liberation.'

Mme Caralp-Jardel's claims marked the start of a long process of rewriting the history of the Grandclément affair, which culminated in the publication of two notable works. The first, *Grandclément – Traitor or Scapegoat?*, was written by a Bordeaux historian in 1996. The second, written along the same lines – *The Grandclément Enigma: The Resistant*

313

Chief Who Sought a Pact between the Resistance and the SS – was published in 2003. Its author was one of André Grandclément's descendants.

Both books question the 'official' Grandclément story in ways which provide a more generous interpretation of Grandclément's culpability, and hint at, and in some cases assert, a wider conspiracy in which Grandclément was merely a pawn. In the 2003 book, a reference by its author to Landes as 'the little Jew' provides an unfortunate echo of the anti-Semitism which was such a feature of wartime Bordeaux.

The propositions put forward by one or other of these books and several articles published around the same time, include:

> That Friedrich Dohse was in fact an agent for the British SIS during his time in Bordeaux.
>
> That Grandclément was probably killed because he was aware of this and of other secret dealings between the British and German intelligence.
>
> That he was executed to cover up the secret relationship which existed between Charles Corbin and the Gestapo, and that Landes married Ginette Corbin afterwards to ensure that this fact never came to light.
>
> That Landes initially wanted to send Grandclément to London until he discovered, during his interrogation, that Grandclément 'knew too much' about secret Anglo-German relations and would therefore have to be killed.

Others followed Mme Caralp-Jardel's line, claiming that Landes personally pocketed the money and jewels found in the Grandcléments' suitcases after their execution and ended the war – apparently – a rich man.

There is no doubt that some of those, British and French, who fought in the Resistance did profit personally from the huge largesse of money parachuted into France by London. SOE's accounting procedures were, to say the least, relaxed. There is even some evidence that an informal rule existed which allowed the members of SOE circuits in France quietly to share out any money left over in their accounts at the end of the war. There is little doubt either that some Resistance leaders led prosperous lives after the war, which many ascribed to their wartime activities. However, with the exception of Léonce Dussarrat, all Landes's key leaders led modest and even penurious existences after the conflict ended. It is, moreover, quite likely that Landes, or one of his team, would have appropriated any valuables found in the Grandclément luggage; it was normal practice for Resistance leaders to use the funds accumulated from operations, such as the execution of a collaborator, to support their Resistance activities and pay their men.

But the accusation that Roger Landes personally profited from his activities during the war seems flimsy, to say the least, given the straitened circumstances in which he lived during the post-war period. It seems very unlikely that the key heads of Landes's Resistance groups, whom he named as his son Alain's godfathers, would have clubbed together to buy the boy new clothes every summer, if they had not known that Landes himself was unable to pay for these. And, by the way, who would be better aware than they, if there were any doubts or suspicions on this matter?

That Dohse himself was a British SIS agent all along seems even more risible. Is it really likely that the British would have allowed one of their key agents to be interrogated (by the British themselves!) at length after his capture? Or that they would have pressed him on numerous occasions to join them, when he already had? Or that they would have permitted such an important agent to languish in a French jail for six years awaiting trial? Or that they would have let him stand accused in that trial on a charge which could have resulted in a death sentence?

Finally, there is the proposition that Charles Corbin was secretly a Gestapo agent. It is very hard to believe that someone in the service of the Gestapo would have gone to such lengths as Corbin and Landes did to get away from them over the Pyrenees in late 1943. Moreover, if indeed Corbin was a Gestapo agent, then Landes, in seeking to cover up the fact, must have been one too. In which case we are asked to accept a scenario which would confound even the most complex hall of mirrors: that Dohse was secretly a British agent, while Corbin and Landes were secret Gestapo ones. The head spins.

The truth is much more simple.

Dohse was a cunning and most subtle counter-intelligence officer who used his remarkable skills in the service of his country, while doing his best to adhere to the standards he believed in as a member of humanity.

As for André Grandclément, he was neither a bad man nor an evil one. He had a deep sense of responsibility – arguably, for a commander in war, too much responsibility – for his men, whom he tried to save, even at the risk of placing in jeopardy his duty to his country. Grandclément may indeed not even have been a traitor in the true sense of the word. Traitors abandon their country for another. But right to the end, André Grandclément was a patriot who loved France and believed he was doing the right thing by it. Misguided, André Grandclément may have been. Ambitious, gullible, vain, egotistical and easily played he almost certainly was. But evil, in the scale of the evil all around him, he was not.

In executing André Grandclément, Roger Landes the soldier was obeying not one, but at least three orders from superior authorities that he was to be killed. During his time in France, Landes did no more and no less than what he had been trained to do, or ordered to do, as an SOE secret agent in enemy territory. That he lived his post-war years unful-filled, largely unrecognised, often unhappy and always poor, only adds to the poignancy of his story.

ACKNOWLEDGEMENTS

In thanking those who have made this book possible I must first, and most of all, acknowledge the huge role played by my colleague and 'collaborator', Sylvie Young. Sylvie is French and has lived in Britain for thirty years, so perfectly understands our strange ways. If this book provides an accurate, warts-and-all account of one of the many remarkable French Resistance stories which were the product of a deep Anglo-French partnership during the Second World War, then that is in large measure because of her.

Naturally, I take full responsibility for the writing and for choosing and assembling the main ingredients in this story; but the overall shape and contents of the book are the product of a genuine working partnership, which, though tempestuous at times, has been one of the most productive I have ever experienced. The mountain of research upon which this book rests has also been conducted on a shared basis. But the fact that we have been able to gain access to so many original French sources, some of which are entirely new, is almost exclusively down to Sylvie Young's determination, drive, charm and commitment – not least by making several trips to Bordeaux to gain access to these documents. It would be remiss of me not to mention here also the contribution of the other members of the Young family, Gordon and Margaux, whose saintly patience and support for Sylvie's three-year rollercoaster dedication to this book I record with profound thanks.

This story itself is in some ways a painful one, for it uncovers, stupidity, weakness, moral turpitude and betrayal on both the British and the French sides. Nevertheless, this is a book which will be more difficult for the French to read, than the British. There is a good reason for this. In the British history of the Second World War the part played by our country in helping the French resistance is small and tangential. But for France the story of the Resistance is central to both their history and their sense of national pride.

Among the letters which came to light from the 'Aristide' archives in the Combined Services Military Museum, East Maldon, Essex, was a detailed correspondence with an academic at Bordeaux University, Professor Michel Bergès, who, it transpired, had spent much of the 1980s finding and assembling an astonishing collection of documents and oral history interviews relating to this story. This includes interviews with all the main players on both sides, written records of these conversations and a prodigious number of official and unofficial documents, such as police records, personal diaries and individual eyewitness accounts – including Dohse's memoirs, the only known surviving memoir written by a Gestapo officer in the Second World War. We would simply not have been able to write this book in its present form without Professor Bergès's unlimited generosity in providing not only access to this cornucopia, but also advice on its contents and support for the project.

The writing of this book has also greatly benefitted from another so far largely unexploited private archive which came to light when I was writing my book *A Brilliant Little Operation*: the family papers and photographs of Jean and Suzanne Duboué held by Suzanne's son, Yves Léglise, at his home near Nice. Once again, Yves and his family have been most generous in providing access to these vital papers.

Chief among the others to whom thanks are due are my readers who have helped most generously with factual corrections, opinions, advice and stylistic suggestions. Some of these are old friends, including Steph Bailey, Rosemary Billinge, Ellen Dahrendorf, Ian Patrick, Steve Radley, Linda Siegle and Janet Smith (who, as in my previous books has once again played the role of my nitpicker-in-chief). Others include some of the foremost experts in the Resistance in France, like Professors Rod Kedward and Robert Gildea, and Messrs David Harrison, Steven Kippax and Neil Cobbett. Peter Lieb, an expert on the German occupation in

France and himself an author of several highly respected works on the subject has also, as with my last book, *The Cruel Victory*, provided invaluable corrections and comments to, primarily, German details in this book. All of these have been incredibly generous with their time and suggestions. Francis Suttill, the author of a recent book about his father, the head of the Prosper network in Paris, has also been kind enough to check the passages which cover the collapse of this key British network.

This book has taken three years to write, of which two years was spent on research in museums, archives and libraries in Britain, France, Germany and Canada. I owe a great debt to those who have helped Sylvie Young and I in this, most notably Richard Wooldridge and his team at the Combined Services Military Museum, the staff at the National Archives in Kew; the staff at the Archives Nationales in Paris; Pascal Gallien and André Rakoto in the Service Historique de l'Armée de Terre in Vincennes; Cyril Olivier in the Archives Départementales de la Gironde in Bordeaux; Jeff Waldron and Fiona Brazil at the BBC Sound Archives in Caversham; Richard Hughes in the Imperial War Museum in London; Fernand Linne in the Médiathèque d'Hendaye; Robert Anthony in the Library of the House of Lords; and Patrick Deane for access to the Cookridge/Spiro archives at McMaster University, Hamilton Canada.

In the course of this research, visits have been made to all the key places where the main actions in this story took place. I am especially grateful for the help and hospitality provided during these visits by Donna Everest, Neil Fleming, Amanda Giles and Steve Barker who helped me visit Room 055 in the Old War Office; Sheila and Richard Souchard and Patrick Yarnold for their information and kindness at Wanborough Manor; Jean-Pierre Lescarret for his help identifying the place of execution of André and Lucette Grandclément and Marc Duluguet; the ninety-two-year-old ex-resistant André Duvignac, for his permission to copy and use his private archive on the assassination of André Grandclément, and his friend Jean-Marie Callen for taking us to the Cazenave villa in Bélin-Beliet; fellow Maquisard Alban Dubrou for access to his papers and for his tour and recollections of Lencouaq; Commissaire-Colonel Francis Clerguerou and his wife for forgiving our unexpected intrusion into their beautiful house on a quiet afternoon and for their kindness in showing us around their house, which used to be that of Madame Jardel (and for not laughing too much when I mistook the door to the lavatory as the front door!); to Juan Carlos Jimenez de Aberasturi for his guided tour of wartime San Sebastián (including finding the old British consulate in the town); and to Guy Lalane, Jen-Michel Sallaberry and Jean-Martin Quatrevieux for their reminiscences and hospitality in the little Basque town of Birriatou.

Others who should be thanked for their contribution to this book include Christine Tochtermann, who, as in my previous two books, has kindly translated documents my poor German cannot cope with, my old friend Jo Ingram who helped me gain access to the Cookridge/Spiro archives at McMaster University; Patrick Canel, who provided some fascinating insights into the life of his forebear Charles Corbin and Roger Landes's son, Alain, who has been unfailingly generous in providing new information, records, photos and insights on his father and finally our steward Ludel Flores on Cunard's Queen Elizabeth, who scoured the ship to find me a table and a shady spot to write in, as we crossed the Indian Ocean.

I am also, as always, greatly indebted to my agent Michael Sissons, who encouraged me to write this, and to all his colleagues at PFD, who have acted as my agents for these last fifteen years or more; to Arabella Pike for her wise guidance and to her colleagues, Stephen Guise and Katherine Patrick at HarperCollins, and to Katherine Johnson, my copy editor for dealing with me so patiently and for her improvements and corrections, especially in reordering certain passages to make them easier for the reader.

Once again, as ever, I want to thank my wife, who has read and re-read these texts as they were written, offering both corrections and advice and who has not only tolerated my three-year obsession with this story but also patiently accompanied us on our visits, especially to the Bordeaux area.

To all of these I owe my thanks. To none should be ascribed any mistakes or infelicities in this book, which are my responsibility alone.

DRAMATIS PERSONAE

ANGELAUD, Robert
Landes's locally trained radio operator on his second mission.

ARTAGNAN, Charles
Business friend of the Grandcléments. Arrested with Lucette.

BAISSAC de, Claude
SOE F Section head of Scientist circuit.

BAISSAC de, Lise
SOE F Section courier and liaison officer of Scientist circuit and organiser of 'Artist' circuit based in Poitiers.

BASILIO, André
Russian Bordeaux resistant and contact of Pierre Meunier, with whom he shared a mistress (Madame Plante).

BERTRAND, Marcel and Mme
Owners of Café des Chartrons, Scientist circuit headquarters and 'letterbox' in Bordeaux.

BÖMELBURG, Karl
SS-Sturmbannführer and head of the Gestapo in France. Dohse's patron.

BONNIER, Claude
Personal representative and Regional Military Delegate of General de Gaulle for southwest France (Region B).

BORDES, Alban
Leader of a resistant group and one of Landes's key lieutenants.

BORREL, Andrée
SOE F Section courier and liaison officer for Francis Suttill's Prosper circuit.

BOUILLAR, André
Leader of a resistant group and one of Landes's key lieutenants. Acted as Landes's guide across the Pyrenees in late 1943.

BUCKMASTER, Maurice
Head of SOE's F Section.

CAMPET, Christian
Roger Landes's second-in-command on his second mission.

CAMPLAN, Eugène
Head of the southwest OCM, after André Grandclément.

CARALP-JARDEL, Marcelle
Owner of one of Landes's safe houses in Bordeaux.

CAZENAVE, Franck
One of Landes's lieutenants. Owner of a villa at Belin-Béliet. Chief of the parachute reception team at Saugnacq-et-Muret.

CHASTEL, Jeanne
Lucette Grandclément's mother.

CHAZEAU, Roland
Key lieutenant of Grandclément.

CLECH, Marcel
Radio operator of the Monkeypuzzle circuit.

COMINETTI, François
Maquis leader who sold Allied escaped pilots to the Germans and offered to sell Landes.

CORBIN, Charles
Police inspector, Bordeaux resistant and Landes's trusted friend. Father of Ginette.

CORBIN, Ginette
Daughter of Charles Corbin; courier for Roger Landes and Marcel Défence.

CRESSWELL, Michael
Organiser of an MI9 escape network through Spain.

CULIOLI, Pierre
Member of Monkeypuzzle circuit and then leader, with Yvonne Rudellat, of Adolphe circuit.

CUSIN, Gaston
General de Gaulle's Commissioner of the Republic in Bordeaux in 1944.

DAUBÈZE, Renée
Cared for Landes for two weeks after his second parachute jump into France, March 1944.

DÉFENCE, Marcel
Sent by SOE to assist Landes as a radio operator on his second mission.

DÉRICOURT, Henri
SOE F Section organiser of landing operations in the Loire valley. A double – or maybe triple – agent who supplied Bömelburg with information.

DEWAVRIN, André
Head of General de Gaulle's Intelligence Bureau in London.

DOHSE, Friedrich
Gestapo head of counter-espionage for southwest France.

DUBOUÉ, Jean
Restaurateur and early Bordeaux resistant; founder with Leo Paillère of a local network which was subsequently subsumed into Scientist circuit.

DUBOUÉ Suzanne
Jean Duboué's daughter. Courier for Duboué–Paillère group and Scientist circuit.

DUBOUÉ Marie-Louise
Jean Duboué's wife.

DULUGUET, Marc
Bordeaux resistant, acted as bodyguard to Grandclément.

DUSSARRAT, Léonce
One of Roger Landes's key lieutenants. Owner of an ironmonger's shop in Dax.

ENZELSBERGER, Anton
One of Kunesch's men; Austrian and known as 'Tony the Boxer'.

ESCH, Pierre
The official French interpreter at KdS Bordeaux.

EXPERT, Michel
One of Landes's radio operators.

FAGET, Marguerite ('Mitou')
Landes's landlady, courier and mistress.

FAYE, Max
Landes's driver and personal bodyguard.

FLOWER, Raymond
SOE F Section head of the Monkeypuzzle circuit.

FOSSARD, Christian
Young resistant in Bordeaux. Interrogated by Dohse.

GAILLARD, Charles

Personal representative and Regional Military Delegate of General de Gaulle for southwest France (Region B) after Claude Bonnier. Worked with Landes before the liberation of Bordeaux.

GRANDCLÉMENT, André

Insurance salesman and early resistant; head of the southwest OCM. Friedrich Dohse's key agent in dismantling the Resistance in the southwest.

GRANDCLÉMENT, Lucette

Mistress and then wife of André Grandclément.

GRANDIER-VAZEILLE, Etienne

Resistance leader of the Alouette group. Arrested in the summer of 1943.

HAGEN, Herbert

First head of KdS Bordeaux.

HAYES, Victor

SOE F Section agent sent to southwest France as a sabotage instructor. Worked with Jean Duboué.

HÈCHE, Gaston

Restaurateur and head of escape line and safe house in Tarbes.

HERBERT, Mary

SOE F Section courier for Scientist circuit. Had a daughter (Claudine) by Claude de Baissac.

JOUBERT, Louis

Early resistant and senior member of southwest OCM. Teacher with connections to Bordeaux University. Leader of local Protestant community. Led the mission to Algiers.

JOUFFRAULT, Paul

Regional leader of OCM group and Grandclément's uncle.

JULIEN, Georges
Senior resistant sent by Paris to reorganise the Resistance in southwest France.

KEIMER, Claire
Dohse's personal assistant and mistress.

KNOCHEN, Helmut
Senior commander in Paris for the German security police and intelligence.

KUNESCH, Rudolf
Dohse's rival in KdS Bordeaux; known as the 'cosher-in-chief'.

LABIT, Henri
SOE RF/F Section sent to southwest France on sabotage mission; Charles Corbin's nephew.

LANDES, Roger
SOE F Section radio operator for Scientist circuit on his first mission; leader of Actor circuit on his second mission.

LARROSE, Jean-Philippe
Official French interpreter for KdS in Bordeaux.

LASSALLE, Josette
Early Bordeaux resistant.

LEROY, Robert
One of the first SOE F Section agents sent to the occupied zone. Linked up with Jean Duboué.

LUTHER, Hans
Second head of KdS Bordeaux after Hagen.

LUZE de, Édouard
Leader of the Arcachon resistant group.

MALEYRAN, André
Key lieutenant of Grandclément.

MANOLITSAKIS, John
Greek SOE F Section agent sent to help Landes.

MACHULE, Walter
Third head of KdS Bordeaux.

MEUNIER, Pierre
Canadian SOE F Section agent sent to help Landes.

MORRAGLIA, Jean-Baptiste
Military commander of all French Resistance forces 1944 (FFI).

NOËL, André
Key French resistant in Bordeaux. Worked with Landes on his first mission. Said to have been close to Grandclément.

NORMAN, Gilbert
SOE F Section radio operator to Prosper circuit.

NOUAUX, Lucien
Leader of one of Landes's Resistance groups in Bordeaux.

O'NEILL, Marc
Key Resistance leader in the OCM, Paris; ex-school friend of Grandclément.

PAILLÈRE, Léo
Early Bordeaux resistant and co-founder of Duboué-Paillère network. One-time chief of the southwest OCM. Worked with Scientist circuit.

PEULEVÉ, Harry
SOE F Section radio operator and later head of the 'Author' circuit in the Corrèze.

POINSOT, Pierre Napoléon
Head of the SAP in Bordeaux and an agent of Dohse's; worked in close cooperation with the KdS.

RIQUET, Michel
Respected Catholic priest and early Paris resistant. A Jesuit who was very influential in Catholic circles.

ROLLOT, Jacques
Key southwest OCM resistant. Son belonged to Lencouacq Maquis.

RUDELLAT, Yvonne
SOE F Section courier to Monkeypuzzle circuit and leader, with Culioli, of Adolphe circuit.

SALLES, Paul
Young Bordeaux resistant and member of the Lencouacq Maquis.

SCHMALTZ, Fernand
One of Roger Landes's key lieutenants. Leader of the Bordeaux railwaymen (*cheminots*).

SOMMER, Marcelle
Head of intelligence section, KdS Bordeaux. Close to Dohse.

SUTTILL, Francis
SOE F Section head of Prosper circuit

THINIÈRES, André
Senior resistant in the southwest OCM. Ex-French army colonel. Accompanied Joubert on mission to Algiers.

TOUNY, Alfred
Head of OCM. Based in Paris.

NOTES

Abbreviations Used in the Notes
ADG: Archives départmentales de la Gironde, Bordeaux
AN: Archives nationales, Paris
CMSM: Combined Military Services Museum, East Maldon, Essex
IWM: Imperial War Museum, London
TNA: The National Archives, Kew, London

Introduction
F. W. D. Deakin: *The Embattled Mountain*, Oxford, Oxford University Press, 1971.
Fitzroy Maclean: *Eastern Approaches*, London, Penguin Books, 1991.

Prologue: The Execution
slingbacks with raised heels: ADG 59J 119.

Chapter 1: Bordeaux – Beginnings
'The population …': Quoting an interview with Colonel Reile of the Abwehr, August 1982, Robert Marshall, *All the King's Men*, London, Fontana paperbacks, 1989, p. 165.
zone non-occupée: Also known as the *zone libre*.
Abwehr: The Abwehr took over all classical espionage and counter-espionage, including intelligence operations in foreign countries. As the war went on, the Gestapo also got engaged in the business of external spying.
Gestapo: The name Gestapo comes from the first letters of their long name Geheime Staatspolizei (State Secret Police).
Geheime Feldpolizei (GFP): The GFP drew nearly all its staff from the Gestapo and also had responsibilities for 'anti-terrorist' activities in occupied territories, as did the intelligence arm of the SS.
'[amongst] the upper bourgeoisie …': H. A. Ree report, December 1943, TNA HS 9/1240/3.
Hôtel de Ville: Known as the Palais Rohan after Archbishop Ferdinand Maximilien Mériadec de Rohan who restored the building in 1771.
'The English, …': Capitaine Charles du Tertre, the head of the Bordeaux chapter of the Centre d'Action Anti-Bolchévique (CAA), Elly Rous-Serra, *Les Renards de l'ombre: la Mission Baden–Savoie*, Paris, Nouvelles Éditions Latines, 1985, p. 529.
'The Jewish question …': Letter from Daniel Gallois to Gilles Perrault, 5 November 1975, AN 72/AJ/68.
requisitioned a nearby château: Château Pérenne, Saint-Genès-de-Blaye.
'Anyone who gives shelter …': ADG 59J 188.
Italian submarines: Italian submarines were excluded from the concrete bomb shelters – a matter which caused great tension between the German and Italian submarine crews.

Atlantic beaches: The US Army under General Pershing had landed here in the First World War.

60,000 German troops: These included Indian Regiment 950 (made up of prisoners from the Indian Army in North Africa and Italy).

two infantry divisions: 708th and 159th Reserve Division.

Panzer division: 11th Panzer Division.

army headquarters: 1st Army HQ.

soldiers' brothels: This was in Rue Laliment. The building, now demolished to make way for flats, was next to No. 22, Kruse's statement, S.I.R 1018, TNA WO 208/3601.

Lion Rouge nightclub: Ibid.

Côtelette: Ibid.

Blaue Affe: Ibid.

rate of exchange: After occupying France, the Germans enforced on the French an exchange rate of 1 Reichsmark for 20 francs compared to 1 Reichsmark for 11 francs in June 1940, see https://halshs.archives-ouvertes.fr/halshs-00652826/document.

'occupied Europe …': Mark Seaman, *The Bravest of the Brave: True Story of Wing Commander Tommy Yeo-Thomas – SOE Secret Agent Codename 'The White Rabbit'*, London, Michael O'Mara Books, 1997, p. 65.

'Bordeaux …': Landes IWM interview, Reel 2 (15' 17"), IWM SR 8641, 03-01-1985.

'Neighbours reported …': Caroline Moorhead, *A Train in Winter*, London, Vintage, 2012, p. 145.

'[They believed] their duty …': Daniel Grandclément, *L'Énigme Grandclément*, Paris, Balland, 2003, pp. 94–5.

spring and autumn fair: *La Fête Foraine*, first held in 1923 to show off the products of France's colonies.

Photographs from 1940: Erwan Langeo, *Bordeaux 1940–1944, la Place des Quinconces traverse la guerre*, Erwan Langeo, 2015, pp. 21–2.

'understand and be resigned': See http://www.liberation.fr/evenement/1997/10/08/bordeaux-1er-juillet-1940-23-heures-l-horloge-passe-a-l-heure-allemande-du-27-juin-1940-au-27-aout-1_218974.

Laiser Israel Karp: Philippe Souleau, *La Ligne de démarcation en Gironde 1940–1944*, Périgueux, Fanlac, 1998, p. 195.

Hans Reimers: Colonel Rémy, *Les Soldats du silence: mémoires d'un agent secret de la France Libre*, Vol. 2, Paris, Éditions de la Seine, 2002, p. 97.

discovered in Bordeaux harbour: He was assassinated at the junction of the Boulevard George V and the Rue de l'Ormeau-Mort in the centre of the city. His briefcase contained detailed plans of the German coastal defences around the Gironde estuary. These, with other plans for the 'Atlantic Wall' Hitler was constructing to protect *Festung Europa* (Fortress Europe, those parts of continental Europe occupied by Nazi Germany), were in due course smuggled back to London in one of the most important intelligence coups of the early part of the war.

257 'Resistance martyrs': René Terrisse, *Face aux pelotons Nazis: Souge, le Mont Valérien du Bordelais*, Bordeaux, Éditions Aubéron, 2000, p. 189.

secret British estimates: Summary of SOE activities for the prime minister, *Quarter*, October–December 1942, TNA HS 8/250. The total numbers for 1940 to 1944 were: about 20,000 executions (including shot and fallen Maquisards) and 67,000 (non-racial) deportations. See Peter Lieb, email to author, 23 February 2016.

foreign-controlled spy networks: These included Mithridate, Jade Amicol, Ajax, S.N., CND Castille, R. Marine, IS-IC, La France Vivra and F2 (run by the Poles).

city backstreet: The Impasse Sainte Ursule, about 400 metres back from the Quai des Chartrons.

He had been wounded: There is some confusion over Duboué's record in the First World War. One document ('History of the OCM', CMSM) records that he was awarded the Croix de

Guerre, while another ('*Histoire Secrète de la Résistance dans le Sud-Ouest*') reports that he was disciplined for deserting his post in the face of the enemy.

the Grand Café ...: Delmas, *Agenda-annuaire Delmas 1944*, Bordeaux, Éditions Delmas, 1943, p. 54.

Café des Marchands: No. 83 Quai des Chartrons. The café was also known locally as the Café du Commerce, but should not be confused with the much larger and more prestigious café of the same name in the city centre, the Grand Café du Commerce et de Tourny, of which Jean Duboué was the manager. Molly's Irish Pub now stands on the site.

at fifty: Information on him (under Payere) in TNA HS 7/13 gives a date of birth of 1878, but TNA HS 9/75 (SOE F Section agent Claude de Baissac's personal file) gives his age as fifty-three in 1943.

next door: In 1940 he lived at 84 Quai des Chartrons, but moved to 20 Rue de Colmar, closer to the centre of Bordeaux, sometime in the early 1940s.

Duboué and Paillère: Duboué's alias was 'Jean-Jacques', and Paillère's aliases were 'Léon Poirier', 'Ludovic Petit' and '84'.

clandestine escape route: The Édouard line was originally set up by SIS in 1940. This route was passed over to SOE, who used it as an escape route for their agents and occasional downed pilots and escaped prisoners on the run.

British consulate: The consul at the time was Sir Henry Farquhar.

murderous enmity: When SOE's prize Prosper network in Paris was rolled up by the Germans in mid-1943, 'Claude Dansey (effectively the head of SIS) marched in, clapped his hands and declared "Great news, Reilly. Great news ... One of the big SOE networks in France has just blown up."' Memoirs of Sir Patrick Reilly, Bodleian Library Ms Eng c6918 (fols 200–50). Reilly was personal assistant to Menzies.

'Though SOE and SIS ...': J. G. Beevor, *SOE: Recollections and Reflections 1940–1945*, London, The Bodley Head, 1981, pp. 75–6.

Colin Gubbins: The titular head of SOE was the Minister of Economic Warfare (Hugh Dalton, and then the Earl of Selborne). Gubbins's title was Director of Operations.

'shrewd ...': Robert Leroy SOE personal file, TNA HS 9/916/2.

codename 'Alain': His alias in the field was 'Louis'.

SOE 'ghost ship': HMS *Fidelity*. *Fidelity* was originally a French merchant ship which SOE purloined for landing agents on the French coast, TNA HS 8/831.

debt and unpaid bar bills: Reports of Egbert V. H. Rizzo, head of the Édouard Line, TNA HS 8/154.

director of warehouses: *Directeur de Manutention*.

Breton marine engineer: called Le Hellec.

'detailed reports ...': Leroy file, French military archives, Château de Vincennes, Paris.

'most vital cargoes': Lord Selborne to the prime minister, 9 May 1942, minute entitled 'Blockade Runners', microfilm, TNA HS 8/897.

'[stop] the trade altogether': Ibid.

'*Bonjour à Mouton*': private archive of Yves Léglise.

Chapter 2: Roger Landes

Piccadilly line towards central London: Landes probably took the tube from Manor House, the nearest station to his parents' apartment, to what is now Embankment station (then known as Charing Cross/Trafalgar Square).

Barnet: He was known to family and friends as Bernard, author interview with Alain Landes, 15 November 2015.

'his smallness ...': Charles Corbin interrogation, TNA HS 9/352/3.

War Office building itself had been hit: http://www.dailymail.co.uk/sciencetech/article-2243951/The-astonishing-interactive-map-EVERY-bomb-dropped-London-Blitz.html.

'We are sending ...': David D. Nicolson, *Aristide: Warlord of the Resistance*, London, Leo Cooper, 1994, p. 6.

Arthur Parks: His father was French sports correspondent for a reputable British newspaper. He once said he got his job because 'he knew how to keep his mouth shut', author email correspondence with Noreen Riols, 7 December 2010. See also Noreen Riols, *The Secret Ministry of Ag. & Fish*, London, Macmillan, 2013.

grand room: One of the common reminiscences of nearly all SOE agents who passed through Orchard Court was of the black marble bathroom, which was regarded at the time as a marvel of decadence and luxury.

Simon was also brief ...: Nicolson, *Aristide*, p. 8.

A30: Now known as the A3.

two giant sequoias: author telephone conversation with Richard Souchard, 1 February 2015. The cast-iron plaques were stolen in the 1980s.

'magnificent, strong ...': SOE F Section agent Henri Déricourt, quoted in Marshall, *All the King's Men*, p. 133.

Meoble Lodge: Special Training School No. 23.

Two ex-Shanghai policemen: William Fairbairn and Eric-Anthony Sykes. These two invented the FS (after the initials of their surnames) fighting knife – more famously known as the commando dagger, which remains to today the shoulder symbol of British commando units.

ex-chartered accountant: 'Killer' Green. He undertook his own mission to France later in the war and also helped with the interrogation of returning agents. His full name was Donald Ernest Farrance Green. See http://www.specialforcesroh.com/showthread. php?30225-Green-Donald-Ernest-Farrance-(Killer).

SOE's 'finishing school': Special Training School No. 31, also known as 'Group B'.

'an excellent operator': Claude de Baissac SOE personal file, TNA HS 9/75.

Gilbert Norman: After an early childhood spent in France, he had been dispatched in his early teens to a minor English public school – Ongar – after which he followed his father into chartered accountancy.

'He has the eye ...': Roger Landes's SOE personal file, TNA HS 9/880/8.

Chapter 3: Friedrich Dohse

his father, Hinrich: Dohse's father's name is stated as Hinrich in Dohse's interrogation by the British, 24 June 1946, TNA KV 3/238.

commercial college: Handels Kollege, Hamburg.

Friedrich joined: On 1 May 1933.

'Golden Party Badge': *Goldenes Ehrenzeichen der NSDAP*.

Hamburg suburb: Altona.

married and with two young children: He was married to Erika, née Jennerjahn, who was three years his junior; his children were a daughter Heidi and a son Harro.

counter-espionage section: Section IV2.a.

BdS: *Befehlshaber der Sicherheitspolizei und des Sicherheitsdienstes*.

'Though not a *political* Nazi ...': Quoting an interview with Hans Kopkow, 3 June 1983, Marshall, *All the King's Men*, p. 166.

one account: TNA KV 3/238.

'little God': Michel Bergès interview with Dohse, April 1985, private archive of Michel Bergès.

another senior SS intelligence officer: Josef Kieffer.

personal driver: Karl Braun.

old spy network: One of these spies was Jean Osvald, a senior police officer in Marseille, whom Bömelburg saw at the Petit Nice restaurant. Osvald was in fact a double agent who worked for the French secret service from the mid-1930s to the end of the war.

'enhanced interrogation ...': Dohse's memoirs exist in two forms. The first, which is more complete, is written in Dohse's own handwriting and was given to the author by Michel

Bergès. The second is an edited version which was typeset and prepared for publication (but never published) by the Swiss publishers Favre and was unearthed by the Bordeaux-based historian René Terrisse. All further references to these memoirs in this book come from this second typeset version, rather than the original in Dohse's handwriting, ADG 59J 209.

'I didn't need …': Michel Bergès interview with Dohse, April 1985, private archive of Michel Bergès.

'did not terrify, he demobilised': Gilles Perrault, *L'orchestre rouge*, Paris, Fayard, 1989, p. 325.

'half French': Walter Machule written statement, ADG 59J 67.

wily and clever …: The French have a single word – *rusé* – which combines all these attributes and is often used to describe Dohse by those who knew him.

'KdS Bordeaux': KdS – Kommandeur der Sicherheitspolizei und des Sicherheitsdienstes.

Avenue du Maréchal Pétain: The buildings were numbers 197, 220, 222 and 224. The road is now known as Avenue de la Libération Charles de Gaulle. It had been first renamed Avenue du Maréchal Pétain shortly before the Germans arrived in 1940.

liaison officer: Dohse statement to Capitaine Stienne, Military Judge, Bordeaux, 13 December 1949, private archive of Michel Bergès.

detective superintendent: *Kriminalkommissar*.

eight weeks younger than Dohse: Born on 13 September 1913 in Neumünster.

'I took …': Michel Bergès interview with Dohse, April 1985, private archive of Michel Bergès.

'everyone in KdS feared him': Hans Bordes evidence, ADG J59 67.

Chapter 4: André Grandclément

Amélia: Her full name was Amélia Marie Céleste Sophie Valérie de Barolet.

'the invisible ghetto': Grandclément, *L'Énigme Grandclément*, p. 15, quoting Perrault, *L'orchestre rouge*.

Franklin Jesuit College: Now Middle School and High School Saint-Louis de Gonzague 12 Rue Benjamin Franklin, 75116 Paris.

period of preparation: What the French call *classes préparatoires* or *prépas*. This is a period of preparatory study before tertiary education to prepare a candidate for the next stage of his/her study.

'So now I am going …': Grandclément, *L'Énigme Grandclément*, p. 19.

'At eighteen …': Ibid., p. 18.

one of his father's friends: Colonel Toussaint.

The couple married …: Grandclément, *L'Énigme Grandclément*, p. 19.

Mnay who knew him: One of those who described Grandclément was Gilbert Comte, see his statement, 23 March 1945, ADG 59J 119.

'intelligent, amiable, …': newspaper cutting, no date, private archive of Yves Léglise.

'He greatly overestimated …': The words of Friedrich Dohse, Jacques Sylvain interview with Dohse, 1987, ADG 59J 65.

'himself badly …': Charles Corbin's interrogatory, TNA HS 9/352/3.

close to the Croix-de-Feu: Police report by Special Inspector Delmas, 24 November 1941, ADG 59J 107.

'a faithful partisan': Ibid.

'official mistress': The French word for the state of official mistress is *concubinage*.

'Their love …': Grandclément, *L'Énigme Grandclément*, pp. 119–20.

covert organisations: A local organisation called Groupe Ouest (Group West) and a right-wing movement of young people, especially students, in the Bordeaux area, which he led, called La France Vivra (France Will Live On).

school teacher from Bordeaux: Jean Ferrier.

escape line to London: Lucienne Souillié, *History of the OCM*, Fonds Calmette, ADG 62J 1.

eau de vie: Alcohol distilled from the leftover of wine pressings. See Aristide archive, CMSM.

'With Lucette …': Grandclément, *L'Énigme Grandclément*, p. 54.

Chapter 5: A Happy Man and a Dead Body

'brutal and stupid': Notes by René Terrisse concerning Kunesch, ADG 59J 67.

'the cosher-in-chief': *Le matraqueur-en-chef*. The rubber cosh is referred to in French as a *nerf de boeuf* because the strand of the whips were often made of the sinews of oxen.

Marcelle Louise Sommer: Née Freierling.

Claire Keimer: Author interview with Michel Bergès, Biscarrosse, 11 June 2015.

108 individuals: Rapport Reillac, pp. 72–81.

'[German] officers …': Simon Kitson, *The Hunt for Nazi Spies: Fighting Espionage in Vichy France*, Chicago, University of Chicago Press, 2007, p. 34.

Johann Dollar: Ibid.

10,000 francs: René Terrisse, *À la botte de l'occupant: intinéraires de cinq collaborateurs*, Bordeaux, Éditions Aubéron, 1998, p. 47.

'murder brigade': '*La Brigade des Tueurs*', Moorhead, *A Train in Winter*, p. 134.

'I said to Poinsot …': Jacques Sylvain and Fabien Pont interview with Dohse for *Sud-Ouest*, June 1987, ADG 59J 65.

paramilitary organisations: Phalange Raciste and Hauskapelle (a German word meaning 'private chapel' – in this context it denotes an intelligence organisation working as a separate organisation within a larger intelligence structure) who were chiefly informers.

197 Avenue du Maréchal Pétain: The French owner was Mme Marguerite Touchard. The house has since been demolished and the site is now the garden of a small house which lies back from the main road. There is some confusion about the number as one British interrogation report puts the address as 189 Avenue du Maréchal Pétain (now Avenue de la Libération Charles de Gaulle), not 197.

The building: See the evidence and sketch maps provided by Kruse, S.I.R 018, TNA WO 208/3601.

interrogation cells: Dohse's concluding interrogatory by Captain Stienne, Military Judge, Bordeaux, 13 December 1949, private archive of Michel Bergès.

'just an administrator …': Michel Bergès interview with Dohse, April 1985, private archive of Michel Bergès.

Dohse's personal chauffeur: Christian Joyaux.

driven to his favourite restaurant: Perrault, *La Longue traque*, p. 324.

'Mr Gutsman …': Harold Goodman, vice-consul in San Sebastián (said to have been SIS). He had close contacts with the Republicans in the Spanish Civil War and was involved in the famous 'dirty shirt affair' of December 1938. Michel Bergès interview with Dohse, April 1985, private archive of Michel Bergès.

'I liked the good life …': Jacques Sylvain and Fabien Pont interview with Dohse for *Sud-Ouest*, June 1987, ADG 59J 65.

'Dohse loved Bordeaux …': Perrault, *L'orchestre rouge*, p. 326.

destroyed a power station: Operation Josephine B.

senior communist: Pierre Louis Giret.

1,600 men and 100 officers: Evidence of Jean Ferrier to Arthur Calmette, February 1948, private archive of Michel Bergès.

almost the whole of southwest France: The Departments of Basses-Pyrénées, Gironde, Landes, Charente-Maritime, Vendée and Deux-Sèvres.

fourteen active units: Case history of the Secret Army group of the Gironde, author unknown, private archive of Yves Léglise.

Café des Chartrons: 101 Quai des Chartrons.

country train: I am grateful to Patrick Canel for his research into Labit's journey that morning, email to Sylvie Young, 19 April 2016.

trained by SOE: Trained and parachuted in by SOE's R/F Section, rather than F Section. His operation was called 'Bass'.

Ginette and her mother: Patrick Canel, email to Sylvie Young, 19 April 2016.

Henri Labit's mother, Henriette: Author interview with Alain Landes (son of Ginette Corbin), 2 November 2015. There is a second version of this story which indicates that Henri Labit's mother recognised her son from a photograph, see KdS Bordeaux, ADG 59J 67, 'Le KdS de Bordeaux: juin 1942–août 1944'.

SOE radio operator: Marcel Clech alias 'Georges', 'André', 'Marcel Cornic', 'Sanction', 'Marcel Lesueur', 'Yves Lebras', 'Georges 60' and 'Bastien'. He landed near Cannes from HMS Unbroken.

Raymond Henry Flower: Alias 'Gaspard' and 'Gaston'.

'no powers of leadership ...': Raymond Flower SOE personal file, TNA HS 9/522–5.

Yvonne Rudellat: Alias 'Jacqueline' and 'Suzanne'; SOE codename 'Soaptree'; false identity in the name of 'Jacqueline Viallat', TNA HS 9/1289/7.

secretly landed: She was landed from the felucca Seadog and was the first female SOE F Section agent to be infiltrated into France after training.

'cold grey eyes ...': Stella King, Jacqueline, London, Arms and Armour, 2006, p. 227.

'investigate the possibilities ...': Claude de Baissac's final instructions can be found in his SOE personal file, TNA HS 9/75.

Chapter 6: Scientist Gets Established

deserted aerodrome: This is now Nîmes airport – Aéroport de Nîmes-Alès-Camargue-Cévennes.

open field: Nîmes golf club occupies the area now.

Claude Boucher: According to de Baissac's file in the French Military Archive in Château de Vincennes, Paris, he also used another alias, 'Michel Roanet', at this time.

'And how long ...': Claude de Baissac debriefing, 13 November 1944, TNA HS 6/567.

Rue Avezac-Macaya: Now renamed Rue Andie Mayer.

Édouard line: Its motto was 'Chercher, Recevoir, Passer' – 'To seek, to receive, to pass on to England'.

password sequence: Claude de Baissac instructions, 24 July 1942, TNA HS 9/75.

two of Dohse's agents: Mme and Mlle Bourdeix, pork butchers at 9 Cours du Médoc. They were members of the Groupe Collaboration, whose names were on a list found after the war in the offices of the Gestapo in Paris, private archive of Yves Léglise.

nearest radio operator: Marcel Clech.

Moulin de Saquet: Also pronounced 'Saquette' in the area. Its exact position is Lat. 44° 42' 30" N, Long. 00° 09' 16" W, operation report, 161 Sqn (RAF Tempsford), TNA AIR 20/8452. The building now on this site, a pretty, low, single-storey farmhouse next to the ruins of the old mill, is run as a chambres d'hôtes by a charming English couple called Val and Vito Traill. The site, which is well sheltered from prying eyes by woods, is now a vineyard. Visit to Targon area by the author, 3 April 2011. See also Michel St Marc, Le Canton de Targon sous l'Occupation 1939–1945, Villenave d'Ornon: AAPA, 2007.

more detailed report: Claude de Baissac report, 19 September 1942, TNA HS 9/75.

Drancy: The infamous French internment camp near Paris where all those awaiting deportation were detained.

Chapter 7: A Visitor for David

Great North Road: Now the A1.

RAF Tempsford: Tempsford was home to the RAF's 138 and 161 Special Duty Squadrons, which carried out all infiltrations and exfiltrations of agents and supplies throughout Europe from 1942 onwards.

Here, after being dressed: This procedure is taken from a description given in King, Jacqueline, p. 170.

Georgian mansion: Gaynes Hall, known at the time as Station 61.

large farmhouse: Gibraltar Farm.

'L' tablets: 'L' tablets came encased in a rubber cover which was placed in the mouth and bitten. Death followed fifteen seconds later.

An hour before departure …: The details contained in this description are taken from the descriptions of the standard preparations for all agents going into France, Freddie Clark, *Agents by Moonlight*, Stroud, Tempus Publishing, p. 77.

Three further attempts: On the first occasion Gilbert Norman was due to jump with Landes. His orders were to join the Prosper network in Paris run by Francis Suttill. Suttill had, however, failed to send a message to London to indicate that he was ready to receive his new colleague, so SOE cancelled the drop.

Bois Renard: Three kilometres southeast of Nouan-sur-Loire, Loir-et-Cher, Lat. 47° 40' 10" N, Long. 01° 35' 89" E.

Gilbert Norman: Alias 'Archambaud'. He was originally assigned to Corsica, but re-tasked to join Suttill.

local mayor: Maurice Dutem, at the time, the mayor of Mer.

first women: With Lise de Baissac.

nearby farm: Owned by a Benjamin and Suzanne Bossard.

'the horse found …': Clark, *Agents by Moonlight*, p. 238.

'more a social event …': Landes's debriefing, 2 December 1944, TNA HS 6/574.

Rudellat: Alias 'Jacqueline' and 'Soaptree', with a false identity in the name of 'Jacqueline Viallet'.

Lise de Baissac: Alias 'Artist', with a false identity in the name of 'Irène Brisse'.

a month previously: On 24 September 1942.

returning to his job: Landes's personal file, TNA HS 9/880/8.

Café des Colonnes: No. 6 Place des Quinconces. It is now an insurance office.

'I have a letter …': Dialogue taken from an interview with Roger Landes published over several days in *Sud-Ouest*. This specific dialogue was published on 29 August 1948, private archive of Yves Léglise.

Café Gambetta: A small backstreet café at the time, in fact Cave Gambetta, No. 36 Rue Bouffard. It is a trinket shop today.

'David is out of town …': private archive of Yves Léglise.

they couldn't hear him: In his debriefing in August 1943, Claude de Baissac comments that 'it is impossible to transmit from Bordeaux owing to the Iron Belt, but it is possible to do so from the other side of the river'. It is not known whether he was referring here to the metaphorical ring of German 'iron' round the city, or some natural phenomenon to do with high concentrations of iron in the soil.

Chapter 8: Crackers and Bangs

Allied landings in North Africa: Operation Torch, which took place on 8 November 1942.

'sabotage …': 'History of F Section', TNA HS 7/121, p. 7, and M. R. D. Foot, *SOE in France: An Account of the Work of the British Special Operations Executive in France 1940–1944*, London, HMSO, 1966, p. 222.

Victor Charles Hayes: Codename 'Printer', field alias 'Yves', his local aliases were 'Charles', 'Charles le Chauve' ('Charles the Bald' – on account of his lack of hair) and 'Charles le Démolisseur'. He landed at a site close to Montbazon.

parachuted into a site: This was Hayes's second mission in France.

Coirac reception committee: This was led by Mme Jeanne Bonnevie, one of the very few women in France who was in charge of a Resistance parachute reception committee. She lived with her husband at Château La Bertrande (now home to winemakers Anne-Marie Gillet and Jean-Marc Bourguinat) opposite the church in the village of Omet.

Mary Herbert: Her SOE codename was 'Jeweller'.

waiting for a flying boat: With Landes and Mary Herbert were Marie-Thérèse Le Chêne alias 'Adèle' and Odette Sansom alias 'Lise'.

'Robert the Tipsy': Robert l'Ivrogne.

'too sophisticated for my new life': Author interview with Denise Hèches, Tarbes, 29 March 2011.

village near Bordeaux: Omet, where he was staying with Jeanne Bonnevie.

in a matchbox …: Mary Herbert debriefing, 30 January 1945, TNA HS 6/567.

set for 12 December: Based on the testimony of SOE's historian Professor M. R. D. Foot on a now lost document. This stated that the Scientist team were carrying out their final reconnaissance for the attack on the morning of 11 December 1942 'before they attacked the following night'. See Dr Tom Keene interview with M. R. D. Foot, 26 January 2004. In a telephone conversation with the author on 25 April 2011, Professor Foot confirmed that, in his researches for his book *SOE in France*, he had had sight of a document which confirmed this.

only recently woken up: Senior Gestapo Commander in France Helmut Knochen statement, 6 January 1947, private archive of Michel Bergès.

demolition team arrived: Author interview with Alain Landes, 3 November 2014.

pandemonium and chaos: Author interview with Jean Trocard, Bordeaux, 30 March 2011. M. Trocard was a conscripted labourer in Organisation Todt.

'to capsize …': Papers of Walter Schnöppe, by kind permission of the Deutsches U-Boat Museum, Cuxhaven, Germany.

'all means necessary': Copies of German signals held at the Royal Marines Museum, Eastney, trans. Christine Tochtermann.

German admiral: Admiral Johannes Bachmann.

Operation Frankton: See Paddy Ashdown, *A Brilliant Little Operation*, Aurum Press, London, 2012.

'difficult to comprehend' …: Keitel's message was sent on 15 December 1942, TNA HS 9/75, trans. Christine Tochtermann.

'At the critical moment …': Scientist target report, 22 March 1943, TNA HS 9/75.

causing serious damage: Though there were some claims that two U-boats were sunk in consequence – see Foot, *SOE in France*, p. 248.

sunk by them: TNA HS 8/22.

conférence de Poitiers: The conference was preceded by a meeting between de Gaulle's BCRA and SOE a month earlier in London in which it was agreed in principle that SOE would provide the arms and equipment needed by French Resistance organisations in France, making Baker Street, in effect, the French Resistance's quartermaster for the remainder of the war.

reorganise the entire underground OCM structure: Tasks were distributed as follows: *1er bureau* (Troop Command): Commandant Paillère; *2ème bureau* (Intelligence): Colonel Camplan; *3ème bureau* (Planning): Commandant Joubert; *4ème bureau* (Logistics): Commandant Souques – see AN 72 AJ 130 A.I.6.

reach an 'agreement': Instruction to Landes, 19 October 1942, TNA HS 9/75.

having control of …: Manuscript document from General Rollot to Henri Michel, 29 October 1959, AN 72 AJ 130 A.I.6.

'[to] establish a new system …': Manuscript document written by André Grandclément when prisoner at Bouscat in September 1943, private archive of Michel Bergès.

'very able and trustworthy': De Baissac debriefing, 6 January 1945, 'Circuit & Mission Reports', TNA HS 6/567.

'an official status …': Ibid.

'a major …': Manuscript document from General Rollot to Henri Michel, 29 October 1959, AN 72 AJ 130 A.I.6.

'In the course of 1942 …': ADG 59J 209, pp. 23–4.

Chapter 9: Businesses, Brothels and Plans

Neither ... was Baker Street: To their fury, SOE were deliberately excluded from the Chiefs of Staff Committee, which essentially ran the war, and were therefore not formally briefed on the results of Casablanca, though they may have heard of its conclusions informally.

'[in] 1943 we had ...': Maurice Buckmaster, *They Fought Alone*, London, Biteback Publishing, 2014, p. 225.

radio engineer: Jacques Bureau – see Jean Overton Fuller, *Déricourt: The Chequered Spy*, Salisbury, Michael Russell, 1989, pp. 356, 358.

20 January: They were wed in a service at the *mairie*. There is some confusion as to whether the date was 20 or 21 January 1943 (for instance, a Wikipedia entry suggests 20 January 1943, while *L'Enigme Grandclément*, p. 119, claims 21 January).

'All André's friends ...': Arlette Caussé – see Grandclément, *L'Énigme Grandclément*, p. 120.

'like a windmill': Michel Bergès and René Terrisse interview with André Maleyran, Reel 2 (18' 50"), private archive of Michel Bergès.

'At that time ...': Michel Bergès and René Terrisse interview with André Maleyran, Reel 2 (20' 45"), private archive of Michel Bergès.

'I left the meeting ...': Landes letter in *Historia*, issue 305, February 1973, private archive of Michel Bergès.

resort to borrowing: See TNA HS 9/462/5 and HS 9/608/8, and ADG 59J 119.

90,000 francs: Bourne-Paterson letter to Venner, 26 January 1946, TNA HS 9/608/8.

'refused to provide ...': Dr Alain Boyau report, started 4 March and completed 11 April 1944, private archive of Michel Bergès.

Sélections Cinématographiques du Sud-Ouest: Guy Penaud, *Histoire secrète de la Résistance*, Bordeaux, Éditions Sud-Ouest, 2011, p. 60, and '*Direction de l'enregistrement des Domaines et du Timbre de la Gironde*', ADG 59J 119.

narrow backstreet of Bordeaux: 11 Rue Fernand Marin – also the home of Madeleine Nicolas, a Scientist agent.

one of Grandclément's close friends: Louis Cassagne, letter from Mlle Rateau passed on to commissaire Lescure, ADG 59J 119.

mistress: Mlle Haderne.

bought a brothel: Letter from Mlle Rateau passed on to commissaire Lescure, ADG 59J 119.

'a lot [of girls] working ...': Landes IWM interview, Reel 3 (05' 15"), IWM SR 8641, 03-01-1985.

'I knew a pimp ...': Michel Bergès and René Terrisse interview with André Maleyran, Reel 1 (15' 18–45"), private archive of Michel Bergès.

wood close to Arcachon: At Lat. 44° 38' 04" N, Long. 01° 10' 17" W – now a patch of ___ wasteground just off the southwestern corner of Arcachon golf course.

spate of parachute drops: Bourne-Paterson report, TNA HS 7/122.

'to arm a Division': Nicolson, *Aristide*, p. 46.

'[in 1943] the supply ...': Hans Luther, *Der französische Widerstand gegen die deutsche Besatzungsmacht und seine Bekämpfung*, Tübingen, 1957, trans. Christine Tochtermann.

'great concern': ADG 59J 209, p. 20.

'I asked the Luftwaffe ...': Ibid.

'We were able ...': Ibid.

Chapter 10: 'Je suis fort – je suis même très fort'

17 March 1943: Operation Trainer.

the Lysander's range: Allowing a 20 per cent contingency for headwinds and diversions, the effective range for a Lysander based on the English southern coast at RAF Tangmere, was 550–570kms. Later versions of the Lysander were fitted with external fuel tanks, but these were only very rarely used for SOE operations.

four secret agents: John Goldsmith alias 'Valentin', Pierre Lejeune alias 'Delphin', Robert Dowlen alias 'Richard' and Mme Françoise 'Francine' Agazarian alias 'Marguerite'.

bring four back: Claude de Baissac alias 'David', France Antelme alias 'Renaud', Raymond Flower alias 'Gaspard' and André Dubois alias 'Hercule'.

Henri Déricourt: There is strong evidence to indicate that Déricourt was in fact a double agent, working both for Bömelburg and MI6.

'*Je suis fort* ...': 'I am strong – I am very strong.'

'*Extremely* intelligent ...': Scientist target report, 22 March 1943, TNA HS 9/75.

Colonel André Dewavrin: Alias 'Passy'.

parachuted into France: On 26 February 1943 (the first attempt was on the 23rd), Colonel Passy, *Mémoires du Colonel Passy*, Paris, Éditions Odile Jacob, 2000, p. 520.

estimated at 42,000: Arthur Calmette, *L'O.C.M. Organisation Civile et Militaire – Histoire d'un Mouvement de Résistance de 1940 à 1946*, Paris, Editions Presses Universitaires de France, 1961, p. 102.

organisation in Bordeaux: This was Mission Arquebuse-Brumaire comprising André Dewavrin alias 'Arquebuse' and Pierre Brossolette alias 'Brumaire'.

'You have your own regions ...': Michel Bergès interview with Christian Campet and Roger Landes, June 1984, CMSM.

'lazy student': Claude de Baissac finishing report, 10 April 1944, TNA HS 9/75.

'state of siege': Suttill report, 9 March 1943, TNA HS 9/183.

D-Day was *not* imminent: Quoted in Francis J. Suttill, *Shadows in the Fog*, History Press, 2014, p. 90, citing Maurice Buckmaster, *Specially Employed: The Story of British Aid to French Patriots of the Resistance*, Batchworth Press, London, 1952.

one of their intelligence agents: Agent 95030 – his identity is not known, Calmette, *L'O.C.M.*, p. 104.

'as the invasion approaches ...': Ibid.

'elaborate camouflage ...': Thaddeus Holt, *The Deceivers: Allied Deception in the Second World War*, London, Phoenix, 2005, p. 477.

highest councils of the war: Specifically the Joint Chiefs of Staff Committee.

visit to Vichy: This probably took place around the end of May 1943.

deciphered a telegram: This telegram appears to have been lost. But an SOE paper of 20 August 1943 analysing the message gives a very clear indication of both its contents and importance, TNA HS 6/339.

roads and bridges ... mined: France Antelme's 'Bricklayer' report, 23 March 1943, TNA HS 9/44.

stay-behind network: Similar German 'stay-behind' networks were created in the Balkans.

Bordeaux midwife: There are some indications – e.g. in the Aristide archive, CMSM – that this may have been Jeanne Chaigneau, a nurse who was one of Dohse's agents and lived at 21 Rue Emile Combes, Bordeaux.

German wireless school: Run by Dr Joseph Götz.

two escape lines: These were in addition to the totally separate escape lines set up by MI9 through the area.

21,000-strong: Basses-Pyrénées, 700 men; Landes, 2000; Gironde, 11,000; Charente-Maritime, 500; Charente, 1,500; Poitou, Vendée, Vienne, Deux Sèvres, 5,000. Reports Nos 1 & 2, brought back by Lysander, 16/17 June 1943, TNA HS 9/75.

'It is ... also undoubted ...': 'F Section History and Agents', TNA HS 7/121.

forest clearing: Lat. 44° 43' 30" N, Long. 0° 52' 24" W, TNA Air 20/8297.

'nights of the full moon': Often referred to by the French by the codename 'Charlotte'.

'Even heaven recoils ...': '*Le Ciel épouvanté, contemple avec horreur, la face de ce monstre.*' Probably derived from Racine's play *Phèdre*, Act 5, scene 6: '*Le ciel avec horreur voit ce monstre sauvage*', http://www.revue-texto.net/Reperes/Cours/Mezaille/theramene.html.

'The full moon period ...': This account is taken from several reports, including ADG 59J 233 and ADG 59J 107. I have slightly altered the quoted text for ease of reading in English.

'Very good ...': TNA Air 20/8287.

'At around one ...': TNA Air 20/8287.

'"Polish pilots"': Many of the RAF Special Squadron pilots were Polish.

Marcel Eusèbe Défence: His SOE codename was 'Weaver'; his various aliases were 'Dédé', 'Maurice Doare', 'Michel Delaplace', 'Marcel Darcy', 'Vasili' and 'Tie'.

calm and taciturn nature: Interrogator's report on Défence, TNA HS 6/436.

'Direct hits ...': *Target Germany: The US Army Air Force's Official Story of the VIII Bomber Command's First Year Over Europe*, HMSO, London, 1944, p. 90.

'revolting aggression ...': The words of Adrien Marquet, http://www.liberation.fr/evenement/ 1997/10/08/bordeaux-1er-juillet-1940-23-heures-l-horloge-passe-a-l-heure-allemande- du-27-juin-1940-au-27-aout-1_218974.

L'Alouette: Landes debriefing, 2 December 1944, TNA HS 6/574.

safe houses: 174 Avenue de la République, the home of Mme Caralp-Jardel; 43 Cours Portal, the home of Paul Masuy; 52 Avenue du Jardin Public, the home of Paul Chevalier; and Rue David Johnston, the home of Robert Furt.

and Marguerite: Alias 'Jacqueline'.

6,200 arrests: Rous-Serra, *Les Renards de l'ombre*, p. 519.

six major sabotage attacks: An attack by a team led by Duboué and Hayes on the main transmitter for U-boats on 5 April; attacks led by Dussarrat on high-tension cables near Dax on 19 April and 20 May; the sabotage by Hayes of pylons at Facture, also on 20 May; the sabotage and sinking of ships in Pauillac harbour by Duboué and Hayes on 13 May. See among other sources Penaud, *Histoire secrète*, p. 121, and Dussarrat's report, 15 June 1944, ADG 59J 117.

Chapter 11: A Birthday Present for Friedrich

'a few seconds ...': Suttill, *Shadows in the Fog*, p. 123.

farm worker's cottage: named Le Cercle.

Canadian agents: Frank Pickersgill alias 'Bertrand' and Ken Macalister alias 'Valentin'.

just above her left ear: Evidence of Comtesse Souris de Bernard, see King, *Jacqueline*, p. 65.

General Charles Delestraint: Delestraint was arrested on 9 June 1943 as he left La Muette Metro station in Paris.

most important intelligence coup: Archives départementales du Loir-et-Cher, 1375 W70, quoted in Suttill, *Shadows in the Fog*, p. 149.

capture of a British agent: TNA HS 9/1430/6.

'particularly dangerous': Josef Kieffer's deposition on oath, 19 January 1947, TNA HS 6/426.

'must be rooted out ...': 'British Circuits in France, 1941–44', by Major R. A. Bourne-Paterson, June 1946, TNA HS 7/122.

He died: Jean Moulin died on 8 July 1943.

Andrée Borrel: According to Henri Déricourt, Francis Suttill also shared her favours – though Déricourt's word on this, as on so much else, is not to be trusted. See Fuller, *Déricourt*, p. 107.

under German control: He was directed by the German radio spymaster Dr Josef Götz, who was a master at playing what the Germans called *funkspiel* ('the radio game') in which captured Allied radios were 'played back' under German direction to the British. Götz had some successes, of which the operation involving Gilbert Norman was one. The British operation Double Cross, already well underway at the time of the fall of Prosper, was far more successful, controlling every single German spy landed in Britain and their radios, for the entire duration of the war – see Ben Macintyre, *Double Cross*, London, Bloomsbury, 2012.

'unusual, hesitant ...': Report, 5 August 1943, TNA HS 9/1110/5.

signal criticising him: Suttill, *Shadows in the Fog*, p. 186, and Charles Wighton, *Pin-stripe Saboteur: The Story of Robin – British agent and French Resistance Leader*, London, Odhams, 1959, pp. 216–17.

in the northwest: He had caught the 0700 train from Gisors, 60km northwest of Paris, that morning.

backstreet hotel: Hôtel Mazagran, 18 Rue de Mazagran. It is now a Chinese massage parlour.

Borrel's flat: 57 Rue des Petites Ecuries.

new restrictions: http://www.liberation.fr/evenement/1997/10/08/ bordeaux-1er-juillet-1940-23-heures-l-horloge-passe-a-l-heure-allemande-du-27-juin-1940-au-27-aout-1_218974.

confined to intelligence-gathering: ADG 59J 209, pp. 25 and 27.

bicycle shop owner: Lucien Ducros.

twenty-two-year-old son: Jean Ducros.

and broke: Jean Ducros, police report, 17 July 1943, AN 72 AJ 131; Rapport Borderie, p. 19; and René Terrisse, *Grandclément: traître ou bouc émissaire?*, Bordeaux, Éditions Aubéron, 1996, pp. 32–3, 36–7, private archive of Michel Bergès.

'an organised … Resistance movement …': ADG 59J 209, p. 28, and Penaud, *Histoire secrète*, pp. 68–9.

his codename – 'Bernard': The other was 'Martin Roland'.

two hundred: Poinsot speaks of about 150 arrests and René Terrisse of seventy-six.

Colonel Grandier-Vazeille: Colonel Paul Étienne Grandier-Vazeille's alias was 'L'Alouette'.

'If you will not talk …': Dohse's concluding interrogatory, 13 December 1949, by Captain Stienne, Military Judge, Bordeaux, private archive of Michel Bergès.

'I hope you now understand …': Ibid.

orders of the time: From 1 June, a new regulation stated that all affairs threatening the security of German troops would be dealt with only by regional KdS.

one of Grandclément's close contacts: Lucien Banizette.

'a bloody mess …': Written statement by Guy Morand alias 'Jules Labat' to René Terrisse, quoted in Terrisse, *Grandclément*, pp. 57–8.

the address: 12 Rue Leberthon.

Chapter 12: The Wolf in the Fold

'to show the Gestapo …': Stanislas report, 21 January 1944, TNA HS 9/76.

ex-police inspector: Inspector of Police Philippe Chatelier.

one of Poinsot's men: Inspector Roger Laffargue.

Lucette's cousin: Arlette Caussé.

one of his key lieutenants: Roger Laffargue.

'Why shouldn't I? …': Laffargue's evidence, 25 October 1944, ADG 59J 108.

'not someone emotionally equipped …': Michel Bergès interview with Dohse, April 1985, private archive of Michel Bergès. The present author has made some alteration to the sentence order for greater clarity.

'in a hurry': Michel Bergès interview with Christian Campet and Roger Landes, June 1984, CMSM.

250 men and women: This number is Dohse's estimate. A French police report dated 23 August mentions 116 arrests, Terrisse, *Grandclément*, p. 61. In Rapport Reillac, p. 135, by André Grandclément's arrest day, 200 persons affiliated to OCM Bordeaux had been arrested.

Fort du Hâ: Now destroyed and built on except for two towers that remain.

1,250 fugitives: Luther, *Der französische Widerstand*, p. 47, translation by Christine Tochtermann (quoting an article in *Paris Match*, 8 December 1951, by M. Bechendari).

'French underground leaders …': Marshall, *All the King's Men*, p. 212, quoting Director of Press and Publicity, War Office Report 19–25 August 1943, COSSC/182X; now in SHAEF SGS 381, pre-invasion file MMR – US NA.

1,061 in August: Luther, *Der französische Widerstand*, p. 49. The British figure is somewhat
   lower at 630, TNA HS 7/10.
977 containers: Ibid.
Twenty-two containers: Parachute drops in 1943, ADG 59J 233.
more than seventy containers: TNA HS 8/225.
2.1 million francs: F Section summary sheet – francs sent to the field – 1943, TNA HS 7/121.
200,000 francs: The equivalent of around £40,000 today.
'to be reimbursed …': Dussarrat SOE personal file, TNA HS 9/462/5.
after the war: The debt was duly honoured.
local businessmen: The other was a Monsieur H. Barraille.
Paris café: The Café Villard, behind the École Militaire. André's ex-school friend, Marc O'Neill,
   was also there.
'live in hiding': Translation of a letter from Artagnan dated 28 August 1946, TNA HS
   9/608/8.
Grandclément had lent: Using one of his aliases – 'Puligny'.
business friend and partner: Charles Michaud.
contact in Dax: Grandclément mentions an 'agent' but it is not clear whether this is a
   commercial or a Resistance 'agent'.
two Portuguese women: Simone Ferrier and Marie-Louise Cunka-Vaz.
A prisoner: Grandier-Vazeille, Rapport Borderie, p. 23, private archive of Michel Bergès.
'some cinema concern …': Extract from Bayswater interrogation of Corbin, 4 February 1944,
   TNA HS 9/608/8.
report to Baker Street: Mary Herbert debriefing, TNA HS 6/567.
'The Gestapo came …': This conversation has been constructed from the Landes report
   ('*L'affaire Jardel*') of this incident, TNA HS 9/76.
'He bent down …': Landes IWM interview, Reel 3 (9' 20"), IWM SR 8641, 03-10-1985.
autumn equinox: 21 September.
field in the Loire valley: LZ Torticolis, 2km east of Couture-sur-Loire, http://www.plan-
   sussex-1944.net/anglais/pdf/infiltrations_into_france.pdf.
one passenger: Nicholas Bodington.
The returning passengers: 'Organisation of David's Circuits', 1 September 1943, TNA HS 9/75.
'This was a woman …': Michel Bergès interview with Christian Campet and Roger Landes,
   June 1984, CMSM.
'of 42 [sic]': She was born in 1903, making her, in fact, forty in 1943.
received the DSO: Claude de Baissac was amongst the first in SOE to receive this medal.

Chapter 13: The Trap Closes
'in a very unstable …': Marcel Défence debriefing, 25/26 January 1944, TNA HS 6/436.
one of them: Benjamin Passet, alias 'Albert', Marc O'Neill's deputy.
Paris restaurant: 43 Place du Trocadéro.
'so obsessed …': René Terrisse interview with Charles Verny, November 1984, private archive
   of Michel Bergès.
senior members: Marcel Pelletier, the Vichy Police Commissioner for Paris, and Max
   Knipping, Milice delegate for the maintenance of order in the northern zone.
'I was extremely suspicious …': Thinières evidence, 29 June 1945, private archive of Michel
   Bergès.
'If there is no invasion …': Jean Sanders report about Grandclément's activities, 1 September
   1944, TNA HS 9/608/8.
several reports: Claude de Baissac reports, August 1943, TNA HS 9/75.
report written by Grandclément: He was later to claim that Rollot had a hand in this.
'All this has been achieved …': TNA HS 9/808/8.
'lucky to survive …': De Baissac report on Gestapo activity, 7 September 1943, TNA HS 9/75.

from Bordeaux to the Pyrenees: The Gironde, Landes and Basses-Pyrénées departments.

464 containers: SOE report, 16–24 August 1943, TNA HS 8/225.

French double agents: Jacques Désoubrie alias 'Jean-Jacques', 'Jean Masson', 'Pierre Boulain', 'Jacques Verge' and 'Capitaine Jacques' belonged to the Lilles Gestapo. In June 1943, Désoubrie had infiltrated and caused the destruction of the Comet network, one of the most successful and largest of MI9's escape networks in France.

another member: Marc Vuillemin.

affording little cover: Fuller, *Déricourt*, p. 214.

Restaurant Monte Carlo: The Restaurant Monte Carlo, Avenue de Wagram, is still there, though its terrace has been covered in.

fellow prisoner: Marc Vuillemin.

Chapter 14: The Deal

Dohse called in: There are many accounts giving details of the progress of Dohse's interrogation of Grandclément. In the main I have followed the account given by Dohse himself, except where this is obviously inaccurate (as for instance in the timings of what happened to Grandclément in Paris). The main sources for Dohse's account are: TNA KV 3/238; the British record of Dohse's July 1946 interrogation; Dohse's own memoirs, ADG 59J 209; his interview with Michel Bergès in April 1985, private archive of Michel Bergès; and Grandclément report written on 10 July 1943, TNA HS 9/608/8.

'One did not see ...': Perrault, *La Longue traque*, p. 324.

'more like a conversation ...': Ibid., p. 326.

'Don't worry ...': Conversation constructed from Dohse's own words, Michel Bergès interview with Dohse, April 1985, private archive of Michel Bergès.

Commandant John: Commandant Alexandre John, a judicial policeman from Lübeck who had arrived in July to head Dohse's department. But he lasted only a few weeks before leaving.

period of freedom: TNA HS 9/608/8. Grandclément claims in his report of 10 July 1944 that he was allowed a whole day out.

'The actions ...': Document given by André Maleyran to Michel Bergès and René Terrisse, 11 January 1986, private archive of Michel Bergès.

German security official: Höherer SS- und Polizeiführer Frankreich (HSSPFF, Commander of the SS and Head of the German Police in France), Carl Albrecht Oberg.

Chapter 15: Arms and Alarms

Rue Robert d'Ennery: No. 69.

'You go ...': Michel Bergès interview with Christian Campet and Roger Landes, June 1984, CMSM.

wash and shave: Although, in Corbin's first account of this event, he says Grandclément showed him the scars from his beating in Paris, his later accounts claim that, when he saw him with his shirt off while shaving, he noted there were no marks on his back.

'insignificant revelations' ...: Conversation constructed from Landes's report, TNA HS/7/96.

'It was a decision ...': Landes (Stanislas) report, TNA HS 9/76.

'ten per cent' ...: Corbin's report, 11 January 1944, TNA HS 9/352/3 (confirmed by Robert Mollié's evidence, ADG 59J 109, and Stanislas report, TNA HS 9/76).

act of treason: Grandclément report written on 10 July 1944, TNA HS 9/608/8.

'In this very grave ...': Rapport Reillac, p. 140, and Rapport Boyau, p. 6, private archive of Michel Bergès.

'I am doing ...': Rapport Boyau, p. 6, private archive of Michel Bergès.

local Resistance chief: Robert Mollié.

Sunday 26 September: Maleyran said it took place on Monday the 27th.

'For the first time ...': ADG 59J 209, p. 62.

'From the moment …': Juge d'Instruction Stienne's confrontation with Landes/Dohse, 5 August 1947, private archive of Michel Bergès.

young Maquisard: Paul Salles.

'Two armed men …': ADG 59J 209, p. 62.

forty containers: Testimonies concerning the amount of arms collected that day differ.

Chapter 16: Progress and Precautions

'fresh and beautiful' …: ADG 59J 209, p. 63.

'The day passed …': Ibid. p. 65.

nine days previously: From thirty-five-year-old documents belonging to Alan and Sue Johnson-Hill, Château Meaune, Maransin, Gironde.

parachute reception committee chief: Pierre Louis Duzon.

'No doubt was possible …': Manuscript version of Dohse's memoirs, pp. 43–4 (it does not appear in the printed version).

changed for each drop: Flight Sergeant Mills report for 18/19 September, TNA Air 20/8500.

DJ342951: Buckmaster, *They Fought Alone*, p. 219.

'the English!': private archive of Yves Léglise.

taken over by the Germans: Speech given on 25 October 1986 when a commemorative plate was inaugurated at Lestiac in honour of Jean and Marie-Louise Duboué, private archive of Yves Léglise.

'there was trouble brewing': Mary Herbert debriefing, 30 January 1945, TNA HS 6/567.

seven major caches: Pissos (Sabres), La Brède, Temple, Lacanau, St Médard, St Jean d'Illac and Blaye, ADG 59J 209.

parachuted British arms: Mary Herbert debriefing, 30 January 1945, TNA HS 6/567.

'Stens by the thousands …': Robert Marshall interview with Horst Kopkow, 30 June 1983, by kind permission of Mr Marshall.

'little gun': This enthusiasm for the Sten, of which 4.6 million were produced during the war, would have come as a surprise to many in British and French circles, who found the Sten clumsy, unbalanced and highly prone to going off accidentally if dropped – as the author can personally attest. Despite the fact that the Sten became the iconic weapon associated with the French Resistance, its habit of unleashing a whole magazine of rounds when handled without respect also cost many Resistance lives.

three other key Resistance leaders: Robert Mollié, Gérard Cazenave [probably Franck Cazenave] and Léonce Dussarrat.

'what threat …': ADG 59J 209, p. 75.

'It was this [step] …': Ibid., p. 77.

gendarmerie: In the Place Hector Serres.

'Too late?': Letter written by Léonce Dussarrat to *Historia*'s readers, probably in 1972, with the kind permission of Alban Dubrou.

German policemen: *Feldgendarmes*.

'Your Resistance activities …': Maleyran testimony, quoted in Terrisse, *Grandclément*, p. 132.

'I lost …': ADG 59J 209, p. 78.

Chapter 17: The Battle of Lestiac

secret letterbox: The letterbox was used by the Confrérie Notre Dame (CND) network of Colonel Rémy.

Jean Paillère's home: 20 Rue de Colmar.

friend's house: Robert Furt.

suburb of eastern Bordeaux: Lormont.

run-down café: Café du Port de la Bastide.

'It wasn't the first time …': Landes report, 21 January 1944, TNA HS 9/76.

'It's them! …': The dialogue here is from a letter from Suzanne Duboué to a friend, 10 May 1993, private archive of Yves Léglise.

battle of Lestiac: This narrative has been assembled from several sources, chief among which is a manuscript account by Suzanne Duboué, Jean Duboué's evidence of 18 September 1945 and a manuscript letter to CND-Castille's Colonel Lecomte, private archive of Yves Léglise.

'Do you know …': Suzanne Duboué manuscript account, private archive of Yves Léglise.

'We are soldiers …': Ibid.

'You have nothing to fear …': From an account written after the war by Jean Duboué, private archive of Yves Léglise.

laid her gently: Manuscript letter from Duboué to Colonel Lecomte, CND-Castille, private archive of Yves Léglise.

'It's time …': Conversation constructed from Jean Duboué's evidence of 18 September 1945, private archive of Yves Léglise; Dohse interview by Jacques Sylvain and Fabien Pont for *Sud-Ouest*, ADG 59J 65; and Michel Bergès interview with Dohse, April 1985, private archive of Michel Bergès.

'I am aware …': Conversation constructed from Jean Duboué's manuscript account, private archive of Yves Léglise.

revelations produced: Poinsot's office (SAP) report, Bordeaux, 20 October 1943, private archive of Yves Léglise.

'at the disposition …': ADG 59J 209, p. 94.

'For only the second time …': Landes report, 21 January 1944, TNA HS 9/76.

one of Landes's men: François Nicolle.

'FROM PEULEVÉ': The signal was sent from 'Mackintosh', the alias for Peulevé's radio operator. In the text aliases were used rather than plain language, e.g. 'Yves' for Hayes and 'Stanislas' for Landes, TNA HS 9/421, vol. 3.

Léo Paillère's sons: See Payère (Pallière) personal information, TNA HS 7/13.

Chapter 18: Maquis Officiels

'The institution …': F Section summary sheet, 1943, TNA HS 7/121.

'[There have been] …': Summary of SOE activities for the Prime Minister, TNA HS 8/250.

Vidal: 88 Boulevard du Président Wilson The building, now a shop selling hearing aids, remains largely unchanged to this day.

'I thought he agreed …': Dohse's interrogation by Military Judge Stienne, 17 August 1947, private archive of Michel Bergès.

policy in Yugoslavia: Similar agreements were also made with Ukrainian nationalists and the royalist EDES in Greece. But these agreements were for strictly limited periods.

Cercle Européen: European Circle.

'as an act of treason …': ADG 59J 209, p. 95.

'It seemed to me …': Ibid.

'A meeting …': Ibid.

Abwehr officer: Erich Vermehren, who defected from Istanbul in February 1944, Macintyre, *Double Cross*.

defect to the British: It is intriguing to note that at exactly this time (September/October 1943) a Spanish agent working for a British escape line reported that Dohse, who always claimed to have an ability to get messages through to London whenever he needed to, was seen in conversation with Michael Cresswell, MI9's representative in northern Spain, at Irun, just over the Spanish border (where he often went on his way to San Sebastián for weekends with Claire Keimer). Unhappily, no MI9 telegrams or reports from Cresswell survive.

secret location: Held at Jean Ferrier's house. Some say this was held at the end of October, but the presence of Hayes indicates that it must have been before his arrest. Others present included Léo Paillère and his son Danny, Colonel (Jean Pierre Tessier, baron) de

Marguerittes, Duboué and – according to some sources – Colonel Marcel Patanchon alias
'Desjardin', OCM Resistance leader for southwest France – see Terrisse, *Grandclément*, p. 133.
official order: Letter of 11 January 1952 from the Service Documentation Extérieure et de
Contre-Espionage (SDECE) to André Dewavrin (alias 'Colonel Passy'), Pascal Convert, *La
Constellation du Lion*, Paris, Éditions Grasset, 2013, p. 132, f/n 51, confirming that: '*à la date
du 28 octobre 1943, la section C.E. (contre espionage) de la DSRA a invité la Section A/M sous
le No. 12.871/BRAL-C à transmettre à CLOVIS l'ordre de faire exécuter GRANDCLEMENT et
MADAME, en suggérant de confier cette mission au groupe 313 de la Charente.*'

Chapter 19: Lencouacq
'under his command': Dohse's interrogation by Military Judge Stienne, 17 August 1947, private
archive of Michel Bergès.
Maquis de Lencouacq: Full name: OCM Groupe Robert Secteur Nord-Landais, from a letter, 8
June 1993, ADG 59J 111.
anonymous young man: Paul Salles's alias was 'Popol'.
Guy Bertrand: Alias 'Le Boulanger'.
control of André Grandclément: And another Resistance commander, Robert Mollié.
local café: The Café Lavigne, Ychoux. The building, now deserted, remains much as it must
have been in 1943.
north of Lencouacq: Lat. 42° 12' 12" N, Long. 0° 26' 44" W. Nothing remains of the farmhouse,
but the two great oaks are still standing.
28 October: Unheaded letter, 20 May 1993, ADG 59J 111.
one other: Henri Lacaze.
'Grandclément explained …': The words of Robert Mollié, quoted in Perrault, *La Longue
traque*, p. 272.
head of the Lencouacq Maquis: Guy Sarramagnan alias 'Le Sergent'.
his commander: Colonel (Jean Pierre Tessier, baron) de Marguerittes alias 'Colonel Pierre'.
but one: Franck Rollot.
'We put the ambush …': Paul Salles evidence, 16 June 1943, private archive of Michel Bergès.
'[Our chief]': Guy Sarramagnan.
local muleteer: His name was Gasparos.
returned to their base: There is an interesting sequel to this story. The German commander at
Lencouacq, a strikingly handsome man, had an affair at around this time with the local
postmistress, who was a notable beauty. Sometime after the Germans left, the postmistress
gave birth to the commander's child. After the war, the woman was divorced from her
husband and was married again to a man who knew and accepted that the father of her son
was the German commander. The son himself, however, was told by his mother only on
her deathbed. Some years after the war the son travelled to Germany to meet his real father,
who acknowledged the boy and took him under his wing. Author interview with Alban
Dubrou, 16 June 2015.

Chapter 20: Of Missions and Machinations
Louis Joubert: Alias 'Ney'.
'He was one …': Notes from Joubert's son, Daniel, private archive of Michel Bergès.
local Bordeaux Resistance command: Eugène Camplan.
'Impossible …': Louis Joubert statement, AN 72AJ 131. B.IV, and another statement by
Joubert, copied to Arthur Calmette, 3 June 1953, private archive of Michel Bergès.
early evening: The time of the meeting was 17.00 hours.
academic friends: Marcel Beaufils, Professor of German at the Lycée Pasteur, Paris, Père
Riquet evidence, 31 March 1950, private archive of Michel Bergès.
'He told me …': Père Riquet evidence, 31 March 1950, private archive of Michel Bergès.
'[He] assured me …': ADG 59J 209, p. 93.

'Grandclément believed …': Report given to Marcel Défence by Père Riquet, 26 January 1944, TNA HS 6/436.

Dohse's villa: 145 Route du Médoc.

one of Dohse's senior colleagues: Närich.

Bordeaux region: Effectively the departments of Gironde, Landes and Charentes.

'You people …': Recollection of Louis Joubert to his son, private archive of Michel Bergès.

'that the protocol …': Michel Bergès interview with Dohse, April 1985, and Dohse interrogation by the French secret services, 21 July 1948, private archive of Michel Bergès.

'Then you'll have …': Dohse's interrogation by Military Judge Stienne, 17 August 1947, private archive of Michel Bergès.

'You are going …': Michel Bergès interview with Dohse, April 1985, private archive of Michel Bergès.

more hard line: Bömelburg handed over to his deputy Josef Kieffer, who was much more 'conventional' in his approach.

'What do you think …': Conversation taken from Larrose's testimony, 1 April 1950.

German tribunal: He had been sentenced to death by the Feldkommandantur's tribunal, Dohse's interrogation by Military Judge Stienne, 17 August 1947, private archive of Michel Bergès.

'in order to …': Penaud, *Histoire secrète*, p. 154.

'Being a respected soldier …': Interrogatory of Dohse, 20 July 1949, private archive of Michel Bergès.

'Our chief aim …': ADG 59J 209, p. 112.

'We were at the end …': Manuscript document from Roger Landes, probably written in the 1980s, CMSM.

'HAVE TRIED …': Penaud, *Histoire secrète*, p. 122.

'escaped Canadian commando': Charles Corbin debriefing, TNA HS 9/352/3

Claude Bonnier: Alias 'Hypoténuse', 'Bordas' and 'Bordin'. Landes met Eugène Camplan on the same day, no doubt for the same purpose. See Landes's letter to Joubert's son, Daniel, 28 January 1990, private archive of Michel Bergès.

'health grounds': Handwritten notes about Charles Corbin with Jean Charlin, fellow resistant, quoted as a source, ADG 59J 111.

burnt his radio codes: Penaud, *Histoire secrète*, p. 122.

Chapter 21: Crossing the Frontier

Izpegui pass: Known in France as Col d'Izpéguy.

24 November: Nicolson, *Aristide*, p. 69, gives 29 November as the date that Landes began his journey out of France, but Landes's own report to SOE (HS 9/76) indicates that it was the 24th.

Fernande and André Bouillar: Fernande Bouillar was known as 'Nanotte', '*Les Passages en Espagne*', ADG 59J 188.

'He immediately inspired …': Extract from one page of a publication (no title), ADG 59J 111. The spelling of Bouillar is probably a French corruption of the Spanish 'Boyar'.

local fisherman: His name was Mattéï; he was apparently paid a retainer of 100,000 francs a month.

cross by the Izpegui pass: The description of Landes's journey, capture and stay at Miranda is taken from a combination of four principal sources: Landes's long manuscript account and his interview with Michel Bergès, June 1984, CMSM; Nicolson, *Aristide*, p. 68 et seq; his reports, TNA HS 9/76; and his letter to Jean Serres, 3 June 1990, CMSM.

'deserter': Probably from the Service du Travail Obligatoire (STO), a compulsory labour scheme for young French people.

single-storey building: It is still there – abandoned and a little the worse for wear, but substantially as it must have been in 1943.

came 'on behalf of Stanislas': '*Je viens de la part de Stanislas*', addendum to Stanislas report, 24 January 1944.

mountain railway: Situated just above the town on its southern edge, this line is now derelict, though the remains of the station can still be seen.

six gold sovereigns: The document specifies 'gold to the value of £6 sterling' but it is clear it refers to sovereigns, SOE internal correspondence concerning Corbin, 7 June 1944, TNA HS 9/352/3.

rickety bridge: The bridge has been replaced by a modern one, carrying the highway at this point, but the piers of the old bridge are still plainly visible as are the buildings of the old frontier posts.

'At this moment …': Jacques Sylvain and Fabien Pont interview with Dohse for *Sud-Ouest*, June 1987, ADG 59J 65.

friend and colleague: Walter Kutschmann, Criminal Komissar in Hendaye. No. 182 on the Nazi War Criminal list, he was tried for the multiple murder of Jews in Poland after the war.

exchanging for francs: About 4,000 francs. The unofficial exchange rate at the time was 5 pesetas for 100 francs.

'*Louis et Charles sont bien arrivés*': ADG 59J 209, p. 108.

'In our heavy boots …': Joubert diary, 20 December 1943, private archive of Michel Bergès.

'The talk was full …': Ibid., 30 December 1943.

'*Louis et Charles sont bien arrivés*': Penaud, *Histoire secrète*, p. 155.

running water … 'German deserters': Landes manuscript account, CMSM.

'[The bath] was …': Ibid.

Chapter 22: Cyanide and Execution

no less than ten: Rollot, Thinières, Joubert, Paillère, Duboué, Maleyran, Mollié, de Marguerittes, Ferrier and Grandier-Vazeille.

Colonel Rollot: Alias 'Arnaud' and 'Jacques'.

Eugène Camplan: Alias 'Vignault'.

Camplan was a man: Thinières's description of Eugène Camplan is from Penaud, *Histoire secrète*, p. 113.

'would bring [the 'traitor'] down': Marcel Défence debriefing, 25 and 26 January, 1944, TNA HS 6/436.

Camplan voted: Joubert voted with Camplan. Others present were Grenier, Patanchon, de Marguerittes and Camplan's deputy, Yves Toussaint, Penaud, *Histoire secrète*, p. 131.

One group: Camplan, Joubert and Toussaint.

'hardliners': Léo Paillère, his two sons and de Marguerittes.

'military dignitaries': *Délégué Militaire Régional*.

'very young-looking …': Jacques Nancy, quoted in Penaud, *Histoire secrète*, p. 136.

Jacques Nancy: Alias 'Sape'.

radio operator: Louis Durand alias 'Kyrie'.

one of Bonnier's closest lieutenants: Jean Lapeyre-Mensignac.

'that Bonnier …': The evidence of Lapeyre-Mensignac quoted in Penaud, *Histoire secrète*, p. 157.

two of Camplan's men: The brothers Lespine – François alias 'Alain' and Frantz alias 'Denis'.

a café in Bordeaux: The Café Clémenceau.

'*Chez Dupont, tout est bon*': 'Everything about Dupont is good.'

isolated wood: Le Bois de Limaux, 6km north of Ruffec, Police Inspector Durand report, 1 April 1947, in Penaud, *Histoire secrète*, p. 180.

'Camplan has been …': Philippe André, *La Résistance confisquée*, Paris, Éditions Perrin, 2013, p. 116.

several signals: Two messages, numbers 35 and 62, sent by de Gaulle's Intelligence Bureau (BCRA) to Bourgès-Maunoury, see f/n 13 in Penaud, *Histoire secrète*, p. 165.

military chief: Maurice Bourgès-Maunoury, de Gaulle's Délégué Militaire National (DMN).

promotion to *Untersturmführer*: TNA KV 3/238.

'He is intelligent …': Joubert diary, 8 January 1944, private archive of Michel Bergès.

early February: ADG 59J 209, p. 108. Machule gives the date as mid-January.

'I was ordered …': Ibid., p. 112.

'urgent family reasons': Machule's evidence, Hanover, 20 April 1953, ADG 59J 67.

café in Bordeaux: the Café Cardinal.

other colleagues: Among them: Marcelle André, Emma, Julien André, Francine Bonnet, Jules, Poinsot's secretary – Penaud, *Histoire secrète*, p. 189.

'Ten or so minutes …': ADG 59J 209, p. 119.

One of Bonnier's close lieutenants: Léon Nautin.

in a bar: La Chope aux Capucins.

one of their senior Resistance colleagues: Banicq (also spelt Bannicq and Banick) alias 'Benoît'.

'Following meetings …': Document signed by Pierre Grolleau, Yves Toussaint and André Banicq, 20 March 1944, private archive of Yves Léglise.

job in Germany: As an Inspector of the Service du Travail Obligatoire compulsory labour scheme. Michel Bergès interview with Dohse, April 1985, private archive of Michel Bergès.

One report: Alain Boyau's report, started 4 March and completed 11 April 1944, private archive of Michel Bergès.

'*Roger reviendra* …': Michel Bergès interview with Christian Campet and Roger Landes, June 1984, CMSM.

Chapter 23: Aristide Returns

'evasive and contradictory': Letter from Maj. R. H. Warden, 22 January 1944, TNA HS 6/436.

Buckmaster was waiting: Buckmaster's diaries, by kind permission of Maurice Buckmaster, and with thanks to David Harrison for his help in gaining access to this document.

'no important divergences …': 'A summary of Principal Points in Actor's Report', 24 January 1944, TNA HS 6/436.

Swiss gold watch: It was also common practice for Scientist agents to wear a gold ring. If arrested, the police would normally allow this to be kept if it was claimed as a sentimental possession. The ring could then be used as a bribe or sold for cash in a tight spot.

'[He is] not …': Letter from MI5 interrogator, TNA HS 9/880/8.

'As far as …': 'A summary of Principal Points in Actor's Report', TNA HS 6/436.

'Do you still …': Nicolson, *Aristide*, p. 88.

'bring together …': Terrisse, *Grandclément*, pp. 207–8, translated from the French.

two main roads: The Route Nationale 137 (now the D137) and what is now known as the E606.

'so rich …': Landes IWM interview, Reel 3 (17' 40"–18' 05"), IWM SR 8641, 03-01-1985.

les naphtalinards: Or *naphtalinés*, the naphthalene brigade.

'the ordinary …': Landes IWM interview, Reel 3 (17' 40"–18' 05"), IWM SR 8641, 03-01-1985.

'The manner …': ADG 59J 209, p. 88.

Around 300: Mme Souques testimony, quoted in Penaud, *Histoire secrète*, p. 196.

two-storey townhouse: 19 Rue du Bocage. According to Charlin, Grandclément had also taken out a lease on accommodation in the Hôtel Graciosa in the Cours Anatole France, Jean Charlin evidence to Police Inspector Borderie, 27 March 1945, ADG 59J 119.

Allyre Sirois: Alias 'Gustave'.

neighbouring SOE circuit: Which would be run by Charles Corbin.

field close to Auch: The actual site was a field on the Montfort property at Nougaroulet, 6km north of Marsan. This was the same parachute site on which de Baissac had landed on his return to France in the spring of 1943.

Landes and Sirois jumped: Because of the wind the pilot dropped his passengers (they were referred to as 'Joes') from a height of 150 metres, instead of the usual 300. Most of the details which follow come from Landes mission report of 4 December 1944, TNA HS 6/574.

Renée Daubèze: Landes's report refers to her as Mme Nougadère, but this is probably an alias.

'When they …': http://sdonac32.pagesperso-orange.fr/1944.htm.

Resistance doctor: Dr Pol Angelé.

'Then he came …': Landes manuscript account, c.1980s, CMSM.

radio and … crystals: Michel Bergès interview with Christian Campet and Roger Landes, June 1984, CMSM. There is some confusion about this event. In his June 1984 interview Landes says he was *not* carrying a radio, only the crystals. The manuscript letter mentions the radio but not the crystals. Landes's report in HS 9/880/8 says he reached Bordeaux 'without incident'.

'ARRIVED SAFELY …': Nicolson, *Aristide*, p. 96.

the man who had driven him: Robert Furt alias 'Fortage'.

flu epidemic: Some sources give the cause of death as a heart attack, which is of course perfectly compatible as a consequence of flu.

one of the key contacts: Franck Nicole, an early courier for Scientist and the keeper of a safe house in Bordeaux.

'Most Frenchmen …': Report on Corbin's interrogation, 10 February 1944, TNA HS 9/352/3.

Chapter 24: 'I come on behalf of Stanislas'

Deputy Supreme Commander West: His area of responsibility covered all of France, Belgium and the Netherlands.

'1. We are not …': Peter Lieb, *Konventioneller Krieg oder NS-Weltanschauungskrieg? Kriegführung und Partisanenbekämpfung in Frankreich 1943/44*, Munich 2007, pp. 263–4.

'The main task …': The italics are in the original: '*Der Militärbefehlshaber in Frankreich*', Ia Nr. 558/44 g.Kdos v. 12.2.1944. Betr.: Banden-und Sabotagebekämpfung, BA-MA, RW 35/551, courtesy of Peter Lieb.

German operation: Operation Wildfang I and II. It is worth mentioning that in the Wehrmacht's report on this operation, they blame the Gestapo in Bordeaux (and specifically Dohse) for heavy-handedness – email from Peter Lieb, 23 February 2016.

Machule instructed Dohse: This is Dohse's own description of this event, which should therefore be treated with caution.

auxiliary units: *Hauskapelle*.

youth labour camps: *Chantiers de Jeunesse*.

'The French workmen …': Dr. 5 and 6. Kontrollkommission Toulouse. Br. Tgb. No.: 137/44g, Toulouse, 24 April 1944, AN 40/1210. Re: Addendum to the report on the campaign against terrorists in the area South and East of Captieux (Gironde), courtesy of Peter Lieb, AN AJ 40/1210.

personal intervention: Dohse claimed to have obtained the release of 1,600 of the least suspect of the detainees, along with a further 190 who were already in prison in Bordeaux awaiting transportation. He also claimed to have turned a blind eye to a minor administrative subterfuge which resulted in the 'spiriting away' of a further 150 of the young men.

His first choice: Pierre Chevalier alias 'Luc'.

Louis Christian Campet: Alias 'Lancelot'.

Commandant Édouard de Luze: Alias 'Marceau'.

reports he received: From Pierre Chevalier.

numbering some 300: 289 men, 15 officers and 35 NCOs, Landes report, 25 September 1944, giving his strengths in May 1944, TNA HS 6/574.

organisation in the port of Bordeaux: Led by Pierre Roland.

another at Mérignac airport: Led by Pierre Chatané, or Chatanet.

their chief Roger Schmaltz: Alias 'Fernand'.

good relations with the *cheminots*: The number of *cheminots* involved with Landes was 145, Penaud, *Histoire secrète*, p. 221.

300 men: Landes report, 25 September 1944, TNA 6/574; he mentions 400 men '*pour les Landes*' in his manuscript account, CMSM, and they are 500 in Penaud, *Histoire secrète*, p. 221.

1 April 1944: Manuscript account from Roger Landes, probably written in the 1980s, CMSM. There is dispute about this date. Landes placed the first drop to his new network as being on 9 April 1944 at Monplaisir, Landes report, 25 September 1944, TNA HS 6/574.

area Resistance chief: Compte Rendu d'activité du groupe Beliet, commanded by Captain Franck Cazenave. The code-phrase was '*Le cercle devient carré*' ('The circle becomes square'), ADG 59J 107.

'run on gangster lines': Pierre Meunier report, 13 August 1944, TNA HS 9/1026/4, and Michael Cresswell dispatches from Hendaye, September 1944, TNA HS 9/880/8.

'dismissal ...': Landes report, 4 December 1944, TNA HS 6/57.

'with a slight ...': Landes report, 25 September 1944, TNA HS 6/574.

Pierre Charles Meunier: Alias 'Moralist', 'Édouard', 'Édouard le Canadien' and 'Le Grandiose'.

John Manolitsakis: Alias 'Jean Manot' and 'Prophet'.

'combination of boy-scout ...': John Manolitsakis SOE personal file, TNA HS 9/984/8.

safe house: The home of Marcel Attané.

7 August 1944: He finally arrived in England on 12 December.

'Gestapo plant': Landes letter, 12 August 1944, TNA HS 9/1026/4.

dispatched Meunier: He arrived back in London on 10 August.

Chapter 25: 'Forewarned is Forearmed'

'This was ...': ADG 59J 209, p. 114.

May 1944: Max Hastings, *Das Reich: The March of the 2nd Panzer Division through France, June 1944*, London, Pan Books, 2000, p. 24.

Jean-Baptiste Morraglia: Alias 'Dufour', 'Acoustique' and 'Lemaitre'.

General Morraglia: Jean-Baptiste Morraglia was promoted to FFI 'brigadier-general' on 22 August 1944, http://www.generals.dk/general/Morraglia/Jean-Baptiste/France.html.

'There were men ...': Gabriel Delaunay evidence, quoted in Penaud, *Histoire secrète*, p. 214.

'We had to be ...': Aristide-Triangle (Landes-Gaillard) activity report, ADG 59J 120.

one commentator: Charles Gaillard alias 'Triangle'.

'of the English': The word 'English' was transposable in the France of the time for 'British'.

'refused to work ...': Reported conversation by Gaillard, Landes report, 25 September 1944, TNA HS 6/574.

'wouldn't last long': Nicolson, *Aristide*, p. 100.

arrest of ... Harry Peulevé: In Brive-la-Gaillarde, 160km west of Bordeaux, on 21 March 1944.

'In my view ...': Dohse's interrogation by Military Judge Stienne, 17 August 1947, private archive of Michel Bergès.

his quarry escaped: At the Bar de l'Oasis on 10 March; Noël was warned by a waitress.

The ambush failed: On 20 May.

sabotage attack: Police report, 1 July 1944, ADG 59J 118.

Landes was 'running': Landes report, 5 December 1944, TNA HS 6/574.

more than 5,000 Maquisards: The full strengths were: Basses-Pyrénées, 150 men; Landes, 4,012 men; Gironde, 1,200; Charente, 100 men – Landes report, 5 December 1944, TNA HS 6/574.

'Dohse had succeeded ...': '*La répression à Bordeaux*', no date, private archive of Yves Léglise.

'forewarned is forearmed': The phrase in French is '*Un homme averti en vaut deux*', which is the colloquial equivalent. All the messages concerning D-Day had been brought to Bordeaux by Claude Bonnier in November 1943. Following Bonnier's suicide, London had wanted to change them, fearing they were compromised. However, as they were not sure the necessary message would get to the Resistance on time, it was decided on 14 May 1944 that both messages (the old and the new) would be transmitted, TNA HS 8/444. The new alert message was '*Tout le monde sur le pont*' ('Everybody go to the bridge') and it was transmitted on 1 June just after '*un homme averti en vaut deux*', TNA HS 8/444, and André, *La Résistance confisquée*, pp. 150–51.

in the southwest: The French referred to this as '*Région B*'.

'Jupiter met Mercury …': '*Jupiter rencontra Mercure et le déluge commença*', Penaud, *Histoire secrète*, p. 223.

'Venus …': '*Vénus! O femme superbe et héroïque*', ibid.

'Cupid fires …': '*Cupidon lança sa flèche et l'amour commença*', ibid.

two-storey townhouse: 30 Rue Méry, Caudéron, home of Marcel Expert.

Léonce Dussarrat's representative: Henri de Mesmet.

a representative of de Luze's men: Robert Duchez.

Chapter 26: 'This Poisoned Arrow Causes Death'

23.15: The time given in most secondary sources is 21.15, but this does not take account of the fact that, at this stage of the war, German time was two hours ahead of British time.

'strike' signals: 'BBC Radio Messages in WWII', TNA HS 8/444.

'The flood team …': '*La brigade du déluge fera son travail.*'

'Don't be tempted …': '*Ne vous laissez pas tenter par Vénus.*'

'This poisoned arrow …': '*Cette flèche empoisonnée causa leur mort*'.

Attacks by Landes's forces: '*Résumé des Services rendu dans la Résistance*', TNA HS 9/880/8.

'The Departments …': Army Group G War Diary, appendix 153, quoted in Hastings, *Das Reich*, p. 76.

'GERMAN TROOP TRANSPORTS …': ADG 59J 116. Given the fact that this report is a compilation of several reports from different sources, it seems most probable that it is the copy of a situation report sent by Landes to London, rather than the report of a single commander to Landes.

'the action taken …': Paul Gaujac, *La Guerre en Provence 1944–1945*, Lyon: Presses Universitaires de Lyon, 1998, p. 66. Gaujac cites Alfred D. Chandler Jr (ed.), *The Papers of Dwight David Eisenhower: The War Years*, Baltimore, 1970, Vol. 3, no page number.

'Morale …': On 20 June; Pierre Meunier interrogation, 17 August 1944, TNA HS 9/1026/4.

'Numerous sabotage attacks …': Diary entry, Monday 26 June 1944, ADG 59J 118.

'Labour Exchange': *Bourse du Travail*.

near Dax: Thétieu.

Milice base: It was a Milice française base

(uncorroborated) source: The original source of this is not known. Moreover, it does not appear in any other source, 'Léon des Landes', ADG 59J 28/1.

'These are our prisoners! …': ADG 59J 116.

'mere sabotage chief': Landes report, 25 September 1944, TNA HS 6/574.

'has the advantage …': Terrisse, *Grandclément*, p. 215.

second radio operator: Robert Angelaud alias 'Julot'.

a third in operation: Bonaparte, alias 'Cheval' and 'Napoléon'. He had actually been recruited and trained on Landes's first mission.

Morse-compatible teleprinter: See teleprinted messages, Aristide archives, CMSM.

'in good faith': Nicolson, *Aristide*, p. 107.

Lieutenant-Colonel Charles Gaillard: Gaillard fled France to London in 1942 where he joined de Gaulle's secret services (BCRA). He was parachuted into France on 14 September 1943 as the assistant to the DMR for the Rhône-Alpes region (Bourgès-Maunoury). Later transferred to the Provence-Côte d'Azur military region, he was finally appointed DMR for the southwest on 11 May, serving until the end of the war.

love of good company: Aristide-Triangle (Landes-Gaillard) activity report, ADG 59J 120.
almost a month: On 7 August 1944, Landes manuscript account, c.1980s, CMSM.
rented apartment: Hôtel Graciosa, 49 Cours Anatole France, Bordeaux. This was not in fact a
hotel, but a building full of furnished apartments for let.
terrace of a café: The meeting took place at the Café Plantier in the Barrière du Médoc, 408
Boulevard du Président Wilson.
one of his group: Georges Fabas evidence, quoted in an untitled document, ADG 59J 118.
cheese shop: Établissements Ballanger, 37–39 Rue Élie-Gintrac. In the Agenda Annuaire
Delmas 1944, it is listed as a *charcuterie*.
tram had broken down: A post-war enquiry – see Rapport Borderie, 1945 – confirmed that
this may indeed have been so, as there was an interruption in the electricity supply that day.
Two days later: At 1700 hours on 28 June.
The following day: This narrative has been constructed from Josette Lassalle's descriptions
given in *Une Bordelaise dans la Résistance*, p. 61, and her evidence, Rapport Borderie, 1945,
pp. 3–4, and ADG 59J 118.
'He didn't ask …': Josette Lassalle, *Une Bordelaise dans la Résistance*, Bordeaux, Mollat, 1996,
p. 61.
two men: André Danglade alias 'Dréan' and Jean Mouchet alias 'Jeannot'.
a narrow sidestreet: The Rue Mouneyra.
'two other men': Henri Capdeville and Georges Fabas.
one of the assassins: André Danglade.
'I am the only …': Penaud, *Histoire secrète*, p. 240.

Chapter 27: A Deadly Charade

'Important information …': Report of Regional Intendant responsible for the maintenance of
order, 8 July, ADG 59J 119; HSRSO, pp. 236–37; and Terrisse, *Grandclément*, p. 262.
'he picked up …': Madeleine Nicolas evidence, 7 April 1945, ADG 59J 120.
one of his Resistance friends: Roger Callot evidence, 5 July 1945, ADG 59J 119.
met with colleagues: The meeting was held in Marcel Ferreira-Texeira's office across the street
from the garage Le Colisée, 104 Rue du Palais Gallien, Bordeaux.
'Moulleau 10 July 1944 …': Grandclément report, 10 July 1943, TNA HS 9/608/8.
ex-army FFI colonel: Jean de Milleret alias 'Colonel Carnot'.
'a Vichy supporter …': Landes report, 25 September 1944, TNA HS 6/574.
sun so hot: Deforges, *La Bicyclette bleue*, p. 178.
ramshackle farm: Richemont Farm. There is a memorial on the site, which is now in open
farmland.
Pierre Poinsot's police: Poinsot himself had in fact left by this time. The SAP were commanded
by René Penot in this operation.
Dohse later claimed: Dohse's interrogation by Military Judge Stienne, 17 August 1947, private
archive of Michel Bergès.
and a friend: Henri Lacaze
his 'bodyguard': Augustine Duluguet evidence, 17 July 1947, ADG 59J 119.
'A couple came …': Ibid.
'restaurant in Biganos': Biganos is 10km east of Arcachon.
'They [the Resistance] …': Augustine Duluguet evidence, 17 July 1947, ADG 59J 119.
hitched a lift: The following account is compiled from testimonies by Georges Lozes, Gilbert
Comte, Pierre Favard, Pierre Tastet and Augustine Duluguet, ADG 59J 119.
Le Volant d'Or: 11 Rue du Hautoir, Delmas, *Agenda-annuaire Delmas 1944*; now the Rue du
Héron.
'fast-response team': Groupe France, whose chief was André Noël.
beyond the range: The Lysander used by SOE at this time of the war (the Mark III, equipped
with long-range tanks) had a maximum range of 1400km for the round trip. Allowing for a

20 per cent contingency for headwinds and diversions, this meant that, for a Lysander based on the English south coast at Tangmere, the effective range was 550 to 570km; that is all north, but nothing south of an arc roughly from the Île de Ré to Limoges. There were several Lysander operations carried out south and west of this at this period of the war, but these were by aircraft based in Algiers, not London. Hugh Verity, *We Landed by Moonlight: Secret RAF Landings in France 1940–1944*, Wilmslow, Air Data Publications, 1995, pp. 224–25.

one of his senior lieutenants: Georges Lozes alias 'Mérillac'.

'We had as yet …': Georges Lozes evidence, quoted in Penaud, *Histoire secrète*, p. 242.

'Neither he …': Jean Charlin report, 22 July 1944, ADG 59J 119.

safe house: The home of Robert Judicie in Rue Chateaubriand.

'We have to leave …': Augustine Duluguet evidence, 17 July 1947, ADG 59J 119.

'a group …': Ibid.

Citroën: The resistant who supplied the vehicle, Pierre Tastet, said it was a '*camionnette Citroën C4*'.

'useful in England': Mme Chastel's testimony after the war, and Pierre Favart evidence, 26 April 1945, ADG 59J 119.

'prisoners' were armed: *Sud-Ouest*, 8 March 1998, by kind permission of André Duvignac.

'If André lies low …': Penaud, *Histoire secrète*, p. 245.

'show signs of nervousness': Pierre Favart evidence, 26 April 1945, ADG 59J 119.

moved again: Pierre Tastet evidence, 29 May 1951, ibid.

27 July: There is confusion about the precise dates here. Landes's reports place the events two days earlier. But I have chosen to follow the dates given in nearly all other French sources, see ADG 59J 119.

'German patrols in the area': Pierre Tastet evidence, ADG 59J 119.

a restaurant: From the restaurant Chez Lagaillarde, 5 Rue des Douves, Pierre Tastet evidence, 29 May 1951, ADG 59J 119.

27 July: The timings given from here on in this chapter need to be treated with caution as they differ in the original accounts, including in the versions given afterwards by those who were actually there, e.g., Landes, Campet, Bordes and Max Faye.

'We have Grandclément!': Penaud, *Histoire secrète*, p. 247.

parachute reception chief: It was Cazenave who had commanded the reception party for Landes's first delivery of arms in late March.

'It's a trap!': Landes report, 25 September 1944, giving his strengths in May 1944, TNA HS 6/574.

'court martial': Landes IWM interview, Reel 3 (3' 40"), IWM SR 8641, 03-01-1985.

Lucette washed …: Police report, 5 September 1946, ADG 59J 119.

'I give you …': Landes report, 25 September 1944, giving his strengths in May 1944, TNA HS 6/574.

arrived at a junction: The spot is called La Layère, Lat. 44° 23' 16" N, Long. 0° 50' 21" W.

'she felt the cold …': Nicolson, *Aristide*, p. 127, and Michel Bergès interview with Christian Campet and Roger Landes, June 1984, CMSM.

finished off: According to later legend, Marc Duluguet murmured '*Vive la France*' as he died.

Chapter 28: The Viper's Nest

Lucien Nouaux: Alias 'Marc'.

one of his men: Pierre Laparra alias 'Lefèvre'.

the driver: Pierre Favart.

the 'departure' of André Noël: There is a double meaning to this word in French. It can mean a literal departure, but it is also, as in English, used as a euphemism for death.

Gaillard's man: Gilbert Comte.

the home of a colleague: Renée Laurent.

'Perhaps you will …': Renée Laurent evidence, 7 March 1945, ADG 59J 120.

sought by and given to: Sent by Gaillard to Comte.

playing cards at a restaurant: The Restaurant de Bayonne.

his mistress: Madeleine Nicolas.

an acquaintance: Jean Izaguirre.

'Please give my apologies ...': Jean Izaguirre evidence, 11 April 1945, ADG 59J 120.

with his lover: Noël left a briefcase full of documents with Madeleine, asking that this should be handed on to Jean Charlin.

lifelong friend: His childhood friend, Jean Barry.

'Have confidence ...': Dr Jean Barry evidence, 30 May 1945, ADG 59J 120.

Resistance contact: Gilbert Comte.

nearby restaurant: The Bar des Ambassadeurs.

five of Landes's men: Alban Bordes, Michel Choisy, Monge, Gaillac and Pierre Soulé. The driver was called Dupin.

Château Grattequina: The château has now been completely renovated and is an elegant hotel. It is situated 200m from the Blanquefort (White Fort) built to protect Bordeaux by the English king Edward the Confessor.

fishing jetty: At Port Lagrange, Parempuyre.

'BRAVO! ...': Telegram 'From Home station to Aristide', 24 August 1944, ADG 59J 120.

'I suppose ...': *'Philippe Henriot Revanche'*. Dohse interrogation by the French secret services, 21 July 1948, private archive of Michel Bergès.

The Rex: The cinema, built in the 1930s, has now been knocked down, leaving an empty space currently used as a car park. The address is 163 Rue Croix de Seguey, Bordeaux.

'to the bar': Le Richelieu, 4 Place des Quinconces.

fifty further escapees: The British record of Dhose's July 1946 interrogation, TNA KV 3/238.

François Charles Cominetti: Alias 'Colonel Charly' and sometimes known as 'Charlie'. After the war there was some confusion as to whether Cominetti was the man behind these transactions and the issue remains disputed even today. However, in an interview with Bergès in April 1985, Dohse confirmed that Cominetti, when they were both in Fort du Hâ prison after the war, admitted to him that he was the person who delivered the pilots.

betrayed by Cominetti: In his IWM interview Landes acknowledges that one of his men tried to sell him to the Germans, IWM SR 8641, 03-01-1985.

a German commander: Colonel Herbold.

the mayor of Bordeaux: Adrien Marquet.

Heinz Stahlschmidt: He later adopted the French name 'Henri Salmide', his Resistance alias.

the port was saved: There are doubts about this story. Some research suggests that the port of Bordeaux was saved because of a deal between the Bordeaux Resistance and the commander of 159th Reserve Division, Albin Nake. This agreed that the demolition of the port would not take place if the Resistance gave the Germans free passage out of Bordeaux. This practice was not uncommon in other places in France, e.g. Clermont-Ferrrand, Cherbourg and, of course, most famously, Paris. Email from Peter Lieb to author, 23 February 2016.

'WE AWAIT YOUR REPORT ...': Telegram 'From Home Station to Aristide', 24 August 1944, CMSM.

After Dussarrat occupied Dax: On 23 August.

especially against women: After the war, Landes commented that he regarded this treatment as deeply unjust as many of the women who suffered these punishments had in fact been working for the Resistance – some of them were, in fact, the prostitutes who had given him shelter from time to time, Landes IWM interview, IWM SR 8641, R3, 03-01-1985.

'as a kind of dictator...': Hendaye 'Dispatch No. 3' to the embassy in Madrid, 19 September 1944, TNA HS 9/880/8.

'the most picturesque ...': Report from Major Ayer on the political situation in southwest France, 'British circuits in France 1941–44', TNA HS 7/122.

'HUNDREDS OF PEOPLE ...': Telegram 'From Aristide to Home Station', 31 August 1944, CMSM.
'NEARLY 1K PRISONERS': Ibid.
'(COMMUNIST FORCES) ...': Telegram 'From Aristide to Home Station', 15 September 1944, CMSM. The communist forces in question were the Francs-Tireurs et Partisans (FTP).

Chapter 29: Two Hours to Leave France
interim mayor of Bordeaux: Jean-Fernand Audeguil.
the new commissioner for police: Commissaire Bonhomme.
commander of the FFI: Colonel Joseph Druilhe alias 'Driant', Commandant of the 18th Region of the FFI.
the French officers: General Chevance alias 'Bertin' and Colonel Jean de Milleret alias 'Carnot'.
newsreels of the day: http://www.ina.fr/video/AFE86002821. Landes identified by his son Alain, email to the author, 5 December.
the French Minister for War: André Diethelm.
'de Gaulle made ...': Allyre Sirois alias 'Gustave' report, 9 October 1944, TNA HS 6/587.
'It is with deep joy ...': Penaud, Histoire secrète, p. 292.
'I hope, mon Général ...': Ibid., pp. 293–94.
What followed: This account has been pieced together from several different accounts by Landes. The core source is TNA HS 6/574.
'You are English ...': Landes IWM interview, IWM SR 8641, R2, 03-01-1985.
the city préfecture: 23 Rue Esprit-des-Lois.
'that he was English ...': Memorandum, 7 October 1944, forwarded by Duff Cooper to London, TNA FO 371.
'Neither you ...': Penaud, Histoire secrète, p. 294.
Bordeaux authorities: The host was Commissioner of the Republic Gaston Cusin.
That same day: 21 September 1944.
a British diplomat: Probably written by Michael Cresswell alias 'Monday' of MI9, who acted as British consul in San Sebastián at the time and clashed swords with Landes.
'the hideous crime ...': TNA HS 7/122, British circuits in France 1941–44, and André, La Résistance confisquée, p. 226.
'refused to obey ...': Duff Cooper telegram to London, 22 September 1944, TNA FO 371.
'YOU HAVE ALREADY ...': Telegram 'From Home Station to Aristide', 21 September 1944, CMSM.
'MY STATE OF HEALTH ...': Ibid.
'IF STATE OF HEALTH ...': Ibid., 22 September 1944.
'KEEN TO RETURN ...': Ibid., 24 September 1944.
sumptuous black limousine: It would be poetic to imagine this was Dohse's old Cadillac – but unhappily there is no evidence to support this.
'secret meetings': Memorandum, 7 October 1944, forwarded by Duff Cooper to London, TNA FO 371.

Chapter 30: Nunc Dimittis
156 never saw France again: 'Historique du Réseau "Denis – Aristide – Buckmaster"' by Jean Duboué, 1951, ADG 59J 107.
'a liability ...': Jean Duboué SOE Personal File, TNA HS 9/452/4.
on a British mission: On the Judex Mission, 1944–45.
'in great need': Manuscript letter from Claude de Baissac to Mme Duboué, 11 December 1944.
25,000 francs: About £5,000 today.
spent the rest of the war: Accompanied by my daughter Kate, I visited and interviewed Suzanne in Nice in February 2011. She was already suffering from mild dementia and mistook me for a Gestapo officer. She refused to tell me anything, but was happy to speak at length to my daughter about her experiences and recollections.

'On 6th February 1944 …': TNA WO 309/1604. Bernau's sentence was subsequently commuted to twelve years' penal servitude which he served in Ostfriesland concentration camp, surviving a mass slaughter when 4,500 fellow inmates were killed wholesale with the use of anti-aircraft cannon. He survived the war.

three other SOE women agents: Vera Leigh, Sonya Olschanezky and Diana Rowden.

evidence gathered by SOE: By SOE's Vera Atkins.

the judge: Lucien Steinberg.

'The most terrible …': Dominique Lormier, *Bordeaux brûle-t'il? ou La Libération de la Gironde 1940–1945*, Bordeaux, Dossiers d'Aquitaine, 1998, p. 56.

to avoid being hanged: Michel Bergès interview with Dohse, April 1985, private archive of Michel Bergès.

'They wanted information …': Jacques Sylvain and Fabien Pont interview with Dohse for *Sud-Ouest*, June 1987.

'It was important …': ADG 59J 28/1.

'Sir, you will …': Letter dated 22 November 1948, ADG 59J 28/1.

'special [police] forces': At that time the French included the SS, the SD and the Gestapo in special-forces category.

'It is not our purpose…': Local newspaper cuttings reporting on the court case, 4 May 1953, private archive of Yves Lèglise.

three policemen: Divisional Commissioner Louis Durand of the Judicial Police, Inspector Guimberteau and Inspector of Photography Pierre Vielcazal.

The captain: Captain Hermann, Direction Générale des Services Spéciaux (DGSS).

'It's definitely Grandclément.': Inspector Pierre Vielcazal report, 7 September 1946, ADG 59J 119.

'without the aid …': Police Inspector Louis Durand evidence, 27 December 1944, ADG 59J 119.

One of the original members: A. M. Cartier, the owner of a local sawmill.

'To the memory …': Grandclément, *L'Énigme Grandclément*, p. 196.

Shenley Military Hospital: On 18 December 1944, John Manolitsakis also arrived in Shenley having spent the five months since leaving Bordeaux wandering around Spain. Manolitsakis claimed he was in the hospital for a shrapnel wound in his back, but Landes concluded that he had had a nervous breakdown.

the town of Grik: In the early 1960s, the author was engaged on jungle patrols in the Grik area, where SOE's wartime operations were still talked about.

an uprising against the British: Two years later, in 1948, the twelve-year jungle war between the British colonial administration in Malaya and Chinese Communist insurgents began. The Malayan Emergency cost the lives of 6,710 Chinese guerrillas, 1,345 Malayan troops 519 Commonwealth personnel and 2,478 civilians.

'As a man …': TNA HS 9/808/8.

They moved to London: 49 Winchester Court, London W8.

in 1949 had a son: 23 June 1949.

rented a flat: 29 Carlton Mansions, Holmleigh Road, London N16.

launching his business: Roger Landes Ltd.

semi in Stanmore: 42 St Andrews Drive, Stanmore, HA7 2NB. It cost £4,750.

firm of London jewellers: Ernest Jones.

retirement home in Surrey: Shannon Court Retirement Home, Hindhead, Surrey.

Epilogue: Post Hoc Propter Hoc

in a local newspaper: *Sud-Ouest*; it was first published in *Sud-Ouest*'s national sister paper, *France-Soir*.

'I am convinced …': Caralp-Jardel evidence to Police Inspector Jacques Reillac, 21 May 1951, ADG 59J 119.

Bordeaux historian: René Terrisse.
one of André Grandclément's descendants: Daniel Grandclément.
German intelligence: The Abwehr and Sicherheitsdienst.
share out any money: See Yeo-Thomas's comments in Fuller, *Déricourt*, p. 36.

SELECT BIBLIOGRAPHY

Archives
Archives départementales de la Gironde, Bordeaux
Archives nationales, Paris
Combined Military Services Museum, East Maldon, Essex
Imperial War Museum, London
Service historique de la défense (French military archives), Château de Vincennes, Paris
The National Archives, Kew, London

Published Sources
Albertelli, Sébastien, *Les Services Secrets du Général de Gaulle: Le BCRA 1940–1944*, Paris, Éditions Perrin, 2009
Amouroux, Henri, *La vie des Français sous l'Occupation*, Paris, Éditions Fayard, 1961
André, Philippe, *La Résistance confisquée*, Paris, Éditions Perrin, 2013
Aron, Robert, *Histoire de la Libération de la France*, Vols. 1 and 2, Paris, Le Livre de Poche, 1967
Ashdown, Paddy, *A Brilliant Little Operation: The Cockleshell Heroes and the Most Courageous Raid of WW2*, London, Aurum Press, 2012
Aziz, Philippe, *Le livre noir de la trahison: histoires de la Gestapo en France*, Paris, Éditions Ramsay, 1988
Bailey, Roderick, *Forgotten Voices of the Secret War*, London, Ebury Press, 2009
Barranx, Serge, *Le Feu est dans la Lande*, Bordeaux, Éditions Delmas, 1945
Baumel, Jacques, *La liberté guidait nos pas*, Paris, Plon, 2004
— *Résister: Histoire Secrète des années d'Occupation*, Paris, Éditions Albin Michel, 1999
Bécamps, Pierre, *Bordeaux sous l'Occupation*, Rennes, Éditions Ouest-France, 1983
— *Libération de Bordeaux*, Paris, Librairie Hachette, 1974
Beevor, J. G., *SOE Recollections and Reflections 1940–1945*, London, The Bodley Head, 1981
Berlière, Jean-Marc, *Policiers français sous l'occupation*, Paris, Éditions Perrin-Tempus, 2001
Bordes, M. R., *Quartier allemand: La vie au fort du Hâ sous l'Occupation*, Bordeaux, Éditions Bière, 1945
Buckmaster, Maurice, *They Fought Alone*, London, Biteback Publishing Ltd, 2014
Bureau, Jacques, *Un soldat menteur*, Paris, Robert Laffont, 1992
Calmette, Arthur, *L'O.C.M. Organisation Civile et Militaire – Histoire d'un Mouvement de Résistance de 1940 à 1946*, Paris, Éditions Presses Universitaires de France, 1961
Cave Brown, Anthony, *Bodyguard of Lies: The Extraordinary Story behind D-Day*, Guilford: Connecticut, The Lyons Press, 2007
Clark, Freddie, *Agents by Moonlight*, Stroud, Tempus Publishing, 1999
Convert, Pascal, *La constellation du Lion*, Paris, Éditions Grasset, 2013
Cookridge, E. H., *They Came from the Sky*, London, Corgi Books, 1976

Crémieux-Brilhac, Jean-Louis, *La France Libre: de l'appel du 18 juin à la Libération*, Paris, Gallimard, 1998

de Gaulle, Charles, *The War Memoirs, Vol. 2: Unity 1942–1944*, New York, Simon & Schuster, 1959

Dear, Ian, *Sabotage and Subversion: The SOE and OSS at War*, London, Cassell Military Paperbacks, 1996

Deakin, F. W. D., *The Embattled Mountain*, Oxford, Oxford University Press, 1971

Deforges, Régine, *101, Avenue Henri-Martin*, Paris, Éditions Ramsay, 1985

— *La Bicyclette bleue*, Paris, Éditions Ramsay, 1985

— *Le Diable en rit encore*, Paris, Éditions Ramsay, 1985

Delarue, Jacques, *Histoire de la Gestapo*, Paris, Editions Fayard, 1962

Delmas, *Agenda-Annuaire Delmas 1944*, Bordeaux, Éditions Delmas, 1943

Delperrie de Bayac, Jacques, *Histoire de la Milice*, Vols. 1 and 2, Paris, Marabout, 1969

Escott, Beryl E., Squadron Leader, *The Heroines of SOE: Britain's Secret Women in France, F Section*, Stroud, The History Press, 2012

Foot, M. R. D., *Memories of an SOE Historian*, Barnsley, Pen & Sword Military, 2008

— *SOE: The Special Operations Executive 1940–1946*, London, Pimlico, 1989 and 1999

— *Six Faces of Courage*, Littlehampton Book Services Ltd, 1980

— *SOE in France: An Account of the Work of the British Special Operations Executive in France 1940–1944*, London, HMSO, 1966

Foot, M. R. D., and Crémieux-Brilhac, Jean-Louis, *Des Anglais dans la Résistance: le SOE en France, 1940–1944*, Paris, Éditions Tallandier, 2011

Fuller, Jean Overton, *Déricourt: The Chequered Spy*, Salisbury, Michael Russell, 1989

Gendreau, Henri, and Regeaon, Michel, *Ruffec et les Ruffecois dans la guerre, de 1938 à 1945*, Ruffec, Éditions la Péruse, 1994

Gildea, Robert, *Fighters in the Shadow: A New History of the French Resistance*, London, Faber & Faber, 2015

— *Marianne in Chains: Daily Life in the Heart of France during the German Occupation*, New York, Metropolitan Books, 2003

Grandclément, Daniel, *L'Énigme Grandclément*, Paris, Balland, 2003

Hastings, Max, *Das Reich: The March of the 2nd Panzer Division through France, June 1944*, London, Pan Books, 2000

Helm, Sarah, *A Life in Secrets: The Story of Vera Atkins and the Lost Agents of SOE*, London, Abacus, 2012

Henry, Jean-Marcel, *Marais sanglants: Le Médoc en guerre – 1944–1945*, Paris, Éditions les Pas Perdus, 1985

Holt, Thaddeus, *The Deceivers: Allied Deception in the Second World War*, London, Phoenix, 2005

Ippecourt, *Les Chemins d'Espagne: mémoires et documents sur la guerre secrète à travers les Pyrénées, 1940–1945*, Paris, Éditions Gaucher, 1948

Jackson, Julian, *The Dark Years 1940–1944*, Oxford, Oxford University Press, 2001

Jamet, Delphine, Bergès, Louis and Laux, Frédéric, *La seconde guerre mondiale en Gironde par les textes*, Bordeaux, Le Festin, 2006

Kedward, Rod, *France and the French: A Modern History*, Woodstock and New York, Overlook Press, 2006

— *In Search of the Maquis: Rural Resistance in Southern France 1942–1944*, Oxford, Oxford University Press, 1995

King, Stella, *Jacqueline*, London, Arms and Armour, 2006

Kitson, Simon, *The Hunt for Nazi Spies: Fighting Espionage in Vichy France*, Chicago, University of Chicago Press, 2007

Koscielniak, Jean-Pierre, and Souleau, Philippe, *Vichy en Aquitaine*, Paris, Les Éditions de l'Atelier/Éditions Ouvrières, 2011

L'A.S.P.E.C.T, *Cessac*, Faleyras's, L'A.S.P.E.C.T., 2011

La Gestapo en France, Vols. 1 and 2, Historia Hors-Serie, 26 (Apr–Jun) and 27 (Jul–Sep), 1972

Lafossas, Franck, *Adrien Marquet: secrets et souvenirs*, Bordeaux, Les Dossiers d'Aquitaine, 2012

Langeo, Erwan, *Bordeaux 1940–1944, la Place des Quinconces traverse la guerre*, Erwan Langeo, 2015

Lapeyre-Mensignac, Jean, *La Résistance dans le Sud-Ouest*, Bordeaux, les Dossiers d'Aquitaine, 2006

Lassalle, Josette, *Une Bordelaise dans la Résistance*, Bordeaux, Mollat, 1996

Le Roy Ladurie, Jacques, *Mémoires 1902–1945*, Paris, Flammarion/Plon, 1997

Legrand, Jean-Michel, *Lysander … from hell into moonlight*, Viverols (France), Éditions Vario, 2000

Lormier, Dominique, *La Résistance pour les Nuls*, Paris, Éditions First-Gründ, 2013

— *Histoires Extraordinaires de la Résistance Française*, Paris, Le Cherche midi, 2013

— *Bordeaux brûle t'il? ou La Libération de la Gironde 1940–1945*, Bordeaux, les Dossiers d'Aquitaine, 1998

— *Bordeaux pendant l'Occupation*, Bordeaux, Éditions Sud-Ouest, 1992

Luther, Hans, *Der Französische Widerstand gegen die deutsche Besatzungsmacht und seine Bekämpfung*, Tübingen, 1959

Lyman, Robert, *Operation Suicide: The Remarkable Story of the Cockleshell Raid*, London, Quercus, 2013

Macintyre, Ben, *Double Cross*, London, Bloomsbury, 2012

Maclaren, Roy, *Canadians Behind Enemy Lines, 1939–1945*, Vancouver, University of British Columbia Press, 1981

Maclean, Fitzroy, *Eastern Approaches*, London, Penguin Books, 1991

Maloubier, Bob, *Les Secrets du Jour J: Opération Fortitude – Churchill mystifie Hitler*, Paris, Éditions La Boétie, 2014

Marcot, François (ed.), *Dictionnaire historique de la Résistance: Résistance intérieure et France Libre*, Paris, Robert Laffont, 2006

Marshall, Robert, *All the King's Men*, London, Fontana paperbacks, 1989

Milliez, Paul, *Médecin de la liberté*, Paris, Éditions du Seuil, 1982

Moorhead, Caroline, *A Train in Winter*, London, Vintage, 2012

Neave, Airey, *Saturday at MI9: The Classic Account of the WW2 Allied Escape Organisation*, Barnsley, Pen & Sword Military, 2010

Nicolson, David D., *Aristide: Warlord of the Resistance*, London, Leo Cooper, 1994

Passy, Colonel, *Mémoires du Colonel Passy*, Paris, Éditions Odile Jacob, 2000

Penaud, Guy, *Histoire Secrète de la Résistance*, Bordeaux, Éditions Sud-Ouest, 2011

Perrault, Gilles, *l'orchestre rouge*, Paris, Fayard, 1989

— *La longue traque*, Paris, Le Livre de Poche, 1975

Perrin, Nigel, *Spirit of Resistance: The Life of SOE Agent Harry Peulevé, DSO MC*, Barnsley, Pen & Sword Military, 2008

Piquet-Wicks, Eric, *Quatre dans l'ombre*, Paris, Gallimard, 1957

Rémy, Colonel, *Les Soldats du silence: Mémoires d'un agent secret de La France Libre*, Vol. 2, Paris, Éditions de la Seine, 2002

— *La Résistance en Aquitaine*, Genève, Éditions Famot, 1974

— *Une affaire de trahison*, Paris, Librairie de Sèvres, 1948

Riols, Noreen, *The Secret Ministry of AG. & Fish*, London, Macmillan, 2013

Rous-Serra, Elly, *Les Renards de l'Ombre: La Mission Baden-Savoie*, Paris, Nouvelles Éditions Latines, 1985

Ruffin, Raymond, *Ces Chefs de Maquis qui gênaient*, Paris, Presses de la Cité, 1980

Saint-Marc, Michel, *Le canton de Targon sous l'Occupation 1939–1945*, Michel Saint-Marc, 2007

Seaman, Mark, *The Bravest of the Brave: True Story of Wing Commander Tommy Yeo-Thomas –
SOE Secret Agent Codename 'The White Rabbit'*, London, Michael O'Mara Books Ltd, 1997

Slitinsky, Michel, *La Résistance en Gironde*, Bordeaux, Cahiers de la Résistance, 1970

Souleau, Philippe, *La Ligne de démarcation en Gironde 1940–1944*, Périgueux, Fanlac, 1998

Stafford, David, *Secret Agent: The True Story of the Special Operations Executive*, London, BBC
Books, 2000

Steinberg, Lucien, *Les Allemands en France 1940–1944*, Paris, Albin Michel, 1980

Suttill, Francis J., *Shadows in the Fog*, The History Press, 2014

Terrisse, René, *Face aux pelotons Nazis: Souge, Le Mont Valérien du Bordelais*, Bordeaux,
Éditions Aubéron, 2000

— *À la botte de l'Occupant: itinéraires de cinq collaborateurs*, Bordeaux, Éditions Aubéron,
1998

— *La Milice à Bordeaux: La Collaboration en uniforme*, Bordeaux, Éditions Aubéron, 1997

— *Grandclément: traître ou bouc émissaire?*, Bordeaux, Éditions Aubéron, 1996

— *Bordeaux 1940–1944*, Paris, Perrin, 1993

Vergez-Chaignon, Bénédicte, *Les Vichysto-Résistants: de 1940 à nos jours*, Paris, Éditions
Perrin, 2008

Verity, Hugh, *We Landed by Moonlight: Secret RAF Landings in France 1940–1944*, Wilmslow,
Air Data Publications, 1995

Walters, Anne-Marie, *Moondrop to Gascony*, Moho Books, 2009

Wieviorka, Olivier, *Histoire de la Résistance 1940–1945*, Paris, Éditions Perrin, 2013

Wighton, Charles, *Pin-stripe Saboteur: The Story of Robin – British agent and French Resistance
Leader*, London, Odhams, 1959

CREDITS

The author would like to thank Mark Bentinck, Michel Bergès, Yves Léglise, Dr Pierre Hèches, Alain Landes and Robert Marshall for kindly allowing the reproduction of photographs from their private collections.

Integrated

Page 97: National Archives, Kew, London

Picture Section

Page 1: Roger-Viollet/Topfoto

Page 2 (top): akg-images/arkivi

Page 2 (middle left and middle right): Yves Léglise

Page 2 (bottom left): Pierre Hèches

Page 2 (bottom right): Musée du 34e Régiment d'Infanterie, Mont-de-Marsan

Page 3: Daniel Grandclément, *L'Enigme Grandclément*. All rights reserved.

Page 4: Robert Marshall

Page 5: Alain Landes

Page 6 (top): Puttenham and Wanborough History Society

Page 6 (middle and bottom left, bottom right): National Archives, Kew

Page 7 (top): Imperial War Museum, London

Page 7 (bottom): National Archives, Kew, London

Page 8: National Archives, Kew, London

Page 9: Deutsches U-Boat Museum, Cuxhaven-Altenbruch

Page 10 (top): Bordeaux3945, www.bordeaux3945.forumaquitaine.
com

Page 10 (bottom): Archives Bordeaux Metropole, Bordeaux

Page 11 (top): Alain Landes

Page 11 (bottom): Michel Bergès

Page 12 (top): Keystone-France/Contributor via Getty Images

Page 12 (bottom): Musée de l'ordre de la Libération, Paris

Page 13 (top): Archives départementales de la Gironde, Bordeaux

Page 13 (bottom): Combined Military Services Museum, Maldon

Page 14 (top): Musée du 34e Régiment d'Infanterie,
Mont-de-Marsan

Page 14 (bottom): Tallandier/Bridgeman Images

Page 15 (top): Yves Léglise

Page 15 (bottom): Michel Bergès

Page 16 (top): Alain Landes

Page 16 (bottom): Mark Bentinck

INDEX

Abwehr 4, 41, 329
'Actor' *see* Landes, Roger Arthur
'Alain' *see* Leroy, Robert
Algiers 123, 189, 190, 192–3, 205–6, 209, 210, 212, 213–15, 227, 301
'Alouette' (Resistance group) 108, 109
Anderle, Leo 53
'Andrews, Peter' *see* Corbin, Charles
Angelaud, Robert 310
Arcachon 86, 87, 93–4, 97, 145, 196, 216–17, 236, 237, 241, 247, 259
Arcachon Resistance 94, 95, 236, 237, 251, 257, 259, 260
'Archambaud' *see* Norman, Gilbert
'Aristide' *see* Landes, Roger Arthur
Armée Secrète 103, 108
Artagnan, Charles 118–19

Baissac, Claude de
  affair with Mary Herbert 71
  airlifted to England 120, 123–4
  alarmed at Borrel's arrest 105–6
  aliases and codenames 23, 54, 106, 111
  arranges ex-gratia payment to Marie-Louise Duboué 297
  arrival in Bordeaux 56–7
  awards and honours 124, 299
  briefed in London on forthcoming invasion 89–91
  character and description 23
  death of 300
  destined for leadership 25
  extracurricular business 85–6
  fails to inform London fully of events in France 127–8
  flees to Paris 115
  funding of 85, 117–18
  furious at Cockleshell Heroes raid 76
  given gold watch by Hayes 222
  Grandclément attempts to send message to 143
  heads up Scientist network 52, 54
  increase in control of landing sites 78
  invited to Grandclément's wedding reception 83–4
  meets Grandclément in Paris 79–80
  meets Landes 66
  organises large quasi-military organisation 93
  parachuted into France 53–6
  reunited with Mary Herbert and his daughter Claudine 300
  sends reports to London 57
  as sole liaison with Grandclément 84
  witnesses American attack on Bordeaux 97
Baissac, Lise de
  alias 106
  awards and honours 299–300
  death of 300
  flees to London 54, 124
  runs support network in the Charente 73
  sent to Poitiers 62–3
Barbie, Klaus 104
Basilio, André 241–2, 247
Bastable, Clement *see* Baissac, Claude de
Baudouinville (ship) 8
Bauer, Ludwig 103–4
BBC 82, 88, 94, 101, 109, 150, 151, 197, 201, 204, 207, 218, 219, 251, 253, 262, 263, 271, 277
BBC Algiers 206
BBC French Service 219, 251, 253
BCRA *see* Bureau Central de Renseignement et d'Action
BdS *see* German directorate of security

Beaulieu, Hampshire (Special Training
  School No. 31 'Group B') 24, 223
Bergen-Belsen 299
'Bernard' see Grandclément, André Marie
  Hubert François
Bernau, Otto 298, 355
Bertrand, Guy 180
Bertrand, Marcel
  deported then vanishes 297
  introduced to de Baissac 56
  restaurant used as clandestine 'letterbox' 48,
    56, 57, 143
  takes letter for 'David' 65, 66
  warned of Grandclément's treachery 144
Blaskowitz, Johannes 255
Bletchley Park 78
Bömelburg, Karl
  agents working for 89, 129
  character and description 29
  death of 302
  masterminds Pétain's escape from Vichy
    302
  as mentor to Dohse 29–30, 45
  transferred to Vichy 191
Bonnier, Claude
  believed to be Gestapo agent provocateur
    213
  briefed by Landes 196
  brings messages concerning D-Day to
    Bordeaux 350
  character and description 211, 212
  commits suicide 217–18, 350
  considers Camplan unreliable and possible
    proto-collaborator 211–13
  cornucopia of documents discovered by
    Dohse 218, 227
  given authority over all military forces in
    southwest region 211, 213
  reports to London that Camplan had been
    'disappeared' 214
Bordeaux
  attacks and sabotage 47, 74–5, 77, 80, 96–7,
    99–100, 107, 116–17, 248, 253–6, 279, 339,
    353
  betrayal, score-settling and manoeuvring
    for advantage in 84, 210, 246–7, 257, 258,
    260–2, 277
  collapse of some Resistance networks in
    107–11, 115–16
  de Gaulle and Pétain meet in 3
  description of 5–7
  execution of hostages in 58

foreign spy networks in 11–12
German intelligence network in 41–8
German occupation of 7–12, 279–81
liberation, reprisals and chaos in 282–5,
  353
parachuting of arms, supplies and men to
  86–8, 93–8, 101–2, 107, 109–10, 117–18
SOE intelligence network in 14–16, 48–52
transportation of Jews from 56, 58, 107
Bordes, Alban 269–71
Borrel, Andrée 62, 83, 104, 299
Boucher, Claude see Baissac, Claude de
Bouillar, André 'Dédé le Basque' 199–202,
  207, 236, 250, 251
  attempts to stop brutality towards Milicien
    256–7
  briefed on plans for D-Day 251
  character and description 199–200
  death of 295
  escapes from Gestapo raid 260–1
  executes Grandclément 271, 272, 273
  given gold sovereign by Landes 202
  hears that Landes has reached London
    safely 207
  helps Landes and Corbin escape to London
    200–2
  payment for his services 250
  re-joins Landes as fearless and able
    commander 236
Brard, Raymond 11, 74
Buchenwald 170, 298
Buckmaster, Maurice James 90–1, 105, 207,
  221, 222, 307
Bureau Central de Renseignement et
  d'Action (BCRA) 14

Café des Chartrons 48, 56, 57, 63, 64, 65, 66,
  73–4, 76, 83, 143, 144, 166, 168–9, 180,
  297
Café des Marchands (aka Café du
  Commerce) 12, 48, 152, 330
'Cagoule militaire' 38
Campet, Christian
  at execution of Grandclément 271, 272–3
  awards and honours 301
  character and description 236
  in charge of arms drop at Saugnacq-et-
    Muret 237
  checks on identity of Morraglia and his men
    245
  commands sabotage and guerrilla echelon
    249

as godfather to Landes's son Alain 310
offers his services to Landes 236
payment for his services 250
Camplan, Eugène
actions considered treasonous 213
ambivalent attitude towards Grandclément
145, 210
believes Bonnier to be Gestapo *agent
provocateur* 213
character and description 209–10
execution of 214
in favour of temporising 'truce' afforded by
Joubert's mission 212
relationship with Bonnier 211–13
takes command of Resistance units in
southwest 209
Cap Hadid (oil tanker) 74
Capdepont, Pierre 251
Caralp-Jardel, Marcelle 121
Caralp-Jardel, Mme 121–2, 304, 313–14
Casablanca 81
Cazenave, Franck 237, 270, 272
Cercle Européen 45
'Charles' *see* Hayes, Victor Charles
Charlin, Jean 266–7
Chastel, Mme Jeanne 153, 306–7
Château Grattequina 277
Château La Brède 149–50
Chatenet, Pierre 251
Chazeau, Roland 138, 145–7, 149–50, 154–6,
172, 174, 176, 180–2
cheminots 6, 76, 237, 248, 251
Chevallerie, General Kurt von der 254
Churchill, Winston
given regular updates from SOE 171
informed of Operation Frankton success 78
meeting with Roosevelt at Casablanca 81
promises help to the French 3
relationship with de Gaulle 194
understands importance of clandestine
operations 13
'Claudine' *see* Herbert, Mary
Clech, Marcel 62
Cockleshell Heroes raid *see* Operation
Frankton
Coirac network 70
Combined Operations 13, 76
Cominetti, François Charles 278–9, 302,
353
Commandant John 136, 140
Conférence de Poitiers 78, 336–7
Corbin, Albertine 142, 173

Corbin, Charles 50
arrival and arrest in Spain 199–203
arrives in London via Gibraltar 206–7
awards and honours 301
as close ally of Grandclément 111
cover identity in Spain 195
death of 301
joins the OCM 73
manages to play Dohse 172–3
passes friendly warning to Joubert 185–6
passes reassuring messages from Lucette to
Landes 119
as possible Gestapo agent 315–16
recognises Grandclément's treachery 141–8
returns to London with Landes 194–7, 301
Corbin, Ginette 50
acts as Landes's courier 72–3, 98
agrees to marry Défence 222, 298
illness and death 310–11
Landes's affection for 73
learns of Grandclément's treachery 142,
148
lives safely in the country 173
love affair with Défence 98
marries Landes 309
Cours de Verdun 83, 85, 110, 111, 114, 115,
117, 118, 138
Cresswell, Michael 200, 283
Culioli, Pierre 'Adolphe'
believed to be a traitor by Flowers 61
character and description 51
compromising documents found by
Gestapo 103–4, 136
joins the Monkeypuzzle circuit 51
meets Landes and Norman 61
sets up parachute sites and reception
committees 101
shot and captured 101–3
survives Buchenwald and acquitted of all
charges 298
'Curtis, William' *see* Landes, Roger Arthur
Cusin, Gaston 287, 288

D-Day 92, 223, 224, 239, 242, 246, 251–2,
253–9, 350
Daubèze, Renée 228–30, 300
'David' *see* Baissac, Claude de
Dax 76, 82, 118, 155–6, 237, 248, 283, 293,
301, 339
Défence, Marcel Eusèbe
accompanies Herbert to Paris 120
eventful journey to Britain 222

Défence, Marcel Eusèbe (*cont ...*)
  executed at Gross-Rosen concentration
    camp 298
  recognises Grandclément's treachery 141–2
  sent to assist Landes 96–8
  unable to return to London due to illness
    196
Delestraint, Charles 103
Démolisseur, Charle le 116–17
Déricourt, Henri 89, 338
Desbouillons, Pierre 159–61
Desbouillons, Raymonde 160
Dewavrin, Colonel André 90
Diethelm, André 290–2
Dohse, Erika 305
Dohse, Friedrich Wilhelm Heinrich
  abandons Grandclément to his own devices
    218–19
  admiring comment on Landes 226
  apocryphal story concerning 281
  appointed personal secretary to Bömelburg
    29–30
  arrival in Bordeaux 27, 31–2
  attempts to ensnare or recruit Resistance
    leaders 185–9, 248
  attempts to establish *Maquis officiels* 174–7,
    179
  aware of increased Resistance operations
    80
  believed to be a SIS agent 315
  captured and sent to British POW camp 303
  captures and interrogates Duboué 160–8
  captures and interrogates Lucette 119
  character and description 27–8, 30–1, 216,
    280, 316
  collects arms and weapons from
    Grandclément and his colleagues 145–8,
    149–50, 152, 153–6
  considers a Grandclément-style deal with
    London 177–8, 344
  continues to sow disinformation and
    mistrust 242, 247–8
  creates network of agents and safe houses
    43–5
  death of 305
  delivers coup de grâce to southwest
    Resistance 226–7
  diminishing of power in Bordeaux 233
  enables prisoners to be moved and
    subsequently freed 280
  enjoys the good life 45–7
  fooled by Corbin 172–3
  given command of Department IV:
    Intelligence and the suppression of the
    Resistance 32
  has access to large number of Resistance
    names 219
  informed of increase in clandestine night
    flights 66–7
  interrogation methods 44, 133–4
  joins the Nazi party 28
  learns of failed Algiers mission 215–16
  leaves Bordeaux and is sent to Eastern front
    281–2
  manages to prevent transportation of young
    men to Germany 235
  meeting with Grandclément cancelled 266
  meets Landes for the first time 304
  negotiates with Joubert on possible
    cessation of attacks 189–94
  orders the arrest of Grandclément in Paris
    129
  organises massacres of young students 265
  outwitted and made to look a fool 156–7
  pays for capture of foreign escapees 278–9
  prioritises finding and capturing Landes
    243
  promoted to full lieutenant 233
  receives reports of arms drops 87–8
  seconded to counter-espionage 28–9, 39
  selects hostages for execution 58
  sent on leave to his family 216
  sent to Bordeaux and imprisoned in Fort du
    Hâ 304
  sets up stay-behind network of spies 92–3,
    280, 293
  sidelined within KdS 216
  smuggles Joubert and Thinières into Spain
    203–4
  sources of intelligence and support dry up
    235, 259
  successful infiltration of Resistance in
    southwest 215
  successful operation at Lestiac 161–8
  successfully interrogates Grandclément
    133–40, 341–2
  successfully recruits German officers and
    French assistants 41–3, 44–5, 93
  survives the Lencouaq episode 179–83
  suspects spy network operating in Bordeaux
    106
  takes charge of Grandclément case 114–15
  threatens to shoot hostages if Grandclément
    harmed 269

trial and release 304–5
unable to break the Resistance movement in
 Bordeaux 99–100
uncovers resistance networks in Bordeaux
 107–11
unsuccessfully interrogates Bonnier 217–18
writes his memoirs 304
Dohse, Heine 216
Dollar, Johann 44
Drancy 58, 335
Duboué, Jean 128
 aftermath of wartime operations 295–6
 aliases and codenames 331
 arranges for Leroy to work in the docks 15
 character and description 12, 330
 death of 296
 given ex-gratia payment by British
  government 296
 gives remarkable testament on behalf of
  Dohse 304–5
 honours and awards 296
 identifies and prepares parachute sites 82–3
 introduced to de Baissac 56
 introduced to Landes 66
 leads series of raids across southwestern
  France 76–7, 116–17
 learns of Grandclément's treachery 145
 moves to the Villa Roucoule 152
 prepares to sabotage blockade-runners 74
 sends reports to London 13, 39
 sets up resistance movement 12–13, 84
 surrounded, captured and interrogated by
  Dohse and his men 159–68
 transported to Buchenwald 170
Duboué, Marie-Louise 12, 161, 162–3, 164,
 296–7
Duboué, Suzanne 12, 152
 acts as guide to SOE operatives 15
 escape and capture at Lestiac 161–3, 165
 falls in love with Hayes 128
 smuggles information out of Bordeaux
  12–13
 survival, marriage and death 297, 354–5
 transported to Ravensbrück 170
Duboué-Paillère network 48, 84
Duff Cooper, Alfred 291–2
Duluguet, Augustine 265–6, 267–8
Duluguet, Marc 1–2, 265, 267–8, 270–2, 293,
 305–6
Dussarrat, Léonce (aka Léon des Landes)
 awards and honours 301
 briefed by Landes on D-Day plans 251

carries out reprisals on female
 'collaborators' 282–3
death of 301
escape from Drax 155–6, 237
as godfather to Landes's son Alain 309, 310
HQ attacked by Wehrmacht soldiers 256
loans de Baissac money 118
payments for his services 250
places his men under Landes's command
 237
shouts abuse at German troop commander
 287–8
wields great power over Resistance leaders
 237–8

Édouard line 55, 334
Eichmann, Adolf 32
Eisenhower, Dwight D. 255, 258
Elizondo 201–3
Enzelsberger, Anton 'Tony the Boxer' 233, 275
 character and description 42
 interrogation techniques 108
 trial of 304
Esch, Pierre 133, 165
Expert, Michel 251

Faget, François 98, 249, 258
Faget, Marguerite 'Mitou' 98–9, 145, 168,
 196–7
 agrees to keep in contact with key
  Resistance leaders 231
 alerts Landes that German unit heading to
  Villa Cazenave 271–2
 briefed by Landes on D-Day plans 251
 codes and decodes messages 258
 denounces Noël 247
 divorce and death of 300
 Grandclément's briefcase burned in her
  garden 274
 house as safe base for Landes 98–9, 145,
  168, 231
 informed of Landes's return 219, 230
 Landes burns his radio codes and crystals
  in her cellar 196–7
 nurses Landes when ill 280
Faye, Max 271, 272–3, 290
FFI see Forces Françaises de l'Intérieur
Flower, Raymond Henry
 character and description 51
 meets Landes at local farm 62
 suspects Culioli and Rudellat to be traitors
  61

Forces Françaises de l'Intérieur (FFI) 226, 244, 258, 262, 263, 276, 283
Fort du Hâ 119, 280, 304
Fossard, Christian 109, 110–11, 115, 155, 217
Free French 11, 14, 126
Fresnes 170

Gaillard, Lieutenant-Colonel Charles
  agrees to work with Landes 276
  arranges ambush and execution of Grandclément 266–7
  arrives in Bordeaux 258
  helps to sort out chaos in Bordeaux 283–4
  introduces Landes to de Gaulle 290
  involved in arrest of German troops 287–8
  ordered to Paris and sentenced to house arrest 291
  orders the arrest of Noël 276
  vanishes from post-war record 301
Gaulle, Charles de
  acknowledged as French leader 192
  attends meeting in Casablanca 81
  Dohse sends emissaries to 203–6
  fruitless interview with Pétain 3
  given control of Resistance ahead of coming invasion 211
  impassioned pleas to fellow countrymen 4
  Joubert and Dohse's proposals to be decided by 190
  London Resistance movement 91–2
  orders Landes to return to England 290
  relationship with Roosevelt and Churchill 194
  visits Bordeaux 285, 287–90
Gaynes Hall, Huntingdonshire ('Station 61') 59, 335
Geheime Feldpolizei (GFP) 4, 329
Gentzel, Hermann 130
German directorate of security (BdS) 28
Gestapo 4, 28, 41, 92, 99, 102, 105–6, 121, 122–3, 130, 168, 171, 186, 194, 205, 227, 247, 248, 259, 263, 329
GFP see Geheime Feldpolizei
Gibraltar 206–7, 221
Gielgud, Major Lewis 20
Giraud, General Henri 81, 126, 212, 244
Gladstone, William Ewart 22
Goodman, Harold 47, 334
Gouyètes, Mlle 282–3
Grandclément, Amélia 33
Grandclément, André Marie Hubert François
  abandoned by Dohse 218–19
  aliases and codenames 80, 84, 111, 130
  alternative version for reasons why he was executed 313–16
  arrest and search of close contact 110
  arrested and interrogated 129–31, 265–9
  at his father's deathbed 66, 77
  attempts to recruit Resistance leaders to work for Dohse 186–8
  attends meetings between Joubert and Dohse 188–9
  becomes head of OCM Southwest 39–40, 48
  body buried, exhumed and re-buried 293, 305–7
  character and description 33–7, 125–6, 127, 316
  commercial operations 85–6
  composes long explanation of his activities 264, 268
  confession statement 139–40
  considered to be a traitor 218, 245, 263–4
  death ordered by local Resistance leaders 178, 261
  execution of 1–2, 270–4
  flees to Paris leaving incriminating documents 113–16
  funding of 85
  invites Charles Corbin to join the OCM 73
  involved in interrogation of Duboué 168
  involved in Maquisards at Lencouacq 179–82
  joins Dohse and Corbin for lunch 172–3
  joins the OCM 38–9
  lack of security 83–4
  learns of Lucette's arrest 123
  lives with his mistress 37–8
  marriage and children 35
  marries Lucette 83
  meets de Baissac 79–80
  moved to safe houses under Dohse's protection 246–7, 259
  risky financial dealings 118–19
  successfully interrogated by Dohse 133–40, 341–2
  tells London he has 50,000 men mobilised for invasion 106
  treachery of recognised by his colleagues 141–8
  works for Dohse 113, 146–8, 150, 152, 174–8, 227
Grandclément, Francine 35

Grandclément, Geneviève Toussaint
  'Myssett' 35, 36, 37
Grandclément, Ghislaine 35, 37
Grandclément, Jeanne 33
Grandclément, Lucette Tartas
  arrested and interrogated by Dohse 118–19,
    135, 153
  body buried, exhumed and re-buried 293,
    305–7
  captured and executed 1–2, 265–6, 268, 269,
    271–2
  character and description 37
  death sentence confirmed by London 178
  dresses stolen by Poinsot's brother Jean 114
  flees to Paris 113
  love affair with Grandclément 37–8, 39, 48
  moves back to Bordeaux 227
  placed under Dohse's protection 247
  stays with her mother 219
  warns Mme Paillère of her husband Léo's
    danger 160
Grandclément, Raoul Gaston Marie 33, 34,
  66
Grandier-Vazeille, Colonel 108–9
Grendon Hall, Northamptonshire 105
Grolleau, Pierre 217, 218
Gross-Rosen concentration camp 297–8
Gubbins, Colin 13

Hagen, Herbert
  overall head of KdS Bordeaux 32
  passive obstructionism of 41
  posted to Paris 46
Hasler, Major Blondie 75
Hayes, Raymonde 70
Hayes, Victor Charles
  aliases and codenames 106, 336
  betrayed by Desbouillons 160
  buys gold watches 222
  character and description 69–70
  executed at Gross-Rosen concentration
    camp 297–8
  given increased responsibilities 128
  leads series of raids across southwestern
    France 76–7
  learns of Grandclément's treachery 145
  meets Grandclément 83–4
  moves to Lestiac 152
  posthumously awarded the Military Cross
    298
  prepares to sabotage blockade-runners 74
  refuses to leave Bordeaux 128

sent to Bordeaux 69, 70
surrounded, captured and interrogated by
  Dohse and his men 160–8
transported to Fresnes 170
warned of possible danger 141, 144
Hèches, Gaston 52
  installs Mary Herbert in room above his
    restaurant 70
  passes messages along escape route 12
  restaurant as local HQ of SOE escape line
    55
  runs successful sabotage network 55
Hèches, Mimi 55
Herbert, Claudine 203, 223–4, 300
Herbert, Mary 'Maureeen'
  acts as courier to Scientist network 70–1,
    98
  affair with de Baissac 71
  aliases and codenames 70, 103, 106
  arrested and child put in an orphanage
    223–4
  arrival in Bordeaux 70
  awarded Croix de Guerre but never
    recognised by British Government 300
  character and description 70
  death of 300
  gives birth to a baby girl 203
  moves to Sussex and teaches French 300
  pregnant with de Baissac's child 89–90, 120,
    123, 153, 222
  reunited with de Baissac and her daughter
    Claudine 300
  takes radio and messages to Paris 120, 123
  travels to Paris with Landes 83
Higgins, Pilot Officer 94–5
Himmler, Heinrich 4
Hitler, Adolf
  demands maximum severity to outrages 11
  destroys the SA 28
  furious at Operation Frankton 75–6
  informed of major British spy ring in Paris
    104
  issues Commando Order 75
  late reaction to Normandy landings 255–6
  new repressive policy set by 233–4
  orders cessation of negotiations with
    Resistance 216

'Ivanhoe' see Suttill, Francis

Jews 7, 10, 56, 58, 107, 187
'The Jews and France' exhibition 10

Joubert, Louis
  character and description 185
  mission to Algiers 203–6, 210, 212, 215
  negotiates with Dohse on possible cessation of attacks 189–94
  placed in indefinite protective detention 215
  postwar employment 301
  refuses to work for Dohse 185–6
Jouffrault, General Paul 39, 78
Julien, Georges 257, 260–2, 263

Karp, Laiser Israel 10
KdS Bordeaux 31–2, 39, 41, 45, 46, 57–8, 66, 74, 76, 80, 82, 87, 107, 110–11, 115, 116, 119, 121, 129, 133–40, 142, 145, 146, 148, 150, 159, 167, 173, 176, 216, 277, 279, 332
Keimer, Claire 43, 46, 110, 179, 203
Keitel, Wilhelm 75–6
Knochen, Helmut 140, 190, 191
Koenig, Marie-Joseph 258
Kunesch, Rudolf
  character and description 41–2
  collects arms and weapons from Grandclément 146
  commands all operations 216
  continued power of 233
  death of 302
  forces information from Desbouillons 160, 165
  interrogation techniques 108, 133, 137, 167, 217
  massacres young students 265
  nick-named 'the cosher-in-chief' 42, 333
  opposed to release of Grandclément 140
  organises anti-Resistance operations 259
  summarily executes six young men 236
  survives Lencouacq episode 181–3
  wishes to arrest Léon des Landes 155–7

La Georgette see Gestapo
La Petitie Gironde newspaper 10
Labit, Henri 49–50, 111, 230, 309
Labit, Henriette 50, 334
'Lalande, Roger' see Landes, Roger Arthur
Landes, Alain Henri Léon 309, 310, 311
Landes, Barnet 18, 309
Landes, Léon des see Dussarrat, Léonce
Landes, Marcel 309, 310
Landes, Margaret 311
Landes, Roger Arthur
  affair with Mitou 99

agrees to execution of Morraglia and his conspirators 280
agrees to meet Gaillard 276
aliases and codenames 20, 59, 60, 106, 111, 166, 194, 195, 196, 224, 243, 279
alternative version for reasons why Grandclément was executed 313–16
arrival and arrest in Spain 199–203, 346
arrives in London via Gibraltar 206–7
attempts to deal with chaos in Bordeaux 282–5
attitude to sex and emotion 73, 99
awards and honours 195–6, 308
briefs his commanders on their tasks for D-Day 251–2
character and description 17–19, 25, 84, 225–6
deals forcefully with unsuitable recruits 239–42
decides to remain in Bordeaux 152–3
dementia and death 311–12
difficulties with command and control 257, 258, 260, 262, 265
difficulties with Morraglia 244–6
eventful parachute landing and return to Bordeaux 227–31
falls in love with Ginette Corbin 72–3
given gold watch by Hayes 222
given increased responsibilities 128–9, 250–1, 262
highly vulnerable to detector vans 87
interrogated by MI5 221–3
interviewed in Room 055 War Office 17, 19–20
involved in unfortunate surrender of German troops 287–8
joins Force 136 in Malaya 307–8
leaves Bordeaux and returns to England via Dax 290–3
marries Ginette Corbin 309
marries second wife seven years after death of Ginette 311
meets de Gaulle and his entourage 288–90
meets Dohse for the first time 304
meets Grandclément 83–4
moves from Cenon to safer lodgings 98–9
narrowly escapes capture in Paris 121–3
ordered to take charge of Scientist 124
organises D-Day attacks and sabotage 253–9
possible affair with Mme Daubèze 228–9
post-war life and employment 308–11

prepares for return mission to Bordeaux 224–6
puts his networks to sleep before returning to London 194–7, 223
re-assembles, trains and arms new organisation 236–9, 248–51
realises he will have to start networks afresh 231
recognises Grandclément's treachery 141–5
refuses to leave Bordeaux 172
sends message to SOE concerning Lestiac 168–9
sent to Bordeaux as Scientist's radio operator 57, 59–67
sent to Shenley Military Hospital to recuperate 293, 307
successfully sends messages to London 71–2, 77, 83
takes charge of Grandclément and executes him 270–4
trains at SOE special schools 21–5, 39
travels to Paris for replacement radio set 83
tries to persuade Hayes not to go to Lestiac 160–1
Lang, Robert *see* Landes, Roger Arthur
Langon 48–9
Larrose, Jean-Philippe 191–2
Lassalle, Josette 261–2
'Le Réseau Adolphe' 101
Le Volant d'Or 266, 267
Léglise, Robert 297
Léglise, Yves 297
Lencouacq 179–83, 210, 344–5
Leroy, Robert
  aliases and codenames 14, 57
  bar bill paid by de Baissac 55
  character and description 14
  demoted to courier 70–1
  involved in sabotage attacks 166, 240
  meets de Baissac 56
  sent to Bordeaux 14–16
Lespine, François 216–17
Lestiac, battle of 159–68
Lime, Flight Sergeant 151–2
London
  64 Baker Street (SOE HQ) 56, 57, 63, 66, 69, 72, 76, 77–8, 80, 81, 91, 223, 239, 244, 255, 264, 284, 296, 307
  Carlton Mansions, Holmleigh Road 17, 57
  Orchard Court, Portman Square 20, 21, 207, 221, 331
  Room 055, War Office 17, 19–20

Whitehall 19
Wimpole Street 90
London County Council (LCC) 18, 309
Longi (Italian itinerant worker) 110
'Louis' *see* Leroy, Robert
Luther, Hans
  agrees to let Dohse deal with Dussarrat 155
  agrees to release of Grandclément 140
  attends executions of hostages 58
  aware of arms drops by London 87
  character and description 46
  oversees transportation of Jews 58
  posted to Bordeaux 46
  removed as chief of KdS Bordeaux 173
  trial and imprisonment 304, 305
Luze, Édouard de 236, 257
Lysanders 78, 89, 91, 93, 120, 123, 195, 210, 222, 264, 266, 267, 269, 271, 276, 301, 338, 352

Machule, Walter
  arrested and placed in chains 281–2
  attends meeting on *Maquis officiels* 176
  character and description 173–4
  closely scrutinises all operations 216
  meets Joubert 188–9
  organises roundup of supposed Resistance members 235
  receives anonymous letter concerning Canadian pilots 277–8
  sends Dohse to city prison to deal with prisoners 280
  takes over from Hans Luther 173
  trial of 304
Madrid 13, 195, 202, 203, 205, 206–7, 221, 291
Malaya 302, 307–8, 355
Maleyran, André 84, 138, 145–7, 150, 154–6, 168, 172, 174, 176, 180–2, 306
Manolitsakis, John 'Cyriel le Grec' 240, 302, 355
Maquis 38, 82, 95, 125, 129, 130, 149, 167, 174, 179, 219, 235, 241, 242, 246, 250, 254, 263, 281
Maquis officiels (or *Maquis blancs*) 174–7, 179, 219
'Marie-Louise' *see* Herbert, Mary 'Maureen'
Mauritius 21
Mauthausen 299
Meoble Lodge, Loch Morar (Special Training School No. 23) 24
Meunier, Pierre Charles 'Le Grandiose' 239–42, 247, 256, 302

Meyer, Colonel Fritz 287
MI5 222
MI6 11, 13
MI9 13, 283
Mihailovic, General Dragoljub 'Draza' 175
Milice 45, 256–7, 274, 284
Miranda de Ebro internment camp 203
Mittelbau-Dora slave labour camp 295, 304
Monkeypuzzle 51–2, 61
Morel, Gerry 207
Morraglia, Jean-Baptiste
  arranges to meet Landes 244–5, 262
  believed to be a traitor 265, 275
  believes he is in overall charge 258
  character and description 244
  in close touch with Grandclément 274
  death of 301
  execution sanctioned by Landes 280
  refuses to work with Landes 246
  regarded as true leader by Grandclément's
    supporters 245–6
  sidelined by Gaillard and Landes 276
Moulin, Jean 103, 104, 211
Moulleau 247, 259, 262, 264
Muggeridge, Malcolm 13

Nancy, Jacques 213, 217
Natzweiler-Struthof concentration camp 299
Neuvy 101–2, 104
New York Times 116
Nicolle (agent of Landes) 14
Nîmes 53
Noël, André 231, 247–8, 260, 276–7
Norman, Gilbert 339
  aliases and codenames 103, 335
  captured and interrogated 104–5, 111
  character and description 25
  fails to alert London of his capture 104–5
  hanged at Mauthausen 299
  parachuted into France 60–1
  persuaded to cooperate with the Germans
    105, 106, 120, 136
  sent to Paris as radio operator for Prosper
    network 61–2, 83
Normandy 254, 255, 258
Nouaux, Lucien 275

OCM see Organisation Civile et Militaire
'Odile' see Baissac, Lise de
Official Secrets Act 21
O'Neill, Marc
  arrested 105

  assured Grandclément would be brought
    down 210
  family background 34
  Grandclément attempts to send message to
    143
  as key member of OCM 39
  in Paris 129
Operation Attila (1942) 69
Operation Cockade (1943) 92, 116, 126–7
Operation Frankton (Cockleshell Heroes
  raid) (1942) 74–6
Operation Torch (1942) 77
Organisation Civile et Militaire (OCM)
  38–40, 48, 77, 78–80, 84, 90, 108, 109, 113,
  115, 139, 185, 189, 193, 212, 219, 226–7
Organisation Todt 59, 63, 224

Paillère, Danny 145
Paillère, Jeanne 12, 160
Paillère, Léo
  alias 331
  appointed Scientist's 'organiser-in-chief'
    77
  arrested/imprisoned for black-market
    offences 39
  betrayed by Desbouillons 160
  character and description 12, 330
  learns of Grandclément's treachery 145
  sends reports to London 39
  sets up resistance network 12, 84
Paris 51, 62, 66, 79, 83, 91, 93, 103–6, 113,
  115, 117–20, 123, 125–6, 129–31, 140, 141
  82–84 Avenue Foch 28, 57–8, 75, 103, 105,
    168, 190
  Franklin Jesuit College 33–4
  Les Invalides 291
  Rex Cinema 58
Parks, Arthur 21, 331
'Père Lefèvre' see Riquet, Reverend Father
  Michel
Pétain, Marshal Philippe 3–4, 38, 69, 135,
  192, 265, 302
Peulevé, Harry
  acts as radio operator 52
  aliases and codenames 23
  character and description 23
  death in Spain 298
  given increased responsibilities 128
  honours and awards 298
  lays low before travelling to the Corrèze
    region 144–5
  parachuted into France 53–4

sends SOS message to SOE concerning
Lestiac 169
survives Buchenwald 298
Plante, Mme 241–2
Poincaré, Raymond 34
Poinsot, Jean 114
Poinsot, Pierre Napoléon
assassination plot against 159–60, 166–7
attacks and kills young students 265
discovers size and extent of spy networks
107–8
executed by firing squad 302
finds green dossier belonging to
Grandclément 113–14
as head of Vichy French police brigade 11,
38, 83
interrogation techniques 44, 108
as paid German informer 44
witnesses interrogation of Duboué 165
Poitiers 62, 78, 223, 336–7
Pol, René see Landes, Roger Arthur
Polish secret service 11
Poole, Hilaire see Peulevé, Harry
'Prosper' network (Paris) 51–2, 62, 83, 98,
101, 105–6, 107, 108, 111, 171, 298, 299
Pyrenees 199, 231, 284, 301

Queyrac 287–8

RAF St Mawgan, Cornwall 207
RAF Tangmere 89, 124
RAF Tempsford (Special Duty Squadrons
base) 59–60, 95, 151, 227
Ravensbrück 170, 297
Reimers, Hans 11, 159
Renaud-Dandicolle, Jean 'Dandy' 124
Resistance movement
arrest, deportation and execution of
members 99, 103, 115–16, 207, 259, 275
attacks and sabotage related to D-Day
253–8
building up, training and arming of 84–5,
236–42
collapse of Prosper and its implications for
Bordeaux 106, 108–11
commanded by de Gaulle's organisation in
London 226
consequences of attacks by 57–8
favourable assessment of 90
financial support for 84–5, 117, 250, 314–15
Grandclément's treachery disclosed to 145
growth and spread 11

help Cockleshell Heroes escape to London
75
interrogation methods 44
lack of security in 83–4
local/regional branches 38–40
martyrs 11
new repressive policy against 233–6
occupation drawing to a close 279
pensions or emoluments given to French
members only 296
problems of command and control 257,
258, 260–2
rivalry, suspicion and betrayal in 84
southwest group in disarray 219
splits, incompatibilities and executions in
209–15, 246–7
Ribbentrop, Joachim von 190
Riquet, Reverend Father Michel 186–8, 222
Rollot, Colonel 181, 209, 212, 284–5
Rommel, Erwin 7
Roosevelt, Franklin D. 81, 194
Rudellat, Yvonne
acts as courier for SOE operatives 51, 56–7
awarded the Croix de Guerre but never
honoured by the British government 299
believed to be a traitor by Flower 61
character and description 51
meets Mary Herbert 71
sent to Bergen-Belsen and dies of typhus
and dysentery 299
sets up parachute sites and reception
committees 101
shot while escaping from Germans 102–3,
104
takes Landes's radio and revolver to
Bordeaux 62–3, 66
Rymills, Flight Lieutenant 'Bunny' 89

SA see Sturmabteilung
Sachsenhausen concentration camp 299
Salles, Paul 180, 182
San Sebastián 46–7
SAP see Section des Affaires Politiques
Saugnacq-et-Muret 237, 269, 270, 305–6
Schmaltz, Roger 237, 248, 251, 310
Schöder, SS-Obersturmführer 43
Schröder, Karl 49
Schutzstaffel (SS) 28
'Scientist' network (Bordeaux) 51, 56, 57, 70,
73, 76–7, 78–80, 83, 90, 105, 106, 117–18,
124, 139, 142–3, 171, 177, 196, 207, 296
SD see Sicherheitsdienst

Secret Intelligence Service (SIS) *see* MI6
Section des Affaires Politiques (SAP) 44
Selborne, Roundell Palmer, 3rd Earl 15
Sélections Cinématographiques du
   Sud-Ouest 86, 115
Service du Travail Obligatoire (STO) 179
SHAEF *see* Supreme Headquarters Allied
   Expeditionary Forces
Shenley Military Hospital, Watford 293,
   307
Sicherheitsdienst (SD) 4–5, 32
Simon, Captain André 331
Sirois, Allyre 227, 229
SIS (Secret Intelligence Service) *see* MI6
Slim, William, 1st Viscount 308
Soldat am Atlantik 160
Sommer, Marcelle Louise 42–3, 304
Soustelle, Jacques 215
Sparks, Bill 75
Special Operations Executive (SOE)
   agrees to arm entire OCM network 78–9
   awards given to female agents 299–300
   aware of dangers of failure to invade 93
   brief de Baissac on invasion 90–1
   brothels as meeting places for agents 86
   criticised for limited contribution to war
      effort 77–8
   divides de Baissac's area between Landes,
      Hayes and Peleuvé 128–9
   establishment of 13
   excluded from Chiefs of Staff Committee
      81, 337
   fails to realise Norman's predicament 105
   fooled into sending information to Avenue
      Foch 103
   French Sections (F & RF) 13–14
   as integrated part of war effort 226
   issues same make/colour suitcases/pyjamas
      49
   loss of Prosper and Scientist networks
      171–2
   messages sent and received concerning
      D-Day operations 253, 254–5
   overview and aftermath of Bordeaux
      operations 295–302
   routes and networks 62, 331
   sanctions immediate sabotage operations
      69
   sends agents and operatives to Bordeaux
      14–16, 49–52
   sends financial support to Resistance 84–5,
      117, 250, 314–15

snobbishness and sense of superiority in
   308
training schools 21–5
Special Training School No 5 *see*
   Wanborough Manor
Sperrle, Field Marshal Hugo 234
SS *see* Schutzstaffel
Stahlschmidt, Heinz 279
'Stanislas' *see* Landes, Roger Arthur
STO *see* Service du Travail Obligatoire
Stülpnagel, General Carl-Heinrich 234
Sturmabteilung (SA) 28
Supreme Headquarters Allied Expeditionary
   Forces (SHAEF) 226, 258
Suttill, Francis ('Ivanhoe') 62, 83, 85, 91, 105,
   299

Tartas, Lucette *see* Grandclément, Lucette
Thame, nr Aylesbury (SOE wireless school)
   25
Thinières, André
   agrees to accompany Joubert to Algiers 193
   excoriating view of Grandclément 126
   mission to Algiers 203–6, 215
   placed in indefinite protective detention
      215
   recommends Camplan as OCM leader 209
   spends time with his wife after her release
      193
Tito, Josip Broz 175
Touny, Colonel Alfred 227
   asks for command of French Resistance in
      all northern France 79
   attends meeting in Poitiers 78
   head of OCM in Paris 39
Tours 51, 56–7, 63
Toussaint, Yves 217, 218, 227

Vaughan-Williams, Flight Lieutenant Peter
   89
Verdon-sur-Mer 287
Verhelst, Louis 159, 174
Vernier, Marie Louise *see* Herbert, Mary
   'Maureeen'
Vichy France 4, 7, 30, 36, 38, 69, 92, 125, 134
Victoria, Queen 22
Von Faber du Faur, General Moritz 5, 7–8

Wanborough Manor (Special Training
   School No 5) 21–4
Wehrmacht 67, 179, 180, 181, 182, 229, 234,
   235, 247, 256, 265, 280, 282